MARTIN KESSLER BOOKS

New York   London   Toronto   Sydney   Singapore

DETUNE .

The Coming Russian Boom

A Guide to New Markets and Politics

Richard Layard
John Parker

THE FREE PRESS
A Division of Simon & Schuster Inc.
1230 Avenue of the Americas
New York, NY 10020

MARTIN KESSLER BOOKS and colophon are trademarks
of Simon & Schuster Inc.

Designed by Carla Bolte

Manufactured in the United States of America

10   9   8   7   6   5   4   3   2

Library of Congress Cataloging-in-Publication Data

Layard, P. R. G. (P. Richard G.)
    The coming Russian boom: a guide to new markets and politics/
Richard Layard, John Parker.
        p.   cm.
    Includes bibliographical references and index.
    ISBN 0-684-82743-3
    1. Russia (Federation)—Politics and government—1991– .
I. Parker, John, 1954– . II. Title.
DK510.763.L39   1996
947.086—dc20   96-2045
                                                  CIP

TO KERRY AND MOLLY

Contents

Figures

Tables

Preface

The future of Russia is important to us all. But most Westerners have a quite distorted picture of what is happening. That is why we have written this book.

We have always been more optimistic than most people about Russia. So far the optimists have been more right than the pessimists. The market system has taken rapid root; there is a functioning democracy; and the Soviet empire has been dismantled with minimal conflict between Russia and the rest. On the other hand there is a serious crime wave, and democracy is less safely established than is capitalism. In this book we try to set in perspective all the features, both positive and negative. Our conclusions are summarized in the final chapter.

For both of us, Russia has been a big part of our lives in recent years. John Parker went to Moscow as the Soviet correspondent of *The Economist* in 1989 and has been involved in writing about Russia ever since. In 1992 he received the Moscow Union of Journalists' award for coverage of Russia, the first Westerner to receive Russia's premier media prize. The generosity of Bill Emmott, the editor of *The Economist*, gave him the time needed to write this book.

All Westerners working in Russia depend on the patience and expertise of friends and colleagues. Among the many Russians who helped explain that most endlessly fascinating and frustrating of countries to John Parker were Sergei Alexashenko, Maxim Boycko,

Mikhail Berger, Olga Dmitrova, Sergei Nazarov, Vera Samarina, Lilia Shevtsova, and Konstanin Trofimov. Among the Westerners with whom it was a pleasure to think through the puzzles were Richard Bridge, James Blitz, Charles Blitzer, Andrew Cowley, Chrystia Freeland, Christopher and Brigitte Granville, John Lloyd, Tony Longrigg, and Quentin Peel. Peter d'Hamecourt and Zoya Ryutina in particular made understanding Russia's reforms a pleasure.

Richard Layard has worked in Moscow for roughly half his time since November 1991, when he was asked by Yegor Gaidar and Alexander Shokhin to become an adviser to the government's economic staff (more recently on a part-time basis). He has worked especially closely with Andrei Illarionov, Sergei Pavlenko, Jeffrey Sachs, Anders Aslund and, above all, Sergei Vasiliev. It has been a great privilege and joy to work with them and to share their remarkable insights.

Layard's work has been made possible through the help of a small and talented team of researchers in the Centre for Economic Performance's Moscow Group, who have done so well in analyzing Russia's economic problems and in producing *Russian Economic Trends*, used heavily in this book. At different times the group has included Michael Ellam, Peter Orszag, Andrea Richter, Pavel Teplukhin, Andrei Lushin, Dmitri Rozkhov, Liam Halligan, Dirk Willer, and Roland Nash, all of them towers of strength. We wish to thank in particular Pavel Teplukhin, the Director of the group, who has been a virtual co-author of the economic chapters of this book.

The group is financed by the European Commission through the TACIS program and is now based in the Russian European Center for Economic Policy. Thanks are due for the Commission's support, especially to the European ambassador in Moscow, Michael Emerson, who has been a constant source of encouragement. Also vital have been those at the Centre for Economic Performance in London who have handled so nobly the problems caused by Richard Layard's absences in Moscow—especially Charles Bean, Nigel Rogers, and Marion O'Brien. Philomena McNicholas did a superb job of typing the economic part of the book.

The whole draft was reviewed by a conference attended by Charles Blitzer, Peter Boone, Sir Rodric Braithwaite, Andrew Cowley, Grigory Glaskov, Jacek Rostowski, and Sergei Vasiliev. It was also read in detail by Michael Emerson, Tony King, and Anders Aslund, whose *How Russia Became a Market Economy* is the authoritative history of the economic reform. We are extremely grateful to all of them for their help, criticisms, and encouragement—and, above all others, to our wives, who shared with us the ups and downs of life in Russia.

London	Richard Layard
March 1996	John Parker

Chapter 1

Introduction

What has been achieved? · *Why the pessimists were wrong* · *The future*

A great nation loses a war and much of its empire. It then plunges into economic turmoil. This is the formula that produced Hitler. Will Russia go the same way? Or will it be a friendly neighbor, with a prosperous new capitalist economy?

Six times in the past three hundred years Russia has turned outward to the West, seeking to modernize its economy and liberalize its society. The first five of those attempts all ended in failure. Will this one succeed?

The answer is crucial for us all. For the reform covers every aspect of life:

- In economics Russia has been trying to build a market economy based on private enterprise. If the attempt continues, Russia will soon offer great opportunities for foreign investment and trade plus a better life for its people. But will the reform continue?
- In politics Russia for the first time in its life has a democratically elected government. But can democracy survive the clashes of interest generated by the process of economic change?
- In international relations Russia no longer aims to defeat the West and is making serious efforts to became a partner instead. But will Russian nationalism rise up again, like German nationalism between the wars, driving the world back to the old balance of terror?

These questions are critical to Western businessmen interested in business opportunities in Russia. They are also vital for Western citizens hoping for a more peaceful world. And they are even more important to every Russian who wants prosperity, freedom, and peace. We shall do our best to answer them.

To many people in both Russia and the West the omens seem bad. They point first to Russia's difficult background. Russia was much more deeply penetrated by communism than any other country in the world. Communists gained power in 1917 rather than after 1945, so nobody in Russia remembers what capitalism was like before they took over. On the political front, Russia has never been a democracy before—tsar and general secretary were both autocrats. And, internationally, Russia always held itself somewhat aloof, an instinct reinforced by three murderous invasions from the West in 1812, 1914, and 1941. After each previous reform failed, Russia turned in upon itself, shunning the social and economic forms of the West.

The pessimists find further support for their case in the current situation. They highlight the return of Communist party power, the continuing imperfections in Russia's economy, the strength of the mafia, and the increasing self-assertion of Russia on the world scene. Many point to the danger that Russia, humiliated by defeat in the Cold War and confused with economic turmoil, will turn to nationalism and corporatism, as Germany did in the 1930s.

In recent years such pessimism has dominated Western comment on Russia and much of the comment in Russia itself. Yet generally the gloomy forecasts have proved false. Instead there has been progress on most fronts—not in a tidy way, but usually by a process of two steps forward, one step back. The one step back is reported more than the two steps forward, consolidating the mood of gloom.

What has been achieved?

So what has been achieved? On the economic front, Russia has established a market economy. Inflation has been high, but by early 1996 was down to 40 percent a year. There continues to be more regulation than in the West, but there is now more private property in Russia than anywhere else in Eastern Europe and privatization has encouraged restructuring.

On the political side, Russia has a functioning democracy with a constitution similar to the French: a strong, directly elected president plus an elected parliament. Unfortunately, up to December 1993 it had an unworkable constitution in which powers were ill-defined but massive power was given to a parliament which had been elected one year before Boris Yeltsin was elected president, in far less democratic days. The parliament tried to block Yeltsin and the economic reform at every step. Yeltsin repeatedly proposed new elections to break the deadlock, and this proposal was supported in a popular referendum. But the parliament would not agree, and eventually Yeltsin unilaterally suspended it. The parliament then took to arms but was defeated when tanks attacked the parliament building. In the ensuing referendum the new constitution was adopted. From then to the time of writing in March 1996, political life has proceeded in a reasonably orderly way.

The third great achievement has been the peaceful dissolution of the Russian empire. Never has a great empire been taken apart with so little loss of life. By great good fortune, the collapse of the communist economy destroyed the power of the imperial Soviet government, allowing Yeltsin to remove Russia from the Soviet Union. The other fourteen republics left at the same time. But many divorces lead to massive rancor. In this case there was no major conflict between Russia and the successor states, because Russia never drove the other partners beyond endurance. There *was* unfortunately a bloody internal conflict when Chechnya tried to secede from Russia. The bloodshed there was cruel, unnecessary, and futile. But the majority of the Russian people opposed the war. Though Russian nationalism is on the rise, most Russians regard the celebrated nationalist Vladimir Zhirinovsky as a joke and do not want their children killed in efforts to reestablish the Russian empire or its power abroad.

Why the pessimists were wrong

So why have the pessimists been so wrong—up to now? They overlook two crucial facts about today's world: the communications revolution and the new institutions that now exist for promoting international cooperation.

The first is the more important. Information and ideas now travel at a speed unknown before. So, once Eastern Europe had rejected communism, it was never plausible, as many people forecast, that Russia would remain communist for five to ten more years. In fact Russia quickly followed Eastern Europe. Russia's economic reform began in January 1992, one year after Czechoslovakia's and two years after Poland's.

The force that has swept Russia forward is exactly the same as the one that destroyed communism in Eastern Europe—the observation that the capitalist West was prosperous and free. No jamming of radio stations could stop that message. Two conclusions followed. First, capitalism must be established in Russia, and second, Russia must be part of the wider capitalist world. Under Brezhnev Russia stagnated from lack of access to Western technology. Now most Russians are avid for all things Western, while well-placed Russians with money abroad understand that their best hope of personal wealth is through contact with the West. That is why Russia is unlikely to choose a ruler who again puts up the shutters.

Fortress Russia is also unlikely because Russia has by now joined most of the world's main clubs for international cooperation—the IMF, the World Bank, and (since 1945) the United Nations. It belongs (with NATO) to the Partnership for Peace and has a "Partnership and Cooperation Agreement" with the European Union, aimed at the goal of free trade. And, most remarkable of all, the Russian president has become the eighth member at political summits of the G7 leading industrial countries.

It would have been impossible for Germany in the 1930s to have joined those clubs, since none of them existed in the disordered world of that time. But in today's world these forms of interaction have enormously helped Russia to become integrated with the rest of the world. What was almost impossible for Peter the Great has been difficult for Yeltsin, but not impossible.

Russia since 1992 is a remarkable story of change. It had to tackle three major problems simultaneously: building a new economic system, creating a functioning democracy, and building a new position in the world. From a situation of chaos, power vacuum, and flux, a new world had to be created. It was rather like 1783 in North America or

1792 in France. Everything had to be remade at the same time. And much remaking has been accomplished.

Rarely, if ever, has a country so turned its back on seventy-five years of its own history. That is what Russia has done. Russia's emblem is once again the eagle, and its flag the pre-1917 flag. Communism is considered an aberration—at least by the young, and even by many who vote communist. But what religion will take its place? That remains to be seen. For the moment the struggle for personal survival dominates everything else. People are deeply cynical about all ideologies and distrust the promises of politicians, an excellent basis for the building of a market economy.

The future

So where will it all lead? What does the future hold for Russia's economy, for its democracy, and for its relations with the West? What happens after Yeltsin? All the world wants to know.

Our reason for writing this book is to provide some pointers for those who are trying to peer into the obscure future. No one correctly forecast the events of 1989 in Eastern Europe, and Russia's future, though less uncertain, is surely not clear. But a balanced look at the recent past can throw much light on what forces are at work (many of them positive, but some negative). In this book we therefore try to answer twelve basic questions:

Is Russia different?
Why did communism fail?
Was there too much shock therapy?
Has the West done enough?
How do people live?
Will Russia prosper?
Can Russia beat the mafia?
Will political deadlock recur?
Can democracy survive?
Will Russia break up?
Will Russia rebuild the Empire? and
Russia and the West: friends or foes?

Figure 1–1. Where next?

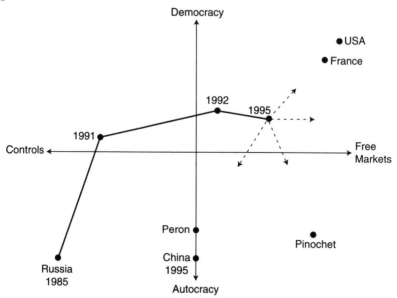

Each question is the subject of a chapter. But behind everything are two themes that dominate all others, in the minds of both Russians and of Western businessmen wondering whether to invest or trade in Russia:

Will the free-market system take permanent root?
Will democracy survive?

Figure 1–1 poses these questions in the sharpest possible way. It shows how far Russia has come since 1985. But, as we move toward the millennium, will Russia continue in the same direction? The presidential election of June 1996 is an important milestone, but what of the basic forces at work after that?

Each of our chapters contributes some clue to this puzzle. In our final chapter we summarize the main points and then discuss what scenarios are possible and how likely they are.

Chapter 2

Is Russia different?

*The political differences · Social institutions: Serfdom and collectivism ·
The burden of geography · The cult of unique destiny*

In his notes for a planned history of Russia, Nikolai Gogol, the first of Russia's great nineteenth-century novelists, jotted down this thought: "The character of the Russians is incomparably more subtle and more cunning than that of the inhabitants of all of Europe."[1] In a poem rebuking those who had gone into self-imposed exile after the 1917 Revolution, Anna Akhmatova, one of the greatest poets of the twentieth century, took exactly the opposite view, yet still concluded that Russians are unique:

*There is no one on earth . . .
more proud and more simple than us.*[2]

Ironically, this poem, which chides the exiles who fled the Bolshevik Revolution of 1917, echoes remarks of Russia's most eminent exile, the political scientist Alexander Herzen, who lived in Switzerland and London for much of the mid-nineteenth century. Compared with Europeans, he wrote, "We are simpler, we are healthier, we are incapable of any sickbed fussiness over food, we are no lawyers, no bourgeois."[3]

Every country, of course, is unique in its own way. Each likes to

7

claim that some combination of history, language, culture, ways of behaving, geography, and so on distinguishes it from all others. And every country likes to compare itself with others; it is part of knowing yourself to know how you differ from other people.

Even so, Russia is unusual. Russia is famous for the wealth of its proverbs. Most such folk sayings express universal guides to behavior ("A stitch in time saves nine"; "Don't spoil the ship for a ha'porth of tar," and so on). Some Russian proverbs are like that, of course ("Don't spit in the well, later you'll want to drink from it"), but an unusually large number are about how the country differs from others: "Foreign countries are like a stepmother. They don't stroke the fur the right way." "The German gets there with his brain, the Russian with his eyes." "Here it is not like in Poland; here we have bigger people."

Children in Russia are brought up on Turgenev's encomium to the Russian language: ". . . you alone are my rod and staff, O great, mighty, true, and free Russian tongue. . . . It is inconceivable that such a language should not belong to a great people." What is known in all Western countries as World War II—an international conflict—is known in Russia as the Great Patriotic War—i.e., a national conflict.

Literature is the clearest barometer of this tendency toward self–definition. An unusually large number of Russia's best-known writers have taken as their subject Russia itself, at critical moments in its history: the struggle against Napoleon (Tolstoy's *War and Peace*); conflicts over the emancipation of the serfs (Turgenev's *A Huntsman's Sketches* and *Fathers and Sons*); terrorism against the tzars (Dostoevsky's *The Devils*); the reign of Peter the Great (Pushkin's *The Bronze Horseman*); and the October Revolution (most of Solzhenitsyn's works from *August 1914* to *The Gulag Archipelago*). Russian writers comparatively rarely identify what makes Russia special by comparing Russia with Britain or France or Germany. Their point of comparison is with Europe as a whole. As a result, Russia seems to emerge from books as a fundamentally different civilization rather than as a member of the European family of nations.

That is also what philosophers and politicians thought. "We do not belong to any of the great families of mankind, neither to the East nor to the West," wrote Pyotr Chaadayev,[4] a contemporary of Turgenev and the most passionate and influential early advocate of the idea that

Russia needed to learn from the West. In 1992, the then Speaker of parliament, Ruslan Khasbulatov, wrote: "While [Peter the Great] imposed elements of European culture in Russia ... the spiritual and cultural fabric of the people remained untouched. As a result, we have Russia, which is neither Europe nor Asia but a very special, very peculiar part of the world."[5]

The history of this peculiar part of the world is littered with the shattered hopes of reform. Russia has alternated between frenzied bursts of change and long periods of tyrannical sloth, rather like a Russian folk character, Ivan, who sleeps on top of a stove for seven years, gets up, gets drunk, briefly terrorizes the village with an axe, and then reverts to another seven-year nap. Over the past three centuries, Russia has seen five great waves of liberalization. On each occasion, the impetus to reform lasted no more than a decade before being crushed by renewed autocracy.

Russia's great attempts at modernization began with Peter the Great, the first Westernizing tsar, who made Russia a European power and who during his reign (1682–1725) transformed Russia in a way that few rulers have ever transformed this country.[6] He created the first national army, fought his way to a warm-water port with Western Europe, and moved the capital from inward-looking Moscow to his new port with the ostentatiously un-Russian name of Saint Petersburg. He allowed foreigners to travel to Russia for the first time relatively freely; imported Dutch, Italian, and French technicians and teachers; founded Russia's Academy of Sciences; and cut off the beards of courtiers to make them look more Western. Russia's modern history begins with Peter. Herzen wrote that "Russia has once had a fundamental revolution: it was made by one man—Peter I."[7] Yet Peter's "opening to the West" was slammed shut again by the welter of dynastic squabbling after his death in 1725.

Catherine the Great said that she had ransacked Montesquieu's *Spirit of the Laws*,[8] the sourcebook of enlightened government in the eighteenth century. But having attempted to introduce the Enlightenment into Russia during the first half of her long reign (1762–96), she reverted to repression in the second half after the crushing Pugachev's peasant uprising in 1774 (Catherine compared the leaders of the French Revolution with "Marquis Pugachev").

Nearly ninety years of repression were to pass before the third effort at modernization, that of Alexander II, the Liberator, who freed the serfs in 1861 and began various legal reforms that brought Russian law closer to that of Western Europe (he introduced trial by jury, for instance). But Alexander was assassinated in 1881, an event that began a period of conservative autocracy that lasted until the fourth wave began under Pyotr Stolypin, who tried to save the dying Romanov dynasty with a series of land reforms in 1906–11. Lenin said that had Stolypin succeeded (he was assassinated in 1911), the Bolshevik Revolution would not have succeeded. As it was, World War I and the 1917 Revolution were periods of chaos, reaction, and repression, interrupted briefly by Lenin's own more limited attempt at liberalization, the New Economic Policy of 1921–24, which attempted to put Russia back on its feet after the Civil War of 1917–21 by encouraging some private entrepreneurship. Stalin put a stop to that.

The sixth wave began to swell under Mikhail Gorbachev in the late 1980s and was unrolled by Boris Yeltsin in January 1991, continuing through 1992. Prices were freed, elections held. Those reforms, for the first time, came from below. Russians were freed to do as they would, not told to do different things by an enlightened tsar. After five years, the reforms are hanging in the balance. On the one hand, more than 60 percent of the Russian economy is now in private hands, the press is uninhibited, and there is full freedom of assembly. On the other, the chaos and crime that have been associated with the reforms seem to be preparing the way for a repetition of the historical pattern. Parliament was shelled in October 1993. Far right wing nationalists won nearly 20 percent of the vote at the general election of 1993.

The damage wrought by these cycles, and Russia's need to break free from them, were expressed in these lines from 1991:

All my life I've rushed between hell and heaven,
today the devil, and tomorrow God . . .
    Stop.

The man who wrote those lines was Ilya Krichevsky.[9] On the night of August 22, he lost his life for Russia's failure: He was one of three people killed during the failed communist putsch against Gorbachev. His death, his words, and the cycles of history that lie behind them alike serve as warnings of how difficult Russia's task is. Will the sixth wave of reform fail like all the others?

The short response is that "history is bunk," that the historical record provides no real guide to present behavior and that historically formed cultural characteristics do not necessarily stand in the way of a country's ability to change. If culture is so important, how can they explain a culture's success in one era and failure in another?

In the nineteenth century, a British traveler had this to say about Japan: "Wealthy we do not think it can ever be. The love of indolence and pleasure of the people themselves forbid it."[10] In the 1940s, few people thought that South Korea could ever be an economic success because of its history of political upheaval and the Koreans' reputation for being happy-go-lucky. At that time, the Asian country with the brightest economic future seemed to be India, because of its competent administration, its democracy, its large middle and merchant class, and its English-speaking elite. In practice, for the past fifty years India has lagged far behind South Korea. China, on the other hand, seemed unpromising because of its communist rule and its long history of isolationism.

Consider Confucianism and modernization. For years, many scholars, notably Max Weber, argued that the Confucian tradition inhibited economic success: Obedience to parental authority discouraged competition and innovation, while the Confucian elevation of the mandarinate was assumed to suppress entrepreneurialism. By the 1980s the treatment of Confucianism had changed entirely. Now, what seemed important was Confucian emphasis on hard work and on cooperation toward a single end, and its encouragement of savings and investment. The moral is not that people have been unsuccessful at explaining countries' behavior in terms of cultural characteristics; it is that cultures are so complicated they cannot be used accurately to predict behavior at all.

The role of destruction. Other countries have been able to change because of defeat in war or internal collapse. In Germany and Japan, military defeat discredited the fascist regimes and provided popular support for a new group of politicians determined to begin again. In China, the self-inflicted chaos and destruction of the Cultural Revolution provided a similar impetus for Deng Xiaoping and his economic reformers. In Poland, as throughout Eastern and Central Europe, the sweeping away of the old communist government provided the opportunity for a new generation to steer the country back toward its earlier alignment with the West.

Some people have argued that Russia has not suffered a sufficiently traumatic defeat to repeat the experience of other countries. Former communists are still in charge, and there has been relatively little bloodshed associated with the transfer of power. That is a one-sided view. While it is true that there has been no wholesale change at the top, in most respects Russia has experienced enormous and destructive change throughout the twentieth century.

It has fought two world wars and a civil war, losing more of its citizens in World War II than any other country. (Most recent estimates put the total loss of life near 20 million.) In 1917 and 1991 it experienced revolutions in its system of government and, on both occasions, lost its empire. Stalin's industrialization has transformed Russia from a largely rural, peasant economy to an industrial one, with the demographic attributes of an advanced Western country: 99 percent of the population can read and write (a rate higher than Britain's); 96 percent go to secondary schools. With such changes, the old patterns of thought die out. Russia is no longer the overwhelmingly peasant country it was when Stalin began his iron rule.

In the 1990s, at the level of government Russia, like East and Central European countries, saw old communists swept from office and a new generation brought in, albeit briefly, in 1991–93. It had experienced the psychological shock of "losing" lands that had long been part of the Russian empire (Ukraine, Belarus, Kazakhstan). That was a big challenge to Russia's sense of itself as a nation. Without those countries, many people were faced with the question, What does it mean to be Russian? To many Russians, and not only those on the communist left and nationalist right, the collapse of the Soviet empire was akin to defeat in war. Considering that Russia is facing these problems while simultaneously trying to build up a democracy and a free market, it is more likely that, in the 1990s, the country was experiencing too much strain, not too little.

It would be an exaggeration to say that Russia was a clean slate in

1991; no country ever is. But it is hardly excessive to say that almost anything was then possible in Russia. And this, too, was historical. "Interruption," wrote Nikolai Berdyaev, the greatest of Russian philosophers between the first and second world wars, "is a characteristic of Russian history . . . the last thing it is, is organic. . . . It is quite possible that there will be yet another new Russia."[11]

And what might a new Russia be like? That is a question that cultural characteristics can help answer. Though Japan's traditions did not prevent its modernizing, they have helped make it a very different country from other industrial economies. Clearly, countries have followed many different routes to modernity, often from a starting point as unpromising as Russia's. What, then, are the distinctive features of Russia's history and culture, and how have they changed?

There are really four main features. First, there are political ones. Russia has an unusually long tradition of autocracy. "His Majesty is an absolute monarch who is not obliged to answer for his actions to anyone in the world" Peter's military regulation of 1710 proclaimed.[12] That was still in force in 1900. The Communist party then took over this function, proclaiming itself to be "the leading and guiding force of Soviet society." It was still doing so until 1990. And it was not just the government that was undemocratic, so was the opposition: Russian opponents to autocracy tended to be revolutionaries and terrorists rather than reformers and democrats. It seems as if Russia somehow has a predilection for anarchy, which has to be suppressed.

Next come the social features. Russia is a land of serfs, of collectivism, not individualism, of a weak and introspective church, and of a curious philosophical-cum-intellectual system of beliefs called Slavophilism. It has been bypassed by many of the formative influences of the West (it had no Renaissance, for example) and as a result has no tradition of the rule of law, no private property. That, it seems, makes Russia bad at business.

Third, there are geographical features. The country is unimaginably huge; its land is also poor (agriculturally) and sparsely populated. Long cut off from the mainstream of Western and Central Europe, Russia seems to have as much in common with Asia as with Europe. In short, it is not "really European."

And fourth, putting all these together, are the cultural features.

Russia has been in the grip of a "cult of unique destiny," which justifies the most dreadful misery and failure on the grounds that Russia is somehow above the petty materialism of other nations and has been lifted up above them by suffering.

The political differences

In 1973, when Soviet communism was at its height and the West was struggling with the impact of the first oil crisis, a Hungarian historian, Tibor Szamuely, compared the eyewitness accounts of Russia by two famous Frenchmen. The first was the Marquis de Custine, who wrote *The Empire of the Tsar* in 1839; the second was Andre Gide, whose *Back from the USSR* appeared in 1939.

Like his contemporary, Alexis de Tocqueville, Custine was the son of one of the great noble families of France and the product of the aristocratic world of post-Napoleonic Europe. His mother had been confidante to one great statesman, Chateaubriand; he himself had been aide-de-camp to another, Talleyrand. "I went to Russia," Custine admitted, "to seek for arguments against representative government."[13] His father and grandfather had both been guillotined.

Gide, on the other hand, went, as he put it, to glorify "more than a chosen land, an example, a guide . . . where Utopia was in the process of becoming reality."[14] The son of a Protestant merchant, Gide was a product of the years of intellectual ferment on either side of World War I: Champion of the poor, and strong supporter of equal rights for women, the great poet and novelist was the foremost literary champion of communism in Western Europe.

Both men were treated as honored guests in Russia. Custine had a private audience with Tsar Nicholas I. Stalin allowed Gide to stand with the Soviet leaders above Lenin's tomb surveying the May Day parade, the first foreigner to have that privilege.

Yet both men returned to France in bitter—and identical—states of disillusionment. "The more I see of Russia," wrote Custine, "the more I approve the conduct of the Emperor in forbidding his subjects to travel, and in rendering access to his own country difficult to foreigners. The political system of Russia could not survive twenty years' free communication with the rest of Europe." One hundred years later,

Gide concluded that "The Soviet citizen has been persuaded that everything abroad and in every department is far less prosperous than in the USSR. . . . For them outside the USSR, night begins."[15]

The salient features of Russian politics were the dominance of autocracy and the instruments of tyranny. "The empire is the emperor," Custine concluded. "His health, his movements, the project with which he is ostensibly occupied, such are the only subjects worthy of the thoughts of a Russian who thinks at all." "Stalin's effigy is met with everywhere," Gide reported. "His name is on every tongue; his praises are invariably sung in every speech."[16]

"In the USSR," Gide continued, "everybody knows beforehand that on any and every subject there can only be one opinion. Every morning *Pravda* teaches them just what they should know and think and believe. . . . So that every time you talk to one Russian you feel as if you were talking to them all." "I marvel," Custine remarked a century before, "at the prestige which the Russian government exercises over minds. It obtains silence not only from its own subjects—that were little—but it makes itself respected even at a distance by strangers escaped from its iron discipline." Or, as Gide put it, "an attempt is being made to obtain an approval that is not mere resignation, but a sincere, an enthusiastic approval. What is most astounding is that this attempt is successful."[17]

The one result was apparent to the two men. "I doubt whether in any other country in the world, even in Hitler's Germany, can thought be less free, more bowed down, more fearful, more vassalized," Gide wrote. "Fear," wrote Custine, "produces everywhere the same result—peace without tranquillity. . . . In that immense empire, the people, if not tranquil, are mute; death hovers over all their heads." "There is nothing like a stay in the USSR," Gide said, "to help us appreciate the inappreciable liberty of thought we still enjoy in France." One hundred years earlier, the same thought had forced itself upon Custine: "If ever your sons should be discontented with France," he concluded in a savage peroration, "try my recipe; tell them to go to Russia. It is a useful journey for every foreigner: whoever has well examined that country will be content to live anywhere else."[18]

Yet things can change, and change fast. When Custine compared Russia unfavorably with a France animated by a spirit of liberty, he was doing so a mere forty years after his native country had been plunged into the terror and confusion of the French Revolution, and little more than a century after the doctrine of absolute monarchy propounded by Louis XIV ("L'Etat, c'est moi"). In the twentieth century, Germany, Spain, Austria, and Italy have all adopted and abandoned authoritarian forms of government, many of them as extreme as Russia's. All those countries have overcome their historical disadvantages and thrived. Russia has no copyright on autocracy: Most European states in the seventeenth and eighteenth centuries had monarchies that also claimed not to be responsible to anyone except God. Absolutism in many European countries seemed then just as deep-rooted as it does in Russia.

All the features of Russian autocracy identified by Custine and Gide were changing in the early 1990s. A modern Gide or a Custine in Russia would find a Russia that has, for the first time in its modern history, an elected leader. In 1991, when he won 57.3 percent of votes cast in Russia's first-ever presidential election, Boris Yeltsin broke a chain that had been continuous in modern Russian history. Russia also has an elected parliament, though this was not the first (there had been one before 1917). But the modern Duma (the lower house), unlike the pre-revolutionary body after which it was named, actually has some power (to pass the budget, for example), which has been defined in a constitution itself voted upon by the population; before 1917, all power had been vested in the tsar, who delegated some authority to the Duma. And, far from being an over-mighty tyranny in which the state can do as it likes, it is so weak that it has only just been able to prevent the country from drifting into anarchy. When the head of government speaks, it almost seems as if no one is listening, not even his ministers. In the first four months of 1994, the Prime Minister complained, he had issued 296 instructions to his ministers; only 156 had been implemented.

As with tyranny, so with foreign influence, censorship, uniformity, and fear. Custine and Gide had found Russia closed to foreigners. The Soviet authorities had stressed Russia's special role in history and the Soviet superiority in everything; children were taught, for example, that a Russian discovered the laws of thermodynamics and invented television. But in 1991, for the first time since 1917, Russia had a government of young people who had worked or studied abroad and who knew foreign languages. The leader of the group, Yegor Gaidar, argued that Western investors should come to Russia because Russians were more friendly toward foreigners than most East European countries. One of his colleagues, Pyotr Aven, then the minister for foreign trade, who had previously worked in Vienna, argued that there was nothing unique about Russia from the standpoint of economic reform and that Russia needed to learn the lessons of other former communist countries, such as Poland.

Instead of censorship, there was a free, often biased, sometimes irresponsible, and always partisan press. Newspapers ranged in policy from strong support of the government to calling openly for its overthrow. Journalists became polarized: One camp wholeheartedly supported democratic reforms; the other regarded Yeltsin's government as "an occupation regime" bent on destroying the country. Because the press was politicized, the government continued to play a role in its activities as ally and (in the case of television and radio) part owner. But this was not the same as censorship.

The uniformity of having everyone think alike had been transformed into the mixture of chaos and anomie that occurs when no one knows what to think. The first years after independence were a period of extraordinary and often disturbing extremes in behavior. Stalinist nostalgics, tsarists, sharp-suited gangsters, Old Believers (schismatics who had broken away from the Orthodox church in the seventeenth century), entrepreneurial grandmothers, raucous casino owners, Cossack commanders, televangelists, public relations officers, private tutors, faith healers—all suddenly erupted into the new Russia. The wildness and extremism reflected an underlying uncertainty. From being a country in which nothing was allowed because everything was certain, Russia had become a country in which nothing was certain and everything was allowed.

Lastly, boundless fear of one thing—the state—had disappeared, to be replaced by anxieties and emotions about many things: crime, making ends meet, children's education. In February 1992 Russia's last ten political prisoners were released from a prison in Perm, a city formerly closed even to ordinary Russians. After nearly a decade of upheaval, turmoil, and miracles, in which everything amiss—from the nuclear meltdown at Chernobyl to the ending of the Communist party's rule—was deemed "a catastrophe" and "a turning point," this reduction of the scale of Russia's problems itself marked a change. Russia was no longer a country of everyday miracles and disasters but of everyday, though manifold, problems. In its difficulties, as in other matters, it was becoming a more normal, workaday country.

Nowhere was that change clearer than in Russians' attitude toward their ruler. Fear of the ruler had begun to erode, then disappear, under Mikhail Gorbachev. In 1991 it was replaced by its opposite, adulation: Millions surged into the public squares of central Moscow to yell support for Boris Yeltsin. Lonelyhearts advertisements appeared in the classified sections of newspapers: "Lady seeks male companion. Only those who share the politics of Boris Yeltsin need apply."[19] By mid-1994, both had given way to the condition of politics in the West in the mid-1990s: open contempt for the government. That became the period of dark disgust at Boris Yeltsin. Opinion polls had appeared in Russia for the first time in the late 1980s, and within a few years, faith in Yeltsin had dropped from 60 percent to under 10 percent. As Mr. Yeltsin himself put it in his memoirs: "The number one man in the government no longer possesses the magic of mystical, untouchable other-worldliness. And oh, how they lambaste me! I'm an Aquarius, which explains this, that and the other thing. I don't know how to work with people. I can only feel alive in a crisis. There is one reason for people's vexation. They can now imagine anyone in my place. The seemingly endless gulf between society and the government in Russia has now been bridged."[20]

The revolutionary tradition. Autocratic government had not been the only aspect of the Russian political character that acted against the development of an open, stable society. So had Russia's penchant for revolution. It was not just the traditions of government that were undemocratic; so were the traditions of opposition.

Though their names are little known in the west, the Russian revolutionaries—Alexander Herzen, Nikolai Chernyshevsky, Pyotr Tkachev, Mikhail Bakunin, Pyotr Kropotkin, Grigory Plekhanov, and others—constituted a flourishing political school with its own theories and controversies. Pyotr Tkachev, for example, engaged in a long dispute with

Marx's collaborator, Friedrich Engels, over the usefulness of revolutionary action in Russia. Tkachev argued that only revolution could effect change in preindustrial Russia, while Engels thought that Russia was incapable of revolution because it lacked an industrial proletariat.

Two observers from a different part of Europe from Custine and Gide were as forcibly struck by Russia's revolutionary tradition as the Frenchmen had been by the autocratic one. The first was Tibor Szamuely himself, the Hungarian historian who made much of the parallels between Custine and Gide. The second was Thomas Garrigue Masaryk, who became the first president of Czechoslovakia.

Like Gide and Custine, Masaryk and Szamuely came from different worlds. Szamuely, born in 1925, came of an eminent Hungarian revolutionary family, and his personal history symbolized conflict between Russia and the West. A Hungarian born in Moscow and educated in Britain (he was a pupil at Bertrand Russell's Beacon Hill school), Szamuely served in both the Soviet army and the Gulag prison camps, where his father, a prominent communist, perished. Escaping from Russia, he became vice chancellor of Budapest University and later a lecturer at the University of Reading in Britain.

Masaryk, born in 1850, was the son of a peasant family and had been apprenticed as a blacksmith. Like Szamuely, he also spent time in Britain, fleeing to London during World War I, when his homeland, then part of the Austro-Hungarian empire, was fighting on the German side. He had little sympathy with revolutionary upheavals and condemned Hungary's 1919 revolution in which Szamuely's uncle played a prominent role. Masaryk's great book, *The Spirit of Russia*,[21] appeared in 1913, in the final efflorescence of the late tsarist empire, just before its destruction by world war and revolution from above. It was one of the first serious studies of Russia by a foreigner. "I have no hesitation in saying that Russia was and is the most interesting country known to me," he wrote.[22]

"Russia has been in a chronic condition of revolution," wrote Masaryk, "and the problem of the revolution is one of the leading interests of all philosophers of history and statesmen in Russia." Szamuely agreed. "The idea of revolution had come to stay," he wrote of an attempted coup by army officers in 1825. "Russia was never again to be free of its presence."[23]

Both historians were fascinated by the personal qualities of the revolutionaries themselves. "Their ardent devotion to intellectual and political freedom, their self-sacrificing enthusiasm for the folk, their reckless disregard of their personal interests and of their own lives, their fidelity toward their comrades—these are brilliant characteristics," Masaryk contended, "which cannot fail to arouse respect and sympathy for individual revolutionists and for the Russian people from which they sprang." Szamuely, more aware of the dark side of the revolutionaries' activity, could nevertheless barely contain his admiration for the early revolutionaries, who "possessed, in the highest degree, those heroic qualities which went such a long way towards creating and nourishing the sanctity of the Russian revolutionary myth: selflessness, courage, manliness, devotion—and a readiness to meet death." He argued that later revolutionaries "reveal all the familiar qualities of youth through the ages . . . its boldness and exuberance, selflessness and optimism, generosity and idealism, its spirit of revolt, intellectual curiosity and general high mindedness. But also the flaws that go to make up the essence of youth: . . . the arrogance and the credulity, the impatience and the implacability, the ruthlessness and fanaticism."[24]

Both were struck by the role terrorism played in Russia's revolutionary movement. "In no other country was terrorism the deliberate strategy of an organized political party," Szamuely asserted. "Russia was the only country where the terrorists enjoyed general sympathy among the educated and well-to-do classes." Masaryk called terrorism "a typical feature of the Russian revolutionary movement."[25]

That two histories are alike might be explained simply by the facts of history. Yet the stress on the nineteenth-century revolutionary tradition was not a staple of Russian historical writing, especially in 1913, when Masaryk published his work. As Szamuley says, "at the time [the revolutionary tradition] appeared to be only a very minor—indeed almost unknown—aspect of [Russia's] life."[26]

Moreover, the parallels stretch to details such as the role of Pyotr Tkachev, a figure practically unknown in the West and a nonperson in Soviet Russia. Masaryk credits Tkachev with being the first to understand the need to seize power at the start and create the revolution later. Szamuely calls Tkachev "the essential link between Chernyshevsky and Lenin. . . . Of all the skeletons in the Bolshevik cupboard, Tkachev's is the most embarrassing—it rudely intervenes into the apostolic success of Marx–Engels–Lenin. . . . Unrecognized in his life-time, unhonored after his death, he remains a central figure of the Russian revolutionary tradition."[27]

To paraphrase what Szamuely said about Custine and Gide, "Two central Europeans, half a century and a revolution apart—two practically indistinguishable interpretations of Russian history."[28]

Two contemporary worries stem from this revolutionary tradition. First, it was damaging in itself. The revolutionaries encouraged a sense that liberty, civic improvement, and modernization were all to be achieved not by compromise, nor by the interplay of interest groups or the inexorable pressure of popular action, but by violence, conspiracy, and terror. Custine argued that the impatient forces of revolution, along with the autocratic tradition, had denied Russia "an essential fermenting process, and the benefits of a slow and natural culture. The internal labor which forms a great people, and renders them fit to rule, has been wanting."

Second, the revolutionaries were damaging not just in themselves but for what they implied about the country and the temper of the Rus-sians. Masaryk put it this way: "Russians are extremely revolutionary, but not very democratic."[29] The argument is that Russia's revolutionary tradition was a product of some warp of the national character that tol-erates bloody and violent struggle, accepts violence for its own sake, and believes the pursuit of political aims through revolution to be more acceptable than seeking change peacefully. Vissarion Belinsky, the archetype of the nineteenth-century anti-establishment Russian intellec-tual, expressed a common view when he said, "A liberated Russian peo-ple would not go to parliament, but they would hurry to the pub to have a drink, to smash windows and hang the gentry."[30]

Was he right? Is it actually true that Russians are so constituted that they are incapable of resisting autocracy except by revolution? The evidence is against it. The power of the tsar and the lack of pow-erful groups supporting evolutionary change (merchants or shopkeep-ers) made it impossible to oppose autocracy in any other way. Russian revolutionaries themselves were always clear on this point.

The clearest explanation of their view came from the Russian terrorist cell *par excellence*, which was called "Narodnaya Volya" (the Peoples' Will). This was the organization that, on its eighth attempt in 1881, blew to pieces Alexander II, the reformist tsar who had freed the serfs. Yet it was also the organization that, in the same year, published the following resolution on the assassination of President Garfield:

> The executive committee, expressing its profound sympathy with the American people on account of the death of James Abram Garfield, feels it to be its duty to protest in the name of the Russian revolutionaries against all such deeds of violence as that which has just taken place in America. In a land where the citizens are free to express their ideas, and where the will of the people does not merely make the law but appoints the person who is to carry the law into effect, in such a country political assassination is the manifestation of a despotic tendency identical with that to whose destruction in Russia we have devoted ourselves. Despotism . . . is always blameworthy, and force can be justified only when employed to resist force.[31]

Even among some of the revolutionaries, then, there was a democratic impulse. And once tyranny was replaced by an elected government, as now, the democratic impulse could be expected to beat more strongly.

But there was a more important reason for doubting that the revolutionary temper of the Russians will determine the shape of the new Russia. It is that the revolutionaries did not represent ordinary Russians, as they claimed. That was clear to Masaryk and Szamuely. "A comprehensive survey of the entire period of reaction under Nicholas and his predecessors," Masaryk wrote, "fills us with astonishment at the incapacity of the Russian revolutionaries. We recognize how little they were competent even to promote their own interests." Similarly for Szamuely: "The Russian revolutionary tradition . . . remained estranged and remote from the Russian people whose cause it had espoused, but who responded to it with indifference."[32]

In the "mad summer" of 1874, thousands of idealistic students dressed in smocks and carrying bundles of books walked out into the Russian countryside to convert the peasants to socialism. "Going to the People," as it was called, was a crusade, an inverted version of Mao's "learn from the peasants" campaign of the Cultural Revolution.

It was an ignominious failure. Porfiry Voinaralsky, one of the campaign's organizers, was arrested while haranguing his audience about the evils of the government; his listeners had summoned the police. Everywhere the student radicals went, they met with incomprehension, indifference, or hostility. Szamuely quotes one would-be revolutionary writing from the sticks: "They don't take it to heart. It all goes in one ear and out the other."[33] That was characteristic of Russian "revolutions": They never had popular support. The Bolshevik Revolution started as little more than a palace coup. In 1825, a group of idealistic army officers attempted to prevent the coronation of Nicholas I. When tsarist reprisals began against them, the reaction of the ordinary people who were supposed to benefit from the uprising was: "At last they've started to hang the nobles."[34]

Social institutions: Serfdom and collectivism

It is one thing to say that Russians have not responded to revolutionary appeals in the past and have now gotten rid of autocracy. It is quite another to say that Russia is ready, socially and institutionally, for democracy. Many people have doubted that it is and point to the historical record as evidence: Russia was not affected by three of the formative experiences of Western Europe. They also point to Russia's history of serfdom and to its strong collectivist traditions, which militate against private property, the prerequisite for a market economy.

Russia was never part of the Roman empire. "We never had feudalism, the more's the pity," Pushkin said. "There was no Renaissance among us" the philosopher Berdyaev pointed out.[35] Those were the three defining historical experiences that passed Russia by. The second, feudalism, was arguably the most important. The feudal system, with its complex structure of obligations and rights, its powerful landed aristocracy, and its bulwarks against tyranny, was fundamentally different from Russia's absolutism-plus-serfdom. Feudalism paved the way for a society in which ruler and ruled were bound to each other by reciprocal rights and responsibilities. The Russian system produced a country in which everybody except the ruler was a slave, including, said Custine, the aristocrats.

But the significance of those three preindustrial features of Russian history seems remote. Types of feudalism varied all over Europe; so did the influence of the Renaissance. It is not clear whether those differences can be related to contemporary ones. Germany and Scandinavia were not parts of the Roman Empire; Romania, Libya, and Turkey were. This does not tell you all that much about the modern conditions of those countries.

If being outside the influence of Rome still means anything, it is that Russia is part of the Orthodox tradition of Christianity. Some Russian reformers have accused the Orthodox church of obscurantism and complain that Orthodoxy tended to accord the state precedence over the individual. But if Orthodoxy is to be considered a misfortune, it is certainly not uniquely Russian: Ukraine, Bulgaria, Romania, and Greece are all Orthodox. More important, the hold of the Orthodox church over Russia seems to be eroding. Despite the huge increase in the number of those who call themselves "Christians in general" (from 22 percent in 1990 to 52 percent in 1992), the hold of the Orthodox church has plummeted: Only 9 percent claim to belong to the Russian Orthodox church, which dominated Russian religious life for centuries.[36]

Insofar as any of those early historical features make a real difference now, it must be that they affect two things: first, the law and attitudes to the law, and second, Russia's collectivist traditions, which have discouraged individual responsibility and private ownership. Sergei Witte, the finance minister who oversaw Russia's first burst of industrialization in 1892–1903 and who became its first prime minister in 1905, wrote in that year: "Russia in one respect represents an exception to all the countries of the world. . . . the exception consists in this, that the people have been brought up over two generations without a sense of property and legality." Was he right?

It is true that from the eighteenth century, Russian attitudes to law came to differ from those of the West. In the early nineteenth century, Count Benckendorff, chief of Nicholas I's secret police, wrote: "Laws are written for subordinates, not for authorities." A few decades later, a group of Russian philosophers called Slavophiles taught that the basis of a well-ordered state is the moral welfare of the people, not the law or institutions. In the twentieth century, some communists preached that the law, along with the state, would die away. In the

1930s a Marxist legal theorist, Pashukanis, proposed abolishing law altogether and replacing it with administration. As a peasant saying puts it, "Where a court is, there truth is absent."

Yet Russia does not lack a legal tradition. Its first legal code was published in 1497, which was early by European standards. Later, the lack of an independent legal system showed the autocracy at work. Since Russia had an autocratic system of government until 1991, it is hardly surprising that it does not now have a strong independent legal system. But that seems to be changing, albeit slowly.

In 1976 the Soviet Union ratified two Human Rights Covenants, which said in effect: We have human rights; the state cannot remove them; that limits the powers of the state. Those covenants were incorporated into the 1977 Soviet constitution. In October and November 1991, the Russian parliament passed two resolutions spelling out what a "law governed state" meant. The first said that a citizen's interests precede those of the state, that the law applies to citizen and government equally. The second reaffirmed that Russians have human rights to which the law must conform, including freedom of speech, freedom of movement, freedom of assembly, and the right to a proper trial. The parliament established courts as the basic defenders of those rights and proclaimed their independence from outside interference.

In 1995 there were three more changes. Parliament passed a new criminal code, confirming private property rights. An independent Constitutional Court was set up as the supreme arbiter on legal matters, with judges appointed for life (and hence in theory free from political interference). And Russia held its first experiments with trial by jury since 1917. Most of these changes were largely declamatory at first. Legal changes, by their nature, take time to become established. But that is because of the nature of the law, not the nature of the Russians.

What about the other social differences between Russia and the West, its collectivist traditions and its history of serfdom?

Until serfdom was abolished in 1861, Russian peasants were little better than slaves. Serfs had virtually no rights. They could not own property, move, or, in some cases, marry and have children. Masters had virtually unlimited powers over their serfs, including impunity from murder. "Baptized property" was Herzen's graphic term. The main difference from slavery was that while slaves could be bought and sold in their own right, serfs were bound to the land and were supposed to be bought and sold only when the land changed hands.

The institution of serfdom is often said to have formed the Russian national character, leaving Russians without initiative and able to act only upon a master's orders. Belinsky claimed that Russia would be freed only by the action of the tsar. Chekhov lamented that "we must crush the slave within ourselves."

Yet this view is odd. Russia was certainly not unique in having serfdom. Romania, Poland, and some other parts of Eastern Europe had it. The southern part of the United States, of course, had slavery. Not all of Russia had serfdom: the northern half of Russia never adopted the system.

Serfdom was established in Russia after it had been established in the Baltic states and in the Carpathians. Restrictions on serfdom were introduced in 1797, which set three days a week as the maximum that a landowner could require of his serfs, and in 1803, when a law on the free tillers of the soil was passed. Serfdom was abolished in Russia earlier than in Poland and Romania and a year before slavery was abolished in the United States. This enormous social transformation was achieved peacefully in Russia, while in America there was a civil war.

None of this suggests that serfdom is an ineradicable feature of Russia and the Russian character.

Russia's collectivist traditions, it is true, look as if they might be. Communism lasted longer in Russia than in any other country and transformed it more completely. In 1917, Russia remained largely a peasant country. Now, Russia is overwhelmingly industrial (more so, indeed, than so-called industrial countries like Britain and America, where services long ago became more important than manufacturing). Only Russia among communist countries underwent the transformation from peasant-based country to an industrial economy under communist rule (though China is following a similar path).

Moreover, communism's roots ran deep into Russia's pre-revolutionary past. Many of the economic arrangements of communism, in particular the denial of private property rights, the most basic of all,were based on tsarist arrangements. Imperial Russia did not know private ownership of land (though factories were often privately owned). After the abolition of serfdom, the freed serfs did not begin to farm the land to which they had been bound as chattels. They held it collectively. In the areas of the tsarist empire that constitute modern European Russia, communal landholding was almost universal. There was nothing like the small-holdings of Britain, France, or Germany, let alone like the cult of the independent small farmer of America, with its nineteenth-century Homestead Act, which granted parcels of land west of the Mississippi free to anyone who could farm it. The village held the land in common; village councils decided on how it would be farmed; periodically, it would redistribute the land so that a family who had been farming a field at one end of the village would suddenly find itself farming a different plot of land at the other. Ironically, perhaps, this preindustrial and collectivist attitude to property may have contributed to the success of the most ambitious program to create private property rights in an industrial country: Russia's mass privatization program, which, looked at one way, was nothing more than one immense property redistribution, which the Russian tradition made familiar. In most ways, however, the tradition was economically damaging. In the West, the desire of a father to hand down to his son a more productive, better-run farm helped improve agriculture. That could not happen in communal Russia.

Communism, in short, was not the alien imposition in Russia that it was in Central Europe—in Poland, say, or Hungary, where those whose memories stretched back before World War II could recall a non-communist past; or even as it was in Ukraine, which harbored a memory of the independent Ukrainian state lost (it had seemed for good) in the mid-seventeenth century. Significantly, even now Russians lack a true equivalent of the verb "to own"; there are only verbs "to have" and "to possess." But is it true that the collectivist tradition means Russians are bad at business because they are temperamentally averse to private property and private enterprise?

It does not seem that way. The reason that the commune system survived so long was that it suited the distinctive feature of Russian geography: It provided protection in a vast and empty land. With the next village often several days' journey away, the communes formed little protective worlds of their own (the Russian word for commune, "mir," is also the word for both "peace" and "world").

There is absolutely no evidence that Russians, given a chance, are in some way psychologically unprepared for a world of competition and private enterprise; nor do they behave as if capitalism were an alien concept.

In the late nineteenth century Russia entered a period of racing economic growth comparable to that of early-nineteenth-century Britain, 1870s America, or China today. In 1880–1917 Russia laid more miles of railway track than any country in the world at that time; its industrial production grew at an annual rate of 5.7 percent over the whole period, accelerating in the four years before World War I to 8 percent. In 1883 its industrial production had been one-third of France's. Twenty years later it was overtaking France as the world's fourth largest industrial power. Such a thing could hardly have been achieved in a country congenitally slothful, anarchic, or capable only of varied forms of collectivism.

Now, Russians have responded to free-market incentives with a vengeance. In the beginning of 1992, a month after the Russian government finally destroyed the communist system of economic management, the center of Moscow was host to one of the strangest sights in the world: Knotted around a children's department store opposite the former KGB headquarters, tens of thousands of Muscovites stood all day long holding up for sale shirts, glassware, or shoes. There were few stalls. People simply stood around, their stock in a bag at their feet. Something similar had happened in Poland in 1989, after the collapse of the communist economic system, but not on this scale. Moscow's giant bazaars stretched for miles, their tentacles spreading into new alleys almost daily. On weekdays, seven thousand people were out selling; twice that number on weekends. On average, they earned about a dollar an hour, ten hours a day, making the market while it lasted one of Moscow's largest enterprises. All this came from nothing within three months: Before the economic system was changed, the market had not existed. It was a veritable explosion of entrepreneurial spirits.

Social science confirms that Russians are no more hostile to free markets, struggling for private gain, and competition than anyone else. The most extensive research on the subject was carried out by an American and two Russians, Robert Schiller, Maxim Boycko, and

Vladimir Korobov, who compared America and Russia.[37] Russians, they found, are just as tolerant of income inequalities as Americans are, and no more attached than they to the notion of "fair" prices; they have a stronger appreciation of the importance of economic incentives. Such differences as do exist—Russians are less likely to count private businessmen among their friends—can be better accounted for by differing political experience than by deep social dissimilarities. There has been an enormous cultural shift toward entrepreneurship. Few things express that so aptly as a new proverb that became popular in 1994: "Those who do not take risks will not drink champagne."[38]

The burden of geography

What about the third set of reasons for doubting Russia's ability to reform, the "geographical" one?

The fundamental fact of geography, some people have argued, is Russia's single most important feature. "We are consumed with geography," Vyacheslav Ivanov, an eminent literary critic, writes, "and we have no real history."[39] Geography matters for several reasons. It has overdeveloped several political institutions, notably the army. It has fostered a laager mentality among the Russians, who feel threatened on all sides by other peoples covetously eyeing Russia's empty and apparently indefensible spaces. And it has isolated Russia from Europe, making it a partially Asian country.

In an age of distance-shrinking telecommunications, it is hard to grasp the immensity of Russia. Driving south from Moscow, it will take all day to reach the Ukrainian border. The landscape of flat fields does not change. You will have driven through three once-independent princedoms. Kiev, the closest of the world's capitals to Moscow, is still another day's drive away. Yet this is a mere quarter-inch on a map a foot wide. When the sun is setting in Kaliningrad, an exclave between Poland and Lithuania, it is rising the following day in Vladivostok. It takes a week to travel by train from Moscow to the Russian Far East.

In 1993, the governor of Vladivostok said that when he wanted to forestall an unwelcome visit from officials in Moscow, "I just tell them the airport is closed." No natural borders interrupt this expanse. The Ural mountains are high but slope gently like hills. The rivers are mighty but do not define international borders. Most of Russia is steppe, forest, or tundra stretching to a flat horizon.

This immense expanse is a fundamental and unchanging feature of Russian life, and the struggle to control it occupies a large part of Russia's historical experience. The parallel is with the Oregon or Santa Fe trails that led through the American West and fostered a frontier spirit of doughty independence. But while those who braved the Oregon Trail eventually reached the rich pastures of California, the Russian settlers reached only a Far East as featureless and barren as the East European steppe they had left behind.

While the settlement of the American West took three or four generations, the conquest of Siberia has taken four hundred years. The first settlements had their foundation in the late sixteenth century, when Tyumen was established in western Siberia (it is now the capital of the country's oil-drilling operations). Within half a century, in 1649, the Russians had established their first outpost on the Pacific, at Okhotsk. Yet three centuries later, the conquest of Siberia and the Far East remains unfinished. The second Siberian railway, the Baikal–Amur line (dubbed by Brezhnev the project of the century), was finished only in the late 1980s. And while the captured territory of the American West had to be defended from tribes and nomads, generation after generation of Russians have waged a relentless, life-or-death struggle against the poverty of the land and the hostility of the neighbors. Here, the parallel is with the Great Treks of Southern Africa, with their laager mentality of ever present danger, their expectation of arbitrary reversals of fortune, and their necessity of sticking together in adversity.[40]

The difficulty of defending these inhospitable lands was immense. Russia, like Germany and Poland, has no natural boundaries, no impassable rivers or mountain ranges. And it is surrounded by past and potential enemies or rivals, such as China or, in the past, Turkey and Poland. The difficulty of defending the land facilitated the growth of a dominant and over-mighty state. A huge army had to be raised to defend the invisible borders. In the sixteenth and seventeenth centuries, the Prince of Muscovy maintained a standing army of more than 50,000 men to defend the state against the Tatar descendants of

Genghis Khan, who would periodically swoop out of the East in raids reminiscent of the barbarian invasion of the Roman Empire more than a thousand years before. To raise 50,000 men was a staggering feat. Cromwell's contemporaneous New Model Army was smaller and was raised in a richer country fighting an all-out civil war. The largest fighting force that Western Europe had ever seen in feudal times—the army of the first crusade, which had drawn on the entire resources of Christendom—comprised only 30,000 men. Those were extraordinary efforts, which beggared the countries that made them. Russia's, in contrast, was a standing army, raised season after season, year after year, in a state scraping a meager living from the poor farmland around Moscow. It is hard not to see a parallel between that mighty effort and the later obsession of the Soviet Communist party with maintaining nuclear parity with the United States, a far richer country, or, even after the collapse of communism, Russia's decision to maintain an army of some 2 million men, by far the largest in Europe. The only way to raise such a huge force and to keep it together was through a strong, centralized power to which the army was loyal.

All those geographical features remain, but it is necessary to put them in perspective. Vast size is not unique to Russia. America, Canada, and Australia are all continental-size countries thinly populated by people of European descent. They do not thereby consider themselves to be anti-Western or antiliberal as a result. Poland, like Russia, lies on flat land unprotected by natural barriers; its borders have shifted throughout history even more wildly than Russia's. This is not usually taken as a reason for thinking Poland is doomed by its geography to autocracy.

Of course, Russia is larger than any of those countries (it is twice the size of Canada, the largest of them). Yet its immense size is somewhat misleading. The overwhelming proportion of Russians—60 percent at the last census—live west of the Ural mountains in European Russia. The rest of the country—more than 70 percent in land area but only 40 percent of population—is like an appendage. Rodric Braithwaite, a former British Ambassador to Moscow, likens Russia to a tadpole pointing left—mostly head, with a long trailing tail. The European part of Russia is smaller than Canada and America and about the same size as Australia.

What has made the difference for the cohesion of these huge countries is the development of modern communications, especially air travel and telecommunications. It keeps Russia together too. In 1991, the last year before it was broken up into separate companies, Aeroflot was the busiest airline company in the world, carrying more than 138,000 passengers and serving 3,600 destinations throughout the former Soviet Union. Russian planes were usually full to overcrowding. Families and businessmen were constantly shuttling back and forth between cities. Air travel and the telephone shrink distance and help tie the country together. No longer is Russia a country of isolated villages, several days' ride from the nearest town, like a huge archipelago of hamlets scattered across an ocean of steppe.

Indeed, it is not a country of villages at all. During the past thirty years, Russians have poured from the countryside into the cities in a way unprecedented in human history. In 1939 two-thirds of the population was rural and gained its living on the land (about the same share as in Morocco today). Now, over three-quarters of Russians live in cities. Many developing countries have seen explosions in their urban populations, but even they lag behind Russia's. Russia is now a country of cities tied together by airlines and telephones, quite unlike the ocean of island villages that made up the old Russia.

Just as the transport revolution helps tie the cities together, so changes in military technology have affected the need to keep an immense standing army. It is no longer all-important to occupy territory physically. Aleksandr Lebed, a popular general who resigned from the army to pursue a political career in 1995, pointed out that the Gulf War of 1991 showed it is possible to inflict a military defeat on an army in vast desert spaces through the use of high-tech airborne weaponry, which Russia possesses. Much of Russia is surrounded by exactly such deserts and open plains. Though Russia in 1995 maintained a large standing army, the changes in military technology would seem to reduce the need for a huge army in the long run. That should, in turn, speed up the demilitarization of the country.

"We are Asiatics, a slant-eyed greedy brood." What about the argument that geography has isolated Russia from Europe and made it a partially Asian country?

Until Peter the Great, Russia was said to be totally isolated from Europe. Actually, the person who said it most often was Peter himself, who fostered the myth of isolation to justify wars against Sweden and to achieve a "breakthrough to the West." In fact, long before Peter's reign Russian merchants had carried on substantial trade with the countries of Northern and Eastern Europe. Novgorod, the largest trading city of Russia's northeast until the late sixteenth century, was a member of the Hanseatic League, the German chain of city-states, which extended to Hamburg in the West.

Nevertheless, it is true that Russia later developed a strong sense of being a partially non-European country. What made it non-European was an admixture of Asian elements.

The clearest expression of this is a cultural movement called Scythianism, which flourished in the years immediately before and after the Bolshevik Revolution.

> *Yea—we are Scythians!*
> *Yea—we are Asians, a slant-eyed greedy brood,*[41]

wrote Alexander Blok three months after the October Revolution in his last great poem, "The Scythians," which came to define what the movement was about. Scythianism was aggressively anti-European. Blok's poem contrasts vigorous, wild Russia with decadent, civilized Europe.

> *To welcome pretty Europe . . .*
> *. . . We shall turn*
> *To you our alien Asiatic face.*

Russians, the Scythians claimed, were as much Asiatic as European; their qualities of spontaneity and fierce emotion came from the Asiatic side. Over the years, they argued, the purer Asiatic tradition had become polluted by a European strain, which, by the start of the twentieth century, had come to dominate the country. Blok and others welcomed the Bolshevik Revolution as a kind of Asiatic revenge upon European Russia. The Scythian, argued Yevgeny Zamyatin in a critical essay published in 1918, is the eternal nomad, in perpetual revolt against established order and the quintessential revolutionary.

On the face of it, there seems to be no obvious reason why the Asiatic strain in Russia's makeup should make it harder to reform and modernize the country. Considering the extraordinary economic successes of Japan, South Korea, Singapore, Taiwan, and other Asian dragons, it might seem that Asian traditions should actually help Russia prosper. In practice, it is true, no one, including the Scythians, thought Russia was really an Asian country. They thought of it as a mixture of Asian and European, falling between the two and acting as a bridge between East and West. The so-called Eurasian movement, a group of Russian émigrés of the 1920s (that is, rough contemporaries of the Scythians), declared that "the Russian people . . . are neither Europeans nor Asians. Merging with the culture and life that surrounds us, we are not ashamed to call ourselves Eurasians."[42] One of their number, Pyotr Savitsky, called Eurasia "a geopolitical civilization" of its own.

But insofar as Russia was Asian, it took from Asia elements that made it impossible to adopt Western forms of democracy and free markets. One such element was despotism. An émigré linguist, Prince Nikolai Trubetskoi, argued in the 1920s that the legacy of Genghis Khan was still alive for the Russians. In the 1240s the princedoms of northeastern Russia became tributary lands of the Golden Horde, a branch of the Mongols' vast empire controlled by Batu Khan, Genghis' grandson. For the next three hundred years, Russia lay, as the Russians call it, "under the Tatar Yoke." Russia's political institutions derive from the system of government set up by the Mongols. Many Russian words associated with taxation and the financial apparatus of government, for instance, are of Mongol origin: *tamozhnya* (customs office), *kaznachei* (treasurer), even the word money itself, *dengi*.

The way in which Russia's non-European features were said to undermine its ability to adopt democracy, the rule of law, and other attributes of a modern state can be seen from a description by Masaryk of the beliefs of the Slavophiles, a movement of intellectuals who began from about 1830 to describe Russia in non-Western terms. "In its intimate nature," Masaryk wrote, "Russia differs from Europe. . . . The Russian state has grown organically out of the commune, the *mir;* the European state originated through armed occupations and the subjugation of foreign peoples. . . . Russian law, too, has developed organically out of the convictions of the people, whereas European law, imposed by the Roman conquerors, finds its climax in outward legalism and in the formalism of the letter. . . . In Russia property is communal . . . for the individual has a value as such; in Europe, the individual is valueless—it is the soil which has value, not the individual."[43]

Many Russians (and some students of Russia in the West) still argue that Russia's non-European features mean the country cannot adopt Europe's market-oriented or democratic systems.

But is it actually true that Eurasianism is a defining characteristic of Russia? Does the country really fall between Europe and Asia, between East and West? Russia's Asiatic influences might seem obvious when you look at the country from Europe. Yet within Russia matters look much less clear.

Russians may like to define themselves as different from Europeans, but they distinguish themselves from Asians just as readily. In the very part of the country where you might expect the Asian influence to be strongest, in Vladivostok and its surrounding province, the local governor has kept his local support strong largely by claiming to be a bulwark against China and by warning that, without him, eastern Russia would be overrun by the yellow peril. Ironically, despite their claim that Russia was partly Asian, the Scythians also saw Russia this way. As Blok put it in "The Scythians":

We were the shield between the breeds
Of Europe and the raging Mongol horde.

Ordinary Russians seem not to have thought of themselves as particularly Asian. In the nineteenth century, when Alexei Khomyakov, one of the leading proponents of Russia's supposedly "Eurasian" identity, took to wearing "traditional Russian" clothes of flowing, multicolored robes, he was laughed at on the street. The Russians thought he was dressing up as a Persian.

Russia's religious traditions are Christian. Its culture is overwhelmingly European. It is hard to think of a single art form that developed in the West to which Russia has not made a large contribution: the novel (Turgenev, Tolstoy, Dostoevsky, Pasternak); drama (Chekhov), the art of acting (Stanislavsky), classical music (Tchaikovsky, Stravinsky,

Shostakovich), classical ballet (Diaghilev, Nureyev, Baryshnikov), painting (Chagall, Kandinsky), cinema (Sergei Eisenstein, Andrei Tarkovsky), and so on.

And despite the Mongol roots of some words, the influence of the nomadic tribes of Asia on Russia's political and social arrangements seems virtually nonexistent. The argument that Russia's autocratic traditions are Asian seems perverse when so many countries in Western Europe also had autocratic forms of government for so long. Insofar as Russia's autocracy had features that were distinctly different from those of Western Europe, those features were the Orthodox church and a system of small communal assemblies, which regulated everyday life in the villages. The Orthodox tradition came from Byzantium ("eastern" to be sure, but Eastern Europe, not Asia). And the village assemblies, according to the Russian historian V. I. Sergeyevich, seem to have come ultimately from Scandinavia, not Asia.

Indeed, there is a good case for saying that the main geographic split in Russia is not between east and west but between north and south. In 1989, at the first real parliamentary session since 1917, the distinguished historian Dmitri Likhachev regaled the deputies with an erudite speech about Russia's place in the world, arguing that the most important feature of Russia was that it lay between the Arctic and Scandinavian north and the Black Sea. "Scandoslavia," he said, made more sense as a description of Russia than "Eurasia."[44]

Whether the Russian past points north, south, east, or west, the Russian present is not constrained by any particular geography. Custine and Gide declared that suspicion and ignorance of foreigners were the norm. Now there are openness to foreigners, knowledge of them, and, if not friendliness, then at least a wary tolerance. In the years after economic reform started, the center of Moscow, like every other city in the world, became ablaze with the marketing of Western goods. As you walk down Moscow's main street from the statue of Alexander Pushkin, Russia's national poet, toward Red Square, the historic center of the empire, you pass shop after shop peddling the icons of Western consumerism. At the start comes McDonald's, which, when it opened in 1991, was the busiest fast-food restaurant in the world. Next come the soft drink stands selling Coca-Cola and Pepsi, a showroom for Western cars, and a couple of casinos. Last, as you approach Saint Basil's, Ivan the Terrible's fantastic dream of old Russian architecture, comes a row of French perfumeries.

What glares brightly in Moscow is reflected more dimly all over Russia. The same limited number of Western products—cigarettes, soft drinks, and perfumes—are available in virtually every town in Russia; advertisements for them, often, for modernity's sake, using the Latin not the Cyrillic alphabet, are papered on billboards, buildings, and buses. The soap operas that are the vehicles for advertising these goods in the West have seen extraordinary television successes. In the spring of 1992 millions of viewers a week turned on their sets for *The Rich Also Cry*, a television soap opera from Mexico about the agonies of the jet set.

In 1994 it was estimated that 200,000 foreigners were living in Moscow, by far the largest group of non-Russians ever to have gathered in the heart of the once-closed country. Their numbers increased dramatically in the first five years after the fall of communism (in 1989 there had been a few thousand in Moscow). From the sixteenth century to the early 1990s, foreigners had been forced to live in gilded ghettos, separated from the Russians around them. That isolation has left its physical mark upon the city. The so-called German quarter, where foreign merchants and emissaries lived, a district of large family mansions and leafy boulevards, is still among Moscow's most gracious areas, retaining an air of bourgeois grandeur at odds with the proletarian gigantism of much of the rest of the city. It was the district in which the great westernizing tsar, Peter the Great, who tried to wrench Russia westward, developed his taste for things European.

As late as 1991 foreigners had no choice about where they could live; they could obtain a flat, and the necessary residence permit, only from a special department of the Soviet Foreign Ministry. Thus the Soviet government corralled foreigners into a couple of dozen state-approved, and state-bugged, apartment blocks.

Within three years, those age-old arrangements for separating Russians and foreigners had broken down. At first a few enterprising Westerners began to ignore the ministry's demands, quietly making their own arrangements to sublet apartments from Russians. When communism collapsed, so did the ministry's ability and willingness to police the old arrangements. Suddenly foreigners could begin to rent apartments wherever they wanted. Of course, since Russia is poor and foreigners relatively rich, in 1991–92, they had their pick of Moscow's districts and were not to be found in the poorest outlying areas of the city. But since Moscow, unlike Western cities, had few exclusive residential areas for the rich only—no Upper East Side, no Belgravia, no 16th arrondisement—within a few years, foreigners became far more widely scattered than they used to be. By 1993, for the first time ever, Russians and foreigners found themselves living cheek-by-jowl in the same buildings.

And Russians' knowledge of foreign lands is not confined to seeing expensive Western consumer goods and expensive Westerners in their own cities. More important, they themselves are traveling to see other countries. In 1993, 9 million Russians traveled abroad, a development of potentially historic significance. For the first time in Russian history, a sizable share of the population (7 percent in a year) was able to see with its own eyes what foreign countries are like. And all this was achieved despite the high cost of travel (the cost of an air fare between Moscow and London was three times higher than the average monthly salary in 1994) and despite the endless inefficiencies and obstructiveness of the Russian authorities, who three years after Russia became independent were still issuing passports stamped "Soviet Union," a country that no longer existed.

The connection with the West produced an explosion of international telephone traffic. In 1994, Russians made 4.5 billion minutes' worth of international telephone calls, a thirty-six-fold increase in just two years.[45]

Russia rejoined the world economy in 1992–93, taking membership in the various institutions that set the framework for it—the International Monetary Fund and the World Bank—and applied to join the World Trade Organization. It also started to trade with Europe and America far more than it had previously. In short, Russia in 1991–94 began to break through the barriers of isolation, ignorance, and xenophobia, becoming awash with foreign influences.

The ending of seventy years of isolation was an important contribution to ending extremism. It has been repeatedly noted that workers in so-called isolated industries—miners, sailors, fishermen, lumberjacks, or shepherds—tend to give overwhelming support to left-wing politics. The requirements of the job produce communities in which everyone is engaged in the same occupation. Such isolation seems to reduce the pressures on such workers to be tolerant of other points of view. Such districts tend to vote communist or socialist by large majorities. If the country is cut off from the rest of the world by its rulers, the phenomenon can operate at the level of the whole country. That is what happened in the Soviet Union in 1917–89. And that is why Russia's opening up is so important.

The cult of unique destiny

All these things together—the political and social changes and the changes in context that make the unyielding facts of geography less important—are combining to undermine what seems the most striking and, to outsiders, most peculiar feature of Russia's national character, the cult of unique destiny.

There were two broad schools of thought in nineteenth-century Russia: Slavophiles who thought that Russia should return to its indigenous roots, and Westernizers who thought it should seek to learn from Western Europe. On most issues, the distinction between them holds good. Yet on the question of Russia's place in the world, there were no real differences between them. Both agreed that Russia had a special destiny, an almost messianic redemptive mission to save mankind.

Alexei Khomyakov, one of the founders of Slavophilism, referred to Russia as "God's instrument"[46] and said that the Russians were ready to become the leaders and saviors of Europe, whose nations would follow Russia willingly. Fyodor Dostoevsky wrote: "Our great Russia will speak its new word, a healthy word, not previously heard by the world, to all the world."[47] In a speech celebrating Alexander Pushkin, the great novelist declared that "the mission of the Russian people is certainly all European and worldwide. . . . To a true Russian, Europe [is] as precious as Russia herself. . . . What has Russia been doing these two entire centuries in its policy, if not serve Europe much more than herself?"[48]

Such messianic views were held just as strongly by Westernizers. Chaadayev, the first of the Westernizers, who damned the Slavophiles as obscurantists, nevertheless maintained: "We belong to those nations who are destined in the future to teach the world some great lesson."[49] Nikolai Mikhailovsky, who translated John Stuart Mill, Auguste Comte, and Karl Marx into Russian, wrote, "We believe that Russia can lay down a new historical path from that taken by Europe."[50] A loud echo of this idea sounded over the crowds gathered outside the Russian parliament on August 24, 1991, to hear the celebratory speeches after the defeat of the attempted communist coup. "Russia," declaimed Boris Yeltsin, the victor of that hour, "has saved the world."

The really peculiar feature of this messianic vision was that Russia would save the world not by virtue of superior government or superior social organization, culture, or force, but by the moral qualities of the Russian people. In them lay the heart of Russia's uniqueness. In one of the best-known poems in Russia, the Slavophile Fyodor Tyutchev writes:

Russia can't be grasped by the mind,
Ordinary yardsticks will deceive.
Her nature is of a special kind—
In Russia one can only believe.

In the Slavophile view, the West was synonymous with rational and scientific inquiry and with self-interest. Those were inimical to traditional Russian values, which respected emotion more than reason. As long ago as 1784 an English visitor to St. Petersburg, William Richardson, observed: "They have certainly more sensibility than firmness. They have lively feelings; but having seldom employed their reason in forming general rules of conduct for the commerce of life, their actions, as flowing from variable and shifting emotions, are desultory, and even inconsistent. . . . This is a character which you may often see exemplified in individuals: But I suppose Russia is the only country where it is so general as to become a leading feature in the *national* character."[51]

In the extreme case, Slavophiles would reject reason and self-interest altogether. Here is Dostoevsky on the subject: ". . . a man, whoever he is, always and everywhere likes to act as he chooses, and not at all according to the dictates of reason and self-interest; it is indeed possible, and sometimes *positively imperative* (in my view), to act directly contrary to one's own best interest. One's own free and unfettered volition, one's own caprice, however wild, one's own fancy, inflamed sometimes to the point of madness—that is one's best and greatest good."[52]

The "I" of that passage is not Dostoevsky but the anonymous narrator of a novella, *Notes from Underground*. This narrator was the great novelist's attempt to portray the "real man of the Russian majority."[53]

So the character of the Russians themselves, as evinced by Slavophilism and the cult of unique destiny, seems to saddle the country with a most peculiar burden. Perversely blind to their own interest—indeed, glorying in acting against them—it is hardly surprising that Russians have failed to fulfil their potential. The word failure does not describe it: Russia has succeeded in avoiding those material achievements which other countries regard as beneficial.

New Russians, new values. That, at least, is how Russia's history seems from the point of view of the cult of unique destiny. Yet despite Dostoevsky's claim to be portraying "the real man of the Russian majority," what he was actually portraying was the viewpoint of a tiny minority, the Slavophiles, who seem so un-European. Like the intellectuals of the "mad summer" of 1874, there is no evidence that the Slavophiles were ever anything more than a few rarefied intellectuals who remained estranged from the people in whose name they claimed to be speaking.

If Russia ever was a country in which appeals to spiritual destiny and the importance of faith stir appreciation, it is no longer. A sense is growing that those qualities have failed Russia. A century after Tyutchev's famous quatrain, another poet, Maria Arakkumova, metaphorically flung the line back in his face:

> *"Russia can't be grasped by the mind,*
> *Ordinary yardsticks will deceive.*
> *Her nature is a special kind."—*
> *But just how much can one only believe?!*[54]

The nearest thing to a popular upholder of Slavophile views in modern Russia is Aleksandr Solzhenitsyn, who returned from exile in

America in 1994 to travel across Russia by train from Vladivostok to Moscow. Respect for a great writer and a man who had always refused to bow down to communists brought thousands out at railway stations to meet him and hear his speeches. Yet Solzhenitsyn's Slavophile political views, propounded in a speech to the parliament, failed to stir popular enthusiasm. Even he rejected the traditional Slavophile support for autocracy in favor of demanding a democratic system of elected village assemblies.

Few serious politicians these days advance the view that the Russian tradition means the country has a unique economy that must be reformed in its own way. The research of Schiller, Boycko, and Korobov has shown that Russians are no more hostile to business or private property than Americans are, nor are they more intolerant of income inequalities. Sergei Glasiev, the chief economist for the unextreme nationalist opponents of Yeltsin's government, whom you might have expected to stress Russia's economic uniqueness, instead criticizes the government for failing to learn from Japan how to run a modern economy.

Above all, Russian nationalism has lost much of its appeal. Many leading Russians claim to be highly nationalistic. Russian politicians of every kind promote the age-old idea of a strong Russian state. Westerners point to the success of the xenophobic Vladimir Zhirinovsky as proof that Russian nationalism is reviving. Yet those who voted for Zhirinovsky hardly ever said they supported him because they wanted to take Alaska back or have Russian soldiers dip their boots in the warm water of the Indian Ocean, as Zhirinovsky promised. Consistently, they said they voted for him because they believed he would do something about crime.

Similarly, the evidence of the opinion polls does not bear out the assumption that nationalism is popular. It points the other way. Sergei Filatov and Lyudmila Vorontsova conducted a series of opinion polls in 1991–94. Their conclusion was that Russians feel not pride in their country, but contempt for it. Citing a "national nihilism," they point out that less than one-third of young people see military service as a "duty and honor" and show that only 10 percent associate "fidelity to national traditions" with the main influence on matters of faith and morals. And they conclude: "People shun identification with this country and this nation."[55]

Such nihilistic attitudes may not survive long. They are best explained as the reaction to the failures of communist rule and the initial difficulties of reform. Sooner or later, Russians will start rebuilding their sense of nationhood. But they are likely to do so on a new basis, not on the rejected features of the old Russia—autocracy, communism, and unique destiny. The qualities they now respect have to do with civil rights: 74 percent of respondents advocated freedom of conscience; 70 percent endorsed full freedom of expression even for detested communists and xenophobes.[56] Those are attributes not of a unique, messianic state but of what Russian reformers have long held up as their aim: a normal country.

Chapter 3

Why did Communism fail?

Inefficiency · Isolation · The defense burden · Good news about capitalism ·
Mikhail Gorbachev · Evaluation · Boris Yeltsin

To understand Russia's present situation, it is essential to begin with the communist system and to understand why it failed.[1] There were four main reasons: it was inherently inefficient; it isolated Russia from the influence of world trade; it crippled Russia with an impossible level of defense costs; and, finally, Russians learned that capitalism works better.

Inefficiency

Communism worked like this. The planners decided what should be produced. They then told each enterprise what to make and where to send it. Thus every enterprise was given output targets plus an allocation of supplies of the necessary inputs. The plan was executed through a set of "state orders," commands to each enterprise to supply such and such outputs to specified customers at such and such prices.

There were two problems. The plan was often ill-conceived, and there was no way to get it executed. The first was a problem of information, the second of incentive. Bureaucrats could never figure out effectively what consumers really wanted, nor could they balance the customer's valuation of what he got against its cost. For example, Russia provided too little housing and simultaneously overheated it. Compared with Canada, which is equally cold, Russia used five times as much energy per unit of total output. As technology became more complex, it became increasingly difficult for planners to select an effective pattern of production.

Even more serious was the lack of incentive to perform. To be promoted, a good communist must of course show that he could achieve his target, and that often involved a good deal of tough negotiation and extra-plan activity. But a good communist should not question whether the target was sensible. If he had a different idea of what could be useful, there was no way he could acquire the resources to do it, let alone be rewarded for his efforts.

The most obvious achievement of communism was full employment. But it was achieved by controlling prices while at the same time printing enough money to ensure that people always wanted to buy more than could be produced. The result was seventy-five years of queues in the shops and shortages of almost everything. By the end of the communist era, more time was spent in queuing for food than in producing it.

However, in the early postwar period communism still inspired some idealism, and many Russians still miss the sense of common purpose that existed then. In the 1950s and 1960s the Russian economy grew rapidly, like many Western economies. There was a postwar catch-up in output; productivity grew rapidly as people moved from the country to the towns; natural resources were increasingly exploited; and there was still a strong sense of national endeavor. But from the mid-1970s onward growth slowed or probably stopped. The figures are extremely difficult to interpret. Russian output was probably exaggerated both by the Russian authorities, to prove Russia's power, and by the U.S. Central Intelligence Agency—for the same reason. Output was also overestimated in the communist part of Germany, where we now know from the experience of German reunification that productivity was only one-third of the West German level, not one-half, as had previously been thought.

Certainly from around 1980 on Russian consumers ceased to feel any clear increase in their living standards, even though official figures record 3 percent annual growth through the 1980s. What had gone wrong? The Russian economic establishment thought the problem was lack of investment. But in fact it lay elsewhere. The root cause was the inherent inefficiency of communism, which had by that stage run out of steam.

Isolation

Another cause was economic isolation. In the West one of the main engines of growth was international trade, which led to the rapid spread of new technology from one country to another. By contrast, Russia was largely cut off from trade with the West.

All foreign trade had to be conducted through a limited number of state foreign trade organizations. If an individual enterprise wanted to import a key new technology, it had to go through those organizations. Currency was not convertible, and scarce dollars were allocated by bureaucratic fiat. No wonder that most Russian organizations relied on Russian technology, which was often decades behind the best practice.

On top of this the U.S. government imposed a set of rules banning exports to the Soviet Union of high-technology goods likely to help the Soviet defense effort. Those rules forced Russia to develop most of its own defense and space technology, which it did with considerable brilliance. Russia's Titan space rocket is better than America's equivalent, the Saturn, and Russia's Sukhoy fighter plane is the best in the world. But those achievements were bought at great cost.

Most Westerners understood that communism was not working. But almost none forecast the speed of its collapse. What brought it down so quickly? The main causes were the burden of defense costs and the spread of information about capitalism—plus the democratic policies of Mikhail Gorbachev.

The defense burden

An important reason for Soviet economic stagnation was the massive burden of the defense effort. Exactly how the Cold War got started is a matter of dispute. It is easy to understand why Russia feared the West, after being attacked in 1914, 1919, and 1941. At least 20 million Russians died in World War II. But Russia's actions in 1945–48 in turn created fears in the West, as did its declared desire to promote communism in the West. Thus began the biggest arms race in history.

But the race was always unequal. Parity in defense capability requires (roughly speaking) equal defense expenditure on both sides. Since the Soviet Union's GDP was roughly one-seventh of NATO's, defense parity meant that the Soviets had to spend roughly seven times more of their income on defense. While the West was spending about 4 percent of national income on defense, the Soviet Union had to spend over a quarter of its income.[2]

Around 1980 the defense burden was further increased by two historic events. The first was the Soviet invasion of Afghanistan in 1979. This act of folly by Brezhnev was a direct replay of America's fruitless intervention in Vietnam, and led after nine years to humiliating retreat. Meanwhile some 15,000 young Soviet citizens had been killed and many more wounded. That failure dealt a heavy blow to confidence in the regime and finally buried the dream of world communism.

At the same time, the Western defense effort intensified. From the moment of his election as U.S. president, Ronald Reagan stepped up U.S. defense expenditure by 3 percent each year. That remorseless buildup included the "Star Wars" program, designed to make America impregnable (and thus able if it had wished to attack Russia with impunity).

Reagan can hardly have expected the "Star Wars" initiative to bring down the "evil empire" within his lifetime, but it must have contributed to that result. For by the late 1980s Russia had decided that it could never again afford to impose its will upon Eastern Europe by force of arms.

Good news about capitalism

But communism would never have fallen unless people had known there was a better alternative. The key here was the spread of information. At the same time as the communist economy was ceasing to grow, Russians became increasingly aware of the success of capitalism. An important influence was foreign travel, one of the main perks available to the *nomenklatura* and their children. It was the children of the *nomenklatura* who first lost faith in communism. The travelers brought back books. American novels in particular pictured a world of freedom, in stark contrast to the constraints of life in Russia. And Western publications of books by dissidents opened Russian eyes to communist oppression in the gulag and in Eastern Europe.

Another influence was films. Some Western films, like those of Fellini, were shown in Russia in order to depict the depravity of capitalism, but they had the opposite effect. More important was Western radio. For a long time broadcasts in Russian were jammed in cities,[3] but broadcasts in English were not, so to understand Western broadcasts one needed to know English. Up to the mid-1970s only a handful of Russians had a working knowledge of English. Western pop music was banned and available mainly through "music on the bone"—pirated records of Elvis Presley and others, made on discarded X-ray plates! But from the mid-1970s on Western pop music began to be played on Russian radio. That created a huge teenage demand for English in order to understand the words. When those teenagers became adults, they tuned in to Western radio news.

This presented a totally different picture of the world. Russia was not, it appeared, the most wholesome country in the world, whose economic system would soon spread worldwide. It was unfree; it ignored consumers' wants; and it oppressed other nations.

Mikhail Gorbachev

Such was the Russia Gorbachev inherited when in 1985 he became general secretary of the party. He took two key decisions. The first was not to intervene if Eastern Europe tried to throw off communism. The second was to reform the Soviet Union by a mixture of political liberalization (glasnost) and economic reform (perestroika). He launched glasnost and perestroika at the same time. That was a key decision and determined much of what followed. Glasnost led inexorably to democracy, and within six years the power of the Soviet state had collapsed.

Gorbachev's economics. But the collapse was hastened by the complete failure of Gorbachev's other policy, perestroika. Economic reform was ineffective, and living standards stagnated, making Gorbachev eventually one of the most unpopular of all Soviet rulers. Expenditure was stepped up to try and increase growth. Meanwhile state revenue fell. When the world oil price dropped in 1985, state revenue from oil exports fell. And domestic revenue from alcohol was cut by Gorbachev's anti-alcohol campaign. As state power ebbed away, enterprises paid fewer taxes, and from 1990 on republics forwarded fewer of their taxes to Moscow. By 1991 the budget deficit was at least 20 percent of the GDP. The deficit was financed by printing money, which led to increased inflationary pressure and ever longer queues. If you went to a typical supermarket you would often find only five or ten types of product on the shelves.

Gorbachev never came to grips with the economic problem. He encouraged debate and the writing of endless reform proposals, and in the summer of 1990 his great opportunity came. The group he had commissioned under Shatalin produced its famous "500 days" report. Had Gorbachev followed its line, he would possibly have led Russia, or even the Soviet Union, into a proper economic reform. But he opted for the policy of ultra-gradualism—nearer to 500 years than 500 days.

The most immediate problem was the growing queues in the shops, caused by the continuous printing of money. Since most prices were controlled, the extra money simply added to purchasing power. At the same time the supply of goods was unchanged, hence the queues. In January 1991 Prime Minister Valentin Pavlov acted to reduce the money supply. He canceled all large-denomination notes. But in the end that reduced the money supply by only a few percentage points. Pavlov's next move in April was therefore to raise prices (an average increase of about 65 percent) in order to bring prices more in line with money. But money continued to grow, and soon the queues came back with a vengeance.

Gorbachev's politics. Thus Gorbachev failed to solve the economic problem. At the same time his policy of glasnost had set in motion a political process he could no longer control. In 1989 he held the first semifree elections to the new all-USSR Congress of People's Deputies. That was a historic event. In March 1990 similar elections were held to the Russian Federation's own Congress, which in turn elected Yeltsin as its Speaker. One year later Yeltsin was elected as president of the Russian Federation in a direct, contested ballot of the Russian people.

Meanwhile political events in Eastern Europe had moved ahead. Because communism had failed to deliver prosperity anywhere, the people of Eastern Europe wanted an end to it. But the speed took everyone by surprise. In the summer of 1989 Poland held a semifree election and, following that, a non-communist government was formed. The Soviet Army looked on, and by the end of the year communism was virtually finished in every East European country.

If Eastern Europe could be free of Moscow, why not the republics of the USSR also? Thus the collapse of the communist economy and the breakup of the Soviet Empire became indissolubly linked, each hastening on the other. The Baltics were the first to declare their sovereignty, followed closely by Russia (in 1990). For a while Gorbachev kept the republics in a state of limbo, but by August 1991 he was ready with a new Union Treaty giving much more power to the fifteen republics. The Treaty was due to be signed on August 20.

For the communists that was the last straw. On August 19 the leaders of a coup took over the government. Yeltsin just made it to the White House, where he was joined by thousands of freedom fighters, including the economist Yegor Gaidar. By August 21 the leaders of the coup were in prison. But their action had speeded the demise of communism and of the USSR. The next day Russia's Communist party was suspended, and from then on Russia was ruled by the government of Russia and not by the government of the Soviet Union.

Evaluation

It is a fascinating story of the interaction of politics and economics. The underlying motive force was the economic failure of communism, and from this stemmed everything else, as Figure 3–1 shows.

In Russia it led Gorbachev to launch his campaigns of glasnost and perestroika, which broke the command system without putting any-

Figure 3–1. How communism fell

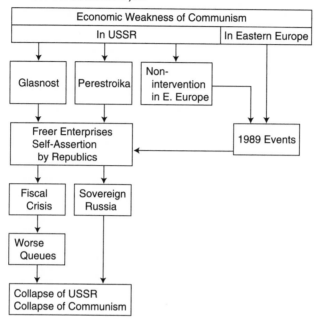

thing else in its place. As enterprises and republics withheld their taxes, the fiscal crisis deepened, and newly printed money led to ever worsening queues.

At the same time glasnost led to democratic self-assertion by the republics, so that the Russian republic emerged as an independent political entity. It was now possible to reject communism not by changing the government of the Soviet Union (a Herculean task) but by replacing it with the government of Russia (and those of the other fourteen republics). Behind this idea of Russian independence rallied many implausible bedfellows, including those whose main aim was that Russia should no longer subsidize half of Europe and a good part of Asia.

In Eastern Europe, meanwhile, discontent over living standards and political oppression led to increasing unrest. Russia no longer had the means to protect the communist governments there. So communism fell. That hastened the process of change in Russia. If Moscow's rule could be challenged in Eastern Europe, why not in Russia too? Thus, by an extraordinary interconnection of events unforeseen by anyone, communism and the Soviet Union collapsed together in the same instant.

Boris Yeltsin

In *War and Peace* Tolstoy discussed at length whether great men make history or whether history is made by great ungovernable forces. He concluded that what matters most are the great forces, like those we have been discussing. But great individuals also make a crucial difference, at least to timing.

Without Boris Yeltsin, Russia might not yet have a market economy. Despite his heavy drinking, his instincts have been generally sound, except over Chechnya. Like Reagan, he often appeared inactive, but at crucial moments he showed himself capable of decisive action.

Imagine that you were born in a peasant family living east of the Urals.[4] Despairing of peasant life, your father moved to nearby Perm and became a building laborer. Your family was so poor that all five of you slept on the floor. You studied hard and became a top student of civil engineering at the Urals Polytechnic. You were also a great volleyball player and team captain.

After graduating, you worked your way up through the construction industry, becoming an enterprise director, and then shifted into local government. By the age of forty-five you were party boss in Sverdlovsk, one of the top regional posts, and by fifty-four party boss in Moscow and a member of the Politburo—effectively a cabinet minister.

However, you found it ever more difficult to achieve anything. In every direction there were obstacles to change. Comrade Gorbachev had already launched his campaigns for glasnost and perestroika. But, though glasnost came, no perestroika followed, and it became clear to you that the system was not working.

At fifty-six what would most of us have done? Yeltsin stepped off the ladder and challenged the system. In a major Politburo meeting he denounced the failure of perestroika and was forced to resign.

But he found his new mode of operation within the Russian Federation. By June 1991 he had become its first democratically elected president. Two months later, in August, the communists played into his hands. They staged a coup but failed to arrest Yeltsin. He made it to the White House (Russia's Parliament building), where he successfully defied the communists for two days and nights. The result was that Gorbachev was humiliated and power fell into Yeltsin's hands.

The immediate problem was the economy, and the first task was to find an economics overlord.

Chapter 4

Too much shock therapy?

*The Gaidar team · Why speed? · Freeing prices and markets ·
Freeing foreign trade · No monetary shock · The curse of the ruble zone ·
Why output collapsed · Evaluation*

One natural candidate for the job of economic overlord was Yegor Gaidar, who had stayed beside Yeltsin in the dark nights of the White House siege. By the end of September Boris Yeltsin had asked him to work on a program for reforming the economy of Russia, and he was busy with his colleagues in the Russian government's dacha colony at Archangelskoye, some miles south of Moscow.

The Gaidar team

Why Gaidar? Born into an establishment family, Gaidar was then thirty-five. A man of great intellect and personal warmth, he had for some time been the leader of Russia's best group of young, progressive economists.

In the 1970s radicals had to keep their opinions to themselves for fear of persecution, but no one stopped them from reading and thinking. Most of them had read Janos Kornai's Western-style analysis of the shortage economy, as well as Paul Samuelson's *Economics*, a standard Western textbook, which had been translated in 1963 and could be found in libraries. Gaidar was especially influenced by Adam Smith's *Wealth of Nations*. Few other free-market textbooks were available, but it was easy to read articles in Western mathematical economics journals, many of which were more seditious than the KGB realized.

From Western economic theory those Russians came to understand how a market system can serve human needs, even though most of them had never seen such a system in action. It was by any standard a formidable leap of imagination. But, though converted to the market system, not all of the reformers believed at first in private property. For many years Gaidar, who as a boy spent five years in Yugoslavia, espoused market socialism along cooperative lines. But eventually he moved on to believe in full-blown capitalism.

In the 1980s it became less dangerous for radicals to talk—at least (as Russians say) "in the kitchen" among friends. Teams of reformist academics developed, including one in Moscow around Gaidar and another, perhaps more radical, in St. Petersburg around Anatoly Chubais. The Moscow group included many members from TsEMI, the Central Economic Mathematical Institute. In 1982 the Moscow and St. Petersburg groups discovered each other, and in 1988 they made their first contacts with Western free-market economists through Ljubo Szirc, a Slovenian émigré associated with the Thatcherite Institute of Economic Affairs in London.[1] But only Pyotr Aven ever stayed long in the West (for three years in Austria), while Anatoly Chubais spent 1988 in Hungary.

In the late 1980s Gaidar was earning his living as economics editor first of *Communist*, the theoretical journal of the party, and then of *Pravda*. But in 1990 he was invited by Abel Aganbegyan, the most far-sighted of the older generation of gradualist reformers, to head a new Institute of Economic Policy. The institute included on its staff all the members of the Gaidar group. Most were under forty, with an average age nearer thirty-five.[2] All were clever.

When on Monday, August 19, 1991, the junta announced it had assumed power, the institute immediately issued a statement denouncing the coup, one of the few organizations to do so, while most just awaited events. Most members then resigned from the Communist party, and many went to defend the White House. They risked their careers and their lives. Given the intellectual eminence of the group and its political loyalty, it was not surprising that soon afterward Yeltsin should invite Gaidar to work on proposals for economic reform in Russia.

But making proposals was quite different from having them accepted or being invited to implement them. There were many other contending sources of ideas (less radical than Gaidar's) and many other contenders for ministerial position. Yeltsin had not reconstructed his government significantly since the failed coup except for the immediate appointment as labor minister of Alexandr Shokhin. Shokhin, aged forty, a highly intelligent labor economist, had been economic adviser to Foreign Minister Shevardnadze for some years. He was a convinced radical, well placed to help the Gaidar group from the inside. But the key figure was Gennady Burbulis, a former philosophy professor from Yeltsin's home city of Yekatarinburg, now acting as chief of staff to the president.[3] Together Burbulis and Shokhin promoted the idea of a Gaidar economic program to be implemented by Gaidar.

On October 28, 1991, Boris Yeltsin at last announced his program in a nationwide address.[4] He used the pure Gaidar draft. There were to be free prices and free wages. The ruble was to be freely convertible. And privatization was to proceed rapidly.

Even so, the battle for power was still unresolved, and in the following days Yeltsin interviewed a number of possible candidates for the post of economic overlord. Other candidates included Yury Skokov, a nonradical bureaucrat, and Yevgeny Saburov, a former minister of economy for Russia. Meanwhile Gaidar's team in the dacha at Archangelskoye produced ever more detailed blueprints for him to take as he drove to the Kremlin for the next interview.[5] At the same time in the Supreme Soviet the deputies from Democratic Russia put intense pressure on Yeltsin, making their support conditional on Gaidar's appointment. Eventually the suspense was over, and on Wednesday, November 6, Gaidar was told he would be appointed as economic overlord, with Shokhin in charge of social affairs.[6] It was time for a party.

A few days later the new government moved into the former Communist party headquarters on Old Square. It was a quite extraordinary moment of history when this group of brilliant and idealistic academics took over the comfortable offices occupied only two months earlier by Mikhail Gorbachev and his Politburo colleagues.

Why speed?

The last blueprint Gaidar had taken to President Yeltsin was a large matrix with rows for the different policy areas and columns for the months to come. In each box the blueprint said what would be done by when—or at least which problem would have been addressed by when. The key issues were:

- freeing prices and markets
- freeing foreign trade
- controlling money and the budget
- reforming the ruble zone
- improving the social safety net
- privatization

On each issue Gaidar proposed rapid action.

There were two overwhelming arguments for speed—one political and the other economic. In any country an incoming government has a honeymoon period. At such a time it can do more in three months than could later be done in three years (once opposition becomes better organized). In Russia in late 1991 there was an additional element, the fear that the government would be ousted at any time. In the previous August Russia had come close to civil war, and many members of the new government did not expect to stay long in power. Some of them publicly referred to themselves as the "kamikaze government," a government that would dive-bomb the command economy and destroy itself in the process. Gaidar himself did not expect to last more than a year. That was an extra reason for immediately changing so many rules of the economic game that the old rules could never be reimposed. To those outsiders, like the authors, who were unwilling to think of Russia as "different," it seemed likely that the new government would have at least one year in power, like the first reform governments in Eastern Europe. But the honeymoon argument was in any case decisive: Speed was vital if anything much was to be achieved.

The second argument for speed was the immediate economic crisis. The Union government was finding it increasingly difficult to collect taxes from the republics, and that worsened after the August coup. So the government financed its expenditure by printing money. The money added to the pressure of demand in the shops, causing the queues to become intolerable. Citizens understood that the situation would eventually lead to higher prices, and their awareness further increased demand. Everyone wanted to buy. If supplies were expected at 6 P.M., queues would start forming at 6 A.M. There were fights in the shops. Only drastic action could deal with the crisis.

So the Gaidar program had to deal with all the problems simultaneously. There could be no question of sequencing—one reform following another in sequence (for example breaking up monopolies before freeing prices). Instead a torrent of activity followed: decrees, laws, programs. Many people in Russia and the West were surprised that the government never produced an overall plan, or even what might be called a program, but there were many reasons for this. At least nine "plans" had already been produced within the past few years—the Abalkin Plan, the Shatalin Plan, and so on. It had become a joke. The reformers therefore believed that concrete measures would impress the public better than a program. A program would not have prevented criticism. Indeed, it would have provoked it, since the program would have had to be debated by the Supreme Soviet,[7] which was making antireformist noises as early as December 1991.

Many people have called Gaidar's policy package a blind application of free-market principles—Thatcherite monetarism applied in a completely inappropriate context.[8] That is quite unwarranted. Russia in 1996 is only approaching what could be called a market economy, and the role of the state is still far more pervasive in Russia than anywhere in the West (including Scandinavia). *Any* Western economist would consider that Russia has still a long way to go in the field of deregulation. So the issue can hardly be whether Russia went too far down the free-market road. The only issue is whether Russia went too fast.

So let us examine how fast Russia went. In this chapter and the next we shall see what has been done to turn Russia into a market economy with a functioning monetary system. Then we shall see in Chapter 6 how this has affected the lives of ordinary people and what has been done to protect them against the consequences of change. And in Chapter 7 we shall look at privatization and the prospects for economic recovery.

Freeing prices and markets

The most important decision ever taken in the reform was the wide-scale freeing of prices on January 2, 1992. It covered not only most consumer prices but also, despite doubts among some reform ministers, the prices of intermediate industrial goods. By the end of the month retail prices had risen by 250 percent. Most of the rise had happened on the first day.

Wages by contrast rose by only about 50 percent, which meant that for a time enterprises were very much more profitable, and families were poorer. That gave the government's critics their main weapon. Grigory Yavlinsky, for example, a reformer who was not included in the government, now criticized the government for having freed prices before dealing with the problem of monopoly. According to such critics monopoly was responsible both for the ongoing price inflation and for impoverishing the people.

Both charges are fundamentally fallacious. Russia certainly has many monopolies, but far fewer than the typical large Western country.[9] But that does not mean monopoly caused the ongoing inflation. If a monopolist is suddenly allowed to raise his price, he may well do so. But having raised his price once, that is it. Freeing the monopoly helped the onetime price jump, but it did not cause the ongoing inflation. Why should the monopolist raise his price again, unless something else changes? If, for example, the government now prints more money so that people want to buy more, then of course the monopolist will again raise his price. But the second price rise has nothing to do with monopoly and everything to do with money creation. It is money creation that caused Russia's ongoing inflation.

But what about the charge that freeing the monopolies to charge what they liked impoverished the people by raising prices faster than wages? There is a little truth in this, as regards the early stages of the reform. For a time profit margins were higher than before, but that phase lasted only a few months while firms were happy to accumulate stocks of their output, anticipating further inflation. After that, profit margins reverted to their former level. (One reason for the fall in profits was the increased competition from foreign imports, which could now enter without red tape; another was increased domestic competition, as firms diversified their products.) In fact, prices in more monopolized industries rose no faster than in those which were more competitive. So the lower living standards from 1992 on reflected not monopoly power but the fall in national output, which we shall discuss later.

Unfortunately, the purpose of freeing prices was widely misunderstood. The immediate purpose was simply to cut back the excessive level of demand in shops, which arose from the artificially low level of prices. Freeing prices did that job extremely effectively, and during 1992 queues shortened to quite normal levels.

But the second purpose of freeing prices was to alter the pattern of production, so that it responded better to what people wanted. Under communism production had been governed by "state orders," telling people what to produce and where to send it, while under the free market those decisions would reflect the wishes of consumers, transmitted through the signaling mechanism of freely determined prices.

But the "supply response" was bound to take time. For a while Russia's rulers did not entirely rely on the free market to make sure that goods got to where they were needed. The system of state orders continued to regulate a large portion of the economy, perhaps still a half of it by the end of 1992. That was hardly surprising. In November 1991 Gaidar's main worry was whether people in the cities would be adequately fed. The 1991 grain harvest had been 20 percent lower than the previous year, and there was a real fear that people would go hungry that winter. But from mid-1992 on there was no further anxiety about food supplies.

Eventually the freeing of prices led inexorably to the end of state orders. Once a free price is permitted in the market, it becomes very difficult to force someone to deliver goods at a lower price. By 1994 few state orders remained, except for some deliveries to former Soviet republics.

Thus the freeing of prices on January 2, 1992, apparently so simple, was an act with permanent revolutionary impact. From it followed the main force that is restructuring the economy and will continue to restructure it for decades, even if no further reforms are put in place. That force is the "invisible hand" of the market.

Not all prices were freed in January 1992, however, and much of the reform effort since has been directed toward further deregulation. Oil prices were not freed till September 1992, coal prices till July 1993, and grain and bread prices till September–October 1993. Each step was a battle against vested interests. Profitability limits originally applied to all enterprises but had lapsed by the end of 1993. The Antimonopoly Committee regulated the prices of industrial monopolies, but that too stopped at the end of 1993.[10] Similarly the Price Committee set the prices of natural monopolies (gas, water, domestic electricity, intercity transport, and communications), but it was abolished at the end of 1993, and thereafter the federal government was setting only the prices of gas, intercity transport, and communications. Local governments (or committees) still regulate electricity prices, public housing rents, public transport fares, and local telephone charges. They can also subsidize food if they want from their own budget, and fix its price.

Thus with few exceptions Russia now has free markets for goods. There are no longer shortages of everything. Now buyers have to find customers. Shops have reasonable stocks of goods on the shelves, though not as much as in the West. And the manners of store clerks have improved markedly. Once they often refused to serve you. Now you may be greeted with, "Can I help you, sir?" and sent away with, "Enjoy your purchase." The switch from a producers' to a consumers' market has been achieved.

Not all Russians like it. They dislike especially the kiosks on the sidewalks, many of which specialize in expensive imports. They ridicule the free market as a "bazaar." But privately they are thankful not to waste their time in queues.

Freeing foreign trade

Russia's price liberalization of January 2, 1992, was one of the most comprehensive ever undertaken on one day. Almost equally daring was the freeing of the foreign exchange market. That same day it became legal for any Russian organization to buy foreign currency on the free market without limit, provided it was to be used to purchase imports. That meant any Russian who could see a useful return from importing could do so.

Thus there was full convertibility of rubles into dollars for purposes of buying imports ("current-account" purposes).[11] In theory dollars were not to be bought as an investment (for "capital-account" purposes) and certainly not held outside the country or invested in property overseas. But in practice this rule was never enforced strongly. In any case, an exporter was always allowed to retain a half of his export earnings in foreign exchange. Thus Russia had close to full currency convertibility (for current and capital purposes) from the beginning of the reform. Moreover, banks today are explicitly allowed to adopt open positions in dollars up to specified limits. That is the position for Russians (though they do not all fully understand it). For foreign firms the right to buy and sell rubles was very limited until mid-1993 (though profits could always be repatriated). Now foreigners have freedom to hold ruble accounts and to convert them into dollars.

Thus Russia has a foreign exchange regime more liberal than France or Italy enjoyed until 1991, or Britain until 1979. According to the critics such freedom is quite unnecessary. As they point out, postwar Western Europe did not achieve even current-account convertibility till 1959. So why expose Russia to a flood of unregulated imports? The reason was quite simple. Unlike postwar Western Europe, Russia had been cut off from the rest of the world for seventy-five years. It desperately needs to import know-how, much of which comes on the back of imported goods. It also, like any country, has many monopolies, and the best way to demonopolize an industry is to expose it to foreign competition.

Because Russia had no foreign exchange reserves, the exchange rate had to be allowed to float. So what happened to the value of the ruble? Under the Soviet Union the ruble had been pegged at a massively overvalued rate (only 0.6 rubles to the dollar), leading to queues of would-be buyers of dollars and massive power for the bureaucrats who allocated this scarce resource.[12] In contrast, the freely floating rate in early 1992 was between 100 and 200 rubles to the dollar. That made imports much more expensive than before (though imports had usually been sold to the final buyer for more than they cost). Nikolai Petrakov, former adviser to President Gorbachev, criticized the government for this, arguing that it was the high price of imports that was causing the high inflation.[13] In fact, however, the opposite was true. It was the inflation that lowered the value of the ruble against the dollar, making imported goods expensive. But the high price of imports in turn protected Russian industry against a too sudden exposure to foreign competition.

In many other ways too Russia kept up its barriers to trade. Under communism producers could sell whatever they produced, but buyers were short of everything. So imports were considered good and exports bad. Trade policy focused on export controls, and imports were duty-free. That has gradually changed. Now producers cannot sell all they produce, so they want to export more and keep out imports. Hence average import tariffs had risen by mid-1995 to 13 percent—from zero initially; the maximum tariff was 30 percent. But, unlike most other countries, Russia has no quotas (or other quantitative restraints) on imports. At the same time export quotas (which have been a serious obstacle to trade) have been progressively dismantled. By early 1995 they had all gone, and export taxes for oil (roughly $4 a barrel) were to be abolished by mid-1996.

Shock therapy? When prices rise 3.5 times and markets are freed, it is a massive shock. And when enterprises no longer have guaranteed customers and suppliers, that is a shock too. On top of all that, the government cut drastically its purchases of military equipment. Those were real shocks, similar to those administered in Poland (where prices jumped 80 percent) and Czechoslovakia (where prices jumped 30 percent). But what Russia never had was a monetary shock of the kind administered in Poland.

No monetary shock

The idea in Poland was that the price rise should be once-and-for-all, to be followed quickly by a period of relatively stable prices. That was roughly achieved. By May 1990 monthly inflation was down to 4 percent. In Russia the reformers never aimed at such a rapid disinflation. One reason was the problem of the Russian rubles in the other former Soviet republics. Under the USSR all the Union had the same currency, which was issued in Moscow. But in September 1991 it became clear that Ukraine would introduce its own currency. Other republics might follow. This meant, Gaidar figured, that Russia would have to introduce a separate currency. Otherwise Russia would be flooded with rubles from Ukraine and perhaps other republics, forcing up prices in Russia and robbing Russia of its wealth.

But introducing a new Russian currency would take time. That led Gaidar and his team to envisage mid-1992 as the moment of monetary stabilization, rather than attempting, as in Poland, to combine the monetary stabilization with the price rise. Thus in November 1991 members of the Gaidar team envisaged inflation continuing to run at 10 percent a month up to mid-1992. And so it turned out.

The path of the inflation after the initial price rise was determined by the rate of monetary growth. As Figure 4–1 shows, the connection

Figure 4–1. Monetary growth and subsequent inflation (3-month moving averages)

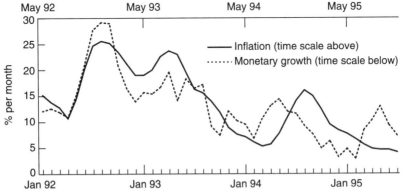

Source: *Russian Economic Trends,* Monthly Update.

between monetary growth and subsequent inflation has been extraordinarily close, and money supply is therefore the best lead indicator to watch when forecasting inflation. Until recently the time taken for this effect has been about four months, so in our graph the time scale for inflation starts in May 1992, and in January 1992 for money growth.

To control the growth of money it was necessary to control the budget deficit, as well as the credit issued to enterprises (via commercial banks) and to other countries in the ruble zone. Gaidar took office with the aim of balancing the budget—in the sense that no rubles would be printed to finance the government's operations. In the event, the cash-flow budget deficit in 1992 was around 4 percent of the GDP. Military procurement was slashed to 15 percent of its previous level, and industrial subsidies were severely pruned. One bad miscalculation was made: The oil price was not raised enough to permit a heavy tax on oil, which would have greatly improved the budget. Gaidar later called this his biggest mistake.[14] Even so, his budget was tough when compared with the previous year's.

The Central Bank's lending to enterprises was also at first reasonably restrained, so that overall monetary growth was held to around 10 percent a month up to May. In consequence monthly inflation was down to 10 percent by August 1992 (see Figure 4–1). There was one other element in the disinflation strategy: the excess wage tax. The argument for wage controls is that if they can dampen inflationary wage pressure, then less unemployment is needed to keep the lid on inflation. To control the growth of wages both Poland and the Czech Republic set limits to the growth rate of wages and then taxed firms on any excess wage growth. President Yeltsin, on the other hand, said in October 1991 that "wages will be free." His statement was politically essential, but in a clever way it was not implemented. From January 1992 Russia operated an excess wage tax of around 30 percent on all nominal wages above some limit. Such a tax on the level of wages is probably at least as effective as a tax on the growth of wages.[15]

To get to 10 percent inflation a month by the summer was not a disastrous performance, given the initial conditions. But what followed was a near catastrophe. After the April 1992 meeting of the Congress of People's Deputies, conservative pressure became intense. Yeltsin felt compelled to broaden the government, bringing in more deputy prime ministers, including three former industrial managers (Chernomyrdin, Khizha, and Shumeiko).[16] Gaidar became acting prime minister.

Even so, the pressure for further subsidized credits to industry and agriculture intensified. The reformers had to make a choice. Either they would agree to highly inflationary policies, or they would have to leave office without achieving the privatization essential for a free-market economy. They decided to stay on. To the agricultural credits for the sowing season were now added extra credits for industrial "working capital," for the agricultural harvest, and for supplies to the Northern Territories—all approved by Gaidar. In addition he agreed to the appointment of a new Central Bank chairman, Viktor Gerashchenko, who was arguing that credits would enable the existing firms to maintain their output.[17]

Russia now paid for having a Central Bank that was more or less independent of the government, though nominally under the Supreme Soviet. The enterprise managers went to the bank and claimed that they did not have enough money in hand to run their businesses. They pointed to the fact that the money supply had increased much less than prices—for example, between December 1991 and June 1992 prices had risen by 900 percent and money by only 120 percent. That was of course precisely what had been intended; it eliminated the excessive demand for goods. Unfortunately Gerashchenko did not understand this. At a famous meeting in 1993 Boris Fedorov, then finance minister, invited some twenty experts to discuss the financial situation. Led by Gerashchenko, all but one urged that money should be expanded in line with the growth of prices—oblivious to the fact that this could only produce hyperinflation.

The monetary squeeze had of course made it more difficult for firms to pay their bills on time. The result was the so-called arrears crisis. By the end of June the overdue debts owed to industrial firms had built up from almost nothing at the beginning of the year to a level equal to one and a half months' GDP. That happened to some extent because firms went on supplying obsolete goods to old customers whether the goods had been ordered or not. But most firms were not only owed money but also owed it to others, so that the situation was less serious than it appeared. The Central Bank therefore organized a consolidation of each firm's net position, and it turned out that the net debts of the net debtor firms were only about one-quarter of a month's GDP. The Central Bank created enough credit for this remaining debt to be cleared. (This was not the main source of extra growth in credit.) Firms were warned that in future they should not sell to other firms that might not pay, and if possible they should get paid in advance. Since that time overdue payments in Russia have never reached as much as one month's turnover, a level typical of Western countries.[18] The notion that monetary discipline will not work in Russia because people do not pay their bills is a clear fallacy.

However, the late summer of 1992 was not a period of monetary discipline. Both the government and the Central Bank were busy pumping out credits, with the aim of sustaining production by providing firms with more working capital. But there was a subtle difference between the government and the Central Bank. The government did it because it was forced to, while the Central Bank governor was acting out of conviction.

The extra credit in its turn simply caused further price increases. Only to a limited extent was it possible to expand the "real" working capital of firms (their credits divided by the price level), because each round of extra credit caused a further round of price inflation. Firms did benefit to some extent, however, at the expense of families. In 1992 and 1993 the Central Bank issued credits in support of firms equal to about one-fourth of the GDP. The interest rates on those credits were below the rate of inflation, so that the credits were largely a gift to the enterprises. But the resulting inflation hurt them by eroding the value of their own bank balances. The net benefit to the firms was about 12 percent of the GDP. At the same time families lost an equal amount, since the value of their savings was eroded, while they received no offsetting credits from the banks.[19]

All this extra credit did little to help production (though from mid-1992 to the spring of 1993 the fall in production was temporarily halted). But the effect on inflation was dramatic. Inflation leaped to about 25 percent a month in October 1992 and fluctuated between 20 and 25 percent for the following year.

Russia was now near to hyperinflation, which is often described as inflation of 50 percent or more a month. In most countries inflation as high as Russia now had would have led to a flight from money—in other words, a large increase in money spending relative to the stock of money. That would have been very dangerous and would have totally frustrated the government's aim of transferring resources from families to firms. But the velocity of circulation of money in fact increased only very slowly, doubling over a period of two years. This was because of the primitive nature of the system for clearing payments between firms and because wages continued to be paid only twice a month, as had always happened before. Thus Russia's cumbersome institutions helped to save it from the worst consequences of its unstable financial policy.

Even so, the velocity of circulation *was* rising,[20] and the economy was becoming increasingly dollarized. By early 1993 the public held as much of their wealth in dollars as they did in rubles. Thus, when Gaidar was dismissed in December 1992 and succeeded by Viktor Chernomyrdin, the economic prospects looked poor.

Chernomyrdin, aged fifty-four, had spent much of his life as an industrial director. His most recent triumph was the creation of the world's largest monopoly, Gazprom, Russia's natural gas producer and distributor.[21] He quickly announced his belief in "nonmonetary methods" of controlling inflation and issued a decree that price controls should be established on key foodstuffs. However, he had broadmindedly retained as economic advisers two outstanding radicals whom Gaidar had put in charge of the government's economic think tank (called the Working Center for Economic Reform). The two, Sergei Vasiliev, aged thirty-six, and Andrei Illarionov, thirty-one, joined with others to persuade the new prime minister that such price controls were unworkable. The decree was repealed, though for many months to come Chernomyrdin remained unconvinced of the link between money and inflation.

As so often in Russia's recent history, things were not as bad as they seemed. Soon after Chernomyrdin replaced Gaidar, Boris Fedorov was appointed as finance minister and deputy prime minister. Fedorov had the ideal background and qualities for the job. He had worked for some years in the foreign department of the Central Bank and then moved via a research institute (IMEMO)[22] to the Central Committee of the Communist party. He became finance minister of Russia in 1990 but disliked the prevailing muddle and corruption and resigned. He was then free to work abroad, first in the European Bank for Reconstruction and Development in London and then as Russia's member of the World Bank's Executive Board in Washington. That experience, together with a tough, no-nonsense character, gave him the independence needed to bring Russia's finances under control.

As soon as he was appointed to his new job, Fedorov drafted a plan for progressively reducing Russia's inflation, with help from Jeffrey Sachs of Harvard University. The plan required a steady reduction in the growth rate of Central Bank credit. After some modifications the plan was accepted by the government and in April reluctantly agreed to by the Central Bank. The plan was, broadly speaking, carried out, thanks mainly to the dogged determination of Boris Fedorov, who when he did not have the money simply refused to pay for expenditure authorized by one presidential decree by invoking another decree limiting the Finance Ministry's borrowing.

Foreigners regularly panic about Russia's finances when they read about some new expenditure authorized by the president or parliament. They should never underestimate the power of Russia's Ministry of Finance, which is as dry and tough as many of its counterparts in the West. Its method of control is not always the most elegant. Most commonly it simply fails to deliver money on time so that employees go unpaid, but this simple expedient has saved Russia from hyperinflation.

Fedorov's austerity drive was reinforced in the autumn of 1993 when Gaidar was once again brought back into the government as economic overlord, five days before Yeltsin called for the new elections. Gaidar made the Credit Commission into the arbiter of all new lending by the Central Bank. To many people's surprise, even when Fedorov and Gaidar left the government after the elections of December 1993, their tight money policy was continued for some months.

By that time Prime Minister Chernomyrdin had become more or less converted. Russian experience pointed clearly to the fact that monetary growth caused a similar growth of inflation four months later (see Figure 4–1). Besides, every time foreigners came to meet with Chernomyrdin, they told him that money caused inflation. Bit by bit, the idea seems to have become acceptable to him. Chernomyrdin needed to be on good terms with the West, especially with the IMF and thus with Russia's creditors, in order to show that he (unlike Russia's conservatives) could be friends with everybody. Sound money was a necessary part of this policy.

Thus from August 1993 to August 1994 Russia disinflated. Inflation fell from 25 percent a month to 5 percent. This was a move from financial chaos to something bearable; in terms of the annualized equivalent the move was from over 1300 to under 100 percent. At the same time interest rates were really high (reaching 700 percent per annum)—among the highest in the world, even after allowing for Russia's high inflation. In early 1994 commercial banks had more or less stopped borrowing from the Central Bank, so the main source of monetary growth therefore become the budget deficit. (In 1992 the main source had been credit to commercial banks.) The new Duma voted a budget deficit for 1994 equal to 10 percent of the GDP, and this was achieved.

The disinflation of 1993–94 led for a time to sharp falls in output, some of which had been artificially postponed by the period of credit expansion. Figure 4–2 shows the official figures of industrial production, which exaggerate output before the coup (because managers needed to "achieve their targets") and underestimate output now (because managers try to avoid taxes). Most of the output that disappeared had to disappear, but did it need to disappear so fast? That depends on how important it is to achieve financial stability. When inflation is high, no one wants to hold money. Barter of one good for another, which is grossly inefficient, becomes more and more common. Almost no one is willing to make loans for more than three, or at most six, months. Such was the situation in Russia—not a climate to foster new investment and new growth. The disinflation of 1993–94 shortened the period of financial instability and thus hastened the day when the areas of growth would exceed the areas of continuing decline.

Once again in 1994, however, as in 1992, the pressure became too great for the policy of disinflation to be sustained. From April on, credit was growing again at 10–20 percent a month, with much of the extra credit going to agriculture. The usual results followed. Inflation rose (to 18 percent a month by January 1995), and the ruble fell on the foreign exchange market. The fall began after the Central Bank had foolishly said the ruble was overvalued. Next thing, the bank was intervening to defend it. Then, having severely depleted its dollar re-

Figure 4–2. Industrial production 1992–95 (Dec. 1991 = 100)*

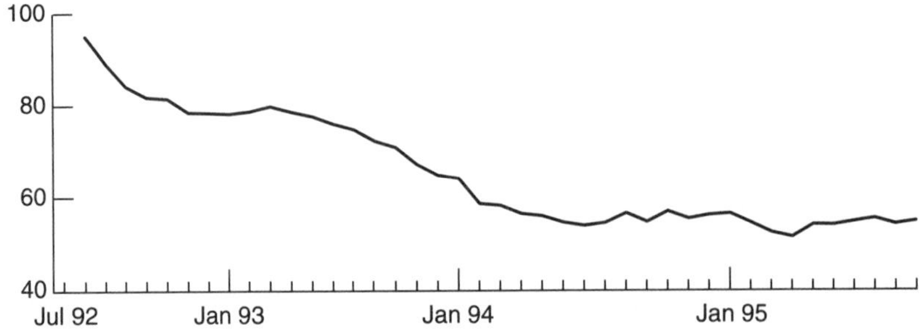

*Seasonally adjusted.

Source: Russian Economic Trends, Monthly Update, December 15, 1995.

serves, it decided it would intervene no more, and again foolishly announced the fact. There followed a debacle. On Black Tuesday, October 11, the ruble fell in one day by nearly 30 percent. It recovered the next day, and the shame of the day's events proved a blessing in disguise. Yeltsin decided to replace the whole economic team. He sacked not only the Central Bank governor, Viktor Gerashchenko, who was primarily responsible, but also the economic deputy prime minister, Aleksandr Shokhin, and the finance minister, Sergei Dubinin. To the relief of all in the West, he appointed as economic deputy prime minister Anatoly Chubais.

Chubais had already proved himself the most effective of all the reformers in his fight to privatize the Russian economy. It is a remarkable testimony to the genius of President Yeltsin that, coming from where he does, he should have selected in turn as economic overlords four outstanding men, Gaidar, Fedorov, Shokhin, and Chubais, all of whom could match in intellect and personal stature most finance ministers in the West. They were all modern men aged 35–45, well suited to carrying the Russian economy into the modern age. The less happy side of the story is that four is too many in four years, but that reflects the state of political division in Russia.

The appointment of Chubais began a new and better phase in economic management. He was strongly reinforced by the financial orthodoxy of the new Acting Central Bank governor, Tatyana Paramonova.

Chubais rapidly set about equipping himself for the task, establishing as his coordinating mechanism a Commission on Economic Reform chaired by him, with two talented deputies, Sergei Vasiliev and Maxim Boycko. Aleksandr Shokhin had already proposed that the 1995 budget deficit be financed without Central Bank credit. The Duma accepted that principle and backed the idea of covering the deficit by borrowing partly from the West and partly from Russians (through the sale of treasury bills). The next issue was the size of the deficit. A budget was drafted in October that provided for a deficit of 72 trillion rubles, which was nearly 8 percent of the level of the GDP forecast at that time. It would be very difficult to stabilize the economy with such a high share of the GDP having to be financed, but Chubais pulled off a brilliant strategy. When it became clear that higher inflation would increase the GDP in 1995 far beyond the forecast level, he persuaded the Duma to leave the budget deficit at 73 trillion rubles (which turned out to be only 5 percent of the actual GDP). The Duma voted that any extra deficit would require a new law.

But there were many other key requirements for a successful strategy. It needed the backing of the president and of the IMF. By good fortune again, the president was by January 1995 feeling increasingly isolated from the West because of the Chechen war. He needed a way to reestablish his reputation outside Russia. Financial orthodoxy was the way, leading to IMF approval. The president decreed that, even though tax receipts would be higher than those in the budget document (due to higher inflation), any item of extra spending must have his approval.

But even that was not enough to secure the IMF loan. Under World Bank pressure, the IMF insisted that Russia remove all limits on oil exports. Quotas had been reducing Russia's exports and thus keeping down the price of oil in Russia, which meant that oil that could have earned Russia valuable dollars was being used for less valuable purposes inside Russia. It also reduced the revenue of the oil industry, which should have been a very valuable source of taxes, as in all other oil-rich economies (see Figure 4–3). But the existing system favored many highly placed people who had the right as special exporters to export oil without paying export taxes.

Figure 4–3. Oil and gas sector tax revenues and output (as a share of GDP)

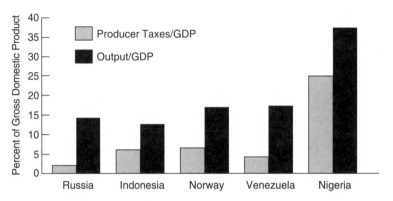

Source: International Monetary Fund (1995).

The battle to remove oil quotas was furious, and the reformers won. Oil exports were freed, and all exporters in principle had to pay export duty. But problems of pipeline allocation remained.

Thus in April an IMF loan of $6.8 billion was approved. By then monetary growth had become very low. In consequence everything in Russia began to change. In May the ruble stopped falling and began to rise. That was a real turnaround. In January the Central Bank had almost exhausted its dollar reserves trying to stop the ruble's fall: from April on it was accumulating massive reserves of dollars trying to stop the ruble's rise. The situation was poised for the next key decision: whether to peg the ruble.[23] The decision was taken in July, when the ruble was pegged within a rather wide band (4,300–4,900 rubles to the dollar) for three months initially, later extended to the end of the year, and later still extended to July 1996 (at 4550–5150 rubles to the dollar).

Thus eventually Russia disinflated. But there was never a moment of shock, as in Poland, when there was a sharp attempt to break the inflationary cycle by fixing the exchange rate and abruptly curtailing the supply of money. In fact no major politician in Russia ever favored what is usually called a "stabilization"—a sudden act on a particular day when a new austere financial package is introduced and the exchange rate is fixed in order to give "credibility" to the counterinflation policy. For that reason it always seemed likely to the authors that, when

Russia disinflated, it would be by the gradualist path rather than by a sudden "stabilization" of the conventional kind.[24] Many economists disagreed with this assessment on the grounds that very few countries had successfully escaped from inflation of 1,000 percent a year by gradualist methods. But by early 1996 Russia's inflation was 40% a year.

Why did Russia never "stabilize" in the conventional way? The reasons were political and economic. Politically, as we have seen, the reformers were averse to grand gestures. They never thought that actions could be made credible by announcement, since the Russian population was so disillusioned by its successive governments. The best thing therefore was simply to pull on the levers (by controlling credits) and let the people see inflation actually fall.

Economically, Russia could never have had a stabilization package (including a pegged exchange rate) without foreign assistance. In January 1992 Russia had no foreign exchange reserves, so there could be no question of fixing the exchange rate. It would also have been extremely difficult to cut down enough on inflationary credit creation, unless enough noninflationary credit had been available from abroad. It was not, until mid-1995 when the disinflation was already well under way.

The curse of the ruble zone

A third reason why Russia has been slow to stabilize is the old imperial role of its currency.[25] Under the Soviet Union all cash (that is, currency) was issued in Moscow, and all Central Bank credit came from the Union Central Bank. When the fifteen republics split up, they continued to use the ruble. But, while Moscow continued to control the issuance of cash, all fifteen national Central Banks began to issue Central Bank credit. The situation was completely unviable, since any republic could now create rubles and use them to buy Russian output.[26] It also meant that, because the rubles created outside Russia ended up inside it, Russia had no control over its money supply.

For a time Russia hesitated about wielding the big stick over the other states. But on June 12, 1992, Ukraine roughly doubled the credits to its firms. To prevent that money from feeding back into Russia, Russia had to limit the volume of credit it was willing to provide to Ukraine—and to all the other former Soviet republics. From July it started doing so by providing only a limited amount of "technical credit" to each former Soviet republic. That did not stop each republic from issuing its own rubles, but it meant that only a fixed amount of those rubles could be converted into "Russian rubles." In due course a foreign exchange market developed between the rubles of different countries.[27]

Once that step had been taken, it was natural for each country to move to an explicitly separate currency with a different name. Ukraine introduced the karbovanets in November 1992, and in the next year all the rest except Tajikistan replaced the ruble. (Estonia went even earlier, in June 1992.) Except for Estonia and Latvia, most of the other countries were on floating exchange rates of one kind or another, though there was usually a different fixed rate for official transactions. There were varying degrees of convertibility. Since the Baltic countries had lower inflation rates than Russia, their currencies appreciated against the ruble, while at first the others depreciated relative to the ruble because their inflation was higher than Russia's.

During the period of the monetary divorce, difficulties of payment created a major obstacle to trade within the former Soviet Union. Bit by bit, however, commercial banks in the CIS countries established correspondent accounts in Moscow commercial banks, and now the majority of payments (at least between Russia and other states) go through commercial banks rather than through the cumbersome machinery of transfers between Central Banks. At last the payments system is beginning to work.

Nevertheless, the breakup of the ruble area was a traumatic affair for everybody. It clearly discouraged trade, and to many Russians it added to the sense of loss involved in the dissolution of the Union.

But in fact it was inevitable. The only alternative Russia would accept was a single currency area, where Russia would have absolute control over the issue of new money. That would require Russian control over the budget deficits of every other state. The states were never going to accept that. Even so, serious efforts were made at intervals to maintain or reestablish the ruble area in one form or another. In June 1992 the IMF pressed the states to agree on a ruble zone based on power-sharing. In September 1993 six of the states signed a treaty on economic union aimed at monetary union, but it soon broke down over details. And in April 1994 came the treaty on monetary union between Russia and Belarus, whose future remains to be seen. With so much ongoing uncertainty, it was perhaps not surprising that monetary control was the weakest element in the Russian reform effort.

Why output collapsed

So there was no monetary shock therapy. But there was major structural shock. And output fell sharply, more than in any Eastern European country. Why?

Could it be because the initial price jump was more than in any Eastern European country? Did not the rise in prices relative to money explain the bigger drop in output? That seems unlikely. In fact, just after the price jump the fall in output in Russia was not as sharp as it was in Poland and Czechoslovakia. The fall was already under way before the price jump, and it went on for at least two years after it.

So why did output in Russia fall so much, and should it have been prevented? We can begin with the similarities to the other countries and then go on to the differences. The first basic change in all the countries has been the move to a free society. That means inflation can no longer be contained by administrative fixing of wages and prices, with high output sustained by the deliberate creation of excessive levels of demand. Instead inflation is controlled by having slack in the economy, with shops finding some difficulty in selling their goods, and workers not automatically finding work. If monetary policy is steady, the slack will automatically emerge, and inflation will stabilize at a level determined by the rate of monetary growth.

We can see this pattern in all the new democracies. When freedom dawns, the first effect is higher inflation. But if monetary growth is kept stable, output then falls, and this brings inflation back into line with monetary growth. The necessary fall in output can take some time, depending on the tightness or otherwise of monetary policy. That has been the pattern throughout Eastern Europe, and something similar happened in Spain when it democratized in the 1970s. Some economists challenge this interpretation by observing that in normal countries financial stabilization does not necessarily lead to falls in output. But that misses the point. The main change in these transforming economies is the change of regime, and the financial stabilization is just one feature of the move from an equilibrium where prices are fixed to one where they are free.[28]

The second common feature in all post-communist countries is the shift from allocation by plan to allocation through the market. That is a painful process. Even though the market is more efficient, the process by which it displaces the old activities is inevitably untidy. In many cases old activities are destroyed before enough new ones can take root. Everyone is looking for something better to do with their time and their property, but they do not move out of the old activities in an orderly fashion. So even in the "recession" many producers complain of lack of supplies, while at the same time people, buildings, and equipment lie idle. It is a problem of "coordination."

Of course, not everything in the old planned scheme of production was irrational (many Russian enterprises still buy mainly from their old suppliers). But even here there is a huge problem of shifting from a command system to one based on contracts. At what price is the deal to be done? Traditional suppliers often spend months withholding supplies, hoping to get a better price from another company or even from abroad. Thus sales were bound to fall for a time as patterns of production and supply were restructured and as new "contractual" relationships developed.

A special case of a new relationship is that between the member countries of the former Comecon—the trading system that operated between the countries of Eastern Europe and the Soviet Union. That arrangement used to work on the basis of bilateral barter between member states. But in January 1991 the countries agreed (at the USSR's suggestion) to conduct their trade in dollars. No one realized that in every country there was a massive shortage of dollar reserves with which to finance the trade. On top of this the USSR raised its energy prices to world levels. There was chaos. Elements of barter continued, but trade shrank suddenly and in many cases irrationally. Between 1990 and 1992 Russia's trade with the former Comecon countries fell by about three-quarters.

Then came the breakup of the Soviet Union. Since the whole Soviet economy had been planned as a single entity, this was as traumatic as the breakup of Comecon.[29] As the Soviet Union collapsed, other former republics acted to limit exports to Russia. Sometimes there were quantitative controls, but more often individual enterprises quoted impossible prices, hoping to find better customers in the West. Sometimes that made sense: The Uzbeks could sell raw cotton more profitably in the West. But sometimes it was based on foolish attempts at national autarky. At the same time the former republics were unable to pay for all the imports they had formerly received from Russia; they were short of money, and the payments mechanism was poor. Thus Russian producers were hit twice—by collapsed demand for their products and by shortages of supplies of inputs.

Another cause of the output decline was the end of the Cold War. In both East and West, demand for military hardware has fallen sharply. But the cutbacks in the Warsaw Pact countries have been steeper, because budgets were tighter. And as a fraction of the GNP the cuts have been very much bigger.

All those changes were more traumatic in Russia than in Eastern Europe. Russia was more highly planned than most of Eastern Europe (except Czechoslovakia and East Germany), so shifting to the market involved more dislocation. And the share of military production in the GNP was two or three times higher in the Soviet Union than in the rest of the Warsaw Pact (except Slovakia).

So it is not surprising that output in Russia, which already fell 8 percent in the year before the reform, continued to fall for three more years. We shall never know exactly how much, for it is increasingly easy for old enterprises to hide their output in order to escape taxes. And, since newly founded enterprises can easily hide, the new areas of growth in the economy go heavily underrecorded.

Perhaps the most reliable figures in the economy are on household consumption. They show that in 1993 household consumption rose by 12 percent and in 1994 by 10 percent. Since consumption is nearly half of the GDP, the fall in the GDP must have stopped in 1994, but by early 1996 there was still no sign of recovery.

Evaluation

In Chapter 6 we shall discuss what the changes meant for ordinary people. For most of them it was tough, both physically and mentally. The changes involved were enormous. But those who criticize the reform should ask themselves the following questions

- What would you have done differently, given the constraints?
- Would you have attempted, like King Canute, to control prices?
- Would you have issued more credit, regardless of the impact on inflation?

Unless one can show that a different path would have yielded better results, it is fruitless to criticize what was done. Some former Soviet republics did go more slowly (Ukraine, Belarus, and the Asian states). But even allowing for their lack of resources, their experience does not compare well with Russia's. So far as we can see, the best that can be achieved is what was done in Poland and later the Czech Republic. Russia has, with some monetary hiccups, followed the Polish model. The outcome so far has been worse, because the initial difficulties were greater and the financial discipline was weaker. But the seeds have been laid for a recovery, which, thanks partly to Russia's faster privatization, may well eventually outstrip Eastern Europe.

The main charge against the reform must be that it was too slow. That is the view of the majority of Russians. When asked in 1995 "What best reflects your attitude toward the pace of economic reform in your country?" 40 percent replied "Too slow," while under 30 percent replied "Too fast."[30] Why did Russia reform more slowly than, for example, Poland? The answer is that the politics were very much more difficult.

Gaidar's team never had a clear political mandate for action, as Leszek Balcerowicz had in Poland in 1990. The Russian team were creatures of a political conjuncture, extremely uncertain about how long they would remain in power or how far the president would back them. They did not have the authority to dispense with the old bureaucracy, though it might have been possible to dissolve the old Gosplan (State Planning Committee) of the USSR (which became the Ministry of the Economy) and to use the old Gosplan of Russia (which could more easily have been packed with reformers). Some bad appointments were made: Barchuk as an early Minister of Finance and Gerashchenko as the second chairman of the Central Bank. Oil prices could probably have been freed earlier than September 1992, and so on. But the room for maneuver was very limited.

However, Gaidar did have a clear idea of what kind of policies were needed. The fact that he and others like him were available in Moscow is an important reason why reform went faster in Moscow than in Kiev or Almaty, where there were fewer outstanding economists.

So why do some people still criticize the reforms for being too fast? Their criticisms are based on two fallacies. The first concerns money: Russia, it says, does not respond to monetary policy the same way a Western economy does. When money is tight, this does not restrain prices. It simply fouls up the system of payments, leading to huge arrears, while prices go their own merry way. As Figure 4–1 shows, this argument is absurd. And payment arrears in Russia are no higher than in the West. But there are still critics who insist that tight money in Russia failed to control prices and at the same time somehow damaged output.

The other fallacy concerns monopoly. It is said to be the cause of inflation. It was therefore a grave error to free prices before dealing with monopoly. The criticism is wrong on three grounds. First, monopoly can only encourage a once-and-for-all price rise; it cannot cause ongoing inflation. Second, Russia is not especially monopolized. And third, it would have been impossible to control prices for much longer in any case—and certainly not as long as the years and years needed to demonopolize an economy.

The case against the reform has simply not been proved.[31] Russian entrepreneurs respond to new freedoms and incentives in exactly the same way as those elsewhere. The situation is more lawless (see Chapter 8), but there is no way in which Western economic ideas can be said to have failed in Russia.

In fact, they have been only partly tried so far, since even in 1996 the reform is only part of the way there. While it is true that the mindset of Russia's reform ministers has been fairly Thatcherite, they are practical men, and the Russia they have helped to create is still more state-controlled than the most socialistic country in the West. In a debate in the Supreme Soviet, Speaker Ruslan Khasbulatov alleged that Gaidar had made a fundamental mistake in introducing the Anglo-American rather than the Scandinavian model of capitalism. Khasbulatov was wrong. The model was neither Anglo-American nor Scandinavian. Gaidar's answer hit the mark: "The choice is not between Anglo-Saxon and Scandinavian models of capitalism; it's between the European and the African."

Chapter 5

Has the West done enough?

The debt collectors · The window of opportunity · Russia and the IMF ·
Economic ideas · Help with restructuring · Western trade barriers · Evaluation

Russia's new reform government was appointed in mid-November 1991. That was a crucial moment in world history. In Russia, the founder of world communism and still a superpower, leadership had fallen to a tiny group of young radical economists committed to building a Western-oriented capitalist country.

If they had wanted to be constructive, the governments of the West could have taken two possible attitudes. They could have said, "Clearly the reform will succeed, and we should help it in the same way we helped Poland." Or they could have said, "The reform is going to be very difficult, but it is vital for us that it succeed. So we should help it in the same way we helped Poland." They said neither. Instead they sent in the debt collectors.

The debt collectors

In mid-November David Mulford, U.S. Treasury undersecretary for international affairs, arrived in Moscow as leader of a G7 debt-collecting mission. The main preoccupation of Western governments was

83

that, as the federal Soviet Union disintegrated, responsibility for the Soviet debt be clearly allocated. Russia made a simple and obvious suggestion, that Russia take over all the USSR's overseas liabilities and its overseas assets. After one year of bickering, that solution was adopted. But in November 1991 the West was unwilling to accept the demise of the Soviet Empire.[1] Its representatives wanted to keep the republics together, thinking that would make it easier to keep the nuclear weapons under control. After two weeks' tedious discussions they forced on the Russians a completely impracticable proposal for sharing responsibility for the Soviet debt among all the republics.[2]

The discussions took a full week and involved Gaidar for hour after hour when he was trying to construct his reform plan. When the rulers of Russia were planning how to liberalize prices without unleashing a hyperinflation, the West did not suggest a collaborative venture as in the case of Poland; it wasted days in achieving an unworkable solution to the debt issue.

There was another disastrous consequence of those meetings. The debt collectors insisted that Russia should for the time being continue servicing its debt, until a rescheduling could be worked out. The completely forecastable result was that the money ran out. By mid-December the Vnesh Econom Bank (the government's bank for foreign transactions) ran out of dollars and unilaterally suspended payments. This incompetent outcome, which blocked the dollar accounts of many Russian and foreign firms, was the first notable failure of the reform government, and it was due directly to Western advice and pressure.

This whole beginning of the relationship was most unfortunate. It led Gaidar to conclude that he was unlikely to get much financial support from the West. He was right. Thus began the arm's-length relationship between Russia and the Western financial authorities, which only really improved from 1994 on. In the meantime Russia failed to control its inflation, thus demoralizing its own people and diminishing its image abroad.

The window of opportunity

If the West had shown more vision, things might have been very different. What was needed was a major cooperative effort between Russia and the West along the lines followed in Poland in late 1989. There, over a four-month period, IMF officials worked with the Polish government to develop a strategy whereby inflation could be brought under control once prices had been freed. The reform government had been established in September 1989 and had to design an immediate reform package to be introduced in the next few months. The IMF (of which Poland, unlike Russia, was already a member) immediately entered into discussions with the government about the structure of the package and the role an IMF loan could play in it. In those discussions it became apparent that in order to stabilize the value of the Polish currency there would also have to be a Stabilization Fund: The G7 governments agreed to provide the necessary $1 billion. Within four months everything was in place, and the program was implemented on January 1, 1990.

To follow that example, Russia needed to take three main steps. First, the budget deficit had to be held at a reasonable level. Second, there should be minimal printing of new rubles to finance the deficit; financing for the deficit should come mainly from borrowing dollars abroad and selling them in the foreign exchange market in exchange for *existing* rubles. Third, the exchange rate should be pegged at some fixed level. The main reason for pegging the exchange rate would be to force the government to stick to its own financial targets.

That theory had been applied time and again in successful financial stabilizations—in Israel, Bolivia, Argentina, Poland, Czechoslovakia, and so on. Indeed, there was almost no case except Chile where a rapid stabilization of prices had been achieved after high inflation without significant untied money being lent to the government from abroad.

But there was also, of course, a history of cases where money was lent from abroad but the financial stabilization failed. The most common symptom in such cases is that the extra foreign finance fails to generate extra imports but simply flows back abroad in the form of capital flight. Since domestic spending has been allowed to increase but there is no increased supply of imports, inflationary pressure remains great.

Fear of such a failure weighs heavily with potential lenders. The basic answer must of course be to produce a credible plan[3]—and more, rather than less, foreign finance may be needed to assure credi-

bility. Whatever is done requires a substantial element of joint planning between the government and the foreign lenders.

In addition Russia, like Poland, had a special problem. It had run
out of foreign exchange. To peg the exchange rate it therefore needed
a stock of borrowed dollars with which it could defend the exchange
rate peg if it came under attack.

Thus a successful strategy required, first, a coherent budget; second, a foreign loan to help finance the budget deficit; and third, a Stabilization Fund to be used (if necessary) to hold the exchange rate.
The sums involved were not huge when compared with the $500 bil-
lion the West was spending on its own defense, mainly against Russia.
In fact, it would have taken a diversion of only about $15 billion of
that huge total to make a massive difference in Russia. Russia's national income in 1992 was only about $100 billion,[4] so that $10 billion
would have financed a budget gap equal to 10 percent of the GDP,
with $5 billion more for a Stabilization Fund.

The key consideration for a successful strategy, however, was that
the Russians should want the strategy and have the power to implement it. There is little doubt that many Russians would have welcomed it. Whether they could have implemented it, we shall never
know. The leaders of the reform could not themselves tell how strong
or weak they were. They knew that they had a honeymoon period,
after which the going would become very tough. If within six months
they had nothing to show, it would be difficult to maintain financial
discipline thereafter. But if a coherent program could have been announced by them, as it was in Poland, that might have altered the
whole climate.

To have reached this position would have required a real act of vision by Western leaders, and even then it might have failed. Indeed,
many Russian reformers believe that extra Western money would
have only gone into extra spending. But that is probably a fallacy
since all the lending would have been conditional on the program's
being followed. The truth is that current perceptions are heavily col-
ored by the confused history of what actually happened.

In the event, Russia never had a reform program of the kind followed in Poland and Czechoslovakia. Instead, reform was achieved by
a series of repeated pushes, like a military campaign, and not by the

implementation of a predetermined strategy. If instead the West had reached out to Russia with offers of support, it might have helped to structure a real program. Its aid would of course have been conditional on sticking to that program. The program might have failed, but it was worth trying. No money would have gone down the drain, like the billions lent to Gorbachev without conditions. Either the conditions would have been satisfied and the Western money provided, or no Western money would have flowed.

Much was at stake, including the whole pattern of future relations between Russia and the West. So a great opportunity for a collaborative effort to stabilize the Russian economy was missed. The window of opportunity was small. By April 1992 the government was under severe attack from the Congress of People's Deputies, and any stabilization plan would need to have been executed before then, if it were to be credible. The planning would need to have begun as soon as Gaidar came to power. Though in the event the worst possible outcome has not happened, things might have been very much better if the West had been more proactive from the start. So what did actually happen?

Russia and the IMF[5]

On December 6, when President Yeltsin asked the G7 for a stabilization fund, the IMF was asked to act as the G7's adviser on all aspects of Russian macroeconomic policy. That was a fatal step, for the IMF is an organization with its own procedures and criteria, which quite naturally it wished to apply to Russia as to other countries. The basic issue for the IMF was: Did Russia qualify for an IMF loan using the standard criteria? Unless specifically instructed to do so by its leading shareholders (the G7), the IMF was not going to take into account Russia's critical role in world politics.

For the first four months the IMF's basic approach was fact-finding and "wait and see." At no stage was there any discussion of sums of money that could have been provided on certain conditions. Thus Russian policy developed independently of Western support. Since Russia's foreign exchange reserves were exhausted, there could be no question of trying to peg the value of the ruble. And without the discipline of a fixed exchange rate, it eventually proved impossible for the government to resist pressure for excessive credit creation. In the event, Russia's finances came near to collapse by the end of 1992, and Yeltsin's presidency came near to collapse the following March. Though the situation improved from then on, Western policy in 1991–92 was a case of dangerous myopia.

The IMF operated through groups of staff who came on missions, with one professional person permanently in Moscow.[6] The Russians had become skeptical of Western assistance as a result of the debt-collecting mission the previous November and made no special effort to engage in joint policy development. Eventually formal negotiations began, with the Russian side led by Konstantin Kagalovsky, a member of the Gaidar team. After two weeks of negotiations, agreement was reached on February 27, 1992, on a Memorandum of Economic Policy. In it, Russia made a comprehensive set of undertakings about its future policy, and the IMF made no undertaking at all. No financial aid to the reform was mentioned. Since there was no quid pro quo, it was not surprising that many of the Russian undertakings were not fulfilled. That was not a good precedent and created a bad impression abroad about the reliability of Russian undertakings.

It is important, however, to understand the difficulty of the IMF's position. It had been asked by the G7 to take the lead role and to proceed much faster than it would normally do. By IMF standards it did precisely that. It admitted Russia to full membership in July 1992 (in time for the Summit), and in the same month provided its first loan of $1 billion. That, of course, was far too late. Already the government had been forced into easy credit by the industrial and agrarian lobby.

1991–92: Whose fault? So whose fault was the debacle? The main responsibility lies on the G7, especially on George Bush.

To any informed observer in November 1991 two things were clear. First, everything had changed. This was the moment when reformers had been given their chance. To make the reform work, now was the moment to act. To "wait and see" would inevitably mean seeing something less satisfactory than could have been achieved by acting at once. The second obvious point was that the window of opportunity was small. The Supreme Soviet was already proposing a full meeting of the Congress of People's Deputies at which the onslaught on the reform would be violent and could be lethal.

Why did the West not act? Russia was not yet a member of the IMF and was thus ineligible for a speedy IMF loan. Thus the main help had to come from governments, most of whom were in fiscal difficulties at the time. However, this explanation does not really wash. When politics dictates, help is provided. In January 1995 more than $40 billion was found for Mexico, some from the U.S. Treasury and some from the IMF, and in both cases money was diverted with scant regard for the formal rules governing its use.

Unfortunately in 1991–92 the politics were bad for Russia. Western policy was dominated by the United States, because of the disorganization of Europe (as usual) and Japanese hostility to Russia over the Kurile Islands. Russia is a long way from the United States, and it was a former enemy. There are few Russians in the United States, whereas Chicago is the second largest Polish city in the world. President Bush was obsessed with the need to keep the USSR together, so that only one government there would have nuclear weapons. As a result he simply failed to notice that after the August coup Russia had become a separate country, and after November it had committed itself to economic reform. He was looking in a different direction while the lightning struck. The Western press must also take some of the blame: Boris Yeltsin's historic speech of October 28, 1991, announcing the reform plan was not reported as a turning point. But to anyone in touch with the reformers it was clear that the moment had come. Western governments did not react that way. They left it to the IMF.[7]

Thus Russia's financial history up to 1994 evolved with little aid from the West. In 1993 the IMF invented a Systemic Transformation Facility to lend to post-communist economies on less exacting performance criteria than would apply to loans to other countries. In July 1993 Russia received a first tranche of $1.5 billion (see Table 5–1). But the second tranche (of equal value), which was due in the autumn, was held back because even the "streamlined" performance conditions had not been satisfied. However, in April 1994 the second tranche was disbursed, after Mr. Chernomyrdin had invited the IMF's managing director, Michel Camdessus, on a private shooting expedi-

Table 5–1. Official financial assistance to Russia ($ billion)

	1992	1993
IMF	1.0	1.5
World Bank	0	0.6
Export credits*	12.5	5.5
Western government grants	1.5	0.5
Total	15.0	8.1
Corresponding headline offer	(24.0)	(28.0)

*Backed by Western governments' guarantees.

Source: IMF Press Release, February 1, 1994, disbursements.

tion outside Moscow. Thus from the beginning of the reform to the end of 1994 Russia borrowed only $4.6 billion in untied money from the West (including $600 million from the World Bank)—less than 1 percent of Russia's GDP in each of the three years.

1992–93: The G7's banner headlines. That was not a lot. So what happened to the massive aid promises that hit the world's headlines in early 1992 and early 1993? Those were political operations, which had mixed effects. In both April 1992 and March 1993 it became clear to the G7 that a large-scale assault on Yeltsin's authority was imminent. Yeltsin sought Western help both because he needed the money and because he believed that a demonstration of Western support would enhance his image at home. Each time, the G7 rallied behind him and provided the kind of demonstration he had asked for.

The Congress of People's Deputies was due to gather on April 6, 1992, for its first attack on President Yeltsin. The day before that, the G7 leaders offered Russia financial support of $24 billion, including a $6 billion Stabilization Fund to be made available as soon as Russia had demonstrated it was ready to fix the exchange rate.[8] In the end $15 billion came (see Table 5–1). But little of it was untied money of the kind Russia needed. It was mainly $12.5 billion of export credit provided by Western firms to help Russia buy the goods that Western firms wanted to sell. (The Western governments just provided payment guarantees.) With those extra credits Russia bought some things it desperately needed, and others of lower priority. Western governments gave only $1.5 billion in grants. And the IMF lent its $1 billion of untied aid. The Stabilization Fund was never put in place, because Russia and the IMF never seriously discussed the possibility of a stabilization.

There was also another form of support in the form of debt rescheduling. Russia's debt to the West (which it took over from the Soviet Union) was about $80 billion.[9] The G7 agreed to a temporary rollover of most debt service. Russians perceived this as a kind of phantom aid, since Russia had already suspended all debt repayment. But it was useful to have the position somewhat regularized, because otherwise there was a real danger that Western firms would altogether avoid operating in Russia. (No proper agreement for rescheduling was reached until mid-1993 when the Paris Club creditors agreed to a ten-year deferral of debt due that year, followed by similar agreements in 1994 and 1995; the London Club creditors eventually offered a five-year deferral in 1994.)

The next, and most intense, challenge to Yeltsin's authority came in March 1993, leading to the referendum held on April 25. By then the Western world had a new leader in President Bill Clinton, with a team much more sympathetic to Russia's needs. The Treasury undersecretary for international affairs was Larry Summers, a Harvard colleague of Jeffrey Sachs and of other economists friendly to the Russian reformers. Clinton also had a special adviser, Strobe Talbott, friendly to Russia. On April 3 Clinton and Yeltsin met at Vancouver, and ten days later the G7 finance ministers meeting in Tokyo made a substantial promise of support to the reform effort: $28 billion of real money plus $15 billion of debt relief, making a banner headline of $43 billion. But very little of the $28 billion was forthcoming. A year later the IMF had lent $1.5 billion, and the World Bank $600 million more of untied aid. Russia decided not to use most of the tied export credits on offer, since (once import subsidies had been abolished) there was insufficient demand for most of the imports. And a year later most of the proposed World Bank loans to support restructuring were still at the stage of negotiation rather than implementation.

The effect of the banner headlines at the time is uncertain, though clearly President Yeltsin wanted them. But their subsequent effects were unfortunate when the money did not come. They simply added to Russians' feeling that the West did not really mean to help.

1994–95: Things improve. During 1994 and 1995 relations between Russia and the Western lenders improved. Russia no longer went with a begging bowl: The Corfu Summit in mid-1994 was the first time a Russian president appeared without a list of financial requests. Over the same period the professional cooperation between the Russian authorities and the IMF improved greatly. The first step was the agreement between Camdessus and Chernomyrdin on the second tranche of the Systemic Transformation Facility in April 1994. But more important was the active joint discussion of the 1995 budget program, between the Russian government and the IMF, whose efforts were now guided and strengthened by Stanley Fischer, the new first deputy managing director and a friend of many of the economists involved in the Russian reform.

Those discussions began in the summer of 1994, when Aleksandr Shokhin was economic overlord and proposed the principle of noninflationary budget finance. The discussions continued even more effectively once Chubais had taken over from Shokhin. The World Bank also played an important role, by insisting on the abolition of export quotas as a precondition for its own proposed $600 million loan. The IMF agreed with the World Bank's suggestion to make this precondition a sticking point for their loan also. That suited the reformers well. That battle won, the IMF agreed in April 1995 to a standby of about $6.8 billion, to be paid over a year in monthly installments subject to Russia's meeting its performance criteria. The main criteria related to the budget deficit and the rate of net domestic credit expansion. Throughout 1995 the Russians stuck to their targets and in February 1996 agreement was reached about the three years to follow, when there is to be an IMF Extended Fund Facility, with again conditions relating to financial and structural policies.

Economic ideas

If so little money flowed until 1995, does that mean Western support played little part in Russia's fight with inflation? Far from it. Western ideas were the basis for the whole disinflation strategy. They were transmitted through myriad channels. The most important was the IMF. Through the process of regular interaction with the IMF, Russian officials learned what packages of macroeconomic measures have been found to work in other countries.

Russia frequently failed to carry out on time the measures it had agreed upon with the IMF. But it is interesting to reread the Memorandum of Economic Policy agreed to in February 1992. Most things foreshadowed there had been done by mid-1995. People sometimes say that the IMF dictated conditions to Russia that were contrary to its interests. The reverse is true. In most cases the reformers wanted the IMF to impose the conditions in order to strengthen the reformers' hands within the government. The IMF did not dictate; it provided important intellectual support in thinking systematically about what needed to be done. As time went on, relations improved steadily, and by 1994 even the Central Bank had become more open and more eager to learn what standard practice was elsewhere. While an early proactive policy from the G7 would have been far better than what the IMF was able to achieve at that time, things would have been worse still without the IMF.

Next in influence were probably the foreign heads of government whom Yeltsin and Chernomyrdin met in Moscow and on their trips abroad. Those people constantly preached the importance of controlling credit, and eventually the lesson sank in.

Foreign advisers also played a role. Jeffrey Sachs of Harvard University was a continuous source of creative and farsighted advice during the first two years.[10] Anders Aslund of the Stockholm School of Economics brought an unrivaled knowledge of the Russian economy, and in 1993 he and Sachs organized a Macroeconomic and Finance Unit of some twenty people at Boris Fedorov's request to help develop relevant economic analysis for the government. Marek Dabrowski, formerly Poland's deputy minister of finance, was an important member of the group, with highly relevant experience. Richard Layard of the LSE's Centre for Economic Performance also worked with the group and with the government's economic think tank to interpret what was happening in the economy and to analyze the available options.

On the strategy of privatization Andrei Shleifer and Jonathan Hay played key roles, bringing economic and legal expertise respectively. And at the World Bank office Charles Blitzer was an influential source of ideas on almost everything. A prime objective of all foreign advisers was to help develop groups of young Russians capable in due course of leading the work themselves.[11]

Help with restructuring

If the West helped on the macroeconomic front, it also helped in the task of restructuring—the building of a market economy based on private enterprise. The main Western organizations involved were the World Bank, the European Commission, the aid agencies of Western governments (especially the U.S. Agency for International Development), and the EBRD (European Bank for Reconstruction and Development). Those organizations played various roles.

They all helped in the design and implementation of the privatization program by financing Western business experts and lawyers to work with the Russian privatization ministry (GKI). The World Bank's IFC (International Finance Corporation), well led by Roger Gale, organized first the pilot auctions of shops in Nizhny Novgorod, then the pilot voucher auctions for larger firms, and finally the pilot auctions of farmland and equipment (again at Nizhny Novgorod).

The World Bank also gave useful advice on a range of problems from trade to energy to the banking system. The European Commission's TACIS program (Technical Assistance to the CIS) supported experts of all kinds in activities from nuclear safety to economic education. The British Government's Know-How Fund supported a smaller number of experts—such as Molly Meacher, who helped to organize Russia's new Federal Employment Service. And so on. One remarkable Western philanthropist, the Hungarian-born financier George Soros, organized his own aid program—first to help save Russian science and then to rewrite the school curriculum.

The contribution has been substantial, but it has also been much less than it could have been and should have been. The most obvious indication of this is that all the aid organizations have been desperately underspent, though to a diminishing extent. For example the European Commission's TACIS program spent under 10 percent of its program allocation in 1992, rising to 70 percent in 1994. In the first four years of the reform the World Bank only managed to disburse project loans of $40 million,[12] and the EBRD disbursed £210 million in loans and equity investment.

All that would not matter if Russia's needs were not so desperate and so urgent. To give just one example, in 1992 virtually no relevant textbooks on commercial subjects were available in the whole of Russia. Teachers and students were crying out for material, and most teaching consisted of the blind leading the blind with the use of newspaper articles. Yet in the first three years of the reform no aid agency could be persuaded to finance the immediate translation and publication of standard Western commercial texts, adapted as necessary.[13] On many occasions the Russian government requested such a scheme, but it never happened. Thus a whole generation of students were frustrated and their chances of unemployment increased.[14]

Flaws in the system. So what went wrong with the organization of technical assistance and project lending? The fault lay on both sides. The Russians were busy trying to create a completely new system of government, with new structures and new people. There were desperately few people with the modern mentality needed for the reform. In the first year there were perhaps fewer than fifty in the Russian government who could think effectively about change (though things have improved greatly since then). In that situation there was bound to be a great deal of disorganization on the Russian side, with key officials often changing and not always available. There was also the endless problem of identifying which Russians could be trusted and which were corrupt.

Thus to succeed in their aid efforts, the Western side needed to be exceptionally well organized. It was not. In all the Western organizations, decisions down to the smallest detail are taken at the head office—in Washington, Brussels, London, or wherever. Lending priorities are determined there. And organizational relations with the Russian government are conducted through missions, when officials fly in to Moscow for (usually) between three and fourteen days. Missions often arrive at very short notice, and often contain different people from the previous mission dealing with the same subject. They then disappear, and a hiatus period passes until the next communication arrives.

The system has two flaws. Though members of the missions take their jobs very seriously, it is hard for them in the time available to get an accurate feeling for the Russian reality they are trying to grapple with: which Russian partner is reliable, who can deliver, what would work, and so on. Second, when the decision-makers spend so much of their time at the head office, the preoccupations of the head office are liable to prevail over the needs of the Russians. For example, at first many of the aid organizations did not consult the Russian partner over which consultant was sent to help them. That partly reflected the fact that their organizations were used to dealing with Third World countries, which may often have a less clear idea of their own needs.[15] But when the aid officials were dealing with the Russians, they were meeting with people as educated and intelligent as themselves. Unfortunately, they did not always recognize this, nor the fact that they themselves needed more local knowledge to be able to offer suggestions that would help.

Thus aid to Russia would be greatly improved if the permanent missions of the aid organizations included field experts with substantial delegated powers over the programs they administer. At least half of all the aid administrators working on Russia should be based in Moscow, instead of the perhaps one-tenth there at present. A large permanent delegation is clearly more economical in Russia than in, say, Bulgaria. But the time has come when all the aid organizations must face the weaknesses of head office centralism and the mission system. If they really have wisdom of value to the world, they need to reorganize themselves so that (as in a diplomatic service) officials expect to spend half their time on assignment, living in another country.

Thus delay in the aid program resulted from weaknesses of organization on both sides. It also resulted from Russia's uncertainty about the wisdom of incurring further debt. Given Russia's exceptional natural resources, those doubts are probably misplaced. Russia now owes roughly $90 billion to Western governments and banks. By contrast the

Novy Urengoy gas field is said to be worth up to $1,000 billion. Russia is currently producing and consuming much below its long-run potential. In such a situation it makes sense to borrow now in order to produce more in the future. Russia has a desperate need to catch up with Western know-how in the practice of commerce and (in some cases) in technology. There are countless activities with high rates of return—investments in both human capital and physical equipment.

But this does not mean that every proposed project is worthwhile. Russian ministers naturally dislike borrowing money to employ Western consultants at fees like $12,500 a month when they themselves earn $250. Inevitably a substantial fraction of consultants fail to operate efficiently, especially if they come for only short periods, much of which are spent learning about Russian conditions. There have therefore been substantial delays while enough Russian agencies are persuaded that a loan is worthwhile.[16]

Things improve. But eventually progress has been made. By the autumn of 1995 agreement had been reached with the World Bank for $4 billion worth of project loans. There were also a number of investment funds using foreign government finance or finance from EBRD. Thus, with the flow of official aid, as with everything in Russia, there has been steady progress in the right direction.

But already the main inflow of know-how to Russia is through the Western private sector and not through official agencies at all. That is exactly as it should be. Russia desperately needs help with expertise in marketing, management, financial control, and certain Western technologies (especially computing). The best form of help is from those who have a commercial interest in successful outcomes, either foreign investors or foreign traders. We discuss such commercial relations in Chapter 7.

Foreign investment in Russia was still small in 1994—including portfolio and direct investment, perhaps $4 billion. One problem is the difficulty of finding the right foreign partner. Russian firms are often in the dark over whether they have a product they could sell and, if so, what. Such know-how is far more scarce than finance to support the necessary investments. One of the best uses of foreign aid would be to finance marriage-makers—industrial experts who could tell individual Russian firms whom to contact in the West and could tell individual Western firms whom to contact in Russia. Provided such knowledge accumulates fast enough, a wave of foreign investment is bound to hit Russia before the century is out.[17]

Western trade barriers

Even more important than foreign investment is foreign trade. To modernize itself, Russia needs to import, and to import it needs to export. Is the West giving Russia the export opportunities it needs?

In the past Russia used at home far more steel, aluminum, uranium, oil, and many other basic materials than it needed to. For example, in 1991 Russia consumed more steel than the United States. Energy consumption was five times greater than in Canada (when measured relative to real GNP). As demand in Russia fell, Russia started exporting more of all those things. The response of the West was less than enthusiastic.

The European Union put a quota on imports of steel from Russia, which in mid-1995 was still as low as 2.2 million long tons, roughly 1 percent of the total European market. Then there was aluminum. When Russia suddenly boosted its sales, the world price collapsed. In response the world's main producers formed a cartel, which included Russia, which effectively put a production quota on everybody. Another problem was space launchers for satellites. Here Russia is a high-class and high-volume producer, but the West resisted Russian exports until an agreement was reached that carved up the world market into roughly equal shares for producers from Russia, the United States, and Europe.

Those are the most publicized areas of conflict. But the greater threat comes from the continuous application of "antidumping" rules on product after product. In mid-1994 Russia was the object of nine "antidumping" or related measures imposed by the European Commission, mainly on various forms of chemicals.[18] The justification for the measures is essentially that Russia is not yet a market economy and therefore has distorted cost structures and even in some cases subsidies. But, since all of this is changing so rapidly, it is to be hoped that such *ad hoc* remedies will soon become less common.

An important step in the right direction has now been taken in the form of a Partnership and Cooperation Agreement between Russia and the European Union, covering both political and economic aspects. It was fortunate that from early 1991 to 1995 the European Union had as its ambassador in Moscow an outstanding economist, Michael Emerson, who had also proved an effective administrator during the dramatic delivery of food aid to Moscow and St. Petersburg in early 1992. The Partnership and Cooperation Agreement pledged both sides to the ultimate goal of mutual free trade. In the meantime they agreed that, though Russia had not yet been accepted into the World Trade Organization, trade between Russia and Europe would be governed by some of the normal WTO rules. That meant Europe would treat Russia as it treated the Most Favoured Nation (MFN) outside the European Community. It also had agreed to extend to Russia the Generalized System of Tariff Preferences (GSP) enjoyed by Third World countries.

Even so, Russia is treated less well than the nations of Eastern Europe, whose "Europe Agreements" are clearing the way to their eventual membership in the European Community. Thus, in the opinion of two World Bank experts, Russia and the other CIS states "face perhaps the most severe obstacles to market access of any group of countries in the world."[19]

How much does this matter? Quite a lot. If Russia is to take off, it needs foreign trade and foreign investment, and both will be greatly affected by the ease of access to the European market. Russia can get around some obstacles by exporting to the Third World. But if we want Russia to be a part of Europe, our trade policy needs to make it possible.

Evaluation

No one could expect the relationship between Russia and its former enemies to be totally straightforward. Given that background, progress has been reasonable. The chief credit must go to one man, Boris Yeltsin. Despite his own provincial background, he stuck throughout to the view that Western aid was important for the reform.

That exposed him to two forms of criticism. First, he was accused of humiliating Russia by becoming a supplicant and allowing Western organizations like the IMF to "dictate" to Russia. Second, he was criticized when the huge sums mentioned in Western communiqués failed to arrive.

Why did Yeltsin get into this position? We cannot be sure, but probably the main reason is that he wanted friends. He was trying to change Russia into a Western type of society and to make it a part of the world economy. He was under strong criticism at home. The most natural source of extra help was from abroad. With some sections of Russian society that was counterproductive, but it impressed others. In the end it surely paid off. When Yeltsin went to the Corfu Summit in July 1994, he put aside his begging bowl. The immediate crisis in Russia was over, and instead he took his place as one of the eight world leaders who as colleagues discussed the political future of the world.[20]

Yeltsin understood that if you want to join the club, you have roughly to follow the rules. Though Western organizations have not given much financial help, the continuous process of interaction has led to a steady change of rules in Russia. A more proactive policy would have been much better. But the constant interaction with Western organizations and firms has become a key mechanism in the reform. Indeed, without it the reform would never have got as far as it did; it could even have failed.

Chapter 6

How do people live?

Before the reform · How living standards fell · Who lost most? ·
Jobs and unemployment · Life and death · Homes ·
The future of the safety net

S o how have the Russian people survived the experience of reform? Even in 1996 intelligent friends ask, Can people get enough to eat in Moscow? *Time* magazine features on its cover a homeless man begging at a train station beside the headline "Moscow—City Adrift." The image of Russia that has been projected in the West is of a society in which Third World destitution coexists with new, vulgar wealth to an extent unknown in the West. The truth is more ordinary. Let us begin with life in Russia as it was before the reform and then see how it has changed.

Before the reform

Russia was always poorer than the rest of Europe and has remained so under communism. In the last years of communism living standards in Russia were somewhere between those in Greece and Mexico.[1] But there was less inequality, so that nearly everyone was adequately fed and clothed. Most families had plots of land where they could grow potatoes, fruit, and vegetables as a buffer against food shortages. Though housing was cramped, most houses were well heated through the Russian winter. Life was hardest in the countryside, where water generally had to be fetched from a well and cranked up by hand.

On the other hand, Russia was unusually well educated, relative to its income. There was almost no illiteracy, the general level of numeracy was high, and as many young people went to higher education as in Britain.[2] Russia has always had a strong intellectual tradition and a deeply cultured intelligentsia. Under communism egalitarian policies spread analytical habits of mind widely through the population. The Cold War led to a massive development of scientific education and research. "Mathematician" was recorded as the most prestigious occupation,[3] and the population developed a preference for being ruled by "good specialists." When Gaidar was replaced as prime minister by Chernomyrdin, more than one taxi driver complained, "But he's not an economist, he's a chemical engineer."

One feature of Russia's emphasis on the life of the mind was the world's highest level of newspaper readership, except for Japan. Most houses had TV: Russia had almost as many sets per capita as Belgium.[4] Those features were a part of the communist legacy. In the early days they had helped to spread communism; at its end they hastened the collapse.

One might have thought that communism would have also been good for health care. Alas, not so. Though Russia had more doctors per capita than almost any other country,[5] their pay and support facilities were poor, and life expectancy in Russia has always been much lower than in the West. In 1991 the expected life span was sixty-nine years—sixty-three for men and seventy-four for women.[6] That was almost as low as in China. Seventy-seven years was the life expectancy in the West (the OECD).[7]

Most Russians drink and smoke, though drug-taking is still not a big problem. Although the statistics show that alcohol and tobacco use is below the OECD average, most drink is hard spirits, and most of it is drunk by men. Accidents by poisoning, drowning, or car crashes are three times higher than in America, and drink is an important cause of road injuries (the highest in the world per mile driven)[8] and of homicide, which in 1991 was already 50 percent higher than in the United States.[9] Alcohol poisoning and drowning were eight times higher.

The most durable institution in Russia is the family—not the two-generation nuclear family of the West but the three-generation extended family. Mothers and their children remain extremely close, and it is often the grandmother (or babushka) who looks after the grandchildren during the day. Husbands are less important in this context, and divorce is more common than almost anywhere else, bar the United States.[10]

To their friends, most Russians are exceptionally warm, but one effect of communism, often noted by Russians and foreigners alike, was that Russians smiled less in public. Life was hard.

Against this background, how have Russians survived the shock of the reform? The trauma has been severe. The clearest indication is the higher death rate, which affected mainly people of working age (especially men). This suggests that the main shock was the psychological shock of adjusting to a totally new work pattern and a new self-image. But there was also a substantial fall in living standards, especially among low-wage working families, and a wholly new phenomenon occurred: unemployment. The greatest triumph of communism had been to provide work for all. Now that guarantee is gone.

So we shall look first at how living standards have changed, and who lost most. Then we turn to unemployment, followed by health and housing conditions. From all this we can form a verdict on the social safety net. Did it fail? What changes are needed? We shall end with a look at the upper crust—the "new Russians."

How living standards fell

As in every post-communist country, living standards fell during the early phase of the reform.[11] In Russia they had in fact already started falling in the previous year (see Figure 6–1). The fall in living standards basically reflected the fall in output, discussed earlier. However, the very sharp drop in 1992 was of course connected with the huge price increase that occurred in January of that year, when prices ran far ahead of increases in wages or pensions. One reason why firms charged such high prices was that they expected prices to go on ris-

Figure 6–1. Quantity of consumer purchases (1985 = 100)

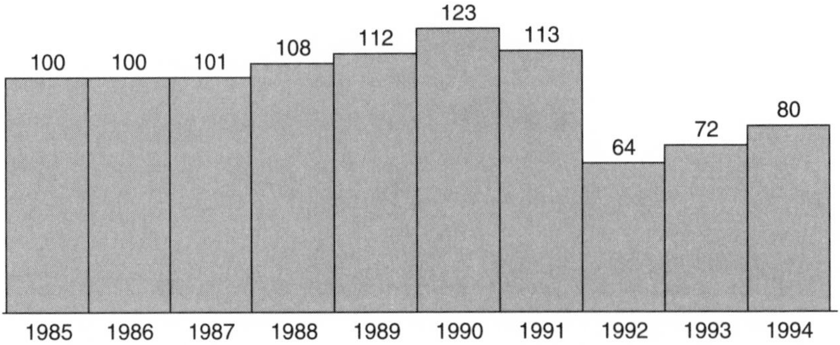

Source: *Russian Economic Trends,* vol. 2, no. 1, p. 35; vol. 3, no. 2, p. 52; vol. 3, no. 4, p. 57.

ing, and they were therefore quite happy to accumulate stocks of goods rather than sell everything at once. However, as time passed, the excessive markup of prices over cost disappeared, and the real value of wages and pensions increased. By 1993 the standard of living was already rising.

But average living standards in mid-1995 were still well below what they were before the reform. How much? It is difficult to be precise. The figures given in Figure 6–1 probably exaggerate the fall, for a number of reasons. First, they basically measure the amount of *goods* people buy[12] (food, clothes, consumer durables, and the like); they underweight *services.*

Consumption of goods has definitely fallen, especially of nonfood items. While food consumption fell initially, it recovered quite quickly to nearly its former level (see Table 6–1). But there was a huge drop in purchases of clothes and consumer durables. So food now takes up almost 45 percent of all spending by workers, and over 70 percent for pensioners.[13]

One must remember, however, that many key services are still very cheap in Russia. Housing rents are still very low, and so are telephone rates. Most Russians pay low fees for housing maintenance and heating, even if they own their homes. Public transport in cities remains extremely cheap and of quite good quality; the uniform fare in the Moscow subway in mid-1995 was 10 cents. On the other hand, there have been sharp increases in prices for some services that were for-

Table 6–1. Food consumption (per capita, kilograms per month)

	1970	1975	1991	1992	1993	1994–Q1
Meat and meat products	4.2	5.0	5.7	5.0	5.5	5.7
Milk and dairy products	27.6	27.7	30.2	27.5	26.6	24.8
Eggs (number)	15.0	21.0	24.0	20.0	26.0	25.0
Bread products	12.0	10.9	9.9	9.5	10.7	10.9
Potatoes	11.6	10.9	8.8	9.4	10.8	10.8
Vegetables	6.8	7.0	7.3	8.0	5.8	6.0
Sugar and sweets	3.5	3.6	3.3	2.8	3.7	3.7

Source: Centre for Economic Analysis and Forecasting.

merly subsidized by enterprises, above all kindergarten and holiday hostels. It is difficult to balance all this out, but almost certainly the real amount of services Russians enjoy has fallen less than the real amount of goods. So, if services were included, the curve in Figure 6–1 would have fallen less.

There are also two positive changes to be considered. First is the end of queues and of shortages. Previously adult women typically spent fifteen hours a week in queues, and even then they could often not get what they wanted. A huge amount of life was devoted to the search for goods—not only food but every item of household use from lightbulbs to building materials. The queues have gone now, and most goods can be found when you want them. That represents a vast improvement in human welfare and is a key reason why there is not more protest, even though, of course, people always complain about the prices.

A second major change is in the quality of goods. Once Russia moved from a sellers' to a buyers' market, producers had to take more trouble to produce a salable product. Thus many products have improved in quality, and some of the worst are no longer bought. The quality of service in the shops is also improving bit by bit. There are more smiles.

Even so, the fall in purchases shown in Figure 6–1 is pretty devastating. Why has there not been more uproar and more complaint? There have been in fact virtually no general antigovernment demonstrations of any significance except the communist demonstration in April 1993 and the pro-parliamentary protest in September–October of that year. That is remarkable, considering that before Gorbachev fell, hundreds of thousands turned out regularly to pro-Yeltsin demonstrations. Some would argue that life has become so hard that no one now has time to demonstrate. But such an explanation carries little conviction, because large numbers are out on the streets in the evening and on weekends and public holidays—and the Moscow subway is full throughout the day.

So what does explain the lack of protest? First, people have lost all faith in politicians and see no point protesting. Second, they have mostly found their own methods of survival.

Two institutions have been crucial to survival: the extended family and the private plot of land. The extended family, as in all less advanced countries, is a strong element in the system of social security. Adult children almost always help their parents in old age, and people also help their siblings if they are in trouble.

But the private plot of land has been another vital safety belt. There are 50 million private plots in Russia, roughly one per household,[14] averaging about a quarter the size of a soccer field. Production on the plots rose by 10 percent in 1992 and the same again in 1993. By 1993 an astonishing 83 percent of all potatoes grown were produced on private plots, and even for meat production the proportion was 40 percent.[15] Yeltsin understood the key role of the plots and issued instructions allowing their enlargement. They were a key buffer against the harsh impact of the reform.

Who lost most?

So who lost most in the early years of the reform, and who, if anyone, gained? Undoubtedly quite a number have already gained. Almost everybody who is directly or indirectly in touch with the dollar economy gained. That includes most individuals engaged in exporting and importing, as well as most workers in export industries (including hotels) and people employed directly by foreigners. People engaged in internal trade have also done well, as have workers in banks and enterprise directors. Gainers are especially common in Moscow, where perhaps half the population are now better off than before. The richest of the gainers are the "new Russians," whom we shall examine more closely at the end of the chapter.

But the harsh truth is that the majority of Russians are still worse off in mid-1995 than they were before the reform. Some are very much worse off.

Old people. Old people are the biggest group of losers. Figure 6–2 shows how the average real income of pensioners has changed. In real terms it has fallen more than the general fall in living standards shown in Figure 6–1. Pensioners have lost especially by comparison with the year 1991, when Yeltsin had given them a large hike. But, even compared with 1985, pensioners are down a lot.[16]

Pensioners have lost not only real income but also real wealth. On January 2, 1992, the real value of their lifetime savings fell by 70 percent in a day because of the sudden rise in prices. Though the price rises affected everyone who had any money, old people generally own more savings than younger people and therefore suffered disproportionately.[17]

Thus, overall, pensioners lost more than the average Russian. Does this indicate the harsh unfairness of the reform? It would only if pensioners originally lay below the average level of living of the popula-

Figure 6–2. Real value of the average pension (1985 = 100)

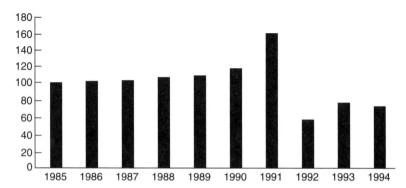

Source: *Russian Economic Trends,* vol. 3, no. 4, pp. 46, 122.

Table 6–2. Percentage in poverty, October 1993

Children (under 16)	39
Adults (excl. pensioners)	28
Pensioners	28
female	29
male	23
Total population	31

Source: Goskomstat, *Sotcialnoekonomicheskoe pologenie Rossii.* no. 11, 1993. pp. 62–63.

tion as a whole. But in fact the average pensioner is not much worse off than the population at large, if you take into account the lower needs of old people. From household surveys one can compute the income per capita in each household relative to its "subsistence" needs.[18] Table 6–2 shows what proportion of people are in households with less than "subsistence" income. Pensioners are no more likely to be poor than anyone else. In October 1993, using the official poverty line, 28 percent of pensioners were in poverty, as against 31 percent of the population as a whole. And of all people living below the poverty line, only 20 percent were pensioners, while 28 percent were children.

Since pensions are roughly indexed to prices, pensioners are protected against inflation. The average pensioner gets about 40 percent of the average post-tax wage, and very few get below 18 percent.[19]

Children. The main cause of poverty, as so often in the West, is not old age but large families, especially where there is only one parent or the parents are low-paid. That has always been a problem in Russia. But the new element coming from the reform is a big increase in the inequality of wages. It has occurred mainly in industry. Health and education workers complain a lot, because their wages are adjusted less frequently than others. But, except for those at the top, wages in those professions have not in fact dropped behind average wages. The real change has been in industry. In sectors like textiles, which are hit by declining demand and rising prices of their inputs, real wages have dropped like a stone; in other industries, like gas, facing strong export demand, real wages have risen. Average wages in textiles are now one-eighth of what they are in Gazprom. Altogether the dispersion of wages across manufacturing industries has increased by a multiple of five since 1991.[20] That astonishing degree of wage flexibility has been good for unemployment (which remains low) but bad for the problem of low incomes.

So what has the state done to protect poor working families? It operates a flat-rate system of benefits for children. In real terms these have fluctuated, but Table 6–3 gives some idea of the scales relative to the average wage. By international standards they are not low, but given the degree of wage inequality they are clearly not giving enough protection. The obvious remedy is to increase the maximum benefit, but then to means-test it, so that richer people do not receive more benefit than they need.

The other remedy sometimes proposed is to raise the minimum wage. It is now very low (about 10 percent of the average wage) and serves mainly as a reference base: All benefits and budgetary wages change in proportion to it. If the minimum wage were raised enough to have a significant effect on enterprise wages, it would almost certainly increase unemployment, which has so far remained low.[21]

Young adults. The main group in the population who have gained are young adults. Russia has become a society more than almost any other where it is an advantage to be young. It is almost an advantage to be inexperienced and thus to have an open mind. In fact the

Table 6–3. Child benefit as a percentage of average wage*

	Aged under 6	Aged 6–16
1992	14	10
1993	5	3
1994	9	8

*1992, May; 1993, February, April, October; 1994, January, April, June, September, December. In 1991–93 separate rates for 0–1.5-year-olds were slightly higher than shown for "under six" and there was an additional allowance for single mothers. All data include allowance for children's clothing.

Source: Russian Economic Trends, 1994, vol. 3. no. 1, p. 45 and no. 4, p. 53.

process of transition has illuminated important features of the human learning process. In economic courses taught by Westerners to a mixture of distinguished Russian professors and their students, the students normally did better. Apparently ideas and behavior that have been learned really do stand in the way of new learning and adaptation. So everywhere in Russia there are twenty-five-year-olds earning more than their parents. This is a traumatic turnaround of relations between the generations in a society that previously respected age more than it is respected in the West.

To summarize the overall position on income distribution, we can turn to Table 6–4. This compares the real income of the person 10 percent from the top of the income distribution with that of the person 10 percent from the bottom. In other words it looks at the ratio of the "upper decile" income to the "lower decile" income. In 1991 the person 10 percent from the top had an income three times as high as the person 10 percent from the bottom. By 1994 the difference had risen to 5.5 times. That is about the same degree of inequality as in Britain

Table 6–4. Inequality and poverty

	Upper decile/Lower decile	Percentage in poverty
Russia		
1991	3.4	
1992	3.6	33
1993	4.2	31
1994	5.3	24
Western countries (mid 1980s)		
US	7.0	
UK	4.5	
France	4.3	
Germany	3.6	

Source: Russia: Upper decile/Lower decile: *Russian Economic Trends*, 1994, vol. 3, no. 4, table 42, p. 50: data relate to individuals distributed according to monthly household income per head. Poverty: *Ibid.*, table 43, p. 51; data relate to individuals according to household income relative to subsistence needs. West: Atkinson (forthcoming).

and well above France and Germany.[22] Indeed, if one takes into account the highest incomes in Russia, Russia may now be almost as unequal as the United States.

However, most people in Russia do manage somehow. The variety of ways by which they manage is amazing. Most underpaid workers in public services and administration use their position to collect extra income from the public. Workers in industry steal goods from the firm or use its equipment to get a second income. And so on. Despite the horror stories in the Western papers, there are fewer beggars in Moscow than in London, let alone New York. And most Russians are adequately dressed—Russia is nothing like Britain in the 1930s, when children went barefooted.

The social safety net is imperfect, especially for poor children, but there has been no general failure. The strain and uncertainty, however, have been massive. And most of the strain revolves around wages and jobs.

Jobs and unemployment

When the economic reform began, horrific forecasts were made—by the International Labor Organization, among others—of likely mass unemployment in Russia. Those forecasts were understandable. After all, in the first two years of the reform in Poland unemployment rose from zero to 10 percent, and similarly in Slovakia, Romania, Bulgaria, and Hungary. By extrapolation the same was forecast for Russia.

But the forecasts were wrong. Unemployment has grown very slowly—from 4.5 percent in 1992 to 8.5 percent by 1996.[23] At the same time employment has fallen by only 7 percent. How is this possible, when industrial production was nearly halved?[24]

First, many jobs *were* lost in the old industrial enterprises, but new jobs sprung up in services, especially in trade, finance, real estate, insurance and tax administration—and also in new manufacturing firms spun off as the old ones broke up. Thus, this was an economy with high job mobility. In 1994 new hirings equaled 21 percent of the workforce.

Even so, in the old enterprises employment fell much slower than output. So how could the firms balance their books? The answer is

Figure 6–3. Wage growth and employment growth across manufacturing industries, 1991 and 1992

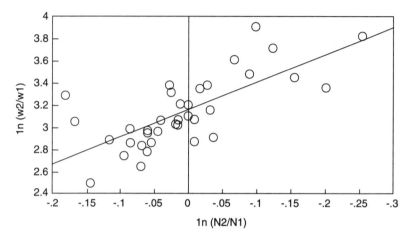

Note: N2 = average employment in December 1992; N1 = average employment in January–February 1991; w2 = Average wage in December 1992; w1 = average wage in January–February 1991; $1n(w2/w1) = 2.41\ 1n(N2/N1) + 3.14$; $R^2 = 0.521$.

Source: Ellam and Layard (1993).

that firms in financial trouble cut real wages drastically or paid their workers late. Figure 6–3 shows how those firms which were cutting employment were also cutting their relative wages. In the extreme case they sent workers home on unpaid or part-paid leave. In late 1995, 1 percent of the nation's workforce were on that kind of involuntary leave at any one time, and 2.5 percent more were working short-time. About half of the industrial enterprises were also behind in paying wages, by an average of one month.[25]

The one thing that firms did very rarely was to sack workers. In 1994 only 2 percent of Russian workers were made redundant—a good deal fewer than in most Western countries. Instead firms kept people on at lower and lower real wages until eventually they left voluntarily for something better. And there was enough hiring in the labor market for a major redeployment of labor to happen in this way.

It was in some ways a model case of how a labor market should adjust, with people moving from old to new jobs directly (through the "pull" of the new job) instead of being "pushed" out of the old job into unemployment. The two contrasting routes are illustrated in Figure

Figure 6–4. Two routes for reallocating labor

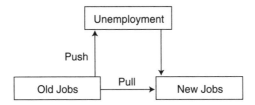

6–4. In OECD countries a large part of the redeployment happens through the "push" route, with typically 15 percent of the workforce entering unemployment each year. That happens because wages are rather rigid, and when a firm finds that its market is collapsing, it is very difficult for it to cut its relative wage. But in Russia, as we have seen, relative wages adjust naturally, so workers are "pulled" from one job to another. This has so far saved Russia from mass unemployment.

But why do Russian workers accept wage cuts with virtually no strikes (work days lost in 1993–94 were below 1 percent of the OECD average).[26] The answer is that they hate unemployment, much more than workers anywhere else in the world. For seventy years Russia had virtually full employment, and unemployment was a criminal offense unless you were old or disabled or a mother of young children. The enterprises where people worked provided not only wages but often also housing, kindergarten, holiday homes, cheap food, and health care, benefits you would not like to lose through unemployment. Of course, if you lost your job you would not lose your home. If the enterprise is in financial collapse, however, it cannot heat or maintain the housing, which makes workers more careful about demanding excessive wages. Being employed also means that you have access to the firm's tools and equipment, which may be very handy if (like at least 20 percent of Russians) you have a second job. But, above all, being attached to an enterprise gives you your sense of social identity and security.

At the same time unemployment offers few attractions. Unemployment benefits are in principle quite generous, but in practice they have not been. Anyone made redundant goes on getting his former wage from his employer for three months. Then he goes to the Employment Service and gets 75 percent of that wage for three months,

60 percent for the following four months, and 45 percent for the last five months.[27] It sounds quite generous, and it would be if there were no inflation. But with inflation the benefits are eroded rapidly, and in early 1995 most unemployed people received the minimum benefit, which was only about 10 percent of the average wage.

To obtain unemployment benefits you have to break your links with your enterprise by withdrawing your Labor Book and handing it to the Employment Office. For most workers it is not worth it. Hence for the workers the top priority is remaining employed.

Managers, if they possibly can, accommodate that desire. Russian managers are to a large extent benevolent dictators in their enterprises.[28] They are important local figures, and their reputations depend partly on their benevolence. On top of that, the enterprise has little financial incentive to fire people. If it fires them, it has to pay them three months' wages anyway. Much better to cut wages so that people leave voluntarily without being entitled to severance pay. The Excess Wage Tax too provides managers with an incentive to press down on pay, thus making it easier to keep people on and to spread the available work over many workers.[29] But financial incentives are not the only issue; they cannot explain why firms with excess labor so often recruit new workers to replace those who leave. This reflects the fact that managers are also concerned about the social role of their firms as local providers of jobs.

At one time managers also had an interest in employing many workers as an argument for receiving cheap subsidized credit. But the days of cheap credit ended abruptly in late 1993. That brought many enterprises near to the edge. Some were saved for a while by industrial subsidies, but by 1994 those were few and far between, except in the defense industry, agro-industry, and coal mines. By mid-1994 the procedure was in place for initiating bankruptcies.

One cannot tell how much Russia will use the instrument of bankruptcy. Few countries in Eastern Europe have done so except Hungary. But one thing is sure: Social considerations will be a leading factor in the outcome. The key decision will be what to do in towns dependent on a single firm or industry. An obvious example is the group of textile towns around Ivanovo, a few hundred miles east of Moscow. Single-industry towns employ quite a small proportion of

Russia's workforce, but the workers there are quite vulnerable because of the huge distances between towns. In 1989, 5 percent of Russia's industrial workers worked in single-industry towns and 13 percent in towns with fewer than five industries (narrowly defined).[30] That is where the crisis will come.

The key issue is to devise local economic development strategies that can stimulate new development fast enough to pick up the pieces as the old industries collapse. The packages will have to include infrastructure development (sites, roads, training), effective business finance, and, in the last resort, effective public works to prevent the growth of mass unemployment. That is one of the greatest challenges now facing Russia.

Life and death

Perhaps the most obvious measure of the harshness of life in Russia is the low life expectancy. It has always been quite low, especially for men (see Figure 6–5). At its peak in 1987 the expectation of life for a Russian man reached sixty-five years. Then it fell steadily. In 1993 it crashed to only fifty-nine. Even allowing for the survival capacity of Russian women, life expectancy in Russia is now lower than in China (see Figure 6–6).[31]

Figure 6–5. Life expectancy, 1985–1992

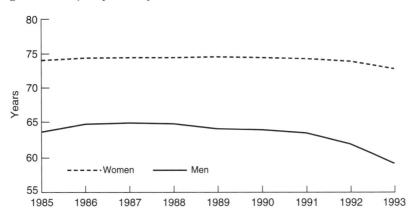

Sources: Ellman (1994, Table 4); UNICEF (1994, p. 90).

Figure 6–6. Life expectancy, 1993*

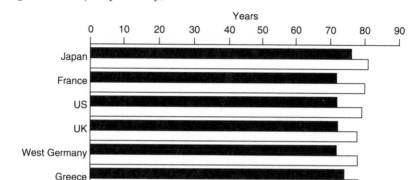

*Russia—1993; other countries—latest available year.
Sources:* Ellman (1994); *Economist* (1990).

Clearly communism was not good for your health. While life expectancy has risen steadily in Western Europe, in communist Europe it stagnated from around 1965 onward.[32] But, equally, the ending of communism has in the short term been even worse for health than communism itself. All over Eastern Europe death rates are up, except in the Czech and Slovak republics. The increase in Russia is the greatest. In 1993 alone the number of deaths increased by 19 percent, and it rose again by 7 percent in 1994.

At the same time the number of births has been steadily falling. Since births are now fewer than deaths, the total population is declining. This pincer action is shown in Figure 6–7. A final indication of the harshness of life is the fall in the marriage rate, down from 8.6 per thousand in 1991 to 6.8 in 1993.[33]

The recent increase in mortality in Russia is without precedent anywhere, except in war or plague. How did it happen? Was it a crisis of the health care services, of nutrition, or simply of psychological stress?

There are various clues.[34] The first comes from the fact that most of

Figure 6–7. Birth and death rates (per thousand)

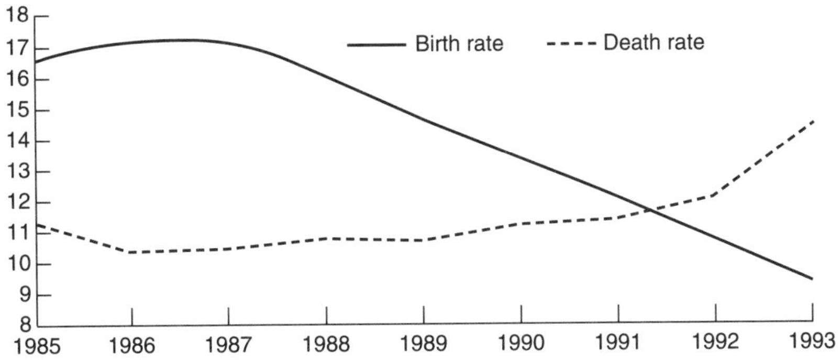

Source: Goskomstat (1994), p. 43.

the extra deaths are among men of working age (and to some extent women).[35] Deaths among old people and among children have barely increased.[36] Yet the main recipients of health care services are the young and the old. So this casts some doubt on the "health care crisis" line of explanation.[37] It also casts doubt on the "living standards" explanation, which should affect all groups and perhaps especially the old and the young—in any case, some people have argued that less meat and milk is better for health.

A second clue comes from the fact that the main increase in mortality was in deaths by violence or through heart disease and stroke (see Table 6–5). All of these causes of death are stress-related.

So the extra deaths reflect above all the intense crisis of identity to which many Russians have been subjected, especially Russian men whose jobs and earning power are so important to them. Between 1989 and 1993 the number of suicides among men of working age rose 53 percent and of homicides 137 percent.[38] By 1993 Russia had nearly three times the U.S. rate of homicide and twenty times the British.[39] Alcohol-related deaths also trebled in three years,[40] partly because cheap vodka can now be bought all day long on every street.

Though stress-related illness has manifestly increased during the period of transition, the life expectancy of men has always been low in Russia. Why is that so? The reasons undoubtedly include alcoholism, smoking, and a fatty diet. In addition, the health service has been of mediocre quality. Though Russia has more doctors per capita than

Table 6–5. Increase in deaths 1989–1993 (by cause)

	Percentage of extra deaths due to:	Percentage increase in deaths of each type:
Violence and accidents	27	78
Heart and stroke	44	27
Cancer	4	8
Respiratory	5	34
Infections	1	35
Other	18	27
Total	100	34

Source: UNICEF (1994), pp. 47 and 49.

any other country except Italy, doctors have suffered from the usual Marxist contempt for "nonproductive" sectors and have had low prestige and low pay.[41] As Russia moves toward a more humanistic society, it will be forced to improve the efficiency of its health care system.

The health care system is currently based mainly on hospitals, with less "primary care" than in Western Europe[42] and very little public health and preventive care. Hospital beds are in ample supply, but the quality of hospitals is highly variable; for example, a quarter of rural hospitals lack sewerage facilities.

Health care is in principle free, but in practice side payments are common. Up to the reform hospitals got their money directly from local authorities,[43] and they were run as nationalized industries. But, as state control weakened, they increasingly took control of their own affairs.[44] The new policy is to recognize this and to organize hospital finance partly through regional Health Insurance Funds. Those levy a 3.4 percent payroll tax, half paid by the employers and half by the workers. The money is then used to reimburse providers by paying a fee per unit of service, or to operate health maintenance organizations. But those funds have not eliminated the need for budgetary support, providing only about 25 percent of total public finance for health care.

So we have a system in extreme flux, with an urgent need to reestablish a degree of cost control. At the same time the system needs to reduce the role of hospitals relative to primary care, and to develop programs of preventive public health. One test of success will be when Russian joggers jam the sidewalks of Moscow.

But, if Russia is to increase its life expectancy toward Western levels, doesn't it need to spend more in total on health? The answer is yes. Except for side payments, Russia spends only 4 percent of its national income on health. Other countries with similar living standards usually spend around 5 percent, while OECD countries average 7 percent. That is clearly an area where more, and not less, state finance will be needed. The opposite is true of housing.

Homes

So what are living conditions like? Most Russians live in overcrowded flats in large apartment blocks built in the last forty years. For almost every Russian family the living room also serves as a bedroom. Including passages and toilets, the average amount of space per person is 17 square meters, which is about half the average in the West.[45]

Under communism the only way to obtain a new flat was if your existing flat was especially overcrowded. So the normal Russian life cycle has been that when a couple got married, the wife moved in with the husband's family. At that point, or when the baby arrived, you became entitled to join the housing waiting list. But then you had to wait on average for ten years before you got a place of your own.[46]

No wonder Russia has one of the highest divorce rates in the world. Thus 10 percent of Russian children live in single-parent families.[47] When a family splits up, the ex-wife generally moves back to live with her mother.

All this makes life sound pretty grim, but it overlooks one of Russia's greatest joys, the dacha. Nearly every Russian family has a plot of land outside the city. For families living in large cities, the plot normally includes a wooden house, sometimes built by family members and generally improved by them. It does not count as housing, because it can be used only from April to September. But during that time most Russians will be at their dachas most weekends, and grandma and grandchildren will be there for most of the school holidays. The dachas are often many miles from the city, involving a substantial train ride and some walking, but that makes no difference. If we want to understand why there are so few political demonstrations in Russia, one reason is that people are at their dachas (or otherwise the weather is freezing).

Up to the reform most urban housing was state-owned, 46 percent by enterprises and 32 percent by local governments.[48] Then came the great giveaway. In December 1992 the housing privatization law was amended to make it mandatory for tenants to be offered the ownership of their flats for free.[49]

However, not everybody wanted to own their flat. Owners are liable for property tax, and people realize that in due course owners will also have to pay for the heating and maintenance of their homes (even if not yet). By contrast, tenants have absolute security of tenure anyway, and rents and maintenance charges were traditionally very low. Rents had been fixed in 1928, and in 1989 averaged only 1 percent of household income, with other charges adding an extra 1.5 percent. Similarly, transport fares were very low—all part of an economy based on low wages and very cheap services.

Maintenance charges are now moving steadily up to economic levels, which they are mandated to reach by 1998. By September 1994, however, only 31 percent of state tenants had claimed ownership of their flats,[50] and rents remain low.

Privatization, of course, makes little immediate difference to the conditions of life, but in due course it will change things as owners begin to improve their properties and as a market for housing develops. When all housing was state-owned, with huge waiting lists, it was difficult for people to move from one city to another.[51] There was no chance of getting a new place, so you had to go and live with friends or relatives. You also needed an official permit (propiska) to take up your new residence. Now the propiska has gone, except in a few cities, and the housing market is developing so that people can rent or buy a new house in the place where they want to live, if they can afford it.

In mid-1995 the market in houses for sale was still very thin. If you sold your home, you would be liable for a massive capital gains tax (on the whole value of the house), and to avoid this most sales go through semicriminal channels—thus restricting supply. In general people prefer to rent out their homes. The average selling price of a

50-square-meter apartment in early 1994 was $40,000 in Moscow and $11,000 in Nizhny Novgorod, which was very high when compared with wages averaging $100 a month.[52]

But in time the privatization of housing will transform life in Russia. Every Russian will find that he has some wealth, and he will thus have collateral against which to borrow money.[53] That will help people wanting to start new businesses and will help to stimulate the next housing boom. Housebuilding has been much reduced since 1991; though there is a housebuilding boom in Moscow, building has slumped in many other areas. The boom will come as soon as financial and political stability is established.

Private ownership of housing will of course lead to more inequality in the use of housing, as the rich buy or rent from the less rich. But it will also lead to much more efficient use of housing, as those with extra space rent it out to people who have too little. And finally it will help to control unemployment, as people leave high unemployment areas to rent a home where jobs exist.

Change, as usual, will be slower in the countryside. There private ownership of housing was always more common than in towns, with more than half of the houses privately owned. Conditions were often quite primitive. Within a few minutes from Moscow along the main road to St. Petersburg you will see women hand-pumping water from the well and carrying it home. In the whole country, nearly half of rural homes are without water and over half without sewerage.[54] All this will take a long time to change.

The future of the safety net

What is the verdict on social policy in Russia? Has the reform been opposed because it ignored the social dimension? To some extent. The old have lost most in real income, and the old vote against reform. But perhaps they would in any case. The most remarkable thing has been the resigned patience of the people. People have not demonstrated but have concentrated on survival. Their expectations have been extremely low in general, and their expectations of politicians the lowest of all.

So long as expectations remain low, the outlook for economic recovery may remain good. Europe had its golden period in the 1950s and 1960s largely because people expected less than the economy could deliver. The trouble came when expectations revived and outran reality. That is when the trouble may come too in Russia. But it could be some years off.

More narrowly, did the social safety net fail? You will hear it said that Russia had no social safety net, and the main mistake in the reform was the failure to construct one.[55] That is absurd. Communist Russia had a well-developed social security system, which has performed reasonably well in the transition, considering the general dislocation of life. Everyone has suffered from the high inflation, and those on transfer incomes have suffered most, since their incomes have been increased at most every three months. But, if inflation now comes under control, what most needs doing to improve conditions of life in Russia?

There are four main priorities. First, pensioners need to share in the rise of living standards. Their pensions need indexing to average household income per head and not to prices. Second, children in poor families need more protection. The only way is to relate child benefit to family income, increasing it for the poor and decreasing it for the rich. Third, much more active help is needed for the unemployed: training and, where necessary, temporary jobs improving the infrastructure. Long-term life on the dole should be prevented at all costs. And fourth, there must be more expenditure on modern health care—health education, preventive health, better primary care, better equipment, and better drugs.[56]

Chapter 7

Will Russia prosper?

*Human resources · Natural resources · Private ownership · Restructuring ·
The banks · When the boom? · Foreign investment · Legal difficulties ·
Trade and growth · Evaluation*

Whether Russia prospers matters not only for Russians but for the whole world. A prosperous Russia will be an important outlet for Western exports and Western capital—and a more peaceful neighbor.

How fast will Russia grow? Other things being equal, countries tend to grow faster the more backward their starting point.[1] Since Russia starts off more backward than the OECD, it should grow faster. But many other factors are also relevant. First, countries with more human capital relative to their income grow faster. Russia is one such. Second, natural resources surely help, provided they are not wasted.[2] Russia has plenty. Third, and most important, a large advantage comes from defined property rights upheld by the rule of law and from free and open markets. Russia is moving rapidly toward full-blown private enterprise and open markets, but the rule of law is still weak.

Those standard factors fail to capture all the reasons why Russia will grow rapidly.[3] It only just threw off the distortions of communism and has therefore more room to grow than countries nearer to an equilibrium growth path. Moreover, Russia was until recently held back by physical remoteness. Sudden integration in the world economy will make possible the rapid importation of new technology, so that Russia can catch up more quickly than the typical country at its income level. Finally, it suffered for two centuries from a military budget greater in relative terms than any other European power's. Throwing off that burden liberates substantial resources for growth.

In this chapter we shall focus on the first three factors: human resources, natural resources, and economic institutions and policies. That will provide a good basis for a minimum estimate of Russia's growth potential.

Human resources

Russian workers are far better educated than workers in other countries at the same income level—except, of course, for the countries of Eastern Europe. Adult illiteracy is 2 percent, as against over 15 percent for other middle-income countries.[4] Russian education is particularly strong in mathematics and physical sciences. Specific education in commerce is of course primitive or nonexistent. But good general education is already proving its value in business. Though the demand for defense-related science has collapsed, many physicists have reached the top in banking and other forms of business.

Natural resources

Turning to natural resources, Russia is without doubt the world's top nation. On a per capita basis it produces more than the United States of natural gas, oil, steel, aluminum, nickel, platinum, diamonds, and many other key minerals. Table 7–1 gives a clear picture of its unique position in the world as a producer of fuel and minerals. In due course Russia's huge area of farmland (third in the world) will also become a significant asset.

Apart from their inherent value, natural resources help in three other ways. They provide finance with which to import new technology and know-how. They provide a potential base for collecting taxes. And they have already created a concentration of wealth that will eventually be very favorable to investment and growth.

Table 7–1. Russia's natural resources

	World rank as producer	Share of world output
Natural gas	1	27%
Nickel	1	23%
Aluminum	2	15%
Platinum	2	15%
Oil	3	11%
Copper	4	10%
Steel	4	8%
Coal	4	6%
Cereals	4	6%

Source: Economist Diary (1993); *UN Statistical Yearbook 1990/1991.*

Private ownership[5]

The best news is on ownership: Russia has privatized faster than any of the East European countries. This is a fairly fundamental difference and has helped to create a rather different type of society. From the beginning of Eastern Europe's transformation in 1990 there was continuous debate about the proper speed of privatization. Everyone agreed that private ownership was the goal. But some people, like the distinguished Hungarian economist Janos Kornai, maintained that the best way to achieve it was to remove all obstacles to the setting up of *new* firms.[6] According to this theory, it was not so important to privatize the *existing* large state enterprises; they would in due course die under the pressure of competition from the new private sector. That was to a large extent the policy followed in Hungary: Enterprises were privatized only to the extent that there were Hungarians or foreigners willing and able to pay an economic price. Thus Hungary adopted a European version of the Chinese gradualist model—letting the new grow up in parallel with the old, rather than deliberately transforming the old.

Poland and the Czech Republic, by contrast, put privatization higher on their priorities, and, partly for that reason, their economies have performed better. The Russian reformers were determined to privatize even faster. They believed the assets of the old state enterprises were of great potential value, provided they were properly used. Those assets were bound to remain the main part of the nation's capital for the rest of the century. They needed owners who would insist on using their property to the best advantage. The privatization of existing assets would also help new firms to grow, as there would then be chunks of old enterprises available for sale.[7]

So rapid privatization was the objective. But how to achieve it? Small enterprises like shops and restaurants could be sold for cash, a process that was largely completed within two years.[8] There was enough private financial wealth available for people to buy those businesses, and in many cases the buyers were the managers or workers. When it came to large and medium-size enterprises, however, it made no sense to auction them for cash. Those few people who had large amounts of cash would have made an unreasonable killing. If such enterprises were to be privatized fast, they would have to be given away for nothing or for a very nominal price.

But to whom should they be given? There were three main groups who claimed rights to an enterprise: the workers in the enterprise, its managers, and the citizens of the country (especially those like teachers, doctors, and bureaucrats who worked outside the enterprise sector).

As soon as he was appointed privatization minister (formally head of the State Property Committee, known as GKI), Anatoly Chubais began his consultations. One day he met with the representatives of the workers; they told him he should give the factories to them. Another day he met with the managers, who also claimed the lot. At the same time pensioners and people employed in the "budgetary sphere" were bound to oppose all privatization unless they themselves got a share. After all, the factories had been paid for by taxes levied on everyone; so, they argued, the factories should be given to everyone, as citizens.

In both Poland and the Czech Republic priority was given to the claims of the citizens. Under Poland's mass privatization proposals, only 10 percent of shares would go to workers, and most of the rest would go to citizens in the form of vouchers. When the workers objected, the proposals became endlessly obstructed in the Parliament. They only began to be implemented in 1995, and other forms of privatization also went quite slowly. Things moved faster in the Czech Republic, where voucher-based privatization went on rapidly from 1992 on. By the end of 1994 half of Czech enterprises had been privatized. But in the Czech Republic it was possible to override the interests of the workers, since workers are weaker than in Poland and the state is stronger than anywhere else in Eastern Europe.

As Chubais looked at the history of privatization in other countries, he concluded that if he wanted to privatize quickly, he had to give enough to *all* the main claimants to secure their support. His first proposal was that the workers should get 35 percent of shares (25 percent free but without voting rights, plus up to 10 percent at a very low price). The managers would receive 5 percent (also at a very low price). And the citizens would, in exchange for Czech-style vouchers, receive most of the rest—a small proportion being kept in state hands for later sale.

That proposal was strongly opposed by the workers and managers and by their representatives in the Supreme Soviet. To salvage the program, Chubais called his initial proposal Option I and introduced an Option II, under which workers and managers could buy 51 percent of the shares at a rather higher price. The workforce of each enterprise now had to choose which option they preferred; except where the firm was very capital-intensive and thus expensive, they chose Option II. Thus the majority of Russian factories were privatized with a majority of "inside" shareholders.

But there were also "outside" shareholders, who had obtained their shares in exchange for vouchers. In the autumn of 1992 a voucher was issued to every Russian citizen. The voucher could then be used in any "voucher auction," at which roughly 20 percent of the shares of the enterprise were auctioned in exchange for vouchers. Most people did not use their vouchers to buy shares directly.[9] They sold them for cash or exchanged them for shares in an investment fund; the intermediaries then used the vouchers to buy the shares of enterprises.

The privatization of factories began at the end of 1992, and within eighteen months the "voucher" privatization was complete. Over 80 percent of Russian industry had been privatized, largely by the dogged determination of one man, Anatoly Chubais, and his talented subordinates Dmitri Vasiliev, Maxim Boycko, and Pyotr Mostovoy. Russia is now in its second phase of privatization, this time for cash rather than a giveaway. By now Russians have enough financial wealth to put up some money. Foreigners too are interested. So the government is selling its remaining blocks of industrial shares mainly through cash auctions and investment tenders, with 14 percent of the money going to the company and the rest to the state. Some important share offerings will be placed abroad, especially of Gazprom, the world's largest energy company. The sectors where much remains to be privatized include not only industry but, even more, fuel and energy, telecommunications, air transport, and banking.

Evaluation. So what overall difference will Russia derive from its drive to rapid privatization? Reviewing the growth of private ownership in post-communist countries, two leading *Financial Times* journalists argued in early 1995 that privatization is much less important to economic success than measures to permit the free entry of new firms. Privatization in Russia, they claimed, "has not transformed the country's economy. By contrast, Poland and Hungary have yet to launch mass privatization programmes but the genuinely private sector in these countries is larger."[10]

It is true that it is difficult to open a new business in Russia. The main obstacles are the bureaucracy (which has to license the uses of space), the lack of a real estate market, and the mafia. The bureaucracy and the mafia will often insist on their own side payment (see Chapter 8). But this hardly settles the issue of whether privatization makes a difference.

Since most privatization was in 1994, there can be no real evidence yet on its effects on economic dynamism. But two serious complaints can be heard: that Russian firms are owned mainly by insiders (leading to a bad system of governance) and that many managers have become excessively rich.

For the good governance of business, two things are important. First, the owners should not be the workers, for otherwise money will be wasted in keeping on too many workers. Second, there should be at least some shareholders who hold large blocks of shares, so that they have a sufficient incentive to press the managers to perform. At first sight the Russian privatization flouts both principles. But in fact things are not so bad.

First, the shares of the workers are tradable. You do not, as in Yugoslavia, have your share automatically as long as you are an employee, and lose it when you leave. It is yours even if you leave, and equally you can sell it even if you remain a worker. Some workers have already sold their shares, either to the managers or to outsiders who often set up shop at the factory gates. But a more potent force that will eventually reduce *insider power* is the need for firms to issue new shares for cash in order to finance investment.

Second, the pattern of *outside ownership* was from the start much more concentrated than the opponents of voucher privatization had forecast. In over half of the voucher auctions one single bidder got a block of at least 5 percent of the shares.[11] Since the shares of at least two hundred companies are now openly traded over the telephone in Moscow, the process of concentration has continued.

Moreover, over the same period as the voucher auctions, there was a separate process of privatization by tender offer. That was limited in scale and mostly covered medium-size enterprises. Blocks of shares were put up for tender for cash. Most of the tenders were won by outsiders, though some by groups of managers.

Thus the "average" privatized company in late 1994 had roughly 43 percent of its shares owned by workers, 17 percent by managers, 29 percent by outsiders, and the rest by the state (now in the process of being sold for cash).[12] In two-thirds of all privatized firms (especially in medium-size firms) workers had over half the shares.[13] However, all these figures overstate the power of workers and understate the power of managers, for in most firms the general manager exercises the voting rights going with shares belonging to the state, and in large companies (which chose Option I) most of the workers' shares are nonvoting.

Thus the whole pattern of ownership is quite diffuse. Up to 1995 banks were not important as owners, but investment funds are becoming important, as are managers. Hence the system is beginning to have elements of ownership by funds (as in Anglo-Saxon capitalism) and by owner-managers (as is common in Germany).

The new owners are increasingly using their muscle. At roughly 10 percent of the first shareholders' meetings the general manager was sacked.[14] Sometimes it took two meetings. Yosef Bakaleinik used to work at the Vladimir Tractor Factory. When he returned from Harvard Business School, he proposed himself as general manager at the first shareholder's meeting but was defeated. By the second meeting, the finances of the firm had worsened and Bakaleinik proposed a restructuring and marketing plan. He was elected as general manager.

Sometimes, however, it took outside initiative to change the management. Yaroslavl Resino Technika is a large producer of rubber products with five thousand workers. One of the voucher funds named Derzhava, which owns 39 percent of the firm's shares, called an extraordinary general meeting of shareholders at which it proposed to replace the management by young whiz kids. Most of the workers supported the proposal, and the management was changed. In July 1995 the first hostile takeover bid occurred. Koloss, a food manufacturer, tried unsuccessfully to take over another food manufacturer, the famous Red October Chocolate Factory on the Moskva River next to the Kremlin. But those examples show the extraordinary importance of Chubais's insistence that the privatized companies be open joint-stock companies with publicly traded shares rather than (as many people had wanted) closed private companies.

Many aspects of the situation are still very unsatisfactory. The rights of shareholders are still insecure. In mid-1995 most Russian companies did not have share certificates. The only proof of ownership was a list called the Shareholders' Registry, which was held by the company. In some cases the record of a shareholder's ownership had been simply crossed off the list of shares owned. In other cases firms have issued new shares free to some of their shareholders without informing the other shareholders. An example is Komi-Neft, one of Russia's largest oil companies, which issued extra shares to some of its shareholders in May 1994. So far the majority of companies have paid no dividend, often a good way of ensuring that enterprise revenues mainly benefit the insiders. Eventually all major abuses that have come to public notice have been corrected. But there clearly needs to be a proper regulating framework requiring among other things share certificates with a secure system for their custody. To deal with all such problems, the government in late 1994 established a Federal Securities Commission with ministerial status and with Chubais as chairman. The commission is creating a central share registry system, with help from the Bank of New York, and will do much to improve the governance of firms.

A second charge against Russia's breakneck privatization is that it has led to a vulgar accumulation of massive wealth by a handful of people, which may lead to economic dynamism but not to a fair society. There have indeed been real cases of abuse. For example, Surgut Neftegaz, one of Russia's leading oil companies, offered 40 percent of its shares for tender. The call for tenders was not made public in the proper place, so only one tender was received. The new owner obtained a major shareholding at a knockdown price. Similarly under the so-called "shares for loans" schemes in late 1995, individual banks secured control of valuable blocks of shares at low cost through tenders that were far from open.

However, we have to consider the alternatives. Without privatization the managers of companies would have been even less subject to external scrutiny. Since the dismantling of central supervision of enterprises by Gorbachev, many managers were engaged in large-scale racketeering. The simplest racket was to set up a trading company of one's own and to sell the enterprise's output to that company at an unreasonably low price. In principle, works councils were meant to prevent this, but worker shareholders have a stronger incentive to do so.

Privatization has indeed created some undeserved fortunes, including for some ministers (not of the reform camp). But the greatest undeserved fortunes have come from foreign trade, especially the privileged export of raw materials. Step by step, Russia is now moving to a more law-based society with fewer licenses. In the meantime it has acquired an ownership structure and a distribution of wealth fairly well suited to economic growth, if not yet to social justice. Through the mechanism of the voucher, Chubais generated an interest in market processes that could not have happened in any other way. Russia is now a nation of 40 million shareholders.

Restructuring

But, the critics say, Russian enterprises are not restructuring. They just go on producing what they always produced. If nobody buys it, they simply pile up debts to their suppliers. Because bankruptcy procedures are ineffective, there is no mechanism to enforce change.

Much of that is fallacious. First, quite obviously the pattern of production has changed hugely across industries (Figure 7–1). Though output in most industries fell in the first years of reform, it is now rising in some; for example, car production has risen. Even in the early days, some individual firms were increasing their output and employment. For example, in 1993 in each month 30 percent of firms increased their output and 40 percent their employment, even though more firms were shrinking.[15]

Faced with the collapse of old markets, the majority of factories altered their products. In the first two years of the reform 29 percent went into quite new product lines, while 60 percent produced new items akin to things they produced before.[16] Russia had always lacked a lightweight truck; GAZ, the producer of the Volga car, produced such a truck, the Gazel. In the aircraft industry Ilyushin produced a

Figure 7–1. Restructuring of output

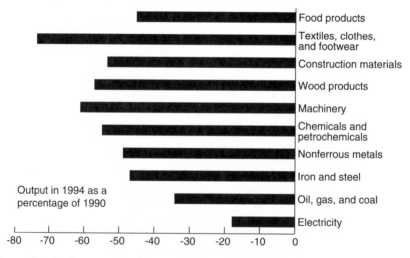

Source: *Russian Economic Trends*, 1994, vol. 3, no. 4, p. 64, Table 5.

newer version of the Ilyushin 96 with engines from General Electric. In machine-building a striking example comes from the giant firm Uralmash, based in Ykaterinburg. It produces oil rigs, earthmoving equipment, foundries, and the like. As investment finance for the oil industry declined, Russia's oil producers could no longer afford to install new oil rigs at each new well, leaving the old rigs to rust on the disused wells; they demanded movable oil rigs. Under new management, Uralmash obliged. Though it has cut employment by over half, it now has a joint venture with Caterpillar and National Oil Wells to produce movable oil rigs. Not surprisingly, 37 percent of Uralmash shares are now in the hands of one of Russia's leading entrepreneurs, Kakha Bendukidze, who has large shareholdings in forty-five companies with 72,000 workers.

The second fallacy is the fallacy about Russian interenterprise debt. Late payment is of course a problem. It is a problem all over the world. In Western Europe the average invoice is paid roughly one month past the due date. In Russia the figure at the end of 1995 was a little less than that.[17] Of course, Russian enterprises consider this a critical situation, because they are not used to worrying about their finances. In some sectors and at some times, things have been particularly bad. The energy sector is always the worst hit, because it comes at the first stage in the production process, while the flow of payments comes from the final buyers and reaches the energy sector last. The overall debt crisis was worst in mid-1992 and has never reached the same proportions again, though there may well be further crises as financial stabilization proceeds.

Workers bear an important part of the problem of nonpayment through wage arrears. In mid-1995 one-third of workers had money owed them, and for them the arrears averaged 1.5 months' wages. All of this is deeply disturbing for workers, but it does not mean that Russian firms are failing to adjust.

They have, for example, adjusted down their stocks of unsold goods. Under communism firms accumulated huge stocks of supplies against the inevitable day when some supply would fail to arrive. Then in the early days of the reform firms accumulated sizable stocks of unsold outputs. But now both are down.

And what about bankruptcy? There is a bankruptcy law, and to some extent it works. Since November 1992 debtor firms could be taken to an arbitration court. At first there were few cases, partly because creditors expected a government bailout. But by early 1995 the courts had put five hundred privatized companies into receivership. To deal with bankrupt state enterprises, a Federal Bankruptcy Agency was set up in late 1993. By early 1995 it had liquidated or privatized roughly one hundred companies.

Though not many firms have been bankrupted so far, the procedure has certainly helped the restructuring. For example, the airplane manufacturer Aviacor makes the Tupolev 154 at Samara beside the Volga. In 1994 it was placed in receivership by the arbitration court. The receiver appointed a twenty-eight-year-old banker, who raised the factory's sales from one plane a quarter to eight, using less than half the workforce.

Problem sectors. Many of Russia's biggest restructuring problems are still to come, as the remaining subsidies are pared down. In 1994 enterprise subsidies amounted to about 5 percent of national income—mainly to coal, agriculture/agro-industry, and defense.[18]

Coal is a real problem. Russia produces more coal than any other country except China and the United States. But most of it comes from mid-Siberia (the Kuznetsk Basin) or the Arctic North (Vorkuta), involving huge transport costs. There will inevitably be a prolonged period of adjustment. Russia has 750,000 miners. Traditionally they have been the heroes of Soviet society and among its highest-paid workers. In 1989 and again in 1991 they had the power to humiliate Gorbachev. Yeltsin made them his friends, but in early 1995 he faced a strike threat and won, with minimal concessions. The adjustment in mining will have to be handled with great care and needs to involve programs of retraining and resettlement like those carried out over the last fifty years in Western Europe.

As for agriculture, under the tsars Russia with Ukraine was one of the granaries of Europe and a major grain exporter. Communism hurt agriculture even more than it hurt industry. Productivity in Russian state agriculture is unbelievably low. That mainly reflects poor organization and, above all, poor motivation. The remarkable fact is that in 1993 36 percent of all agricultural production came from production on small private plots, which still comprise only 2.5 percent of agricultural land.[19]

Given the passion for private farming, it is remarkable how difficult it has been to privatize the state and collective farms. The problems are political and technical. Politically the power of the farm directors is formidable, and most peasants are conservative. There has been tremendous opposition to the notion of privately owned land. In principle the problem has now been largely overcome. Since October 27, 1993, it has been legal to buy and sell land and to use it as collateral. That applies both to rural and urban land.[20] But even in towns the land market has barely started. In the countryside, the main forms of private farming are the 50 million small family plots and the 280,000 family farms set up since 1990 on unused land, often for the benefit of people leaving the army. The family plots average a quarter of an acre each (though for rural families they are somewhat larger). The family farms average around 100 acres and add up to only 5 percent of all farmland.[21]

When it comes to the breakup of the old collective farms, there are clearly technical problems of assembling for each new farm a piece of land of reasonable size and a minimum collection of tractors and equipment. In principle any individual has been entitled to withdraw his share of the land and equipment from the collective since 1992, but in practice any such action would have been impractical, since the resulting ostracism would have made the new farm inoperable. Farms can be broken up only in a concerted fashion. The most promising model is that now being implemented in the Nizhny Novgorod region. Here the privatization committee first splits the land of each collective into a set of viable farms. Members of the collective are then supplied with points with which to bid for the separate farms (either individually or in partnership). The same happens for the buildings.

But to implement such a process over the whole of Russia will take years, probably decades. A land registry is only just beginning to be constructed, and the political obstacles are formidable. The basic legal framework is there, but agriculture is sure to be the last part of the Russian economy to be restructured.

Social role of enterprises. In the enterprise sector, a major problem has been the social responsibilities of the enterprises, especially for housing, kindergartens, cafeteria, and health care. Those responsibilities confuse the objective of the business, taking up an excessive fraction of top management time. They make it harder to enforce external financial discipline on the enterprise, and they also discourage outside investors.

Altogether social expenditures of enterprises in 1994 added roughly 20 percent to their labor costs.[22] Much the biggest cost is housing, especially the cost of heating and maintenance. Under communism 46 percent of all housing in towns was owned by enterprises. When privatization happened, the idea was that the housing should be transferred to the municipalities. But many enterprises kept their housing. In principle the cost of housing formerly owned by enterprises is borne by the federal government, independently of who owns the housing.

To facilitate labor mobility, eventually all these homes should eventually be privately owned, but families will not be able to pay the cost until their real wages rise. A simple arrangement to raise wages and housing charges simultaneously would not work, because a third (or so) of those who live in enterprise housing do not work for the same enterprise.[23] So the final resolution will be approached by a number of routes. Probably the best would be a quick privatization with subsidies continuing but declining. Administrative responsibility for housing issues needs somehow to be removed from top management and given either to separate agencies or municipalities. Firms need to concentrate on their core activities.

Too many giants, or not enough dwarfs? People often say that the worst thing about Russia is the degree of monopoly, so that the top priority is to break it up. That is a fallacy. Though the average size of all Russian firms *is* larger than in the West, that is not because there are many huge firms but because there are very few small ones. The twenty largest firms in the United States are four times larger than the twenty largest in Russia (in terms of employment).[24] And 40 percent of American factory workers are employed in firms of more than 10,000 workers, as against only 20 percent of Russians. At the other extreme, however, over a quarter of Americans work in really small firms (fewer than 250 workers), while only 6 percent of Russians do.

Table 7–2. Russia's top ten privatized companies

	Employees	Industry	Implied dollar value, $mn
Avtovaz	551,817	Motor vehicles	45
United Energy Systems	216,278	Electricity generation	647
Norilsk Nickel	161,520	Non-ferrous metals	466
Gaz	109,036	Motor vehicles	27
Magnitogorsk Metallurgical	108,526	Metallurgy	47
Zil	103,000	Motor Vehicles	16
Lukoil	102,700	Oil	293
Surgut Neftegaz	80,200	Oil and gas	81
Nizhnevartovsk Neftegaz	65,780	Oil and gas	168
Yugansk Neftegaz	60,823	Oil and gas	72

Note: Value at the end of voucher privatization.
Source: The Economist, April 8, 1995, p. 16.

What is wrong in Russia is the lack of small firms, not the predominance of large ones (see Table 7–2).[25] In the future many of Russia's large enterprises may well, and should, split up spontaneously. But the main problem is the lack of small businesses, some of which should provide the seedlings for the great businesses of the future. Many things are needed to promote the development of small business: first, business know-how, provided through advice centers and training; second, financing through a proper network of local banks; third, sites— instead of obstruction from local bureaucracy and mafia, whenever new business is proposed; and fourth, better communications.

Bad communications have been a huge obstacle to economic progress in Russia. Under communism a limited telephone network and a poor road system helped to keep the nomenklatura in charge. In 1990 only 1 percent of freight ton-miles went by road, as against 33 percent in the United States.[26] The market depends critically on the flexibility that comes with a good road system and good telecommunications. Telecommunications are improving rapidly, roads more slowly.

The banks

Another key requirement for a modern economy is an efficient financial system to facilitate payments and to channel savings into the most productive lines of investment. At the center of any financial system are the banks. Their development in Russia is one of the success stories of the transition. In the communist period there was essentially one monobank plus the Savings Bank, which took in household deposits and lent them back to the government. In the late 1980s the monobank was split into a number of sectoral banks for agriculture, industry, construction, and so on. In addition in the late 1980s private banks became legal. Those have sprouted like mushrooms. Altogether there were about 2,500 banks in mid-1995. Most of them were small. Some, but not many, were owned by enterprises, which had set them up as a channel for securing depositors who would in effect lend to the enterprise.[27] Depositors, however are insured only at the Savings Bank (Sberbank).

Apart from the Savings Bank, there are three main forms of bank (see Table 7–3). First, there are chunks of the old monobank (for example, the foreign trade bank, Vneshtorgbank, and the agricultural bank). Next are the new banks created by enterprises (for example, Imperial, owned largely by Gazprom, and Stolichny). Finally there are new independents, such as Inkom, Unexim, and the International Company for Finance and Investment (IFC). The last are the most dynamic banks. Two (Unexim and IFC) are managed by the thirty-four-year-old Vladimir Potanin, who put together a powerful banking consortium of eight banks, which in April 1995 offered to lend the government $2 billion on terms that were eventually rejected.

In the first four years of the reform, banking was very profitable because of higher spreads in periods of inflation. So banking has become the elite profession in Russia, even more than in the West. Bankers earn much higher salaries than their former colleagues who stayed in government or research. Successful bankers have come from many quarters. Many of the most successful are former physi-

Table 7–3. Top ten Russian banks

	Assets (trillion rubles)
Sberbank	44.3
Vneshtorgbank	18.8
Agroprombank	18.3
Inkombank	9.2
Rossissky	7.7
Uneximbank	7.1
Moscow Industrial Bank	6.1
Imperial	5.8
International Co. for Finance & Investment	5.8
Stolichny	5.3

Source: The Economist, April 8, 1995, p. 14.

cists or mathematicians, who have moved from one elite to its successor. Most young people would like to work in a bank, because the pay is many multiples of that in industry or education.

The main economic functions of banks are to facilitate transactions (by holding people's money and making their payments) and to channel finance into investment. How well are the banks performing their role?

The payments system has been transformed. Payments used to be cleared through the Central Bank. In 1991 the process averaged around a month, and between Moscow and Siberia it often took twice as long. Now payments are cleared directly between banks and average four days.

By contrast, the system of financing private investment is still rudimentary. Banks have little expertise in assessing the risks involved in each loan. Since the risks are often large, they charge very high real interest rates, and the risk of bank failure in turn leads depositors to require high rates on deposits.[28] Because loans are so risky, banks lend only for very short periods, usually six months or less, which also ensures that there is a continual stream of maturing loans with which to fight a run on the bank. High and volatile inflation reinforces the tendency to shorten the time horizon, and banks have been loath to take equity stakes.

None of this is good for investment, but it is inevitable in the early stages of transition that investment is mainly financed by retained profits and by equity stakes taken directly by rich people (and not via the stock market, which is rudimentary). But so far even rich people hang back, preferring to put most of their money abroad.

When the boom?

So when will things change and the boom take off? There are four main conditions that would be favorable to an investment boom:

- Increased demand in the economy
- Financial stability
- Availability of finance
- Certainty of taxes, legal title, and law enforcement

The prospects for the first three look quite good, but the fourth is a huge problem.

Demand in the economy had already bottomed out in 1994. After the drastic fall of real spending by households in 1992, private consumption rose somewhat. It rose by about 10 percent in 1993 and the same in 1994. However, investment was falling sharply. Even in 1994 it fell by 26 percent compared with the previous year.

The consumption boom has already led to a miniboom in housebuilding in the larger cities. It will inevitably lead in due course to a wider investment boom, especially because Russia has been largely isolated from the rest of the world for seventy years, leading to a huge technological backlog. Russian industry needs desperately to invest in order to produce new products that consumers want, as well as to produce old products more efficiently. With the high level of general education in Russia and the low wage level, there is no reason why Russia should not be a competitive location for production. Such a boom, once it starts, could be expected to last a long time, as we have seen with the long Chinese boom.

But it will start sooner and go more strongly, the more stable the financial environment. In early 1996 the prospects for stability looked good. In its Monetary Program, agreed upon with the IMF and subject to monthly monitoring, the government had committed itself to a strong disinflationary course.[29] There were, of course, significant political uncertainties ahead, and one cannot be sure that all possible future presidents and prime ministers will have learned the lessons from the high inflation of the last four years. But it would be surprising if annual inflation did not fall further, after the following history:

1992	2,500%
1993	800%
1994	200%
1995	130%

Foreign investment

But where, some might say, will the financing for investment come from? The greater part, as throughout the world, will come from retained profits. Some will come from private savings, which have hitherto financed the government deficit, now sharply reduced.[30]

But an important part will undoubtedly come from a turnaround in the capital flows between Russia and the West. Despite its "need" for capital, Russia in 1992–94 was a net exporter of capital. The reason was quite simply the low appetite for undertaking real investment projects in Russia. Since Russians were not themselves investing in Russia, their saving went into foreign assets (either foreign securities or cash dollars, or real property abroad). The scale of the capital flight has been truly enormous. In 1992–94 Russia "exported" some $45 billion, which could otherwise have been used to finance machinery and other imports that could have brought forward the modernization of Russia.[31] In the process, the price of imported goods was pushed artificially high through a devalued exchange rate for the ruble, and the high price of imports in turn discouraged the purchase of investment goods.

If such a capital exodus were to stop, one can easily imagine the consequences. It would liberate billions of dollars' worth of savings to finance investment in Russia, much of which would be devoted to the purchase of foreign goods. And, going further, if the capital flight were to be reversed, there would be even more financing for investment. The capital then flowing in from abroad would include not only foreign-owned wealth but also Russian wealth that had previously been exported.

All the evidence suggests that capital is highly mobile between Russia and the West.[32] It can flow in and out with ease. The actual flow depends upon how much real investment is being undertaken in Russia. People sometimes complain that foreigners do not invest in Russia, but so long as Russians are not investing, why should they? The truth is that all investment in Russia, whether by Russians or by foreigners, is determined by the same forces.

A well-tested indicator of the investment climate in the country is the standing of the stock market. If the stock market is high, people are more likely to invest, and vice versa. Figure 7–2 shows the value of the shares of Russia's top two hundred corporatized companies, measured in dollars. These companies produce well over half of Russia's national income, and the shares include those still held by the government (valued at the market price per share).

Figure 7-2. Market value of Russian businesses*

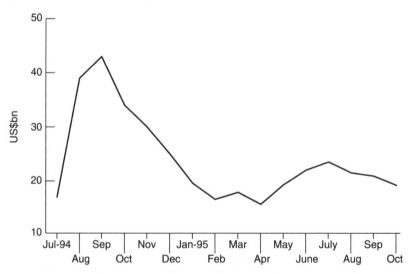

*Market capitalization of 200 Russian firms, including Gazprom, but excluding banks.
Source: Russian Economic Trends, Monthly Update, December 15, 1995.

Two facts leap out. First, in late 1995 the estimated value of the shares was incredibly low. At $20 billion, Russia's main companies are valued at about 7 percent of one year's national income. By contrast, the shares of U.S. companies are valued at around 70 percent of national income, and those of U.K. companies at over 100 percent. Putting the same point more concretely, in April 1995 the Russian stock market valued oil companies at 10 cents per barrel of proven oil reserves, while the comparable figure for Western oil companies was $5.50.[33] Even more extraordinary is the case of Gazprom, Russia's huge gas monopoly, which produces about a quarter of the world's natural gas. If its resources were valued in the same way as those of Western gas companies, Gazprom would be worth at least $250 billion. Its market value in Russia in April 1995 was $5 billion. This clearly reflects a gloomy underlying view of Russia's current prospects.

Second, the value of shares has moved up and down considerably. There was a sharp boom in 1994, with share prices doubling in August 1994. But between September 1994 and February 1995 share prices fell to less than half what they had been. Those movements reflect strongly the perceived level of stability, both financial and political. Inflation was falling up to September 1994, but it then rose. The ruble crisis of October was a symptom of financial instability, which was then augmented by the political crisis over Chechnya. The stock market stayed low throughout 1995 and into early 1996.

The Russian stock market, though a sensitive indicator of confidence, is so far largely dominated by foreign buyers. In 1994 it acted largely as a vehicle for the first large influx of foreign capital into Russia, with foreign investment funds buying up the shares of newly privatized companies from Russian voucher funds. It appears that altogether about $2 billion of foreign portfolio investment flooded into Russia in 1994, with the flow peaking in September and falling sharply after that.[34]

From the standpoint of restructuring, however, the private foreign investment that matters most is not "portfolio investment," which is largely speculative, but "direct investment," where a Western firm assumes a substantial stake with the view to creating a new type of operation. Such investment, mostly in the form of "joint ventures" with a Russian partner,[35] has been building up steadily: $100 million in 1991,

$800 million in 1992, $1.1 billion in 1993, and $2.3 billion in 1994.[36] Most Western companies that have started up in Russia have as their prime objective supplying the potentially huge Russian domestic market, and they want to do so from inside Russia, because costs are low (wages around $100 a month) and most imports are taxed. In addition there are the Western oil companies, which would like to get their hands on some of Russia's huge oil reserves but so far have been largely confined to the least choice fields. As for other goods Russia can export, few Western companies have begun to manufacture in Russia for sale abroad, except perhaps to the communist bloc.

Western companies can now be found operating in almost every sector of the economy. In food and drink Mars, Pepsi, Coca-Cola, and Philip Morris are having a field day, because Russians love Western products. The same is true of household goods (Procter & Gamble, Johnson & Johnson). But Westerners are also active in engineering (ABB, Otis, Caterpillar), paper and pulp (Herlitz), and other manufacturing industries. The French PTT, Deutschetelekom, and British Telecom have important stakes in the modernization of telecommunications, and Lufthansa and others in the new air transport system. But in business services the impact is perhaps the most significant, with all the six main accounting firms providing a mass of locally based consultancy services. But almost no sector is untouched, from housebuilding and hotels to fast food, where McDonald's is a household name.

When the opportunities are so great, it is perhaps surprising that there has not been more foreign investment. In most lines of business (but not defense, energy, or banking) foreigners have the same rights and obligations as Russians.[37] They can become sole owners of enterprises and, if they do, can buy the land beneath, like any Russian owner.[38] They can repatriate both profit and capital.

The reasons for low investment differ somewhat between direct investors and portfolio investors. Direct investors are discouraged by the general difficulty of doing business in Russia: taxes, the mafia, and problematic relations with local governments and business partners. Many joint ventures have run into trouble because the Russian partner has tried to increase its share of the takings. So increasingly direct investors go for 100 percent control, with the Russian partner as a subcontractor.

Portfolio investors are concerned more with legal and financial uncertainties affecting shareholders' rights and returns. Our colleagues Liam Halligan and Pavel Teplukhin carried out a survey of the forty-two leading Western investment banks, brokerages, and accounting firms operating in Russia and asked them to rank the various disincentives.[39] It emerged that the biggest disincentive was legal insecurity, followed by financial uncertainty. Interestingly, political risks ranked only third. The consequence of those uncertainties is that Russian shares are very cheap compared with what they will eventually reach. Even though profits are quite depressed, the average price is around two years' profits, a real bargain.[40]

Legal difficulties

The legal uncertainties are certainly legion. First, there are the weak rights of shareholders—to vote at meetings, to extract a dividend, and even, in the extreme, to have their title properly recorded. Second, there are the legal uncertainties affecting the enterprise itself. What can it really do with its assets? Can it, for example, really sell its land? And what taxes and regulations is it likely to face? Finally, how will it be able to enforce its rights? Will there be a functioning system of courts that will uphold any contract the firm has signed?

To develop a clear and consistent set of laws for the market economy takes time. In early 1995 the first part of the new Civil Code was adopted, but further parts will follow. At the same time there is little tradition of contract enforcement by the courts. Most contract enforcement is done by cruder means. To develop an effective system of civil courts trained to operate the new laws will also be a matter of time. But here, as on all other fronts, things are moving forward.

What about the mafia and corruption? This is such a big subject that we are saving it for a separate chapter. But without a doubt it is now a big, perhaps the biggest, impediment to new business development in Russia. Doing business in Russia is tough.

So what is the scorecard? By mid-1995 Russia had achieved

greater financial stability than in the previous five years, and there is step-by-step progress in securing property rights. Political uncertainty continues, at least up to the presidential election in mid-1996. But the economy has now bottomed out and it is poised for an upsurge. Even political instability cannot prevent this, and it would be surprising if by the end of the century Russia was not growing at 5 percent per annum, as Poland is now.

Trade and growth

And what of the longer future? History shows that countries grow fast if they start behind (like Russia), if they have high educational standards relative to their income level (like Russia), and if they follow good policies (sound finance, private ownership, and open trade).[41] Russia's privatization policy has given it a dynamism that many countries lack. But on foreign trade the line remains unclear. Protectionist forces are strong. They argue not only for tariffs and a devalued ruble but also for the formation of giant companies "able to compete in the world market."

The best evidence shows that competition is the engine of productivity growth. That shows up from looking both at firms and countries.[42] Russians sometimes say, "Why should we keep our economy open if the West blocks entry to our aluminum, uranium, space launchers, and food products?"[43] The answer is simple: The record shows that it is better for a country to keep itself open, even if others do not. It is too early yet to be sure that Russia will heed this lesson.

At this stage Russia is not very open, for an economy of its size. Imports from the West are only about 13 percent of the GDP. They come from (in descending order of volume) Germany, the United States, the Netherlands, Finland, Italy, Japan, and a few others.[44] Another 4.5 percent of GDP is imports from the former Soviet Union. Of Russian imports, machinery to modernize the country amounts to less than a third.

But trade is a vital engine of growth, because it, even more than foreign investment, is the vehicle that carries know-how from one economy to another. Russia needs more imports. Fortunately it should have no difficulty at all in paying for them. Russia's export capacity is huge. It already exports 18 percent of GDP to the West and 5 percent to the former Soviet Union. Nearly half of Russian exports are oil and gas, and most of the rest are other raw products (metals, diamonds, and timber). The exports of oil and gas were artificially contained by quotas up to 1995. If those quotas have now been truly removed and pipeline capacity is expanded in response to demand, Russia could enormously expand its raw material exports. At a later stage manufactured exports, which have so far failed to grow as they have in most of Eastern Europe, could also grow.[45] The extra export earnings plus foreign borrowing could then fuel a surge of imports to modernize Russian industry, which would in turn boost manufactured exports. Developing manufactured exports will certainly take time, and long before that Russia's production for the domestic market will have surged ahead.

It is tempting, but probably idle, to speculate about which industries will be likely to prosper in Russia. In other words, where is Russia's comparative advantage? Various economists attempted to predict which industries would prosper in Eastern Europe, and their models turned out to have no predictive power. Industries that use raw materials, which are abundant in Russia, will surely tend to prosper—industries with a heavy content (by value) of energy, metals, or timber. But beyond that little can be said. Within each industry some firms will prosper because they are well managed, and others will fail. The firm-specific element, more than the industry-specific element, will determine who succeeds. And Russia, like other advanced countries, will be found exporting and importing goods produced within the same industry.

Evaluation

So how rich will Russia become? Khrushchev predicted that under communism Russia would overtake the West. It failed to. Could it do so without communism?

In the next century this is surely unlikely. But Russia has a lot going for it. As in all of Eastern Europe, the workforce is highly educated. On top of that Russia has natural resources unparalleled on a per capita basis except in the oil states. As a large country of 150 million people (plus 100 million more in its surrounding sphere of influence), Russia will exert a special appeal to foreign capital. And it has a new dynamism, based on rapid privatization and substantial concentration of wealth. Given all this, Russia is likely to experience growth averaging at least 4 percent a year for a decade or more. In living standards Russia by 2020 may well have outstripped countries like Poland, Hungary, Brazil, and Mexico, with China far behind.[46]

Chapter 8

Can Russia beat the mafia?

*How bad is crime in Russia? • What is the mafia? • The effects of crime •
Why is crime so bad? • Breakdown of honor among thieves • Corruption • Will
crime remain big? • Does this apply to Russia? • Can the mafia be defeated?*

In February 1993, just thirteen months after the start of economic reform, Boris Yeltsin lamented, "Crime has become problem number one for us. [It] has acquired such scale and character that it poses great danger for . . . the whole Russian state. Crime is destroying the economy, interfering with politics and undermining public morale."

Some people went even further, claiming that criminals were not just threatening the state but had already taken it over. Everywhere, it seemed, corrupt politicians and officials were selling government contracts to the highest bidder; policemen were in the pay of gangsters; businessmen were making fortunes from extortion and settling disputes by murder; when cases did go to court, crooked judges used their influence to get crime bosses acquitted; and everywhere, criminals were able to go about their activities almost with impunity. That was the impression both of ordinary Russians and of people in the West.

This chapter looks at the extent to which criminals have won the battle for Russia and suggests answers to the following questions: How big is the crime wave? (Very big, but the worst part of it is domestic rather than organized crime.) What is organized crime? (Russians have a much wider definition than Westerners.) What are its effects? (Damaging to both the government and business.) Why is it so big? (Partly because criminal gangs were deeply entrenched in the Soviet Union and partly because the transition to a market economy occurred when the state was weak.) And will it remain big? (Not necessarily; much depends on how quickly Russia can write for itself a coherent body of laws.)

How bad is crime in Russia?

More than 32,000 people were murdered in Russia in 1994. That was twice as many as in 1991, the last year of the Soviet Union. In 1992, the first year of economic reform, it leaped to 23,000 and to over 29,000 in 1993. This period saw the worst upsurge of criminal activity. Rates for the main crimes of violence—rape, aggravated assault, and robbery, as well as homicide—rose more slowly or even fell in 1994–95.

Nevertheless, 32,000 was an enormous number, even for a country of Russia's size. It works out at 21.8 murders per 100,000 people. That was more than twice as high as in America, which has one of the highest murder rates among rich developed countries (9.3 per 100,000 in 1992). The rate is about 4 per 100,000 in Germany and France, and less than 1 per 100,000 in Japan. It was also higher than in any other post-communist country. Poland's murder rate was just 3.0 per 100,000 in 1994.

Russia, in short, has worse than American-standard homicide rates but without the drug problems and inner-city gang warfare with which much of American homicide is associated. America displays a kind of apartheid world of crime, with safe places coexisting often side by side with places that are as dangerous as anywhere in the world. Russia, in contrast, is more pervasively dangerous: You can be shot anywhere.

Or robbed, assaulted, or raped. Rates for virtually all crimes of violence are extremely high in Russia, though not as high as in America. In 1993, there were, for every 100,000 people, 124 robberies (as against 264 in America); 27 "aggravated assaults" (America: 442) and 9.7 rapes (compared with 43 in America).

When Russians put crime at the top of their list of public problems, they are not reacting to exaggerated fears of public safety. The threat to ordinary citizens is real.

The overall picture, however, distorts the real threat that crime poses to Russia. When Russians talk about crime, they distinguish between two different kinds: street and domestic crime on the one hand, organized crime on the other.

Domestic crime accounts for the larger part of Russia's high murder rate. Though the minister of the interior claimed "the bulk of [murders in 1994] were contract killings," in fact the ministry's own figures suggest otherwise: 14,000 of the 32,000 murder victims were women killed by husbands, lovers, or former partners.[1] Similarly, many of the murdered men were victims of street or domestic crime too. Domestic crime is strongly associated with Russia's huge alcohol problem. Anecdotal evidence suggests that many, perhaps most, domestic crimes are alcohol-related.

When Russians describe their country as "a mafia state" or say that criminals dominate the government and control business, they are talking about the second category. "Organized crime," Yeltsin claimed, "has become a direct threat to Russia's strategic interests and national security." It is organized crime that poses the big threat to Russia's reforms.

What is the mafia?

But what is "organized crime" in Russia? When Westerners talk about it, they refer to groups who use violence to extract income. But when Russians talk about "the mafia," they are actually using a far wider definition, embracing four groups who in reality are distinct. Only the first group is really "mafia" in the usual Western sense of an organized gang using violence to extract income.[2] The second and third groups are not criminals in the ordinary sense at all. And the last group is involved not in criminal violence but in the related area of corruption—that is, the sale by officials of government property, whether trading licenses, passports, or permits to build roads or houses, for personal gain.

The first group, the real mafiosi, are the thugs in sharp suits with bulging armpits that any visitor to Russia can see lurking in expensive German cars outside hotels. They are the violent enforcers who collect protection money, run prostitution rings, peddle drugs, and sell weapons. In August 1995, the head of the interior minister's department for organized crime said that more than eight thousand criminal gangs were operating in Russia, with 35,000 members in all. That is slightly fewer than in Italy, if you take account of the size of the country. The organized criminal groups in the three southern Italian provinces of Sicily, Calabria, and Campania had just under 17,500 gang members in 1995, organized into four hundred families.[3] Their Russian equivalents are the type most like criminals elsewhere.

The second and third "mafia" groups in Russia would not be called criminals elsewhere. The second group consists of the small businessmen who own shops or sell goods from a kiosk on the street. Customers call them mafia even though in reality they are more often victims of gangs than members of them. Russians do so partly because shopkeepers have regular contacts with the criminal gangs "protecting" them, partly because prices are extortionately high—as they need to be if the shop is paying extortionists—and partly because of communist indoctrination. Russians were taught at school that the only worthwhile part of economic activity was manufacturing and production; everything else, especially trade and finance, was to be looked down upon. Many forms of private trading were illegal. That still plays a residual role in popular perceptions.

The third type is like the second writ large. They are the big businessmen with large Mercedeses and troops of "assistants" with bulges under their left arms. Their business methods are rough; they avoid paying taxes when they can and make liberal use of bribery. But their business itself is usually legal. They resemble the robber barons of late-nineteenth-century America, the Rockefellers and Vanderbilts, rather than outright gangsters like Al Capone. And like them, they employ large numbers of private security guards, often for defensive purposes rather than criminal ones—that is, to provide the security that the ordinary police cannot be relied upon to give. Russia has huge numbers of such private security guards. Their association claimed there were 800,000 in late 1995, over twenty times more than the number of members of organized criminal gangs. This third category consists first and foremost of businessmen, who are criminals because it is hard to make deals in Russia without becoming involved with crime.

The last type is the state mafia, corrupt officials who sell licenses to import or export at controlled prices, licenses that bear with them the chance to siphon off goods for sale at uncontrolled and highly profitable prices. They may sound less noxious. They are not usually directly responsible for crimes of violence. But they are perhaps the most deadly of the four groups, because they are mainly responsible for the corruption that is becoming pervasive in Russia. Some estimates suggested that between one-third and one-half of all hot money in Russia went through the hands of corrupt officials in 1994.

The use of the blanket term to cover all these groups leads to some exaggeration in the scale of the problem of organized crime. In reality, the difficulties have been caused mostly by the first and fourth groups, the thugs and the corrupt officials.

The effects of crime

By calling into question the ability of the elected government to provide law and order, the thugs who commit murder and extortion are undermining one of the basic functions of government. Max Weber gave a famous definition of the state as an agency that successfully claims a monopoly over the legitimate use of physical force within a given territory. In parts of Russia, it often seemed as if the agency with the monopoly of violence was not the government at all but a criminal gang. By that definition, Russia is not a state at all, just a collection of "given territories" controlled by criminals.

The corrupt officials have damaged the government directly. Virtually no institution of government—not the civil service, the police, not even the courts—has been free of their influence. This has undermined popular confidence in democratic rule.

A poll taken in the Russian Far East in the summer of 1992 found that one-third of all residents believed that criminals "determined the course of events in their region." A year later, another poll found that 49 percent of Russians put crime higher on their list of concerns than unemployment, while another poll taken that year in the city of Yekaterinburg in the Urals found that three-quarters of the residents thought their city was ruled by the mafia.[4]

Fear of crime could have effects that were almost as worrisome as the crime wave itself. Vladimir Zhirinovsky won 22.9 percent of the seats for the lower house of parliament in December 1993 on a platform of aggressive nationalism. He used the crime wave as an argument for returning Russia to authoritarianism and in his last pre-election television broadcast advocated shooting criminals on sight (something Lenin had permitted during the Civil War of 1918–22). The respected All-Russian Center for Public Opinion Research found that Zhirinovsky's strongest support had come from young, relatively skilled industrial workers on good wages. They had voted for him not because they wanted to reverse economic reform (they had not been adversely affected by it), nor because they wanted to incorporate Finland into the Russian empire (as Zhirinovsky proposed), but because they wanted to restore social discipline, create a strong state, and prevent incipient anarchy. The crime wave was high on their list of concerns.[5]

In contrast, the main reformist party in this election campaign, Yegor Gaidar's Russia's Choice, was far less effective at running on an anticrime ticket, perhaps because, as a pro-business party, it worried about being accused of hypocrisy because of the popular association of business with crime. That enabled opponents to argue that reformers were themselves to blame for crime, even though, in fact, the reformers were among the least corrupt politicians in Russia.

This hurt both the reform and support for it. Capitalism, which the reformers were trying to build, needs a basic sense of justice and fairness. People must feel that they get from the system what they put into it. Otherwise the system will lose its support. Crime drives honest people away from business or limits what they are willing or able to do in it. If mafiosi are successful, that encourages the assumption that any successful manager is a crook. It blackens the reputation of honest managers and overturns the notion that you get what you deserve. Indeed, it has the opposite effect: If business is extensively criminalized, law-abiding citizens will assume that if you have anything, you don't deserve it.

The crime wave also became the biggest single problem for most consumers and businessmen, outstripping even inflation.

In 1993, Yeltsin commissioned Pyotr Filippov, the head of his analytical center (the Kremlin's think tank), to look at how crime was affecting the Russian economy and society. Filippov's report, presented in January 1994, painted a picture of a society in which no one trusted the police, few believed that laws would be enforced and "every, repeat every, owner of a shop or kiosk pays a racketeer"; 150 such gangs, it claimed, controlled 40,000 private and state-run banks, including most of the country's 1,800 commercial banks.[6] In another report, the Ministry of the Interior claimed that organized crime controlled as much as 40 percent of the GDP in 1993.

That hurt all companies because of the amount of protection money they had to pay. Filippov's report claimed that three-quarters of all private enterprises were being forced to pay between 10 and 20 percent of their earnings to criminal gangs. They had to hire small private armies to defend themselves against rival racketeers. They were unable to trust the courts to enforce contracts and had to resort to criminals themselves to collect loans. A director of the Round Table of Russian Businesses, set up to lobby the government on behalf of three hundred leading companies, complained: "There are no precise or detailed legal procedures for resolving economic conflicts. A banker cannot be sure that his loan will be repaid, a businessman cannot be sure that he will be paid for his goods."

It all hit small businesses especially hard. Big companies could afford this sort of private protection. Small companies could not. That discouraged would-be entrepreneurs from going into business, which was particularly unfortunate at Russia's early stage of capitalist development, when there were many economic opportunities to exploit. One academic went into business for himself in 1992 and set up an oil consultancy. In mid-1994 he admitted that he had not gone into oil trading because it was too dangerous and said he did not advertise and kept as low a profile as possible (no fancy offices in the city center) in order to escape the attentions of criminals both inside and outside the government.

Crime hurt not only the companies but the government as well, because it imposed such a tight squeeze on firms that they had less money left over to pay taxes. The government's revenues would have been higher than it was without the extensive crime; had it been able to collect more taxes, it is possible either that its budget deficit would have been lower or it would have spent more money in the real economy. Either way, the state's public finances would have been better off. That in turn has contributed to inflation, which hurts everyone. So the effects of crime are not just confined to businesses.

Corruption damaged the economy further. Corruption was rife in the former Soviet Union, of course, and has continued to exist in Russia. But, as was pointed out by Andrei Shleifer and Robert Vishny, two American economists who have acted as advisers to the Russian government, the form of corruption has changed a great deal—and for the worse. In the Soviet Union, officials had reason to believe that they would be in power for a long time and had an incentive to keep bribes reasonably low so as not to scare "customers" away. They also had to keep a low profile to avoid being noticed by higher officials. Not so in Russia. Officials could not be certain how long they would stay in their jobs, which gave them an incentive to steal as much as possible as fast as possible. Worse, the relaxation of discipline from the higher levels of government meant that officials everywhere were competing to grab as much as possible for themselves. This drove up the total cost of corruption. Shleifer and Vishny describe how a businessman wanting to start a company in Russia has to bribe officials of both central and local governments, the fire and water departments, the local police, and criminal gangs as well. Each group charged as much as it could, taking no account of other bribe seekers. That imposed a much higher cost on business than if the corrupt officials had had a monopoly over government services.[7] In short, disorganized crime and corruption are more damaging than the disciplined sort. That is important, because it corrects the intuitive belief that, once officials have sorted out their differences, and once gangs have settled their wars, the winners will have a stranglehold on the economy and will be able to impose huge monopoly costs on the country. In fact, as the disputes subside, the costs on the economy are likely to fall. From this point of view, organized crime is better than disorganized crime.

Lastly, crime and corruption damaged the Russian economy because it scared away foreign direct investment. Considering that foreigners have the same rights of ownership as Russians, and that Russian assets are extraordinarily cheap (in terms of reserves, for example, oil companies cost about one-fiftieth the price of Western ones in April 1995), foreign investment has been low. Direct investment—that is, buying a Russian company or building your own—was particularly low. A survey of forty-two top Western investment banks, brokerage houses, and accountants showed that legal insecurity was the biggest disincentive to investment. Crime was not the only legal problem (others included the weakness of the courts and of shareholders' rights), but it was among the worst.

Why is crime so bad?

The crime wave seemed to come out of nowhere. One minute, Russia was a stable, law-abiding sort of place; the next, it was the Wild West. Of course, it was not that way. One reason that crime has proliferated is that criminals were well dug into society during the Soviet period.

The rulers of the Soviet Union liked to claim that crime and corruption were features of Western capitalism. In fact, both were widespread in the Soviet Union. Because crime was supposed not to exist, it was rarely reported in the state-controlled newspapers or on television. That made the postreform crime wave the more inexplicable. But it did not mean there was little of it before 1991. Between 1974 and 1991, Arkady Vaksberg attended all but a few closed sessions of the USSR Supreme Court, the country's highest court, to hear its reports on crime in the Soviet Union. "Invariably, the picture was depressing," he wrote. "The growth of crime, especially the rise in serious crimes (homicide, armed robbery, burglaries, gang rape), far exceeded the average levels reported over many years by the developed and even by the less developed countries. The statistics of death sentences passed and executed were particularly horrifying. The press release issued after each session contained no hint of the depressing facts."[8]

In addition, the KGB and other communist organizations, which did not balk at genocide, were not shy of criminal acts in the ordinary sense too, if they served their purpose. Thus, before 1991 crime was either hidden or was perpetrated by the secret police themselves.

During the Brezhnev regime, criminal gangs entrenched themselves further for two reasons: their connections with corrupt local Communist party bosses and their usefulness in compensating partly for the ever-widening shortages in the centrally planned economy, thus deflecting some public dissatisfaction with communist economic failure. Lev Timofeev, a former dissident, went much further when looking at Soviet crime: "In the last decades in the USSR, not a single product has been manufactured and not a single paid service has been performed outside the confines of the black market."[9]

That said, there were differences between the criminals of the Soviet era and their modern Russian counterparts. Speaking of the old Soviet mafia, General Gennady Chebotaryev, the number two to the Interior Ministry's organized crime directorate, says, "Theirs is a very old and traditional profession, which predates the revolution." A true Russian godfather "is opposed to laws in the most fundamental way." He will never do an honest day's work. He will never serve in the army, never cooperate with the police, often not even own much. In the Soviet period a thief was prohibited from having anything to do with the Communist party, which was not an easy task. "Even if you were only seven years old and had to join the Young Pioneers [a sort of communist scout movement that almost all children were obliged to join], that was just too bad," said one mobster.[10] "Wearing a Communist pin or a badge with Lenin's portrait even once in your life meant you could never become a *vor v zakone* (godfather, literally 'thief in law')."[11] Thieves were banned from holding a job, thus cutting them off from the housing, educational and other benefits of the party-state that required everyone to have a job. In the Soviet period, the thieves would not even grow rich from their spoils. "Thieves in the Soviet Union are generally indifferent to the accumulation of wealth," Valery Chalidze, an emigré dissident, wrote.[12] The gang's earnings all went into a general fund, called the *obshchak*, from which all drew their salaries alike. Soviet thieves were outlaws in the deepest sense of the word, with their own codes of behavior, isolated from what they called "the civilian world," brutally violent and with rituals so bizarre that they seemed to belong to some strange, previously undiscovered tribe. Like the *yakuza* of Japan, Russian thieves would even cut off a finger or cover their bodies with tattoos as part of gangland ritual.[13] Some of those codes continue today. Killers, for example, leave their murder weapons at the scene of the crime as a calling card; it is considered bad form to use a murder weapon more than once.

Yet, though the underworld shunned communism, it turned out to share many communist features. As with most other aspects of life in the Soviet Union, the underworld was planned, organized, and cartelized, with one group having a monopoly on one form of criminal activity, and other groups others. In Moscow, for example, there were about twenty big gangs. The Lyubertsy ran prostitution; the Dolgoprudny controlled big protection rackets; the Ingush gangs controlled smuggling; the Azeris ran drugs. In addition to this professional specialization, there were also regional monopolies, usually for smaller-scale protection racketeers. The city was divided into some dozen regions, each controlled by one gang or another.

The gangs existed within a stable underworld, often controlled and coexisting in a symbiotic relationship with the bosses of the Communist party.

The Soviet gang was one of the few institutions to do well from reform. When Russia began its lurch toward the free market in 1992, criminal gangs had the easiest access to large amounts of capital. They were among the richest and best organized of all Russian institutions. That gave them enormous opportunities. But reform also overturned the old criminal certainties. Groups that had been rich now became poor; groups that had been poor became rich. Suddenly, the old criminal ways were in turmoil, and the criminal gangs with them. The old modus vivendi was over.

Breakdown of honor among thieves

That was the moment when the mafia probably posed the greatest danger to the Russian state. At that point, given its assets, it might have been able to buy up virtually every large business in the country and to take control of the economy. It blew its chance. At the end of December 1991, only days before the Soviet Union finally dissolved, thirty of the top criminals gathered secretly in a dacha of the Vedentsovo Borough of Moscow.[14] Their subject was the place of the mafia in the new Russia, but instead of planning how to take over the economy, they spent their time thinking about other matters: the opportunities that all those new unpoliced borders would afford the smuggling business; whether they could bribe the politicians and officials of the coming political order, as they had the Soviet order; and, above all, the challenge to their businesses coming from relative newcomers—gangs from Georgia, Chechnya, Armenia, and elsewhere in the Caucasus. "The assembled *vory*," wrote Steven Handelman, in the first full-length study of the Russian mafia, "agreed to combine their forces in a war against the Caucasian intruders."

Gang warfare erupted. That was both a symptom of the competition between gangs and the means by which it was conducted. It accounted for part of Russia's high murder rate. By the middle of 1994, General Chebotaryev estimated, smaller, weaker gangs in Moscow were beginning to unite together to defend themselves. About a dozen gangs emerged from the score or so that used to run the capital's underworld. What might be called criminal rationalization continues. It can be seen in the Far Eastern city of Khabarovsk. There, most of the city's trade is controlled by one man, Vladimir Podiatev, known locally as the Poodle. A man who had spent seventeen years in prison camps for criminal offenses, he has his own political party, his own television station, and a letter from the Patriarch of the Russian Orthodox church blessing his charity work.

Some of the old gangs were among the victors, but not all. Many of the criminal groups that came out on top were a quite different breed. Far from waging war on those in power, they went into business with them, bribing officials and using corruption as a way of making money. And far from living modestly out of collective funds, they flaunted their wealth, driving around with fast cars and women.

The breakdown of control by the old groups was exemplified by the fate of one of them, the Kvantrishvili family, a Georgian group influential in Moscow's underworld in the late 1980s. In August 1993 Amran Kvantrishvili and three of his followers were shot dead by a group of Chechens. In March 1994 the head of the clan, Otari Kvantrishvili, a former wrestler, was picked up by the police. The transcript of his interrogation is a long lament for the lost influence of the old thieves-in-law of whom he had been one. A few weeks later, Otari was shot by a sniper as he emerged from a bathhouse.

A new breed of criminals emerged because the roots of crime in the new Russia were different from those in the Soviet era. The difference lay in the ending of the state's monopoly control over the economy.

Under the Soviet Union, there had been little private property, no private businesses, and no private contracts. So problems such as protecting your company from thieves or enforcing contracts on defaulters did not arise.

The establishment of private property rights and the creation of millions of private companies changed all that. Suddenly there were such problems. And they arose before an independent judicial system was up and running.

There were two results. First, criminals stepped in as enforcers. Hence the large number of contract killings which Viktor Yerin, the interior minister in 1994, ascribed to "conflicts in the sphere of commercial and financial activity arising from the struggle for markets."

Murders were particularly common in banking, partly because Russia had so many small banks (2,500 in 1995) competing fiercely in a business where it was hard to enforce contracts, and therefore resorting to criminals to collect debts. In 1993 thirty-five bankers (many of them prominent) were murdered. In the twelve months up to August 1995, the number rose to forty-five, including three members of the ruling body of the Round Table of Russian Businesses, the country's top lobbying group for large firms. Even the most respected businessman could fall victim to criminals. On August 4, 1995, murderers broke into the heavily guarded office of the Round Table's chairman, Ivan Kivelidi, one of Russia's most respected businessmen, who had been struggling to improve the country's political and business ethics. They poisoned him and his secretary by putting cadmium salts in his telephone.

The second result was an upsurge of corruption.

Corruption

Just before his death, Otari Kvantrishvili told the police that "the Moscow city authorities are the most corrupt government that has ever existed." The signs of decay were not confined to the capital's city government. Corruption has infected the very heart of the Russian government.

In July 1993 the wives of the security minister and the deputy interior minister were invited by an emigré Russian businessman named

Boris Birshtein on a three-day shopping trip to Zurich (his firms were based in Switzerland). As Yeltsin put it in his memoirs, "there the ladies scooped and ladled tons of perfumes, fur coats, watches, and everything else—a total of $350,000 in purchases. The wives took twenty baggage claim checks to Moscow; Seabaco [Birshtein's company] paid $2,000 for the overweight luggage."[15] The security minister, Viktor Barannikov, was fired.

Government regulations, where they existed, were vague and left room for abuse. Public servants were underpaid, demoralized, and hungry for bribes. Hundreds of government regulations and licenses remained in place, providing opportunities for corruption and crime. The most egregious examples came from the oil business, which is at once one of the most regulated and most criminalized parts of the economy.

The most spectacular example occurred in television. Rights to television advertising in 1995 were sold by the broadcasters at below market prices to middlemen, who resold them at full market rates and pocketed the difference. In the spring of 1995, Vladislav Listeyev, one of Russia's best-known television personalities and presenter of several of the country's most respected current affairs programs, was appointed to head one of the country's nationwide television networks. Soon afterward he was gunned down at his home in a classic contract killing, designed, it seemed, to prevent him breaking up the racket. His murder produced an outpouring of public grief; thousands of mourners attended his funeral.

Corruption and lack of legal guarantees made the privatization program, in particular, a bonanza for gangsters, partly because, in the rush to privatize, the authorities rarely had time to check bidders' documents or the source of their cash. In Nizhny Novgorod, armed riot police protected potential investors, keen to intimidate rival bidders for cheap assets. At an auction in Saransk in early 1994, the police were not on hand to discourage rival gangsters from "advising" rivals not to bid. Those who persisted were, it was said, mutilated. The head of the privatization committee in Chelyabinsk (the man who arranges the selloffs) thinks that gangsters threw him off a train.[16] At least thirteen mafiosi were killed in disputes over the privatization of a large aluminum enterprise in the Siberian city of Krasnoyarsk in the summer of 1995.

The question is, Was this upsurge in business-related crime a passing feature of Russia's political and economic transition? Or will criminals become entrenched in the new Russia, as they were in the Soviet Union and are in Italy?

Will crime remain big?

As we have seen, capitalism gave criminals opportunities they did notchave under communism, providing a chance to compete for control of property, allowing criminals to come out into the open, and breaking up cozy relationships with each other and with the communist elite. Mafiosi flourished because they were wealthy to begin with, because the state was too weak to suppress them, and because it was easier and more profitable to make a living by crime than by working.

That, together with the gangs' secretive and often archaic organization and rituals, makes it natural to think of the Russian mafiosi as simply predators, emerging from a world of their own to prey upon the economic activities of others, rather like the Morlocks in H. G. Wells's *Time Machine*, who lived in the bowels of the earth and emerged intermittently to eat those who lived on the surface. Businessmen, in this view, are forced to pay protection money to buy off the threats from the mobsters. But is that really so? An intriguing account of the Sicilian Mafia by Diego Gambetta[17] suggests that it may not be all there is to it.

The Mafia in Sicily, he argues, grew up in response to a particular set of circumstances. The state was weak, nonexistent, or, on occasion, punitive. That meant there was no legitimate body that could enforce contracts, agreements, and property rights. Nor could markets work properly without proper laws and property rights. A businessman could not be sure, if he bought a plot of land, for example, or a business, that the seller actually owned it. So businessmen could not trust either the markets or each other. Such a lack of trust was critical to the development of the Mafia, Gambetta contends.

Trust is an essential lubricant of free markets. Without it, they cannot work properly. Gambetta argues that, where there is no trust, protection becomes a substitute for it, albeit a poor and costly one. He recounts the core of this idea in the words of a cattle breeder in

Palermo: "When the butcher comes to me to buy an animal, he knows that I want to cheat him. But I know he wants to cheat me. Thus we both need, say, Peppe [a third party] to make us agree. And we both pay Peppe a percentage of the deal."[18] "Peppe" is the Mafioso taking his cut.

That is fundamentally different from straight extortion, in which businessmen pay simply to avoid being beaten up, robbed, or killed. In the case Gambetta describes, the cattle dealer paid willingly. During his interrogation, Tommaso Buscetta, a Mafioso turned state's evidence, argued that this is common. He told the magistrates that

> . . . around the Mafia families and the men of honor there is an incredible number of people who, even though they are not themselves Mafiosi, cooperate, sometimes even unconsciously, with the Mafia. . . . With regard to the nature of these relationships, I must stress that they cannot be explained as the result of coercion. . . . It is like courting a woman: if a relationship gets started, it is because the woman has cooperated in being chosen; she has agreed to be courted.[19]

This was what gave the Mafia its staying power in Italy. It has become an economic enforcement agency similar to the state and is sometimes regarded, in the absence of anything else, as legitimate. It has turned from a hunter—who kills his prey and moves on—into a rancher, someone who lives off his herd but also "protects" it.[20]

Does this apply to Russia?

The Mafia began to flourish in Sicily when feudalism collapsed there. In feudal societies, only a few people had private property. The same few also held a monopoly over the use of force. When feudalism came to an end, there was a sudden dramatic increase in the number of property owners. Peasants acquired their own land, but they did not inherit the former owners' monopoly over force, even though the aristocracy's military might declined. And the new postfeudal state did not acquire the monopoly of force either.

The parallels with post-Soviet Russia are obvious. In the Soviet Union, there were no owners of private property. Russia's privatization program gave the entire population a right to buy the former state-owned assets and transferred ownership to anyone willing to invest. By 1995 Russia suddenly had 40 million new property owners. At the same time, the monopolists over the use of force—the Communist party, the KGB, the police, and the army—all collapsed.

Gambetta concludes that in both Russia and Sicily the "consequence is a phenomenal increase in the fear of losing property and of being cheated and, correspondingly, in the demand for trust: trust in other people and trust in whoever has the power to enforce property rights."[21]

Russian gangsters also claimed to be people providing a service, rather than acting simply as predators. Two young girls who washed car windshields outside the Kropotkinskaya subway station in Moscow described how:

> The lights there change slowly and you can wash more cars. Only we have to pay protection money to bigger boys. One is called Dude. . . . He makes sure adults don't take our money away and chases off competition. Further down the road, two boys work at the crossing next to the embankment. They pay the traffic police there 25 rubles for each 100 they earn. They do not bother us because Dude makes a deal with them.[22]

In other words, Dude is not simply extorting money from the girls, that is, providing protection from his own threats. He provides some security from thieves, from competition, and from corrupt traffic policemen.

In Sicily no real government appeared after feudalism collapsed to meet the sudden surge in demand for protection of property rights from the millions of new owners. The Mafia appeared in a vacuum. In Russia, though there was a government, the situation was in some ways even worse: The government added to the prevailing sense of mistrust. It was slow in moving to secure property rights in law. A new civil code, with a new company law, did not appear until January 1995. Licensing and other government controls were a breeding ground for corruption. Pyotr Aven, Yeltsin's first foreign trade minister, who subsequently became the boss of Alpha Bank, explained what this could mean: "One fine day, your insignificant bank is authorized to conduct operations with budgetary funds, for instance. Or quotas for the export of oil, timber, and gas are generously allotted to your company, which is in no way connected with production. In other words, you are appointed a millionaire."[23]

And just as in Sicily the armed retainers of the aristocrats' private armies found roles as "men of honour," so in Russia decommissioned soldiers, policemen, and KGB agents, their ties with the old regime broken by economic reform and the new politics, started queuing up to sell their skills. Most of the ubiquitous bodyguards of Russia's new rich were former soldiers or security service employees. One of Russia's richest men, Vladimir Gusinsky, employed his own private security force of more than a thousand people. One of the people who worked for him (as an adviser, not in security) was Filipp Bobkov, a former deputy chairman of the KGB, who had been the boss of its notorious Fifth Directorate, the part that had conducted Brezhnev's campaigns against dissidents.

That is not to say that the mafia is providing a service that is really beneficial to the public, somewhat like insurance companies, but only that people could find it in their individual interests to cooperate with the mafia. Nor is it to say that this is the mafia's only activity; mafiosi also engage in extortion, drug smuggling, forgery, illicit arms trading and plenty of other crimes. But those operations are not what make the mafia the force that it is. It is because people cooperate willingly with the mafia, and because it is performing a necessary economic function that would otherwise be absent, that the mafia has become so deeply entrenched in both Sicily and Russia. The mafia makes its money from distrust as well as from crime.

Can the mafia be defeated?

The Sicilian example shows that organized crime becomes established quickly if law enforcement is weak in a country where there is a sudden change in property rights and a dramatic shift in who the owners are. That applies in Russia.

But there are differences, of which the most significant is simply time. The Russian mafia is newer. The Sicilian Mafia is more closely woven into the island's life. Russian criminals have established connections with politicians, civil servants, and businessmen, which will make them hard to dislodge. But those connections are, for the most part, recent. Relatively few of them go back to the old Soviet criminal system. In contrast, connections between criminals and the established order in Sicily have grown up over decades, even centuries.

The other difference is that the biggest opportunities for crime in Russia have arisen because of government failure in the early stage of economic reform: the failure to protect private property rights and the continued existence of economic regulation in the form of licenses and quotas to trade particular products. This implies that the consolidation of property rights, further deregulation to cut corruption, and the establishment of a proper law enforcement system could do much to undermine the Russian mafia. If businessmen can trust the markets, can trust contracts to be enforceable, can trust prices to be free, not distorted, then demand for the mafia's "services" will fall away.

The previous chapters have looked at what more needs to be done to advance economic reform and to improve the operation of markets. Here, we conclude with the last change that is required to defeat the mafia: reform of the legal and judicial systems.

In 1990–93, as the crime rate soared, the police were hopelessly ill equipped to take on rich gangsters with expensive cars and weaponry. In mid-1993 policemen were receiving 30,000 rubles a month in pay, then equivalent to $30, less than most factory workers and less than a small kiosk usually paid in protection money. Not surprisingly, they became fabulously corrupt. The chief of Moscow's police force said in 1994 that 95 percent of his men were on the take, a view seconded by Yuri Nikishin, a police chief in the capital, who claimed: "Every criminal has high connections in the police and officialdom. I would guess that about 90 percent of the militiamen who operate out of local police stations in this city are on the take. It gets a little better as you go up the line: maybe about 15 percent of the middle-ranking police bureaucracy are on the take."[24] Yevgeny Novikov, the head of the economic crime directorate at the Interior Ministry, says that the younger officers are the worst; they see the chance to take bribes as the main reason for joining the police. There were virtually no background checks on new recruits, so criminal gangs could simply send members to become policemen. In 1992 more than two thousand policemen were charged with criminal offenses, which (policemen and prosecutors being what they are worldwide) was at most a small fraction of the total number actually committed by them. Filippov, the president's adviser, believes that the only way to clean out the police is to start from scratch, as the Americans did in Japan in 1945. He suggested sacking all serving police officers and hiring army veterans, of whom there are hundreds of thousands looking for work.

While there was no wholesale replacement of the police by former soldiers, by 1995 there were signs of improvement in the conditions of policemen. The 1994 budget sharply increased spending on law enforcement, doubling policemen's wages. Spending on equipment rose too, enabling the police to give chase in cars as fast as the criminals' getaway cars (and not, as occasionally happened before, by bus). Those measures may have been behind the modest improvement in the crime figures: the slowdown in the growth of serious crimes in 1994 and 1995 and an increase in the proportion of reported crimes solved, from 47 percent in 1992 to 60 percent in 1994.

Progress has been slower with reform of the courts, where the problem is, if anything, worse. Under communist rule, judges were under the thumb of the local party secretary, whom they consulted before handing down sentence. They started to become more independent. In 1994 they released 13,000 of the 65,000 people who claimed that they were being held in prison illegally. The ending of communist control, however, did not really leave the courts independent, even though parliament passed laws mandating punishments for anyone interfering with judicial impartiality. Instead, it left judges, who are ill paid in Russia, vulnerable to threats and bribery, enabling mobsters to use the law as a weapon.

The constitution says that judges are supposed to be appointed by the president. In reality, in 1995 most were still being appointed by regional governors. Judges were often provided with cheap housing, telephones, and even holidays by local governments to compensate for their low salaries.

While judges, by Western standards, were too weak, public prosecutors were too strong. In most Western countries, the prosecutor conducts the case against a defendant, but the judge is responsible for the conduct of the trial itself. In Russia, it was for the prosecutor, not the judge, to ensure that the trial was "fair." The constitution says that only judges may issues warrants for arrest. In practice, in 1995 prosecutors were still having people arrested without asking anyone's permission. Prosecutors' offices often maintained "general surveillance" departments with spies in factories, schools, and businesses.

In general, Russia in 1991–95 had too few lawyers, since the law had been a relatively lowly profession in the Soviet Union. In 1995 there were only 28,000 public prosecutors and 20,000 independent lawyers for a population of 148 million. America then had 800,000 lawyers in all, seventeen times as many lawyers for fewer than twice as many people. Russia's 50,000 lawyers were not enough to make the courts work properly.

The collapse of the party left law enforcement weak, so entrepreneurs turned to racketeers rather than courts to enforce business agreements or to settle a dispute. Filippov's report concluded: "An entire generation is growing up . . . who in such circumstances will not turn to official authorities but to unofficial ones. These people are more likely to hire a murderer to punish a guilty or even an unpleasant partner than to go to court or arbitration."

Recognizing that the courts were overwhelmed, Russian politicians advocated impatient and draconian measures against crime. In 1993 Yeltsin ordered all "unregistered aliens" to be thrown out of Moscow, a move aimed at gangsters from Chechnya and other parts of the Caucasus. In the spring of 1994 he issued a decree on fighting organized crime that violated an article in the constitution requiring suspects to be charged within forty-eight hours of arrest or released. The head of the counterintelligence service dismissed criticism of his agency's campaign against organized crime with the remark: "As regards talk that human rights may be violated to some degree—well, probably yes, but only so that the rights of 99 percent of the citizens are defended."

Measures like that militated against respect for human rights, though it must be admitted that other countries, faced with a challenge from organized crime, have also resorted to extraordinary measures. Italy, for instance, promulgated effective anti-Mafia laws that granted pardons to criminals who turned state's evidence.

In the long run, however, almost everyone recognizes that the only solution is to establish a stable, impartial body of law, presided over by independent courts. This is proceeding gradually. In 1994 the so-called arbitrage courts, which settle commercial disputes, were made into real courts, that is, branches of the judiciary. Before that they were not courts at all, but branches of the administration, and the judges who presided over them were civil servants. Businessmen are now turning more frequently to those courts to settle disputes.

Then, in early 1995, Russia took two important steps toward a "law-governed state." On February 13 a new Constitutional Court resumed work, more than a year after the old court had been abolished after splitting over the political struggle between the president and parliament in 1992–93. Its chairman had controversially thrown in his lot with the old parliament. The court's new chairman, Vladimir Tumanov, for many years had been a Soviet professor in "bourgeois [Western] law." Like America's Supreme Court, Russia's Constitutional Court has as its main task to determine whether or not laws and government actions conform to the new constitution.

The other step had been taken a month earlier, when a new civil code came into effect. It was a 650-article body of laws that laid down, almost from scratch, the laws that regulate the economic relationships essential to the proper workings of a market economy—laws on contract, ownership, and property, intellectual property, inheritance, and the application of foreign law. It followed the overhauling of individual items of legislation in the previous three years, which established new laws on, for example, ownership and property and the decision, made in July 1992, to incorporate into Russian law a late-perestroika-vintage body of legislation, called the fundamental principle of civil legislation, which updates the old civil code by a quarter of a century.

Russia now has what might be called first generation laws on companies, pledges, joint stock societies, leases, ownership, patents, and foreign investments. If they can be implemented properly, they will create the trust that will enable businessmen to dispense with the "services" of the mafia. That is something that can be tested only over time and will depend on the improvement in the quality of the judiciary.

The main grounds for thinking it can succeed is that there is considerable, and often unrecognized, pressure to succeed. Businessmen of all types are coming to see the virtues of legitimacy for reasons of self-interest. "Every mafioso wants to hand his business to his son," says Igor Smolkin, the director of one of Russia's largest fund management firms, Alfa Capital. "The mafia used to be strong because there was no private property, which meant that access to goods was decided by who you knew or who you could scare. Now there is private property and the mafia will become one of the strongest defenders of property rights."[25] This is what happened in parts of America, where mobsters, having built up business empires (like gambling in Las Vegas, created by Bugsy Siegel), went straight and sought the protection of the law against younger more ruthless mobster rivals.

It seems to be happening in Russia too. In December 1994 a group of top Russian businessmen, led by Vladimir Gusinsky, the chairman of MOST Bank, one of the largest in the country, held a one-day Congress of Russian Entrepreneurs in the Kremlin. All of them argued that, as one American observer put it, no matter what the rest of the country or the world might think, the new wave of Russian entrepreneurs craves a legal order; chaos is bad for the country and bad for business.[26]

That new wave, Gusinsky claimed, showed the transition of Russian business from criminality to legitimacy. "The first wave," he explains, "began with people who were 100% creations of the system. Many of them tried to make some money and then hide it. . . . I would say that about 80% of that first wave that made some money went abroad—the nouveau-riche money wave I call it. They left because they did not trust the state." This was the wave of those who made their money in the last gasp of communism, under a regime that regarded private property askance, at best, and as a crime at worst. They are the forty- and fifty-year-olds, who are geriatric by modern Russian business standards.

"The second wave was the toughest and most criminalized. They were people who came to the market on a wave of aggression. We have to reap the fruits of their criminal activities." They are the profiteers of the post-communist chaos and of corruption. They are the thirty-year-olds.

The third wave, Gusinsky said, "is different. It is perfectly legal. These are young people who came to the fore in the last two years. They are fearless and are not involved in criminality. They are ordinary people, fully educated, full of energy."[27] They include many of Russia's richest men, who find that law and order are in their interest.

As one businessman, Lev Weinberg, commented: "I know of no case in history when millionaires stole from thieves."

Russia, then, has a broad base of legal principle, many good laws, and a substantial interest in making them work. "We are on the way to a state ruled by law," says the procurator of St. Petersburg, "but we are not there yet." What is still needed is that Russians should come to believe that the law is a friend, or at least neutral—something that will depend partly on further judicial reform, partly on the impartial operation of the laws already in place, and partly on the creation of a reasonably stable constitutional system. The last condition is a political question, a matter of creating a legitimate political order. It is the subject of the next two chapters.

Chapter 9

Will political deadlock recur?

*The war of laws · The constitution: 1977–93 · The players in the crisis ·
Attempts at compromise · Confrontations: January 1992–October 1993 ·
Showdown: October 1993 · Aftermath: December 1993 · Evaluation*

Within two years of the failed communist putsch of August 1991, tanks were on the streets of Moscow, the Russian parliament had been shelled into a smoldering ruin, and hundreds of people had been killed in the fighting. This chapter looks at why that violence broke out and weighs the chances of a constitutional crisis recurring.

To many people, both in the West and in Russia, the fighting demonstrated that political violence is endemic in Russia. They argued that Yeltsin's government was highly unstable and could hold onto power only by force. Since it seemed doubtful that violence had ushered in stable government, it followed that Russia would either slide toward a new dictatorship or experience another bout of violent conflict between government and opposition. This chapter questions those arguments, beginning with the assertion that violence is endemic in Russia.

The whole period from Russia's "declaration of sovereignty" in June 1990, through the failure of the communist coup against Mikhail Gorbachev, to the public approval of a new constitution in December 1993 was comparable in some ways to the period of American history

173

from the Declaration of Independence, through the Revolutionary War, to the political struggle over the Constitution in 1787–89. Those were the birth pangs of a nation, combining the fight for independence with the struggle for a new political order.

The revolutionary nature of the change in Russia was disguised somewhat because the president himself, and many of his ministers and officials, had held high rank under the old regime. Nevertheless, by most standards Russia was going through a real revolution. It confronted three immense tasks: to create a market economy, to create a democracy, and to become, for the first time, a nation-state rather than an empire. It tried to tackle them simultaneously. The system of government was transformed from an autocratic state controlled by a powerful monopoly party to an elected government with the forms of democratic rule. This government instituted drastic reforms to the country's economy and undertook one of the most radical distributions of property the world had ever seen. Russia also lost its former empire, which dramatically changed the shape of the country. Half the population of the former Soviet Union split off into other independent states.

Considering the immensity of the change, Russia's transfer of power was peaceful. Three people were killed during the coup of August 1991. About two hundred lost their lives in the fighting in Moscow in October 1993, and thousands were killed later in Chechnya, a corner of the Russian Federation that took advantage of the collapse of communist rule to declare independence. By comparison, the Russian Revolution of 1917 was followed by a bloody three-year civil war. The French and Chinese revolutions were even more violent. The struggle for independence or for a new political order has rarely been as bloodless as it was in Russia.

That said, it would be wrong to dismiss the violence as historically trivial. In practice, it did much to determine the politics of post-communist Russia. So it is important to ask, Why did it happen in the first place? And what does it say about the new Russia?

The answer begins with the condition of the Russian government in August 1991. The state that emerged into independence from the Soviet ruins was desperately, almost terminally, weak. The most immediate threat was that Russia would run short of bread, as it had in 1917 and again at the end of the 1920s, when Stalin introduced central planning. In the week after the putsch, grain purchases by the Ministry of Procurement, the agency for supplying the bakeries, fell to about a quarter of what they had been before the attempted coup; the government then had only five months' worth of grain reserves left in stock. The failure of the coup had almost destroyed the authority of the Communist party and the institutions of the Soviet state. The army and the KGB were then at their weakest. Weapons were being stolen from barracks with impunity, and the top brass, chastened by the involvement of the defense minister and the KGB chief in the failed coup, refused to involve themselves in internal politics. Yeltsin was racing against time to prevent both the breakup of the government and—as would have followed—the breakup of the country.

That is little understood in the West for two reasons. First, people have been brought up for more than fifty years to think of Russia as a stable superpower, with a huge army and a totalitarian government. In fact, the possibility that Russia would go from superpowerdom to misery was there almost from the start. In 1947 George Kennan, later America's ambassador to Moscow, argued: "If . . . anything were ever done to disrupt the unity and efficacy of the [Communist] Party as a political instrument, Soviet Russia might be changed overnight from one of the strongest to one of the weakest and most pitiable of national societies."[1] That is exactly what happened in 1991.

The communists had identified the state with the party. The Communist party, said the Soviet constitution, was "the leading and guiding force of Soviet society." So long as the party was strong, so was the state. When it collapsed, the state collapsed too.

In some ways, Russia was even worse off than other former Soviet republics, for it did not even have shadow local communist institutions to fall back upon. In an effort to stamp out Russian nationalism, the Bolsheviks denied Russia attributes of statehood that they allowed for the others. All other republics had their own Communist parties, KGBs, academies of science, and other identifying features of nationhood. However fraudulent those institutions were in reality (and they had limited freedom of action), it was still significant that Russia alone had none. Its own Communist party was not set up until 1990. There was no Russian Academy of Sciences, no ministry of internal affairs, no police force, no trade union, and no Russian television station. The great French historian of the Soviet Union, Hélène Carrère d'Encausse, characterized the Soviet suppression of Russia as follows: "Soviet libraries were filled with books about World War II, such as *The Contribution of the Karakalpaks to the Second World War* and *The Uzbeks in the Second World War*. No people, however small, lacked national institutes that extolled their glory and exploits, except the Russians. . . . The Russian people as such did not exist."[2]

So when Russia became an independent state, Yeltsin had no choice but to take over the discredited Soviet institutions. The Speaker of the Russian Parliament, Ruslan Khasbulatov, complained, "Other union republics had much greater independence than the Russian Federation. The lack of rights and the grievous condition of Russia itself were results of the deliberate policy of the central administration, which 'dissolved' the republic in All-Union [i.e., Soviet] party, economic, and administrative structures."[3]

The second reason why the weakness of the state was not understood in the West was that people were accustomed to thinking of Russian politics as incomprehensible anyway. "Like bulldogs fighting under a carpet, every so often the carpet is lifted to see who is winning"—Churchill's apt description of the Kremlin expressed the general view of Russian politics. No one quite knew who was up or down. But, though you did not know who was in charge, it was certain that someone was.

So when, in 1991–93, no one could tell who was in charge, outsiders still assumed that someone was, a belief encouraged by Russian politicians themselves, who, like nature, abhor a vacuum. Guessing where power lay, or claiming it, became a national pastime. In July 1992 Arkady Volsky, a lobbyist for Soviet industrial bureaucrats, boasted: "Power belongs to those who have property and money. At present it is not the government but industrial managers who have both." Actually, at that exact moment Volsky was unable to stop the government's plans to privatize Russian industry, which he disliked; other managers were disputing his claim to be the industrialists' leader; and in the general election of 1993 Volsky's party failed to win a single seat.

In short, when Yeltsin became president of an independent Russia, he faced a vacuum of power, amid competing claims to leadership from other (similarly powerless) groups, and had no ready-made administration to work with. Ironically, that may have encouraged him to implement radical reform.[4] His government simply lacked the authority it would have taken to solve the bread shortage by, for example, introducing rationing or cracking down on the grain-producing regions.[5]

But it also meant that, at the outset, the new Russian government lacked two essential attributes of democracy: effectiveness and legitimacy. Legitimacy requires persuading people that the existing political institutions are the best for the country, not only those who support the government anyway, but especially those who do not. Yeltsin did not have this. Even though he himself had won a personal mandate by winning an election in 1991, his opponents increasingly often denied his right to govern. As early as January 1992 they began referring to him and his ministers as "traitors to Russia," "fifth columnists," and "agents of America." That went far beyond exaggeration for political effect.

Even more worrisome was the question mark over his government's effectiveness—that is, its ability to meet the basic expectations of most citizens. As would be proved again and again in the months after economic reform began, the government's power to conduct policy was limited to abolishing communist restrictions. Its decision to begin by abolishing communist price controls was an example. Unfortunately for the government, that in turn reduced living standards by more than almost anyone had expected and made the government even more unpopular. It soon became clear that the police, the courts, and other law enforcement agencies were alike unable to stop the crime wave. Indeed, corrupt officials were contributing to it. Thus the state failed to perform a basic function of government, providing law and order.

In late 1991, Russia exemplified Tocqueville's graphic description of a general loss of legitimacy—"epochs sometimes occur in the life of a nation when the old customs of a people are changed, public morality is destroyed, religious belief shaken, and the spell of tradition broken. . . . The citizens then have neither the instinctive patriotism of a monarchy nor the reflective patriotism of a republic; . . . they have stopped between the two in the midst of confusion and distress."[6] Russia after the communists' failed coup was in just this state, suspended between democracy and dictatorship, with belief in communism destroyed and public confidence confused.

The history of the next two years was a struggle for power, but not in the sense of an attempt to wrest power from someone who already had it. It was a competition to establish power from scratch, to be first to rush into the political vacuum. To win power, you first had to establish a regime.

It was disguised as a fight over economic reform and the powers of president and parliament. Those were real problems, of course, but the arguments over them in 1991–94 were phony. The economic dispute was not between two equally plausible economic policies. Part of the government had a clear understanding of what needed to be done and a program to do it. Parliament had no alternative but to postpone change as long as possible. The real battle was in effect over whether the economy could be reformed at all. Similarly in the political sphere, the dispute between parliament and government was not just a battle over who should be in charge and who should run the program. It was a battle over whether anyone could stay in charge long enough to make a difference. And, to make matters more urgent, it was not really a two-way battle between president and parliament. It was a three-way battle involving also the regions of Russia, who added their agenda to the mix, raising doubts not only about relations between the central and local governments but about whether Russia could stay together as one state.

The war of laws

The biggest political problem caused by the vacuum of power was that no one took any notice of laws or decrees. In the West it is taken for granted that once a law has been passed, it will be implemented, or should be. Not so in Russia. "I don't see decrees from Moscow" one official said in Tatarstan, a republic 500 miles east of the capital. "Perhaps they're sent and registered in the office somewhere. We've really forgotten about this kind of thing. We only carry out the decrees of our president" [i.e. Tatarstan's]. The phenomenon was not confined to the rebellious republics, such as Tatarstan, anxious to thumb their noses at the central government in the Kremlin. In one remarkable episode in

August 1994, when some of the government's opponents were trying to organize a referendum that the government opposed, a civil servant at the Ministry of Justice (no less) was quoted as advising Russians to forget about the law on referendums for the moment: The government did not want to hear about it just then.[7] Ironically, that was the very law that Boris Yeltsin had used to introduce the office of the presidency in Russia in 1990. When Viktor Chernomyrdin became prime minister at the end of 1992, one of his first actions was to issue instructions to ministers requiring them actually to carry out government orders. It did no good. In 1994 he was complaining that of the 296 instructions he had issued to his own ministers, only 156 had been implemented.

The most important reason for the legal chaos was that too many people were issuing orders in the first place. Russia has not only laws issued by parliament, but also decrees, directives, and instructions, which often had the force of law. Under the old constitution, the list of those allowed to issue decrees and directives included the president and vice president; the prime minister and any first deputy prime minister; plus the top four parliamentary officials.[8] That was in addition to the laws passed by central and local parliaments.

That cast produced a bewildering welter of decisions. In 1992 the president issued 1,727 decrees and 811 directives. The vice president issued seven directives. On the parliamentary side, Russia got 59 decrees from the Congress of People's Deputies plus two laws; 290 decrees of the Supreme Soviet plus 112 laws (which required 85 supporting decrees); 70 decrees from the Council of Nationalities and 41 from the Council of the Republic; 66 directives from the chairman of the Supreme Soviet and 20 by his two deputy chairmen—a grand total of 3,290 legal decisions from the center. On top of that, there were an estimated total of 40,000 laws, directives, and regulations issuing from local authorities every week.[9] Russia had a lot to do in 1992, but issuing 166 laws per working day was ridiculous.

Not surprisingly, many of them were badly drafted. In July 1993 Sergei Filatov, the head of the presidential administration (Yeltsin's chief of staff), admitted that decrees were not being prepared properly.[10] In June 1994 Yeltsin, sacking the government's chief civil servant, complained that the government had passed "so many bad documents that it will take half a year to put them right."[11]

It was not just the sheer number of muddled laws and decrees that was problematic. What was even worse was that many of the decrees were not issued on the basis of existing law; they were just free-standing decisions. There was no hierarchy of legal order. And because of this, as we shall see, disputes about the validity of laws and decrees proliferated.

Even if all the decrees and laws had been mutually consistent and harmonious, those responsible for implementing the law would have been stretched. But the government itself was not even capable of acting in concert. In a speech to his cabinet, Chernomyrdin said that in the first six months of 1993, 167 ministerial directives had contradicted presidential or other government instructions.[12] In November 1994, the president sacked the prime minister's chief aide with the complaint that "of 300 presidential instructions to the government, only 10% were carried out."[13]

As for relations between government and parliament, they were disastrous. To take examples from foreign policy: In 1993 parliament tore up Russia's international commitments under the treaties that followed the collapse of the Soviet Union and claimed the Ukrainian port of Sebastopol as Russian territory. The president was forced to dissociate himself and his government from the actions of Russia's own parliament. In a move unprecedented in international relations, the Russian government supported a resolution of the United Nations Security Council condemning the parliament's vote.

Lastly, there was a problem of straightforward incompetence. Government officials were trying to do everything at once, working sixteen hours a day, seven days a week. No one, it seemed, thought they were doing their job properly unless reduced to a state of permanent exhaustion. Matters got so bad that at one point Yeltsin (former professional volleyball coach) even ordered his ministers to play soccer or tennis regularly to keep fit.

The constitution: 1977–93

In democracies, constitutions settle disputes about competence. Tested by time and practice, they are templates against which to measure basic questions of government: Who rules? What powers should they have? In Russia, the constitution could not do that.

The constitution in force in Russia when it became an independent state dated back to 1978. On paper, it made Russia a state in which parliament was supreme, like Britain, rather than one in which parliament and president were balanced. The Soviet constitution was based on the Leninist precept "All power to the Soviets." "Soviet" means "council" in Russian; Soviets were the elected councils that existed in every town and region. At the apex of the hierarchy sat the Supreme Soviet, the main legislative body, which was elected from the ranks of the Congress of People's Deputies, which met only a few times a year and was the only body that could change the constitution. On top of that arrangement, Boris Yeltsin established the office of the presidency and won an election for it in 1991. On paper, both president and government were subordinate to parliament.

In contrast to the American president, Russia's was not in charge of the day-to-day management of government. The prime minister was. The president nominated the prime minister; parliament had to approve his choice. He was able to veto a law of parliament, but his veto could be overruled by a simple majority (in America, it needs a two-thirds majority to override a presidential veto). He could not legally dissolve the Supreme Soviet. This restraint was to have important implications later. In short, parliament was the sovereign body.

Nothing problematic about that, you might think. Actually, there was a problem. All democracies, whatever their system, need to strike a balance between government and parliament. The government is supposed to make the system effective and efficient; parliament keeps it representative and maintains popular consent. You need both. If government dominates parliament, there is a danger of authoritarianism; if parliament dominates government, the danger is that nothing gets done. Even in Britain, the model of the parliamentary system, the parliament does not dominate the government. The two are intertwined.

That was not the case in Russia. There, on paper, parliament really did have the upper hand. Recognizing this as a potential problem, Russian politicians lighted on a tactic to avoid stalemate. In November 1991 parliament granted emergency powers for one year to the president to carry out economic reform. That enabled him to push through privatization, change trade regulations, and take many other decisions on his own. After one year, however, parliament could take away his authority.

Presidential decrees were valid only as long as there was no law on a similar subject. When a relevant law was passed, it superseded the decree. That undermined the force of all decrees on subjects parliament was discussing. A local government official who disliked a particular presidential decree could postpone implementing it on the grounds that a parliamentary law was imminent—which often happened. In October 1993 an official in Novosibirsk, for instance, justified his city's refusal to push ahead with privatization by arguing that "not all is clear on this matter in Moscow." Even when parliament was not discussing a law, anyone faced with a decree he did not like could simply postpone enforcing it and hope that a law would come along sooner or later to contradict the decree. It usually did. In short, local officials could pick and choose which decisions from Moscow they wanted to implement and which to ignore. Those sympathetic to the government implemented decrees and ignored laws; those who supported parliament ignored decrees. The "war of laws" (as it was called) provided an opportunity to increase local power at the expense of both parliament and government by playing each off against the other.

As if that were not bad enough, the constitution's failure to separate the powers of executive and legislature caused endless arguments between them over who controlled what. Until 1994, for example, the central bank reported to parliament for the monetary policy it was conducting. Since parliament and government were feuding, that made it possible for the central bank to conduct one kind of economic policy while the government conducted a different (and tougher) one. That, too, proved a recipe for economic disaster in 1991–93.

With so much to fight about, it was not surprising that politicians were unable to resolve conflicts smoothly. But their failure contributed further to the democratic failures at the outset of reform. In "Stability, Change, and the Democratic Creed," Professor Robert Dahl of Yale University argues that for democracies to work, it is essential that politicians be strongly committed to the democratic process. They must be more consistent about their views, more ideological, and more completely in agreement about the rules of the political game than ordinary voters are. Citizens may be the ballast of democracy, but politicians provide the sense of direction.[14]

Over time, Dahl argues, the two groups interact. Politicians understand what voters want. Voters accept what is possible. Everyone comes to accept a system of established rights and responsibilities. That is what happens in a normal democracy. But it was not happening in Russia. The professional politicians were too divided and, often, not committed to democracy.

The players in the crisis

In the summer of 1993, at the height of the battle between president and parliament, the balance of political forces was as follows:

First, the parliament. Constitutionally, it was the center of power. Its laws took precedence over everyone else's. Its popular legitimacy, however, was not great. So quick had been the pace of political change in 1990–93 that mandates were soon lost: Whoever had been elected most recently had the best claim to legitimacy. The Russian parliament's election had taken place in early 1990—another era compared with Boris Yeltsin, whose authority had been regularly renewed since he first became Russia's leader on his election as Speaker of the Russian parliament in June of that year. In July 1991 he was directly elected president; in August 1991 his authority was redoubled by the failure of the attempted putsch; in April 1993 he won a vote of confidence in a nationwide referendum on his performance as president and on his policies. With Yeltsin, voters knew roughly where they were: He stood for reform. Parliament, in contrast, was all over the place. Before 1990 it had been the epitome of stagnation, with deputies showing up twice a year obediently to rubber-stamp Communist party decisions by hundreds of votes to nil. Then, in the heady days of August 1991, it became the symbol of democratic resistance to the dying regime. In 1992–93 it changed again, into a battlefield in which old guard politicians uncertain of their future gradually wrested control of the lawmaking process from reformers who supported the president. Those fluctuations raised popular doubts about what, if anything, parliament stood for.

Second, the government. It was in flux too. Ministers came and went. Between the start of economic reform in January 1992 and the end of 1994, Russia had three prime ministers, four economy ministers, five finance ministers, and six reshuffles. Departments also came and went. In September 1992 Russia had 137 ministries and departments, many of them tiny. This was over fifty more than the Soviet Union had had. Even the Soviet figure of eighty-five had been extraordinarily high. America has fifteen "cabinet agencies" (such as, for example, the Department of Defense). Moreover, the government was doubly divided, first between reformers and apparatchiks and second functionally. The majority of ministries concerned themselves mostly with the economy and reported to the prime minister. But the ministers of defense, interior, and security and the foreign minister (a quartet collectively called "the power ministries" in Russia) went straight to the president on issues of policy.

Third, there was a body called the security council. Its responsibilities embraced "Russia's vital interests," which could mean anything. The council, on occasion, could overrule the government. It was on the advice of the council, not the Foreign Ministry, that the president controversially canceled a trip to Japan in 1992 because of the two countries' territorial dispute over the Kurile Islands (which Japan calls the Northern Territories).

Fourth came the president's retinue in the Kremlin, influential in its own right, which controlled access to the president, like courtiers to a medieval monarch. This organization was proliferating. By 1995 it would have as many civil servants working for it as the government did, having doubled in size since 1991.

Fifth came the central bank, nominally responsible to parliament and supposed to coordinate its policies with the government (there was a committee for this). In practice, the central bank was often conducting a monetary policy flatly opposed to the broader economic policies of the government.

Sixth, the army was not completely under the president's control. In the summer of 1992 the army refused to implement his promise to withdraw troops from the Baltic states. In Moldova, the commander of the Russian 14th army stationed there (Aleksandr Lebed) was in effect running his own foreign policy and using the position of Russian-speakers in Moldova as a weapon with which to assail the president's foreign policies.

Seventh, the vice president, Aleksandr Rutskoi, displayed the extraordinary phenomenon of open opposition to the president. He publicly insulted government ministers (calling Yegor Gaidar and other young reformers "boys in pink shorts") and finally called for a military insurrection against the president.

Last, and not least, was the president himself, who mediated among those various groups more like a feudal monarch than the head of a modern state.

Many countries display tensions between the parliament and president. Not all exercise full control over their armies. But few had quite so many competing centers of power as Russia had in 1991–94. Fewer still combine multiple centers of decision-making with an almost complete lack of separation of powers, as Russia did then. By itself, Russia's plethora of decision-making centers would have raised a formidable obstacle to political stability. So would its constitutional vacuum. Together they reinforced each other to make Russia ungovernable.

Attempts at compromise

So it was hardly surprising that compromise could not be reached among the competing forces. Some politicians were fighting old battles—to defend communism or to re-create the Russian empire. Others were fighting new ones—against organized crime or to create a market economy. With so many fundamental issues at stake, it was impossible to resolve them all at once. Russia's failure here points not to a fundamental failure of Russian democracy but to the circumstances the country faced at the start of reform.

The conflicts overwhelmed attempts at compromise. Khasbulatov, the parliamentary speaker and one of Yeltsin's toughest opponents, argued that parliament had granted the president emergency powers for one year to conduct economic reforms. In mid-1993 it voted to hold a general election in the middle of 1994, a year earlier than it needed to. Parliament felt it had offered olive branches to the president.

Similarly, the president had tried to work with parliament. In the spring of 1992 he responded to parliamentary criticism of the reforms by appointing four new ministers at parliament's request. In the summer of 1992 he did an abrupt U-turn in economic policy, increasing industrial and farm subsidies as parliament had demanded. Then he stood by for eighteen months without effective retaliation while parliament stripped him of one power after another, which it was allowed to do under the constitution. As Yegor Gaidar said in the spring of 1992: "Compromise is usually better than confrontation. At a time when Russian democracy is very young—an infant really—it is probably not the best idea to begin with drastic confrontation between the executive and legislative powers."[15]

Confrontations: January 1992–October 1993

So deep were the issues at stake, however, that confrontation proved unavoidable. The crisis played itself over a series of political battles between the spring of 1992 and the autumn of 1993. Ruslan Khasbulatov, the parliamentary Speaker, began the attack almost immediately. Ten days after the start of economic reform, he declared that the policy had failed and that it was time to begin again. In the summer of 1992, listening to complaints from industrial managers, parliament forced Gaidar to relax his economic policies and to take in three new ministers with close ties to industry. One of them was Viktor Chernomyrdin, who would soon succeed Gaidar as prime minister.

The end of 1992 may have been the last time compromise was possible. Certainly it was the last time it was tried. At the seventh Congress of People's Deputies, which took place December 1–14, president and parliament did make a deal: Parliament would shelve its constitutional amendments to reduce presidential power, and in exchange the president would throw Gaidar to the wolves and would choose Chernomyrdin to replace him.

Either it really was too late, or at that point the speaker made what proved, in retrospect, a decisive error. At the start of 1993 Khasbulatov and the parliamentary leadership tore up the compromise. Having refused to renew the president's emergency powers at the seventh Congress, they now said they would take away his ability to appoint the four "power ministries." Parliament had voted for that change at the seventh Congress in December, but shelved it under the compromise. Henceforth, parliament would confirm or reject the president's nominees. The eighth Congress marked the beginning of parliament's attacks on the president himself.

Until then, parliamentary critics of reform had concentrated their fire on the economic and foreign policies of his government, and especially on the ministers responsible for them, Yegor Gaidar and Andrei Kozyrev. Now, they had Mr. Yeltsin himself in their sights. Layer after layer of his authority was stripped away. He was soon to lose the right to issue decrees with the force of law and the right to appoint prefects in the provinces. To undermine his authority over the government, parliament allowed the government to submit proposals for legislation to it directly, not, as before, through the president.[16] Both the seventh and eighth Congresses refused Yeltsin's demand for a referendum on the issue of who rules Russia, president or parliament.

Even some of Yeltsin's closest advisers were unsure how he would react to parliament's assault at the eighth Congress when he went on television on the evening of March 20, a week after the Congress had ended. In the hope of breaking both the political deadlock and the parliament, he decided to appeal over the heads of his opponents and (not for the first time) took his case directly to the voters. He announced that a vote of confidence in his presidency would be held on April 25, adding that, until then, he would rule by decree—and parliament be damned. Six days later, at a hastily called ninth Congress, Yeltsin narrowly escaped impeachment.[17] Most of his remaining powers were stripped from him. That, arguably, was the critical period of his presidency, more dangerous even than the violent autumn to come, because in the spring of 1993 parliament retained some popular support, and the outcome was uncertain, which it was not as soon as the sides resorted to force and the army came out for the president. When the results of the referendum came in, they vindicated Yeltsin's faith in Russia's voters: 59 percent of those who voted said they had confidence in him, as against 39 percent who said they did not; surprisingly, considering the pain of reform, 53 percent said they approved of his economic policies; 67 percent called for early parliamentary elections.

On the face of it, the referendum settled nothing, as parliament ignored the results and refused to hold elections. In fact, though, it saved Yeltsin's presidency. There was no second impeachment vote. Yeltsin was able to summon an all-important Constitutional Assembly to draw up a new constitution. It convened in Moscow on June 5, with the wind in the president's sails. For a few critical months, the referendum ensured that parliament could not move against Yeltsin directly.

Instead, it moved against him indirectly. On July 24, with the president at a holiday retreat outside Moscow and the finance minister out of the country, parliament's ally, the chairman of the central bank, announced that he was withdrawing from circulation all banknotes printed before 1993. There was public uproar at the decision, because it originally restricted the number of old rubles that could be exchanged for new ones. The ruble was being used as ammunition in the political battle. In August parliament adopted a budget with a deficit twice as large as the one the government had planned. That threatened to drive the country into hyperinflation. At the same time, parliament began debating an "amendment" to the privatization program that would have wrecked the idea of having popular capitalism in Russia. The amendment would have allowed the existing managers to grab full control of their firms.

During the summer of 1993 the Speaker of parliament followed this up by purging his opponents from parliament's hierarchy. He also packed the presidium, which determined parliament's agenda and order of business, with his friends. It was a classic revolutionary maneuver: to win control of the antechambers of government by stealth and then to exclude your opponents. When parliament reconvened in September, those deputies who supported the president had no means of influencing parliamentary business.

There is some evidence that at this point Ruslan Khasbulatov was planning a "constitutional coup" against Yeltsin, which aimed to abolish the office of the presidency and to return Russia to the system of government that had existed (on paper) before 1991. That accusation was made against Khasbulatov not only by the president's supporters but by one of the Speaker's own deputies, Nikolai Ryabov, who said that Khasbulatov had ordered local councils to neutralize all the various presidential representatives throughout the country,[18] and by an-other senior parliamentary figure, Yevgeny Ambartsumov,[19] a frequent critic of Yeltsin, who nevertheless accused Khasbulatov of seeking to become a new dictator.[20]

Showdown: October 1993

Parliament's counterattack marked the beginning of the final, uninter-rupted, phase of the struggle: All pretense of compromise was dropped, and every attempt to work together ended. In July Vice Presi-dent Rutskoi, who had broken with the president, called upon troops in the Far East to support him in his political struggle against the pres-ident.[21] At that time Gaidar and Fedorov also accused Khasbulatov of seeking to destroy the apparatus of the Russian government by appeal-ing to all the parts of the country not to pay taxes.[22] In a speech to par-liament, Khasbulatov attempted to win over the army, police, and security forces to parliament's side by promising them unspecified fi-nancial benefits. The president's supporters attempted to halt parlia-mentary proceedings by staging walkouts; parliament responded by reducing the quorum required for business. It debated a bill that would have permitted criminal prosecution against ministers who failed to carry out parliamentary orders. The chairman of one of par-liament's two chambers proposed to transfer all economic decision-making from the government to parliament.

Under the assault, the government wavered. Chernomyrdin criti-cized privatization and shock therapy. Oleg Lobov, a supporter of the industrial lobby who had been appointed first deputy prime minister in the spring, proposed that further reform be junked. On September 22 parliament was due to resume its business with three items on its agenda: final approval of the planned hyperinflationary 1993 budget; the amendment of the privatization program; and a clutch of bills de-priving the president of his power to dismiss ministers, taking away his power to veto legislation, and making failure to carry out parlia-mentary laws a criminal offense. For Yeltsin, this was the last straw. On September 21 he disbanded parliament and called new elections.

To many, this was unforgivable. Many Westerners thought the dis-solution of parliament would set democracy back years, perhaps decades. Within Russia, Vitaly Tretyakov, editor of *Nezavisimaya Gazeta*, one of the most influential new newspapers to appear after the ending of censorship, asked: "If Yeltsin can dismiss one parliament, what is there to prevent another from being dismissed?"[23] Were those views justified? Had parliament won, it would almost certainly have ended reform, since parliament was opposed to it. But reform, essentially an economic policy, is not democracy, though it makes a big contribution to it. It would have reduced the president to a figurehead, but the president could not claim to embody Russian democracy. It would also have ended any notion that Russia has two branches of government, executive and legislative, with a real separation of powers. That too, though regrettable, might not necessarily have been antidemocratic.

The real justification for the president's actions was that Russia had become ungovernable. Compromise was not possible. One side had to win the confrontation. In those circumstances, elections were the only democratic way of deciding the outcome. France faced a similar choice in 1958 and resolved it the same way. Confronted with the threat of civil war over Algerian independence, parliament recalled Charles de Gaulle to supervise the drafting of a new constitution. The constitution he drew up, with its vastly increased presidential powers, was criticized by parliament, which accused him of trying to reinvent the monarchy. That set off of a bitter presidential–parliamentary dispute, eventually resolved by elections and a constitutional referendum. Yeltsin's own summary of the issue in Russia is not far from the mark: "Formally, the President was violating the constitution, going the route of antidemocratic measures and dispersing the parliament—all for the sake of establishing democracy and the rule of law in the country. The parliament was defending the constitution—in order to overthrow the lawfully elected President and establish total Soviet rule."

There is also evidence that the population supported the president against parliament. The referendum six months earlier showed it. So did opinion polls taken at the height of the confrontation. They were overwhelming: On the eve of the final crisis, 72 percent said they supported President Yeltsin, 9 percent the parliament.[24] The support of the population barely wavered. Immediately after the storming of parliament, 68 percent of those asked whom they supported said President Yeltsin; 6 percent said parliament. Asked whom they held responsible for the bloodshed, five people blamed Rutskoi and Khasbulatov for everyone who blamed Yeltsin.[25]

In his memoirs Yeltsin claimed that he had hoped to take parliament by surprise and force it to surrender meekly. If so, he failed. Khasbulatov and Rutskoi had got wind of the planned dissolution and called an emergency Congress, which announced Yeltsin's impeachment and the assumption of the presidency by Rutskoi. The parliamentary leaders, most of the parliamentary deputies, and many armed supporters occupied the building. A two-week standoff followed. Police surrounded parliament. The head of the Orthodox Church arranged talks; the electricity was cut off, then restored. The culmination came on the afternoon of October 3. Rutskoi appeared on the balcony of the parliament calling for an insurrection to overthrow the president. As the lights came back on, armed insurrectionists, believing that their opponents' resolve was cracking, gathered in the center of Moscow, sacked the mayor's office, and then attacked the main television station 5 miles from the Kremlin. After a stunned moment of indecision, Yeltsin ordered a military response: On the morning of October 4, tanks moved on the White House. Guns pounded the building's large tower, reducing it to blackened hulk, while the Speaker of parliament and the vice president took shelter inside. The resistance of the parliamentary leaders collapsed when they realized that the armed insurrection they had been expecting had not materialized. Five hours later, bedraggled and unshaven, the leaders of parliament gave themselves up. Yeltsin had promised to use force to defend democracy. He had fulfilled the first part of his promise.

Aftermath: December 1993

The second part was made good on December 11 and 12, two days of nationwide elections. But now the popular mood was changing. The "Liberal Democratic Party" of Vladimir Zhirinovsky, which is neither liberal nor democratic, won 22.9 percent of the popular vote, 7 percentage points more than Russia's Choice, the reformist party led by Yegor Gaidar. The old Communist party and its allies in the Agrarian party between them won nearly a quarter of the seats in parliament.

The results were a severe disappointment to those who had expected the election to confirm the reformers as the largest force in parliament. The four main reformist groups (Russia's Choice; the Yavlinsky–Boldyrev–Lukin bloc nicknamed Yabloko, or Apple; the Party of Russian Unity and Accord; and the Russian Movement for Democratic Reform) won a combined total of 164 seats in the lower house as against the 182 for the three main antireform parties.[26] The new lower house contained more extremist politicians than did the old Russian Congress of People's Deputies. Interpreting the results as a protest against shock therapy and radical reform, Yeltsin told Chernomyrdin to slow the reforms down. Gaidar resigned as first deputy prime minister, along with the pillar of the financial stabilization, Boris Fedorov. (That caused the German foreign minister, Klaus Kinkel, to argue that market reforms were over in Russia.)[27] Many people wondered whether Yeltsin would have taken such drastic steps against the old parliament had he known what the election results would be. That matters had come this far—tanks on the streets of Moscow, attacks on parliament, followed by the reformers' defeat—seemed a terrible setback for Russian democracy.

That same day, however, Russians voted for a new constitution. That was the more important vote. The makeup of the government could change, and so could the pace of reform. But this vote concerned the basic rules of politics. The constitution passed narrowly (the vote was announced to be 58.4 percent for, 40.3 percent against). That laid the basis for Russia's first period of relative political stability since the collapse of communism.

Despite widespread fears to the contrary, politicians of all sides accepted the new rules of the game. Though many of the actors were the same, the new political order proved more stable than the old. This was strong evidence that the confused rules of the game, rather than ideological differences or some innate inability to understand democracy, had brought Russia to the brink of anarchy.

Either from sheer exhaustion or from a sense of defeat, or else— most likely—because they hoped to win the presidential elections of June 1996, Yeltsin's opponents by and large accepted his new constitution. In the spring of 1994 Yeltsin and the leaders of all the main political parties in the country signed a political truce, which, unlike all previous attempts at compromise, was not immediately broken. Its signatories said they would not seek to change the constitution or otherwise to upset the balance of power between president and parliament for two years, nor would they call for presidential elections before 1996. The truce was kept.

That was a step toward stability, not stability itself. Not all groups were reconciled to the new constitutional arrangements, and the unreconciled included some that had signed the truce. The Communist party, for example, said that it wanted to reduce the authority of the president considerably and to make parliament the dominant power. That raised a possibility of a renewed tussle over the constitution. This time, however, the possibility was much narrower than it had been before. In 1992–93 parliament was the only body capable of amending the constitution, a power it used frequently in its battle with the president: by the end of 1993 the constitution had been amended around about a thousand times, considerably more than one amendment per working day. The new constitution not only laid down the basic rules of the political system but also made it hard to change them. Anything to do with the federal arrangements now requires a vote of approval by two-thirds of the lower house of parliament and three-fourths of the upper house, plus the agreement of the president, and no less than two-thirds of all the eighty-nine regional governments of Russia. Any alternative constitutional arrangement, in short, would have to command near unanimity. That seemed unlikely.

So, for the first time since the collapse of communism, the basic rules of politics in Russia seemed stable and had broad, though not universal, support. Combined with the voucher privatization program, whose completion in mid-1994 had transferred over three-quarters of Russian industry to private hands, this meant that Russia had gone some way toward mitigating the three great historical divisions that had been bearing down upon it in 1991. Then it had been trying simultaneously to create a market economy, build a democracy and a state, and rid itself of an empire. With each step toward political stability, it was inching away from that terrible inheritance, which required it to solve everything more or less at once. It had begun to create a market economy, with owners and private property rights, all essential corollaries to democracy. Supporters and opponents of the government had begun to accept their political institutions as appropriate. There were even some signs, as Chapter 12 will show, that Russia was beginning to accept its loss of empire. None of the divisions had been healed for good, of course. But if Russia's need was to resolve some of the conflicts to make others easier to handle, then that had been achieved.

Evaluation

A new Russian political order was born of muddle and bloodshed between the summer of 1991 and the autumn of 1993. The dissolution of parliament by decree and tanks by the man who had sworn to uphold it had damaged the country's faltering steps toward constitutionality. So did the actions of the Congress, which had used its authority as the only body empowered to amend the constitution with irresponsible frequency, turning the constitution, which should have set the basic ground rules of politics, into a weapon to attack the president. Those opposed to Yeltsin's policies thought he had shattered Russia's fragile democracy. Even those who supported his policies thought the result an unsatisfactory second best, a cutting of losses. As so often in recent Russian history, their pessimism proved exaggerated. Russia continued to muddle through, and 1994 saw a more stable political climate than at any time since the 1980s.

Chapter 10

Can democracy survive?

*A political balance sheet • Where democracy failed • An overmighty presidency?
• Weak bulwarks against autocracy • The Duma of 1994–95 compared with the
Congress of People's Deputies • How parties failed • The initial conditions •
Russians against democracy? • Democrats against democracy? • Why did
parties not develop? • Is there a military threat? • Possibility of
serious setback • Will democracy persist? • Evaluation*

In Nikolai Gogol's short story "The Overcoat," a downtrodden clerk, with vast self-sacrifice and expense, buys a fine new 80-ruble overcoat with a fur collar[1] to replace his threadbare old one, which had made him a laughingstock at the office. At first, he is ecstatic. He starts eating meals again with relish after half-starving himself to save the money. His colleagues throw a party in honor of his new purchase. But the overcoat brings him nothing but grief. Returning home from the party, he is set upon by thieves as he crosses a vast, shadowy St. Petersburg square. They strip the coat from his back. The next day, he returns to work in his old dressing gown to face humiliation, first from his colleagues and then from an unnamed Very Important Personage whose help he asks to track the culprits down. Mortified by their mockery and rebuffed at every turn in his search for his precious overcoat, he dies.

The great worry about Russian democracy is that it will prove to be like Gogol's overcoat—something external to the real Russia, an inappropriate piece of finery that costs too much and brings disaster in the end. This chapter looks at these doubts by considering three sets of

195

questions. First, what is the political balance sheet? Is Russia a democracy, and does it observe the normal principles of democratic life? Second, why do the nondemocratic features of modern Russian politics persist? Is it because Russians are reverting to autocracy, or is there some other reason? And third, does Russia have the basic requirements to sustain a democratic regime, such as a network of civic institutions and reliable popular support?

A political balance sheet

Stable democracies develop over years, even decades. Robert Putnam of Harvard University argues that it took Italy generations to create robust democratic institutions.[2] Clearly, Russia will not have passed that test for years to come. Nor has it yet passed even the narrower test suggested by Samuel Huntington of Princeton. He argues that democratic regimes can be considered to have consolidated themselves only after two changes of government: "if the party or group that takes power in the initial election at the time of transition loses a subsequent election and turns over power to those election winners, and if those election winners then peacefully turn over power to the winner of a later election."[3]

Nevertheless, even in the years immediately after the fall of communism, it was possible to see the first stages of democratization taking place. After the collapse of communism, the system of government in Russia was genuinely democratic and not, as is sometimes alleged, a fake.

Robert Dahl of Yale University argues that there are seven essential features of democratic rule: an elected government; free and fair elections; universal franchise; no restrictions on standing for public office; freedom of speech; access to alternative sources of information; and freedom of association.[4] Russia after the collapse of communism had all seven.

All important political decisions were in the hands of elected representatives in government or parliament. The presidential election of 1991 gave Russians their first-ever opportunity to choose a leader democratically. Parliament had been elected in 1993 and again in 1995. The constitution of the country had also been approved by popular vote in 1993. There were few areas of policy run by the secret police or some other unelected body, such as the army. Force had been used to settle two disputes, between parliament and the president in October 1993, and between the Russia Federation and the breakaway republic of Chechnya in December 1994. But on neither occasion did the army act independently: It was brought in by the president after negotiations had failed. By and large, the army's leaders made it clear that they did not want to be involved in domestic political disputes. Perhaps the biggest exception to the rule that officeholders were elected was Viktor Chernomyrdin, who became prime minister in 1992. At that time he had never stood for public office and, in the election of 1993, ostentatiously refused to have anything to do with the election, claiming to be above party politics. Nevertheless, he had been elected by parliament and, in 1995, decided to enter the popular fray, setting up his own political party—a turning point of sorts.

Elections were fair, free, and frequent. In the four years starting in April 1989, Russia held nine nationwide ballots,[5] an exhausting exercise in popular consultation. With one exception, those elections were free and fair. Even the negative case—an important one, the constitutional referendum of 1993—was an example of distorting the legal meaning of the vote rather than a rigging of the result itself.[6] Those elections took place both at the national level, for parliament and president, and at local levels, for provincial and town councils. Everyone had the right to vote; everyone had the right to run for public office—even those who had called for the overthrow of the government by force in October 1993. They were released from prison on the orders of parliament and permitted to run for office again.

Russia had full freedom of assembly and expression, with ferocious criticism of all politicians from the president on down. On the one occasion when newspapers and journals were closed by order of the state, in October 1993, the order specified newspapers and magazines that had issued calls for armed mutiny and racial hatred, cases that raise genuine difficulties regarding the limits to free expression. The government did not control the press, though it owned a powerful and influential national television network. In 1995 there were hundreds of independent radio stations and newspapers and dozens of private television stations all over the country.

Finally, Russians had freedom of association: They could join political parties and interest groups independent of government. Again, such restrictions as existed were little different from those in Western democracies: Political organizations calling for public violence were banned (for example, Yeltsin banned the Communist party in September 1991 after it had been implicated in the attempted coup against Mikhail Gorbachev; in November 1993, after the parliamentary uprising, he banned nine organizations implicated in the killings. In all but two of the cases the bans were lifted, and the organizations returned to normal political life).

Dahl argues that those features—a government chosen by free election under universal franchise; freedom of speech; access to alternative sources of information; and freedom of association—are what make a government responsive to its electors. If democracy means allowing people to make up their minds about what government they want and giving them a chance to vote it into power, then Russia by 1994 was a democracy.

Where democracy failed

But it remained a most peculiar democracy, one which lacked several essential safeguards for democratic rule. What might be called "rule by due process" had not been fully established, partly because the law itself remained weak and partly because the system of government that had emerged from the constitutional crisis of 1992–93 gave immense powers to the president and government. The countervailing powers against autocratic rule were weak and disorganized, especially the parliament and the political party system. There was little organized support for democracy at the grass roots, something that was demonstrated both by the weakness of the party system and by the lack of consistent popular support for any of Russia's politicians.

An overmighty presidency?

The issue of due process of democratic rule pertains in particular to the relative strength of president and parliament. As Chapter 9 showed, Russia settled its constitutional crisis by setting up a political system in which the executive branch triumphed over the legislative. The huge complex of marble buildings on the Moscow River, Russia's so-called White House, symbolized the shift. In August 1991 it had been the site of resistance to the attempted communist putsch, where Boris Yeltsin had clambered onto a tank to defy communism and where, in blazing sunshine that late summer day, crowds had gathered to hear their elected president celebrate "the victory of democracy over reaction." In October 1993, however, it had become a killing ground where more than two hundred people died while tanks pounded the parliament into a blackened wreck. Six months later, the same buildings, cleaned and spruced up, reopened as the offices of government, surrounded now by a 20-foot-high spiked metal fence, a symbol of the shift from government by popular representatives to government by ministers and civil servants, fenced off from the people.

The salient characteristic of Russian politics in the first years after the collapse of communism was Yeltsin's construction of a strong independent presidency. "Russia must be strong," he announced in his New Year's message of 1994. "To have a strong Russia," he said, sounding like Louis XIV, "you need a strong president." *L'Etat, c'est moi.*

In office, the most important questions of public policy after the Soviet collapse—the confrontation with parliament and economic reform—were centered on the presidency. For the first year of Russia's post-communist existence, Yeltsin had emergency powers to rule by decree; for six months he was his own prime minister. With the approval of a new constitution in late 1993, the president has enjoyed strong (critics said dictatorial) powers, at least on paper. Only a dictator, it seemed, can rule in the Kremlin. Russian democracy seems to be a contradiction in terms, like military intelligence.

The constitution of December 1993 enshrined the pattern of strong president and weak parliament. Under it, the Russian president has authority greater even than that of the French or American president, the two examples in the West of a strong executive separated from the legislature. He combines the advantages of both.

He is head of state and commander-in-chief. He chairs meetings of the government and, in essence, leads it. He may declare war and parliament, provided it is "informed" of his decision, cannot overrule him. In America, by contrast, it is Congress that formally declares war. The

Russian president controls the foreign and defense ministries directly, not through the prime minister. As in France, but more than in America, the president has the upper hand in making foreign and defense policy. The so-called power ministries (defense, security, the interior, and foreign affairs) report to him directly and not to the prime minister.

In Russia, the president nominates his prime minister and may (with certain restrictions) dissolve parliament if it rejects his nominee three times.[7] The French president has comparable powers. The American president, in contrast, cannot dissolve Congress. The power to dissolve parliament was given to the Russian president to stop its undermining of presidential policies by dictating ministerial appointments, as it did in 1992–93. The prime minister is supposed to pick his team of ministers, as in France, but in practice the president can conduct reshuffles by himself.[8] He can also sack the government without asking parliament's permission. He appoints the head of the central bank, the prosecutor-general, and high court judges, subject to parliamentary confirmation. He may declare states of emergency or martial law, subject to confirmation by parliament's upper house. In all those cases, then, parliament has to give its consent. But the constitution is unclear what happens if it refuses. That ambiguity suggests a weak point of defense against authoritarianism.

What if the president tries to become a dictator? The only ground for impeaching him is treason or serious crime; at least one-third of the lower house of parliament must be willing to start proceedings against him; two-thirds are needed to make a formal charge stick; even then, the Supreme Court must uphold the charge. The process is intended to stop a replay of 1992–93, when parliament repeatedly threatened to impeach the president for infringing the old constitution. Under the new one, it will be hard to impeach him, though not impossible.

In office, Yeltsin did not use his potentially overweening presidential powers, except during a government reshuffle in 1994, when he appointed ministers over the prime minister's head. In practice, the exercise of his power to dissolve parliament would have provoked a major constitutional crisis, which he could not be sure of winning. So he continued to work with parliament over economic policy, and parliament continued to pass legislation the president opposed.

But Yeltsin used his power in another way: by building the office of the presidency into an independent, parallel branch of government. The president in 1995 had a staff of roughly 2,000 professionals, much of which was financed "off budget" and was therefore, in essence, not accountable to parliament. It included presidential commissions and task forces that replicated the work of government departments. During 1995 many disputes over policy—for example over the privatization of remaining state-owned assets—turned into arguments between the staffs of the president and their ministerial equivalents.

The existence of a strong presidency is not necessarily antidemocratic. France also has a strong presidency with powers that, on paper, could be used dictatorially. Under emergency provisions in the French constitution, for example, the president can abolish parliament on his own say-so. In practice, of course, France is a democracy because there are strong bulwarks against autocracy at every level of society.

Weak bulwarks against autocracy

In contrast, the countervailing powers in Russia are weak. The least weak among them is local government. The new constitution turned Russia from a highly centralized state into a federal one. Under the new arrangements, local governments—provincial and republic—won considerably increased powers. They became, for example, the main bodies responsible for privatization. Considered as institutions for encouraging democracy, they are weak. The regions are the bastions of the old local elites, former local communist leaders and heads of old state enterprises, who have adapted reluctantly to democracy and whose main interest lies in the often highly corrupt exercise of power. But considered purely as countervailing forces against the president, they are strong. Any new Russian autocrat would be a strong centralizer, because he would need to stamp his authority on the whole country. The local elites would be likely to resist that.

From the standpoint of encouraging democratic rule, parliament is most important. The Russian parliament's principal weakness is that it cannot form the government: The prime minister does that, and the president, who chooses the prime minister. Parliament's role is re-

202 Coming Russian Boom

stricted to confirming (or rejecting) the prime minister. It cannot reject ordinary ministers. Nor can it turn down nominations to other executive posts (such as ambassadors), though they are supposed to be chosen after ill-defined consultations with parliamentary committees.

Parliament, however, is not powerless. Its upper house, called the Council of the Federation, which has two members from each region and republic of Russia, rather like American Senate, has jurisdiction over relations between the center and the regions, including border changes. It may also examine legislation passed by the lower house; any law involving financial or defense policies—that is, the most important ones—needs its approval.

The lower house, called the State Duma, has to approve the prime minister and, most significantly, the budget. Thus Russia has one of the essential attributes of democracies everywhere, a parliament that controls the basic spending of the government. The Duma can override a presidential veto of one of its laws by a two-thirds majority (as in America). The Duma is also the body that holds votes of no confidence in the government (which it threatened to do in mid-1995 after the government bungled an attempt to free hostages taken by Chechen terrorists in a small town in southern Russia). The first time around, the president may simply ignore the vote. If the Duma passes another no-confidence motion within three months, the president must either dismiss his government and propose a new prime minister or dissolve parliament and call a new election. Two clauses provide the Duma with protection against arbitrary dissolution. The president may not dissolve it after a no-confidence vote during its first year (otherwise the president might try to dissolve parliament repeatedly until he got one he liked). And the Duma cannot be dissolved if it is considering impeachment charges or during a nationwide state of emergency.

The Duma of 1994–95 compared with the Congress of People's Deputies

The makeup and professional competence of parliament are almost as important as its formal powers. On this score, Russia's second parliament, which sat in 1993–94, showed itself to be a considerable improvement over the first one.

The old parliament, the Congress of People's Deputies, had been a kaleidoscope of shifting alliances between part-timers. Most deputies were directors of state companies or state farms; few thought of themselves as career politicians. They rarely identified themselves with any party, and they voted as they pleased.

At the seventh Congress of People's Deputies in December 1992, one-third of the 1,033 deputies said they did not belong to a party and most of the rest would not specify any allegiance. Instead, they organized themselves into factions, which were groups of deputies who claimed similar views but had little or no voting discipline. At the start of the seventh Congress there were fourteen factions; four formed during the session, making eighteen by the end. Of those, the largest by far had only 158 members out of 1,033 deputies; the next largest had 80. So the largest faction had 15 percent of the deputies and fourteen of the rest between 28 and 64 deputies (or 3–6 percent of the total each). By the time of the eighth Congress in March 1993, four factions had broken up.

The second parliament was far more coherent. In the 1993 election there was a voting threshold: A party had to win 5 percent of the vote for candidates on its list of representatives to gain seats in parliament. That narrowed the number of parties in parliament to eleven. Now, each of the top five all controlled 10 percent or more of the seats. So while in the old Congress the top five factions had controlled 41 percent of the seats, now the top five controlled 67 percent. The process of consolidation was taken a step further by the election of December 1995. Then the operation of the 5 percent threshold meant that only four parties won enough votes for people from their lists to enter parliament.

Many people thought the 1993 parliament would be hard to deal with, because it had more legitimacy than the old Congress and contained more extremists—both neofascists and free market liberals—than the old Congress. It did not turn out that way.

Extremists were sidelined. When the parliamentary faction leaders met for negotiations on January 12, the day after the ceremonial opening of the State Duma, many of them walked out in protest at the demand of the neofascist Vladimir Zhirinovsky to chair the meeting. He failed to win control of any of the parliamentary committees for his party. Other members of parliament, it seemed, wanted no more to do with Zhirinovsky than Yeltsin did.

Partly as a result, conflict with government became a debate, not a battlefield. For this, the chairman of parliament, Ivan Rybkin, was largely responsible. At the end of 1993 Rybkin had been one of the bitter-enders led out of the blackened shell of parliament under armed guard. He had spent his previous career as a low-level communist apparatchik messing about with tractors in southern Russia; listing his skills as "peasant, farm worker, tractor driver"; and boasting "75 publications on the improvement of agricultural machinery." Yet the man whom many feared would be a new hard-line non-cooperator proved exactly the opposite. Whereas his predecessor as parliamentary chairman, Ruslan Khasbulatov, had been a democrat who became a hardliner, Rybkin was a hard-liner who mended fences with Yeltsin and the reformers.[9] Thanks to him, the ruinous conflicts over policy that occurred in 1992 and 1993 did not recur. In 1994 and 1995 parliament amended the budget rather than adopt a fundamentally different one.

Russia's second post-communist parliament, then, was a reasonably coherent body. It was able to function independently of the government and was not cowed into submission by the constitution. It showed that a modest degree of parliamentarism was still possible even under the strongly presidential system of government. All the same, it could not be relied upon as a bulwark against autocracy.

That would not matter quite so much if other countervailing powers, such as the courts and the political parties, were strong. But they are not. As the previous chapter showed, the law courts and the criminal justice system were little better than in the last days of communist rule. Though the judiciary began to improve in 1995, when parliament finally approved the new Constitutional Court, legal independence and the rule of law inevitably take time to establish. The political party system was also slow to develop. In the first five years after the Communist party eschewed its monopoly on political power, Russia threw up at least a hundred parties, only one of which (the

Communist party) had more than a few thousand members. By one estimate, thirty-eight of them had the same program.[10]

How parties failed

Russian parties fell short of being proper parties in the Western sense in several ways. They had no real role in the exercise of political power, and the makeup of the government did not reflect electoral success. After the election of 1993, the two parties with the largest number of seats in parliament had two ministers between them, even though that government was a coalition. But the Party of Russian Unity and Accord, which came seventh in the election, had six ministers. After the election of 1995, Yeltsin sacked the two most prominent reformist ministers, but the government of early 1996 in no sense reflected the outcome of the election, which made the Communists the largest party in parliament.

Parties made little attempt to control their members. It was not until late in 1992 that any party said that it would require its members to vote for party policy in parliament. Even then, few took any notice, because not many parties had any coherent policies anyway. Most Russian parties started as clubs of intellectuals discussing the affairs of the day. And most stayed like that.

Worse still, personal rivalry hampered political organization. Politicians saw parties as vehicles for personal ambition, not as ways to organize popular backing for their ideas and policies. The reformers were like cannibals. Five of the best-known founded five different parties: Yegor Gaidar (Russia's Choice), Boris Fedorov (Forward Russia), Anatoly Sobchak, the mayor of St. Petersburg (the Russian Movement for Democratic Reforms), Sergei Shakhrai (the Party of Russian Unity and Accord), and Grigory Yavlinsky (the Yavlinsky–Boldyrev–Lukin bloc, popularly known as Yabloko, or Apple). Ego divided those parties, not ideology. Vaclav Klaus, the Czech prime minister in the 1990s, thought that the reformers' biggest mistake was not to pay enough attention to generating grassroots support by building up parties.

The descendants of the Communist party were better organized. There were only two of them in parliament, the Communist party itself, which appealed mainly to pensioners and bureaucrats, and the Agrarian party, which represented the collective farms and the Soviet-era agro-industrial complex. As happened in every other former communist country, the communists attracted support because of public disillusionment with reform. But Russia's communists had a narrower public appeal than the Polish or Hungarian ones (both of which won the second post-communist elections). It was less thoroughly reformed than they were and contained more unreconstructed Soviet-era nostalgics (the reformers of the Gorbachev era mostly left the party, abandoning it to hard-liners). It also depended, far more than did the Hungarian or Polish socialists, on its bedrock supporters. Outside parliament, several breakaway communist parties sprang up to challenge it.

The centrist parties were the biggest losers in the election of 1993. Only one of three competing parties, the Democratic party of Russia, crossed the threshold of 5 percent needed to win seats in parliament. It was also the only party to take the notion of voting discipline seriously. But its attempt to create a coherent united group failed: The party collapsed in 1995, torn apart by personal rivalries. The center ground in the parliament was represented not by organized parties but by independents, especially representatives of local interest groups, such as, for example, businessmen from the oil and gas industries, or directors of big privatized firms, or bankers and local bureaucrats, all of whom won their seats on the basis of local name recognition.

So it seemed that whenever two or three members of a Russian political party gathered together in one place, one of them walked out to form another party. This phenomenon has been common throughout Russian political history—so common, in fact, that the language even has a word for it: *krugovshchina.*

In short, Russia's political system combined a strong, almost authoritarian presidency with democratic forms of government, and considerable power to elite interest groups who resisted organization into political parties. That produced a democratic balance that was evenly poised. On the one hand, Russia had free and fair elections; the president, parliament, and constitution had popular mandates. There was an independent constitutional court to ensure that Russia's lawmakers stuck by the rules. The country also had free speech and freedom of assembly. On the other hand, rule by due process was not secure because of the dominance of the president over the parliament. Parliament could not be considered a real bulwark against the abuse of power by the president. Political parties were weak.

It was hardly surprising that Russia failed to create a full-fledged stable democratic system immediately after the collapse of communism. As Chapter 9 argued, the creation of an independent Russia from the ruins of the Soviet Union was in many ways a genuine revolution. It is hard to think of any great revolution that established a stable political system right away. Even America's first constitutional arrangement, the Articles of Confederation of 1781, was a failure and had to be replaced by the present constitution eight years later. The French (and Bolshevik) revolutions opened with periods of revolutionary turmoil, followed by imperial autocracies to restore order.

In one crucial respect, Yeltsin's Russia was more like postrevolutionary America than postrevolutionary France: After the initial upheaval, it established a reasonably stable government. In the first two years of the life of the constitution, 1994 and 1995, Russian politics were calmer than at any time since the Communist party began to collapse in the late 1980s.

But it cannot be assumed that the system will remain stable. It seems unlikely that political parties, for instance, will remain in their embryonic state. More probably they will either collapse completely or become better organized.

More important, the stability owed a great deal to Boris Yeltsin himself, who, like a medieval monarch, kept a balance among the various groups in the coalition government, slapping down this faction and building up that. Having established a strong presidential system, he did not use the mighty powers of the presidency in such a way as to disrupt the constitutional balance further. But there could be no guarantee that another president would not seek to do so.

Which way, then, will Russia go? Will the balance tilt more toward a full-fledged, stable democracy, with stronger institutional bulwarks against autocracy? Or will it go the other way, toward a yet more powerful presidency, unfettered by parliament?

The initial conditions

One can talk only of likelihoods, but the starting point must be the basic attitude of the Russians themselves. A full-fledged democratic system by definition depends on the population. It cannot not be established without their support.

So perhaps the biggest worry about the long-term prospects for Russian democracy is that Russians themselves do not seem fully committed to it. In December 1993, 22.9 percent voted for the party of Vladimir Zhirinovsky, a man espousing openly fascist views. That was 7 percentage points more than the vote for its nearest competitor and a larger share than Hitler gained in the German general election of 1930. "I will establish a dictatorship," Zhirinovsky boasted. In the parliamentary election of December 1995, the party which emerged as the largest single group was the Communist party, which had denied Russia democracy for over 70 years. Suddenly the prophecy of Vissarion Belinsky, Russia's greatest nineteenth-century literary critic, seemed to be coming true: "A liberated Russian people would not go to parliament, but they would hurry to the pub to have a drink, to smash windows and hang the gentry."

Russians' apparent distaste for democracy seemed to be confirmed by later evidence. In August 1994 a poll conducted by the Russian Public Opinion Research Center found that only half the respondents thought Russia needed democracy and a quarter didn't. Russians did not appear to agree even on what democracy actually was. Only 19 percent of those polled thought the system Russia had then was democratic; more than half thought that Russia's leaders were not democrats.[11] Politicians themselves were held in contempt. In November, asked to say which politicians they trusted, 47 percent replied no one. Though other polls found higher levels of support both for democracy in general and for individual politicians in particular, the findings generally suggested a grumpiness, tending toward hostility, about the democratic process. Aleksandr Lebed, a general who went into politics in the summer of 1995, characterized the electorate thus: "They are like sheep. They will run after anyone who barks at them but protects them."

There was an even more powerful force at work: apathy. Polls in

1994 showed that under 5 percent of Russians said they were inter-ested in politics; 40 percent said they had no interest, and the rest could not make up their minds.[12] That was an enormous change from 1989–91. At the height of the anti-communist demonstrations, three-quarters of a million people surged into the largest square in Moscow to shout, "Yeltsin! Yeltsin!" By 1995 Yeltsin had lost almost all his sup-port, and so had everyone else. Opinion polls at that time found that no one could command the support of more than about 10 percent of the population. The most popular, the reformer Grigory Yavlinsky, got between 9 and 11 percent. Lebed got about 8 percent. Yeltsin got less than 5 percent.

What explains ordinary Russians' indifference? Did the collapse in public confidence show that Russians were rejecting their fledgling democracy? Did voters turn to Zhirinovsky because they wanted dic-tatorship?

The answer to the last question seems to be no. After the parlia-mentary election, the Russian Public Opinion Research Center asked Zhirinovsky's supporters why they had voted for him. The answers were surprising. The majority of those who had voted for him turned out to be young industrial workers with jobs, frequently on higher-than-average wages. They were not losers from democratic or eco-nomic reforms. They seemed to be registering protest votes against the abuses of the early years. Most of them said they had voted for Zhirinovsky because he seemed like the candidate who would do most about crime (he certainly would have been: he promised to shoot criminals on sight). Clearly, his supporters were not particularly wor-ried about his dictatorial ambitions. But neither, it seemed, did they want fascism or even a reversal of market reform.

So if the vote for Zhirinovsky does not necessarily show that Rus-sians are rejecting democracy, what explains their indifference? Per-haps the most convincing answer is that Russia after the collapse of communism was suffering from the same phenomenon that Alexis de Tocqueville diagnosed in France after the Revolution and in America in the early 1830s, after the extension of voting rights under Andrew Jackson: "atomization."

"It is . . . commonly at the outset of democratic society," Tocqueville wrote, "that citizens are most disposed to live apart . . . democratic revolutions lead them to shun each other, and perpetuate in a state of equality the animosities that the state of inequality created." The reason, he argued, is that "those members of the community who were at the top . . . cannot immediately forget their former greatness. . . . Those on the contrary who were formerly at the foot of the social scale . . . cannot enjoy their newly acquired independence without secret uneasiness . . . they stand aloof . . . with an expression of fear and triumph."[13]

Tocqueville's description fits Russia closely. Those members who were at the top were the old Communist party members, the elite of the former society. They treated the new governors, that is, Yeltsin's team, as oppressors, calling the president and his ministers by every imaginable epithet. Conversely, "secret uneasiness" and "fear and triumph" informed the attitude of the new men, Yeltsin's supporters. They were little disposed to mutual support and solidarity after communism fell.

Russians against democracy?

How much does the lack of strong support for democracy matter? It is natural to assume that it matters a lot: Democracy, it seems, needs widespread support to be stable, and that in turn requires popular agreement about what democracy means in practice.

Yet surprisingly, the evidence from stable democracies does not bear out those assumptions. In fact, widespread agreement seems to exist only at the most basic level. Voters accept that democracy is the best form of government. When it comes to what this means in practice, there is little agreement.

In one of the most influential articles of modern political science, James W. Prothro and Charles M. Grigg tested the assumption that stable democracies need consensus on the basic rules of politics—and found it wanting.[14]

They chose two American towns, Ann Arbor, Michigan, and Tallahassee, Florida, where they asked voters questions about democracy as an abstract principle and about how it should work in practice. Almost everyone agreed with the proposition "Democracy is the best form of government" and "Public officials should be chosen by majority vote." But equally, people also thought that "if a Communist were legally elected mayor of this city, the people should not allow him to take office." They also thought that "in a city referendum deciding on tax-supported undertakings, only taxpayers should be allowed to vote." Supporting democracy, it seems, is one thing; defining what constitutes democratic behavior is another.

Yet no one thinks that democracy does not exist in Ann Arbor or Tallahassee. Democracy, it seems, can work even though many people are not committed to every aspect. That in turn seems to cast doubt on the idea that democracy depends on universal support. Instead, the conclusion must be that, so long as people have a general commitment to the principle, however vague, the everyday workings of a democratic system actually depend on something else—the way politicians behave, for example.

How do the Russians compare? The evidence suggests that they may be less wholeheartedly committed to democracy than Americans are, but they nonetheless have a core of support for democratic norms. Mass demonstrations for free elections took place in Russia's large cities in the late 1980s, involving millions, not just a politically committed elite. A huge number of political parties sprang up, which does not seem consistent with indifference about democracy. Despite the extraordinarily large number of elections in 1989–94, the turnout remained reasonably high (it was over 50 percent even in the ninth election in four years, which was about the same as in American presidential elections).

Russians' support for reform held up remarkably well throughout this period, despite the hardships it involved. In June 1991 Yeltsin, the candidate of reform, won 57.3 percent of the vote. In April 1993, in a nationwide referendum, 58.7 percent of voters said they had confidence in him as president and 53 percent said they approved of his socioeconomic policies. Then, in December 1993, 56.6 percent[15] voted in favor of the new "reform" constitution. Considering the traumatic change that Russia had seen in the thirty months after June 1991, the constituency for reform proved remarkably resilient. Reform, of course, is not the same thing as democracy. In Russia, however, it does imply a pluralist system as opposed to the old autocratic one. At a minimum, this seems to provide a safeguard against the balance of political power's tipping sharply away toward dictatorship.

The actions of the electorate provide a corrective to the opinion poll evidence that only half of Russians think their country needs democracy, and that less than half think they have one. It suggests the glass is half full, rather than half empty. On balance, then, the evidence about public attitudes suggests that while Russians fall short of providing full-blooded support for democracy, they also tend to favor an ill-defined "reformist" agenda. Given the evidence from other countries of how much public support is really required to sustain a democratic regime, that suggests the Russian support for democracy is weak but adequate.

Democrats against democracy?

The same extreme individualism that Tocqueville said afflicts ordinary citizens in the aftermath of a democratic revolution also helps explain the "antidemocratic" behavior of some Russian politicians. It also helps explain Russia's initial failure to develop political parties.

The flight of former democrats to authoritarian nationalism shows that at least one group of Russian politicians was not strongly committed to democracy. In October 1993 Aleksandr Rutskoi stood on the balcony of the White House calling for an armed uprising against the government. Yet a little more than two years before he had campaigned alongside Boris Yeltsin in the presidential race and had fought alongside him during the abortive putsch of 1991, organizing the defense of the Russian parliament against the KGB. The same path was trodden by Ruslan Khasbulatov and many others. It was not surprising that four generations of communism should mean that many politicians were unenthusiastic about democracy from the very start. But to see politicians who had espoused democratic principles at the start abandoning them later suggested that some top politicians were not really ready for democracy.

More generally, Russian politicians seem to have a somewhat different attitude to power from those in the West. In the West, politicians usually see the cut and thrust of the democratic process in terms of compromise, tradeoffs, and coalition-building. Those are necessary to get anything done. In the United States, for instance, it has become rare for the same party to control the presidency, the Senate, and the

House of Representatives. To conduct government business requires cross-party agreement and bipartisanship. The same is true in much of continental Europe, where it is rare for any party to win an outright majority in elections and where you need to build a coalition to form any sort of government. Politics is the art of the possible.

Some Russians, in contrast, appear to see the democratic process in terms of power, victory, and defeat. For them, politics is a zero-sum game. Those who opposed Boris Yeltsin's economic policies in 1991–95 were called, significantly, the "irreconcilable opposition." In early 1994, a few months after the attack on parliament, four hundred Russian politicians and more than 150 parliamentary deputies gave interviews for a radio series on democracy produced by Radio Russia and the BBC. In the course of hourlong interviews, many of then mentioned the word *vlast* (power) more than two dozen times. Some of them repeated it a hundred times. Sergei Stankevich, an influential parliamentarian, says of the battle between parliament and president, "We were too Russian. First we had to know who was in charge."[16]

What was the explanation for this behavior? It is partly, no doubt, the genuine appeal of Russian nationalism. But part of the explanation also has to do with the sheer newness of democracy in Russia. In "Consensus and Ideology in American Politics," Herbert McClosky points out that new participants in democracy tend to behave differently from experienced ones.[17] The examples he gives comes from the 1960s and 1970s in America, when opposition to the Vietnam War and the civil rights movement were drawing activists into politics for the first time. America then saw the rise of groups such as the Black Panthers and militant antiwar groups, which pursued their own demands uncompromisingly, with low tolerance for the views of others.

No Russian in the early 1990s had firsthand experience of how democracies worked, except as a foreign observer. More than that, many politicians who came to prominence in 1991–92 were not politicians at all. Many of the members of Yeltsin's first cabinet, for example, were academics from the Moscow-based Institute for Economic Policy or its St. Petersburg affiliate. In the parliament, many of the deputies were factory managers or chairmen of state farms.

Considering this, Russian politicians proved themselves skilled at the arts of compromise and accommodation. For the first five years after 1991, Russia's governments were coalitions containing radical young technocrats, old-fashioned Soviet bureaucrats, and everything in between. It was remarkable that coalitions so broad managed to hold together at all, especially considering the bitter political turmoil around them. They did so because, in practice, reformers accepted the bureaucrats' demands when it was unavoidable and the bureaucrats often allowed the reformers to draw up the main economic strategy. Thus in the spring of 1992 Yegor Gaidar gave in to demands to relax his austerity to stay in office and see through the privatization program. The privatization chief, Anatoly Chubais, made concessions to the managers and workers in order to buy their support for the privatization program as a whole. He even allowed the mayor of Moscow to run a different program in the capital to guarantee that his own scheme would be adopted everywhere else.

On the other side, in 1993 the prime minister, Viktor Chernomyrdin, accepted the need for monetary austerity even though the old-fashioned apparatchiks, of whom he was one, were opposed to the idea. Above all, Boris Yeltsin proved himself a compromiser, skilled at balancing competing forces and able to keep ramshackle coalitions together. It was largely thanks to him that the Russian governments managed to avoid provoking confrontations with the public, despite intensely unpopular economic policies.

Why did parties not develop?

But if the "atomization" of the political elite did not kill the art of compromise, it does help to explain the failure to develop a coherent party system.

It is important to bear in mind that political parties are not synonymous with democracy. Indeed, democracies, especially in their early stages, are possible without parties.

Most of America's founding fathers disapproved of parties, which they dismissed as "factions." James Madison's Federalist paper no. 10 argues that "factions" breed corruption and can prevent the population from judging issues on their merits. The American constitution makes no provisions for parties, and a coherent two-party system did not really get going until the 1830s. Yet America in its first fifty years of independence was one of the most democratic countries in the world. A modern example comes from France. There, political parties have never been durable organizations. The parties that dominated politics in the 1980s and 1990s were all recent inventions. The Socialist party was founded in 1971, the Rally for the Republic in 1976, and the Union for French Democracy in 1978. They were all, in different ways, vehicles for the men who founded them, respectively François Mitterrand, Jacques Chirac, and Valéry Giscard d'Estaing. French parties are constantly breaking up and being reconstituted. But France is a democracy.

That casts doubt on the argument that Russia's endless political squabbling and the proliferation of its parties show that Russians are somehow deficient in the qualities of sustained effort and social coherence needed to make democracy work. The same point can be seen by looking at other countries. "Atomization" was not unique to Russia. It was characteristic of all post-communist politics. Throughout Eastern Europe and the former Soviet Union, communism was overthrown by coalitions that included virtually every social group, even (in Romania) the secret police. Coalitions that broad would be unlikely to survive in the best of circumstances. The early years of economic reform were not the best of circumstances. The coalitions everywhere held together long enough to stage the mass demonstrations that threw out the communists and to form the first governments. They then exploded: Witness the decomposition of the main dissident organizations—Solidarity in Poland, Sajudis in Lithuania, Civic Forum and Public Against Violence in Czechoslovakia, as well as Democratic Russia, the broadly based anti-communist movement that had organized Yeltsin's presidential election campaign in 1991. Unprecedentedly large numbers of parties emerged from the ruins everywhere: sixty-seven parties fought in the Polish election of October 1991, seventy-four in the Romanian election of September 1992. Indeed, in the aftermath of World War II, before the emergence of two large groups, West Germany also initially saw a proliferation of political parties as it struggled to build a democracy from the ruins of Nazism.

Comparison with those countries suggests that while Russia's ill-developed party system will cause political confusion, it is not necessarily evidence of an underlying social instability. Poland and Romania were not atomized into seventy or so groups in need of someone to save them from anarchy. The proliferation of parties, however, did produce chaos in the first parliaments. In Poland, the first post-communist parliament had twenty-nine parties, none with more than 14 percent of the seats; Poland had three governments in 1992 alone. That was an extreme case, but in only one Eastern European country (Albania) did any party win more than half the seats in parliament, and in all of them, three or four party coalitions, often quite unstable ones, were the norm.

This produced the impression that politics was so unstable that democracy itself might be in danger. But it was not. In Poland and elsewhere in Eastern Europe, democracy was entrenching itself. That may also be true in Russia, though it lags behind Eastern European countries in the formation of coherent parties and has even more parties than its neighbors.

Some of the reasons are transitory. The Communist party provoked a strong reaction to the very word "party" and made the concept of party discipline synonymous with purges.

Political parties find their reason for existence in parliaments. But Russia's first parliamentary election, in March 1990, took place only six weeks after the Communist party had forgone its constitutional monopoly of power, too early for parties to become established. Then came the battle between president and parliament, which made party rivalry secondary. Only after the election of 1993 have matters begun to change.

In addition, Yeltsin, like General de Gaulle, chose to stay above the political fray, to give himself as much room for maneuver as possible. In 1990 he announced that he would not join any party so long as he was Russia's leader. In 1992 he refused all attempts to create a "presidential party" to help fight parliament and turned down an invitation to attend the founding congress of Russia's Choice at the end of the year. Many observers said that Yeltsin's refusal to give his blessing to Russia's Choice, the party that carried the banner of his reforms to the electorate, contributed substantially to its failure at the polls. While that criticism may well be justified, Yeltsin's refusal to enter the factional fray enabled him to do something no less important: keep the coalition governments together and not split an already divided society further.

There is some evidence that Russian politics is slowly changing. By 1995 embryonic political parties based on different social groups had begun to establish themselves. The Communist party, for instance, represented the members of the old bureaucratic elites who were doing badly from reform and those on state welfare payments who were doing even worse, pensioners above all. The Agrarian party represented the state and collective farms. The shift to clearer interest group politics was represented above all by Viktor Chernomyrdin, Yeltsin's second prime minister. He refused to have anything to do with the election of 1993, saying that, as prime minister, he was a nonpolitical technocrat. In 1995 he changed tack and set up his own political party, rather oddly called "Our Home Is Russia." That was an attempt to set up a party for the managers of Russia's new big businesses, such as Gazprom, the gas monopoly he used to run. Bankers called the new party "Our Home Is Gazprom." It offered economic competence and stability; it came third in the 1995 election.

Doubts remain over this particular party's long-term future: Other attempts to represent the corporatist center have failed, but Chernomyrdin's decision to enter the political fray still marked a significant change. He was the most important member of the political establishment that emerged under the 1993 constitution to take the plunge into party politics.

By 1995 Russian party politics was beginning to take on a faint resemblance to the interest group politics of eighteenth-century Britain. There were few real parties, an immense amount of corruption, and lots of horse-trading. But the most important players in the political establishment were beginning to use parties to advance their interests and ideas. It was not full-fledged party-political democracy, but it was at least possible to see where the support for multiparty democracy would come from.

Is there a military threat?

In contrast, it is harder to see where support for full-fledged authoritarianism would come from.

It is true that democratic regimes will not be stable if they are openly opposed by powerful groups who can threaten the political system, such as the army, police, or security services.

It is also true that the Russian army is a powerful and dissatisfied group of men. Russia's army is one of the largest in the world. In 1994, 25 percent of the national budget was spent on it, yet there were still thousands of officers living in tents, the pay of ordinary soldiers was derisory, and quartermasters complained that they did not even have enough money to buy food.

Yet the traditions of the army are firmly against intervention in politics. In Russia, the army has always been closely controlled by civilians. Under the communists, all officers had to be members of the party, which maintained "party cells," i.e. small groups of loyalists who kept tabs on what was going on. In the 1930s Stalin was able to decimate the officer corps in a series of purges.

Indeed, the Russian army has been reluctant to intervene in domestic politics even when the authorities have called upon it to do so. In 1962 General Matvei Shaposhnikov, a hero of World War II who won the Gold Star for bridging the Dnepr River in 1943, ruined his career by refusing a direct order from the Politburo to fire on striking workers in the southern city of Novocherkassk.[18] He did so in order to maintain the Russian army's proud tradition of staying out of politics. Indeed, the tradition was nearly the undoing of Boris Yeltsin, who describes in the second volume of his autobiography how the army reacted when, during the night of October 3, 1993, parliamentary forces tried to seize control of Moscow. "I saw," he wrote, "that the army, despite all the assurances of the defense minister, for some reason was not able to come quickly to Moscow's defense and fight the rebels. . . . All of us—me, the defense minister, the government, and our society— have become hostages to the idea that the army is outside politics. But now, when the army had been called to defend society from bandits, fascists, and criminals, we were surprised: why is the army finding it so difficult to react? Why is it so poorly obeying orders?"[19]

The answer seems to be that, unlike in Latin America in the 1970s, the Russian army does not see itself as a guardian of the nation. Its generals may grumble about the way they are treated, but they do not think they know how to run the country better than politicians do.

The chances of their trying to take over the country are falling further as military morale sinks. The bloody and bungled operation in Chechnya in 1995 showed that the army could not take control of a small part of the Russian Federation, except at enormous cost. In the light of that event, taking over the entire country looked even more perilous, especially considering the amount of local armed resistance that the army met in Chechnya. The lesson was not likely to be forgotten quickly. Any would-be coup leader would have to reckon that any attempt to impose the central government's authority by force would be resisted all over the country by dozens of regions acting independently. As Richard Pipes, a Harvard historian, has remarked, "a future dictatorship would be confined to two cities [Moscow and St. Petersburg]. The rest of the country would get on with its own life." Russia's army, remember, is a largely conscript force. Its conscripts seem extremely unlikely to respond to the idea that the army can save the nation. Opinion polls have found that less than one-third of young people see military service as an honorable duty.[20]

The one thing that would make a difference is if Russia were at war and the army were dragged into politics because of it. Hence the significance of one of the great differences between Russia's current reforms and all its previous attempts at modernization: Russia is at peace. All its earlier reform programs took place at a time when one of the government's primary tasks was the maintenance of a strong army because of the threat or reality of war. For the first time, the threat of the military looks reasonably containable.

Possibility of serious setback

All that said, Russia's short-term prospects remain highly uncertain, because its politics are so fluid and because, by 1995, living standards were beginning to recover. As Tocqueville famously put it, "evils which are patiently endured when they seem inevitable, become intolerable when once the idea of escape from them is suggested."[21]

The parliamentary election of December 1995 was the country's second after the start of economic reform. Elsewhere in Eastern Europe, the second post-communist election produced a strong showing for reformed communist parties. Russia's communists were not reformed but they duly became the largest party in the 1995 election, taking one third of the vote and giving their leader, Gennady Zyuganov, a strong platform for his run at the presidency. In the 1993 election, the biggest threat to democracy had come from the nationalist right. Now it appeared from the communist left (which was also aggressively nationalist). Zyuganov himself claimed to be a moderate, claiming that communists accepted the idea of private property, welcomed foreign investors, and wanted only a "voluntary" new Soviet Union. Others in the party, however, spoke of a secret "maximalist" program far more wide-ranging than the "minimalist" campaign manifesto. Disputes over what the communists stand for make conflict probable between the 50 or so disparate groups supporting Zyuganov. Even more probable are conflicts between the communists and Russia's new elites if the policies are fully implemented. These elites are powerful: the communists will not be able to ignore them even if they try, though any attempt to do so would be destabilizing enough. Their influence will limit the damage the communists can do to the post-Soviet settlement.

In these circumstances, the likelihood is that a handful of parties with roughly equal support will continue to muddle through, running the country with coalition governments.

But it is also possible that the deadlock among the competing groups will pave the way for a populist promising quick fixes. This is the Bonapartist phenomenon, in which a strong, perhaps a reforming or a communist, leader comes to power with public support to restore order and not mess about with democratic institutions. Such a man might well use the presidency to pursue a more aggressive foreign policy and might seek to impose more bureaucratic controls over the economy. That would unquestionably upset the balance of Russian politics, perhaps for a considerable time.

Nevertheless, the range of possibilities open to a Bonapartist is narrowing. The instruments of the Russian state remain relatively weak. Popular support is inconsistent, and the army wants to stay out of politics. It is highly unlikely that a populist would be strong enough to reimpose anything like a planned economy or to renationalize swaths of the economy. Russia's emerging business class would oppose such a thing strongly. An extensive, and almost certainly corrupt, licensing system is the most that could be achieved. Nor could he manage to turn Russia back into a highly centralized state. The regions would resist.

It is also unlikely that a populist presidency would be stable. Because the state remains relatively weak, he would need to retain popular support. A corrupt system of economic licensing would damage the economy, benefit a few rich people, and erode public confidence. So, to judge from the revulsion that set in after the attack on Chechnya's bid for independence, would an aggressive military foreign policy. A Bonapartist could come to power in Russia. Whether he could stay there long is another matter.

Will democracy persist?

What about the long term? Many of the social and economic supports for democracy would remain in Russia even if an authoritarian regime were to take over. So the long-term prospects for Russian democracy look better than its short-term ones. Here we reach the basic underlying supports for democracy.

Russians have the right kind of society for democracy to flourish in. Democracy is more likely if a country has a wealthy and complex society; if it is not riven by deep ethnic divisions; if it is well educated and urbanized; and if it has a strong underpinning of clubs and informal associations that make up "civil society." Russia has all those characteristics.

Wealth. The connection between wealth and democracy is strong. With several notable exceptions, the world's richest countries are democracies, and most of the poorest ones are not. If you were to draw a map of the world classifying countries into free, partially free, and unfree, it would be remarkably like a map classifying them into rich, middle-income, and poor. The rule of thumb is that wealthy countries tend to be democracies.

In 1959 an American professor, Seymour Martin Lipset, became the first person to test whether there was any empirical evidence to support this rule of thumb. There was. After classifying forty-nine countries from Europe and the Americas, he concluded that "the average wealth, degree of industrialization and urbanization and level of education is much higher for the more democratic countries."[22] This was confirmed by later, more rigorous studies using better data.[23]

That says nothing about cause and effect. Wealth could promote democracy, so that, as people become richer, they demand free elections, civil liberties, and so forth. That is what happened in the Soviet Union. Or it might be the other way around: Democracy could promote wealth because it limits the ability of rich rulers to steal and waste money, or because it promotes social stability and better economic decision-making. But whichever way round it is, the correlation between the two is what matters to the question, Will Russia remain democratic? Russia's per capita income in 1993 was $2,340. That puts it into the upper-middle category, poorer than established democracies such as Britain and America, richer than some of the fast-developing Asian democracies such as Thailand or Malaysia. If wealth is important (as it seems to be), then Russia should be rich enough to be a democracy.

Pluralism. The main reason wealth tends to make countries democratic is that richer countries tend to have more complex economies. In a subsistence village, most people are concerned with the harvest or the farm animals, either growing and processing food or making tools for farmers. It is a world that is closed to the outside, a world of few occupations and mutual dependency. The modern industrial or postindustrial world is far more complex. It is a place of diverse economic interests, of competition, open communications, and occupational diversity. It is the economic counterpart to a diverse civil society.

This kind of society makes it harder for any one group to concentrate power in its hands and to hang onto it indefinitely. Instead, it disperses power away from the center of authority, toward individuals and groups, who see themselves as having equal opportunities and rights ("all men are created equal with certain inalienable rights").

Russia in 1991 was already a much more dynamic and complex society than it was in 1917, when Lenin took over a peasant economy; it was more complex than it was in the 1930s, when Stalin began his crash course in industrialization. And it became still more complex after 1992, when economic reform did away with the forced simplicities of central planning, in which all aspects of economic life were subjugated to a single, overarching five-year plan.

Cities and education. Russia displays the features of a dynamic modern society in two other ways: urbanization and education. During the past fifty years, Russians have poured from the countryside into the cities in a way that was every bit as dramatic as that which occurred in many developing countries. In 1939 two-thirds of the population was rural, earning their living from the land (about the same share as Morocco today). Now, three-quarters of Russians live in cities. It has also taken on many of the demographic attributes of an advanced western country: 99 percent of the population can read and write (this rate is higher than Britain's); 96 percent go to secondary schools.

Education is an indispensable feature of the complex, pluralistic world that produces democracy. Educational achievements, one study of five countries concluded, had "the most important demographic effect on political attitudes";[24] the more education people had, the more likely they were to engage in politics and the more confident they become in seeking to influence governments. Educationally, then, Russia has the makings of a democracy.

Civil society. Tocqueville argued that the most important reason for the success of democracy in America was "the customs of the people . . . the peculiar cause which renders that people the only one of the American nations that is able to support a democratic government." He singled out, in particular, America's flourishing "civil society": the world of Rotary Clubs, bowling leagues, churches, and so on. A robust civil society, he argued, checks and balances the power of the state. It implies pluralism; no single group can claim to represent everyone's interests, as the Soviet Communist party did. There must therefore be many parties to represent people's political views.

The Russians in 1986–95 have seen an explosion in "civil society," triggered first by *glasnost* (openness), and encouraged further by the abolition of the Communist party's monopoly of power. For seventy years, the Communist party had crushed not only competing parties but any form of independent public organization, even boys' clubs. Instead, the party ran its own clubs, such as the Young Pioneers, a Soviet cub scouts' organization, to which virtually everyone between eight and thirteen years of age was supposed to belong, or the Young Communist League, which they were supposed to join after the Pioneers. The party also set up clubs for the appreciation of Maksim Gorky or for hiking in the Pamir Mountains. Nothing was too small to escape the party's attention. Perhaps, people hoped, when it gave up its power, everything would be able to escape.

It did. The abrogation unleashed a wave of activity. Literally thousands of independent groups sprang up: Cossack regiments; writers' associations; ecological movements concerned with, for instance, the poisoning of Lake Baikal by a furniture factory that was pouring bleach into it (Baikal is a natural wonder, containing one-fifth of the world's total supply of fresh water and the world's only freshwater seal). There were Tupperware parties and political parties—these and thousands more participated in the revival of civil society. When the Russian-American University undertook to classify them all, it needed ten volumes for the job. In the aftermath of *glasnost*, Russians rejoined the world of independent clubs and associations.[25]

The renewed vigor of Russia's clubs was both an indispensable breeding ground for democracy and, at the same time, the expression of the extreme individualism that made it anarchic.

Ethnic unity. The last important social feature that has a bearing on the future of Russian democracy is its ethnic makeup. The prospects for democracy are reduced if one part of the country thinks its way of life is being threatened by another. So there is a rule of thumb: The more a country's national or cultural groups increase in distinctiveness, and the more they come into conflict, the more difficult it is to keep democracy stable.

Ethnic instability looks, on the face of it, to be a serious worry, because Russia seems more like a multiethnic empire than a nation-state: 27 million people belonging to dozens of ethnic groups live in twenty "republics" inside the Russia, i.e., self-governing provinces with their own constitutions and laws.

But the question is not, Is Russia a single-nation state? Clearly, the answer is no. The real issue is, Can it limit ethnic conflict so that democracy can survive (as it has in Belgium, America, and even

India, none of which is a single-nation state)? The evidence suggests the answer is yes. For one thing, the challenge of ethnic instability is not as great as it was. Though not a single-nation state, Russia is still a relatively homogeneous society. Ethnic Russians accounted for 83 percent of the population in 1989; Russian is a universal language; among the Russians, there is either one church (the Russian Orthodox) or none, but not two or more.

The next chapter will argue that Russia in 1991–95 made progress, albeit slowly, in developing a proper federal system able to withstand ethnic strains. Russia is more a coherent unit than it has ever been. It may not be a nation-state, but it is more like one than it has ever been in the past and as much like one as several European countries are.

Evaluation

It would be wrong to argue that Russia will be a democracy simply because it is relatively rich, urbanized, well educated, and ethnically coherent. In the 1930s Germany and Italy were all those things. Because Russian politics in 1995 was evenly balanced between a half-built democracy and a potentially overweening presidency, democracy could still be knocked off course, and a populist demagogue could come to power. But it does not seem likely that he could stay there long if he forfeited the support of the voters. The evidence from public attitudes, from the behavior of politicians, and from the gradually developing political parties, is that democracy will not crash into dictatorship because it is inherently flawed in Russia. By 1996 Russia's chances of sustaining democracy were stronger than they had ever been.

Chapter 11

Will Russia break up?

*Russia and the USSR: likenesses • Russia and the USSR: differences •
The Federation Treaty • The invasion of Chechnya • Who won and lost as a
result of reform • Reform in one province: Nizhny Novogord • The Brezhnevite
paradise of Ulyanovsk • How can the center help the laggards? • Evaluation*

To grasp the immensity of Russia is an essential part of understanding the country's reforms. Moscow and St. Petersburg no
more constitute the whole of Russia than New York and Washington
make up all of America. Yet many people continue to think of Russia
as if they do. Moscow, its politics, its intrigues, its fashions, and its
concerns, pass for those of the country at large. That may have been
understandable in the Soviet era, when the politics of the Kremlin
were all-encompassing. But it is no longer.

One of the most significant results of the first few years of reform
after 1991 was a decisive shift in the balance of power from the central government to the regions. The shift was sometimes chaotic, often
haphazard, and always confused. But power was unmistakably eddy-
ing out from the center to the periphery. The importance of that can
scarcely be exaggerated. For the whole of its history, Russia had been
under the iron grip of the Kremlin, and whether tsars or commissars
were inside made little difference. The power of local barons, where it
existed, was constrained by their need to lobby the central authority
and to accommodate its demands. They had virtually no power of ini-

tiative. That was one of the main reasons why previous attempts at reform in Russia collapsed. All were imposed from above. They failed to win the support of officials at the grass roots who were expected to implement reform but who often ignored or sabotaged instructions from the Kremlin. This time, things were different. Local officials had discretion. Some rushed ahead of the central government. Others fought reform tooth and nail. All were protagonists.

In 1995 about half of all public spending went through Russia's local governments, which spent 80 percent of the money that went on social welfare programs of all kinds, including schools, hospitals, and public housing. In just eighteen months in 1993–94, they were responsible for selling 100,000 small state-owned firms into private ownership and all but the largest of the 16,000 medium and large-scale ones. They were responsible for the millions of housing complexes, hospitals, and kindergartens that, under central planning, had been the responsibility of companies but which, after privatization, were got rid of by the firms. To take just one example, a capital-goods firm in Yekaterinburg called Uralmash owned what was to all intents and purposes a company suburb, having been responsible for all the apartments, the schools, and even the public transport system in the area. Its new boss transferred the ownership of 44,000 apartments to a holding company. In 1995 Uralmash financed 95 percent of the maintenance costs, the local government 5 percent. But the company planned to cut its contribution by 20 percent in each of the next five years, so that by 2000 the local government and the residents will be responsible for the whole thing. That sort of arrangement was being repeated all over Russia. Local authorities are responsible for deciding whether or not to allow the sale of land, still publicly owned in 1995. In sum, they were responsible for carrying out the reform that created 40 million shareholders almost overnight—the reform that did most to change Russians' lives—and because of their responsibility for welfare spending and land sales, they are the bits of the government that will do most to determine the success or failure of the second stage of economic reform, which involves getting the initial changes to work consistently. Yegor Gaidar, the main architect of radical reform, was right when he asserted: "The whole decision-making process has been reorganized. The country is no longer run from Moscow."[1]

"Organized" was perhaps not the *mot juste*. The delegation of power to the regions was, like most things in Russia, muddled, arbitrary, and improvised. It came about in the first instance because of opportunism. As the central government collapsed, local politicians took advantage to grab power for themselves. The so-called war of laws, in which parliament and president passed rival articles of legislation, gave local governments a chance to pick and choose, adopting those laws they liked, ignoring those they didn't. The failure of the central government's powers of coercion provided the opportunity for some areas to keep more of the taxes they collected and to press claims for more autonomy, or even for full independence. Such disorder in relations between center and periphery led many observers to doubt that Russia would even survive as a single state. The Soviet Union, they argued, had broken up because of the nationalist and ethnic demands in its constituent republics. They had wrecked Gorbachev's attempt to reform the Soviet system by withholding taxes from the center, bankrupting it. Now here was Russia being threatened by its ethnic constituents who were also using their tax-raising powers as a weapon against the central government.

This chapter begins by asking whether Russia will go the same way as the Soviet Union. Or has Yeltsin managed the problem of secessionism better than Gorbachev? It then goes on to look at the questions: How well does Russia's new federal system work? Which regions gained from reform and which lost? Are the regions part of the problem or part of the solution? And how can the problems of the regions be overcome?

Russia and the USSR: Likenesses

It was hardly surprising that many people thought Russia was doomed to break up, like the Soviet Union before it. There were many similarities between the two. The Soviet Union was an empire, not a nation. Russia is more like the carcass of that empire than a functioning nation-state. The Soviet Union consisted of fifteen republics, each with a dominant nationality, around a Russian core. Russia includes a score of so-called republics, each with a titular nationality (Tatars in Tatarstan and so on), around a Russian core. Russia, the 1989 census showed, contains 126 different nationalities. In both countries, some areas wanted much faster reform than the central government was willing to allow, while other wanted the center to slow down. In both, ambitious local politicians emerged to challenge the authority of the president, and they played important roles in two critical events—the Soviet coup of August 1991 and the dissolution of the Russian parliament in 1993. And disputes over taxes were important in both cases.

Between November 1988 and July 1990 a succession of Soviet republics issued "declarations of sovereignty," which said their laws took precedence over the laws of the Soviet Union; four declared independence. That eruption of sovereignty affected the internal politics of Russia too. In 1990, trying to drum up support in his struggle against Gorbachev, Yeltsin visited Tatarstan, the second largest of the Russian republics. He told his audience, "I reckon the Tatar people are entitled to decide for themselves what kind of autonomy they need." In 1992, they decided they needed the maximum amount. Tatarstan adopted a constitution that said it was a sovereign state with laws that took precedence over Russia's. The referendum on Boris Yeltsin's constitution was declared invalid there because of lack of interest: Only 14 percent of the Tatar electorate bothered to vote. In that same poll, 53 percent of the electorate of the neighboring Muslim republic of Bashkortostan voted against the Russian constitution, and almost immediately the republic parliament adopted a constitution which, like the Tatar one, claimed precedence over Russia's. Neither transferred any significant amounts of tax to the central government during 1993. Nor did two other republics, Chechnya in the Caucasus and Yakutia in the Far East.[2] In another republic, Tyva, sandwiched between Russia and Mongolia, less than one-third of the electorate voted for the Russian constitution in December 1993, but a majority approved a constitution that allows the local parliament to suspend Russian law in the republic. In October 1991 one Russian republic, Chechnya in the Caucasus mountains, which had been added to the tsarist empire in the same southward expansion that had also conquered Georgia, Armenia, and Azerbaijan, actually did declare independence. In 1992–93 it did seem just possible that Russia would break up.

Russia and the USSR: Differences

Yet the differences between Russia and the Soviet Union were more important than their similarities. There were five main ones.

First, despite decades of propaganda, the Soviet Union never managed to create what Lenin called a "new man," a kind of *Homo sovieticus*, with a sense of Soviet identity to replace the old national ones. In the last years of perestroika the Soviet identity collapsed altogether, and the old national or ethnic identities reasserted themselves. A sense of being Russian was never lost. Unlike the Soviet Union, Russia has a heartland: most of European Russia west of the Urals and most of Siberia and the Far East. That was largely unaffected by ethnic strife: 82 percent of the Russian Federation is ethnically Russian. There were differences between local governments in this heartland and the central government. The local governor in Sverdlovsk Province (where Yeltsin was born) talked of setting up a "Urals republic." Regional leaders toyed with the idea of a Siberian republic in Novosibirsk and a Far Eastern one in Vladivostok. But their disputes with the central government concerned economics—tax rates, subsidies to local industries, and control over resources. The nationality issue did not arise in the heartland. In contrast, there was no such thing as a Soviet heartland. If you excluded the fifteen Soviet republics, there was nothing left for Mikhail Gorbachev to rule. If you exclude the twenty-one Russian republics, that would still leave Boris Yeltsin in charge of most of the country, with 123 million people out of the total population of the Russian Federation of 148 million.

The second difference between Russia and the Soviet Union is that, Russia itself apart, the Soviet republics were mostly old nation-states. The Baltic states, Moldova, and Ukraine had once been nations within something resembling their current borders. By 1991 they were all arrayed against Gorbachev in a more or less united front. In contrast, the Russian republics are neither like nation-states nor united against the center. Only one of them has ever actually been independent, Tyva, between 1917 and 1944, though the Tatars like to claim descent from the great Tatar empires that trace their ancestry back to Genghis Khan's heirs. Russia's republics were for the most part relics of

Stalin's divide-and-rule policies. Their names—Tatarstan, say, or Yaku-tia—make it sound as if they are dominated by the eponymous ethnic group. That is misleading. In the Komi republic and Yakutia, vast areas of steppe and permafrost in the north named after two Inuit peoples, Russians account for more than half the population. In three republics between Russia and Mongolia, they account for between 60 and 70 percent. Taking all twenty republics, Russians account for half or more of the population in nine and 30 percent or more in eight others. In only six of the twenty-two republics is the titular nation more numerous than the Russians.

The interests of the Russian republics are very different. The republics fall into three main categories. The ones that appear most like the old nation-states crushed into the Soviet Union are eight that might be called ethnic trouble spots. By Russian standards, all have small Russian minorities, between 9 and 40 percent of the population. All are poor, with average incomes between one-third and one-half the Russian average. All but two are in the Caucasus, between the Black and Caspian seas. They include four of the six republics where the titular group outnumbers the Russians, notably the most troublesome of all, Chechnya. This is the region where independence is certainly conceivable. Among nationalist Russians, there is no a strong constituency for keeping them all inside the federation. Even Aleksandr Solzhenitsyn, though a strong nationalist, says that southern Chechnya should be allowed to leave Russia. Vladimir Zhirinovsky calls the whole region "an abscess on the Russian body politic." In fact, however, the demands for independence are weak among all but one of the Caucasus republics themselves. The exception is Chechnya, which is something of an oddity among the southern republics. It is the only republic that is both relatively large (more than 1 million in population) and reasonably homogeneous ethnically. The other Caucasus groups tend to regard the Chechens, and to some extent their neighbors the Ingush, as different from the rest, more militant, more intractable, more militaristic. Chechen leaders have been far more determined upon secession than the others and more confrontational toward the authorities in Moscow.

The second group comprises large resource-rich republics—Komi and Karelia (next to Finland) in the north and Yakutia in the Far East.

They have above-average incomes and ethnic Russian majorities. Their demands are almost entirely economic. They are using their ethnic differences as bargaining chips to wring tax concessions and subsidies from Moscow. There is no serious risk that they will secede. The president of Yakutia even supported Yeltsin's 1993 decree abolishing the parliament and calling new elections, though he was the only republic leader to do this. Their Russian majorities make relations between these Russia's republics and Russia itself very different from the relations between the Soviet republics and the Soviet Union. Yakutia is no Lithuania. It is not even a Latvia, a country in which 30 percent of the population is Russian. The Russian republics are often more than 50 percent Russian in population and less than half nationalist in sentiment. That acts as a powerful brake on anti-Russian secessionism by the small non-Russian nations.

The real threat to Russia's integrity comes from the third group, the Muslim republics on the Volga, such as Bashkortostan and Tatarstan, the two most populous republics, with more than 3.5 million people each. They have oil, straddle the railways that connect Siberia to European Russia, and are home to most of Russia's 18 million Muslims. Accommodating their demands proved extremely hard. In 1992 Tatarstan refused to sign a treaty defining the powers of the central and local governments. It spent 1993 claiming to be a sovereign state subject to international law which just happened to be voluntarily "associated with" Russia (and could therefore decide to leave at any time). Bashkortostan did sign the treaty, but only after signing a secret clause that granted it special tax and other economic concessions. Nevertheless, full independence, while conceivable, would prove even harder for them than accommodating their demands has been for Russia. Ethnic Russians account for between 40 and 60 percent of their populations and oppose independence. All are landlocked and would depend on Russia for defense and communications.

The third big difference between Russia and the Soviet Union, which should also prove a brake on secessionism, concerns taxation. The Soviet republics collected and controlled all taxes and had the power to bankrupt the Union government. They claimed the right to determine their own tax rates and exemptions. Russia's regions are also responsible for collecting taxes, which they then pass on to the central government. But they have few independent tax-raising powers. Under the tax law of January 1992, virtually all taxes are determined centrally and then assigned to one or another level of government. Value-added tax goes to the center; personal and corporate income taxes go to the regions. So local authorities' revenues come from fixed shares of federal taxes. A similar system prevails in Germany. The local authorities have little scope for determining their own tax base and tax rates. Russia has nothing like state income or sales taxes, as in America. Even Moscow, which ought to have more potential than most of Russia for developing its own tax base, actually derives 90 percent of its revenues from taxes determined by the federal government. That limits its fiscal independence and the fiscal powers of local authorities generally. With the exceptions of the four republics already mentioned (Tatarstan, Bashkortostan, Chechnya, and Yakutia), the Russian republics and regions continued to stick by the rules of this revenue-sharing arrangement.

The fourth difference is not directly connected with underlying ethnic or political differences. It concerns the background against which the differences were played out. In the Soviet Union, the processes of disintegration were reinforced by economic collapse and political chaos. The Soviet authorities' unwillingness to come to grips with economic reform encouraged regional reformers to break away and mend their own economies independently. And the Soviet Union's galloping economic destabilization soon destroyed any remaining public support for staying in it. At the end of 1989, when Gorbachev went to Lithuania and tried to dissuade the people from seeking independence, he gave them a warning: "If you leave, you'll be in the soup." "We're in the soup now," someone in the crowd shouted back. In contrast, the gradual movement of Russia toward political and economic stability in 1994–95 reinforced the processes of integration. The economic decline began to bottom out; the ruble stabilized; there was some measure of political stability. That reduced the incentive to secede.

The Federation Treaty

The last and perhaps biggest difference between Russia and the Soviet Union lay in the differing approaches of Yeltsin and Gorbachev to decentralization. Largely because the problem of separatism was smaller in Russia, Yeltsin was able to begin dealing with it earlier than Gorbachev. He was also able to be more accommodating to the regions. Hence, he was much more successful.

Russia's initial attempt to resolve arguments between the center and the periphery took place in March 1992, when Yeltsin persuaded eighteen republics to sign an agreement called the Federation Treaty, a rudimentary division of powers between the central and local governments, which was later incorporated into the constitution.

The Federation Treaty pointed up the contrast between what was possible in Yeltsin's Russia and what could be achieved in Gorbachev's Soviet Union. Yeltsin was able to give the redistribution of power early priority and managed to have an agreement signed within three months of the time economic reform began in earnest in January 1992. In contrast, negotiations over the equivalent Soviet arrangement, called the Union Treaty, did not begin until four years after Gorbachev took over the Communist party and more than a year after the Baltic states first demanded radical changes in the distribution of Soviet power. Negotiations then dragged on for two more years, while the demands of the Soviet republics for autonomy became demands for outright independence. Gorbachev seems to have been slow to recognize the danger that nationalism posed to the Soviet Union. But he might never have been able to delegate Soviet power anyway: The opposition from the communist old guard was simply too strong. His Union Treaty never came into force. The putsch of August 19, 1991, was designed to prevent its being signed, as planned, on August 20. The coup was successful in that narrow aim, if in no other.

Yeltsin's Federation Treaty set up a broad and ambiguous distribution of powers. It gave the central government responsibility for defense, the ruble, long-distance communications and transport, basic science, and the like. Regions were solely responsible for social services and most privatization. Center and regions were jointly responsible for the development of natural resources. The treaty got off to a rocky start when Tatarstan refused to sign it.

What made the difference was the defeat of the old parliament, which helped Yeltsin both directly and indirectly. Not only was he no longer fighting on two fronts, but he also did not have to worry about local authorities playing off president against parliament to win more powers. A number of local councils had backed the parliament in its battle with Yeltsin and had declared his decree suspending parliament to be unconstitutional. In the aftermath of the parliament's defeat, all revoked those declarations. The Federation Treaty won a popular mandate of sorts because it was incorporated into the new constitution, approved by voters throughout Russia in December 1993. Then, in February 1994, after three years of negotiation, Russia and Tatarstan finally signed a treaty, which brought the Tatars back into line with everyone else. Tatarstan retained its constitution, but the treaty said it was "united" with Russia, not "associated" with it. Out went any mention of Tatar sovereignty or Tatarstan as a subject of international law. The republic's president, Minitimer Shaimiev, said that Tatarstan had no desire to leave the Russian Federation and that, indeed, it wanted to preserve Russia's integrity. The federal arrangements looked to be settling down.

The invasion of Chechnya

There then occurred one of those events that seemed to threaten the gradual progress that was being made toward a more stable federation: the invasion of Chechnya.

Chechnya was in many ways a special case. Not only are the Chechens regarded by their neighbors (and by the Russians) as intractable and militant, but the republic's leadership pursued its bid for independence in a way that made negotiation exceptionally difficult. The man who led the independence movement, Jokar Dudaev, a former Soviet Air Force colonel, overthrew the local communist boss in the aftermath of the coup against Gorbachev in August 1991. Dudaev declared independence soon afterward. The regime he set up fell far short of the normal standards of acceptable conduct. He armed his supporters with weapons taken from the local Russian military base. His government was implicated in several notorious frauds perpetrated upon the Russian Central Bank. It was also implicated in cases of drug and weapons smuggling inside Russia.

That did not mean his government lacked popular support in its bid for independence. There is little doubt that the Chechens wanted considerably more autonomy than they had and more than would later be offered them under the Federation Treaty (which they refused to sign). Had Dudaev put the issue of independence to the electorate, they might well have approved it. But he never did. Instead, when the local parliament organized a referendum on the question in mid-1994, Dudaev disbanded parliament and forcibly cleared out those demonstrating support for the referendum in a mini-Tiananmen Square; several of the demonstrators were killed. That gave the Russian government a chance to present the Dudaev regime as a group of bandits rebelling against the legal order. In October 1994 it attempted to foment a rebellion against Dudaev by giving arms and soldiers to the local opposition in a covert destabilization operation. That failed ignominiously.

Three months later, in December 1994, Russia sent 30,000 soldiers (mostly raw recruits) to Chechnya and, on New Year's Eve, launched what turned into the longest, bloodiest assault on any of the smaller ethnic groups in Russia since Stalin's mass deportations during World War II (from which the Chechens suffered hugely too). The sheer brutality of the assault seemed quite disproportionate: The Chechen capital, Grozny, was reduced to rubble, and more than one-third of the republic's 1 million people were turned into refugees. The attack led to near-universal condemnation not only in Western capitals but in Russia itself.

The invasion renewed fears in the West about the breakup of Russia. In Russia, leaders of the Muslim republics denounced the "fratricidal war." The republics in the Russian Caucasus, overwhelmed by Chechen refugees and with virtually no emergency assistance from Moscow, seemed as though they might respond to Dudaev's appeals to fight a *jihad* (holy war) against Russia. It even seemed possible that they might follow Chechnya and pass their own declarations of independence.

In the event, none of those things happened. There were no copycat declarations of independence. The regions waited to see who would win before backing one side or the other (a common reaction in Russia). No one went to the barricades for Chechnya, not even in the Caucasus. Everywhere, the argument of overwhelming force had had its sobering effect.

The capture of ruined Grozny gave Yeltsin another chance to flesh out the half-formed federal system. He took it. In February he convened a meeting in the Kremlin to work out what new reforms were needed in the federal system. A law on local self-government was the result. It dealt mostly with technical matters, such as the size of local councils and parliaments. It was not enough to establish a workable federal system on its own. Its importance lay less in what it did than in what it showed: that Yeltsin was still trying to make local government work, rather than, as might have been imagined after Chechnya, re-creating a centralized Russia by force.

Despite Chechnya, Russia's post-communist federation was a significant improvement over what had gone before. Russia had been an overcentralized state under commissars and tsars. The new arrangements redressed the balance. Previous attempts at reform had failed in Russia because they were imposed from the top and failed to engage the support of local officials. The new arrangements gave local authorities an incentive to become involved in the reform and a stake in the outcome. Decentralization was also the only possible response to the fact that a chronically weak central government could not hold a huge state like Russia together without help.

But the new arrangements were a long way from ideal. For one thing, they were unclear about the division of responsibilities between central and local governments. How, for example, was "joint sovereignty" over natural resources supposed to operate? Who in practice would be in charge of issuing, say, oil-prospecting licenses? Answers to such questions called for a raft of additional laws and regulations to create a workable federal arrangement. By 1995 they had hardly even begun to be discussed. The deputy speaker of the upper house of parliament, Ramazan Abdulatipov, himself from the Caucasus and a specialist in the "minorities question," complained that parliament discussed his draft law on the question for just fifteen minutes before dismissing it as not urgent.

The new federation failed to match the local government's revenue-raising powers with their new spending responsibilities. In an attempt to cut the budget deficit, the central government shifted large amounts of spending to the regions. Most social welfare policies, subsidy programs, and investment financing—even of highways, military barracks, and airports—fell to the local governments. But there was no guarantee that the necessary revenue would be there to pay for it all.

In theory, the tax-sharing system was supposed to be enough. But the regions' two main taxes (personal and corporate income taxes) varied greatly, and there was no formal transfer system to top up local shortfalls. Moreover, the tax law was rarely implemented properly. So in practice the tax system, far from being clear and transparent, as the law suggested, became a jungle of *ad hoc* bargaining arrangements.

Lastly, Russia took over wholesale the administrative structure of the old Soviet Russian republic. That had divided up the country into eighty-nine basic administrative units (that is, the first level down from the central government). Those units came in half a dozen separate categories, each with slightly different formal powers. Their boundaries were arbitrary and had been drawn for the purpose of running a centralized dictatorship, not a democratic federation. All eighty-nine local government units survived into post-communist Russia, which means there were eighty-nine "subjects of the Russian federation." That was too many. While there can be no hard-and-fast rules about the "right" number of such units, comparison with other federal systems suggests that Russia has far more than is normally required for a federation. America, which has nearly twice Russia's population, gets by with barely half as many states. Germany, with about half Russia's population, has only sixteen states. The states sometimes need to band together against the central government, or just to agree between themselves on policies to pursue. That is much harder with so many states. The excess number of states also means that, as the economic power of any one region grows, it may not be able to have its new demands represented to the central government; it will be drowned out by the other states.

Who won and lost as a result of reform

Because of the sheer size and variety of Russia, wide differences exist between one part of the country and another. With seven time zones, it could hardly be otherwise. The richest areas—Moscow, St. Petersburg, Yakutia—are about three times richer per capita than the poorest, the Caucasian republics. By Western standards, the difference is large. By the standards of developing countries, however, it is small (the richest provinces of China and India are about ten times as rich as the poorest). The economic divisions do not seem deep enough to threaten the unity of Russia.

They are likely, however, to become greater over time, because economic reform affected different regions differently. Under the old Soviet system, heavy industrial production was encouraged, and prices for steel and other industrial raw materials were kept artificially low. Energy was an extreme case: The domestic Soviet price for oil was one-third of the world price. Copper was half the world price; scrap steel a mere seventh of the world market price. Next came food, which was also artificially cheap: Pork was also only one-seventh of the world price, and bread was cheap. In contrast, consumer durables were exceptionally expensive. An average car cost twice what a similar one might cost in the West; a video recorder cost more than three times as much; a personal computer, sixty-five times as much.[3] Central planners, it seemed, minded little if no one could afford consumer goods.

Price liberalization unraveled this system. Companies that produced favored goods suddenly lost their privileged position. Those that had been producing artificially cheap goods saw prices boom. Since the planners had had tidy minds and had exaggerated the tendency of similar firms to concentrate together in one place, this meant not only that certain firms suddenly lost and gained; whole areas did. Regions that produced energy, finished steel, or processed food benefited strongly from reform. They included the oil-producing region of western Siberia. Regions with consumer-goods factories lost out. So did those areas which specialized in what the architect of Poland's reforms, Leszek Balcerowicz, calls "pure socialist production," i.e., the sort of thing that could be imaginable only under central planning—fantastic quantities of military equipment of every kind; endless amounts of steel (proportionately, the Soviet Union produced seven times as much as America); incredible numbers of oil wells (Uralmash in the mid-1980s was producing more giant stationary oil rigs than the whole non-communist world put together). And, as a special category of "pure socialist production," Russia also inherited nearly all the economy of the Gulag, the slave-labor camps of Stalin. In the mid-1990s, several million people were still living and working in appalling conditions in or near the Arctic circle, digging coal under the northern tip of the Urals or smelting nickel at Norilsk, the largest nickel town in the world. Such places would never have existed on such a scale in the West. Over the coming years, people are likely to leave them if they can, which implies huge movements of populations and the emptying of whole cities.

Some of those cities will have to be kept alive artificially through subsidies. It would be socially explosive to let them collapse overnight. Whether reform can cope with these changes will depend more than ever on the regions. As time passes, the focus of reform has shifted from the center to the periphery. "At the start of the reforms," Aleksandr Belyakov, head of the council for the region around St. Petersburg, said, "the central government was the more important. It developed the strategy and plan at the macroeconomic level. As reform progresses, the fate of Russia will be solved at the local level." The question then is: How is reform taking root locally? Who gained and who lost?

Reform in one province: Nizhny Novgorod

Two cities on the Volga exemplified the winners and losers. Both were large cities, with roughly one million people, well-developed and varied industrial bases, and surrounded by the fertile farmland of the Volga basin.

The city that became Russia's laboratory of reform was Nizhny Novgorod, Russia's third-largest city and one of a string of trading posts that grew rich in the nineteenth century on the Volga's river traffic. Nizhny Novgorod, whose name in Russian means Lower New Town, boasted the biggest trade fair in pre-revolutionary times but was best known in the West under its Soviet name, Gorky, as the city to which the great scientist and dissident Andrei Sakharov was dismissed into internal exile. The province has a population of 1.4 million, of whom most live in the big city.

Unusually, as economic reform began in 1991, Nizhny Novgorod found itself with a strongly reformist administration led by two men in their early thirties, the governor of the province, Boris Nemtsov, and the mayor of the town, Nikolai Bednyakov. They were the pioneers of local reform in Russia. In late 1992 Nemtsov claimed, "Everything—demonopolization, forming financial markets, privatization—depends practically 100 percent on local government. The federal government only determines the rate of the ruble and supports the KGB and the army."[4]

In April 1992 the city held the first public auction of government-owned property in modern Russian history, a jubilant affair overseen by a flamboyant auctioneer who had been a former horse trader, with a big bow tie and a sense of occasion. Within three months 84 percent of the city's restaurants, 40 percent of its shops, and 38 percent of its other service establishments had been privatized. Within six months it became the first place in Russia to break up and sell off a medium-size state firm when it turned the local public bus and freight-truck monopoly into 20 firms, each of which it auctioned. Part of Nizhny's success lay in getting good advice: The sales were managed by the International Finance Corporation (IFC), a branch of the World Bank. It was the first such public intervention by any Western agency in Russia since the revolution.

Nemtsov also turned for advice to his friend Grigory Yavlinsky, a rival to Yegor Gaidar as reformer-in-chief. With Yavlinsky, he devised the first sales of local municipal bonds and a local land bank where farmers were permitted to use land as collateral for their loans (at the time the scheme was devised, using land as collateral was illegal). Between 1992 and March 1995 Nizhny Novgorod raised 65 billion rubles through three municipal bond issues. Nizhny was the only region in Russia to have worked out a system for breaking up collective farms; it privatized ninety of them in the first three years of its experiment.

The city was a heavy engineering center, with many defense-related businesses that were no longer viable (MiG jets are made there; it is one of the half-dozen largest defense centers in Russia). Those plants needed to be converted to civilian production. So the city set up a special "conversion" bank to help its defense industries. It negotiated a special arrangement with the federal government allowing it to keep half of the profits tax and value-added tax paid by local defense firms. The money was used to build up the capital of the bank.

But perhaps Nemtsov's greatest achievement lay in what he did not do. "The key to the Nizhny experiment is that the authorities have been willing to step aside and let the market work," was the verdict of Tony Doran of the IFC. That earned it rewards from outsiders. In March

1995 a paper plant in the city, called A.O. Volga, which makes one-third of Russia's newsprint, won a $150 million foreign investment deal. Herlitz International Trading, a German paper company, bought a controlling stake with the help of the IFC and a Western investment bank, CS First Boston, which had acquired 26 percent of the firm when it was privatized. The result was a firm 90 percent owned by foreigners; the bonus for the 4,800 workers was that they were paid three times the going rate. Herlitz said it would not have become involved in the deal if the Nizhny government had not been so reformist.

The Brezhnevite paradise of Ulyanovsk

In contrast to Nizhny Novgorod was the case of Ulyanovsk. Like Nizhny, Ulyanovsk is on the Volga, about 500 miles downstream. The province is the same size, also smaller: 1.4 million people, 72 percent of whom live in the main city.

Unlike most others, however, its local government stayed true to the memory of its most famous son, Lenin (whose real name was Ulyanov). The city fathers refused to reform. For two years they maintained a crude system of price controls and rationed basic foods. In the autumn of 1993, residents of the city were entitled to 1.5 kilos of meat, 2 kilos of sugar, 400 grams of butter, and fifteen eggs a month, all at well below market prices. This was far from unique. At that time, 40 percent of cities were controlling the price of bread, 26 percent the price of milk, and 11 percent that of sugar. But Ulyanovsk went further than most. The regional authorities had self-consciously gone about making themselves more self-sufficient, investing in local (publicly owned) farms, food processing plants, and fuel. Some of the republics apart, Ulyanovsk was the place in Russia that privatized the least. In Yeltsin's expressive phrase, the city was "living on an island of developed socialism."

For a while it looked as if the citizens of Ulyanovsk might benefit. Life there was easier than in Nizhny Novgorod because, though wages were roughly the same, food cost less.

That changed at the end of 1994. At that point Ulyanovsk ran out of money and was forced to abandon much of its rationing system. "In Ulyanovsk, the economy is still going down," Mr. Nemtsov claimed in

February 1995, "but now we're growing." One piece of good news, therefore, is that, given time, local reform will work.

The other piece is that reform could be adopted anywhere. It did not matter much if a region had inherited the sort of factories that benefited from price liberalization. Whether it adopted or rejected reform seemed largely a matter of will. This was surprising. It might have been expected that the pace of reform would be dictated by fundamental factors, such as whether the region had the kind of economy that would benefit or suffer from changing relative prices. Self-interest would dictate it.

In practice, however, it did not turn out that way. Philip Hanson of Birmingham University looked at privatization in seventy-seven regions during 1992. He concluded that "of an array of possible influences, only the distinction between local leaders' policy orientations and the percentage of non-Russians in the population was statistically significant. Possible influences, such as the degree of the dependence of local employment on the military industry and the percentage of the urban population did not appear to be significant, nor did an index of regional dependence on industries likely to 'lose' heavily through reform."[5] In other words, regions with a large non-Russian population tended to be slow in adopting reform. Otherwise, the only thing that made any real difference was the attitude of the local authorities. Nizhny Novgorod, with its array of defense industries, was exactly the sort of region that might have been expected to adopt reform last. Instead, it was among the first to change. That too was good news for Russia: The large regional disparities did not seem to be obstacles to reform. What matters is the people.

But too much rested upon people like Nemtsov. While mayors and governors were able to adopt reformist policies if they were determined enough, the second, more ticklish stage of reform depends on persuading those who are not strongly committed to reform to adopt it. Given that most of the regional leaders in Russia had worked their way up the communist hierarchy and were typical products of the Soviet bureaucracy, such uncommitted people were in the majority.

Here lay a paradox. Decentralization was part of the political solution—the solution, that is, to Russia's overcentralization, to the chronic weakness of the center, and to the failures of previous reforms

from above. But economically, decentralization was part of the problem, the problem, that is, of opposition to reform from the old communist elites. By and large, most local politicians were not
enthusiastic about economic reform which, through privatization, had
reduced their power to boss about local factories they once controlled, and, through fiscal reform, had laid on them spending responsibilities without sufficient taxes. They were also usually even more
corrupt than the central government. This meant that giving powers
to the regions tended to slow reform down.

How can the center help the laggards?

The task for the central government, then, was to alter the federal system to overcome the economic problems. It had to do so without jeop-
ardizing the political achievements of decentralization. In principle,
that should be achievable, because part of the responsibility for the
failures of the federal system lay with the central government itself.

The biggest problems were in the tax-sharing arrangements. They
often broke down into secretive and arbitrary bargaining between
center and regions that had nothing to do with fairness, efficiency, or
impartiality. A secret agreement between Tatarstan and the federal
government enabled the Tatars to transfer only one-tenth the amount
per person that Nizhny Novgorod has to pay each year. "It's a crazy
system for the basis of relations between the regions and the center,"
Nemtsov complained.

Block grants made by the center to help finance local government
welfare spending were made regardless of whether the local government was spending the money wisely or wasting it. "The principle that
you should get more if you want to do something is hard to explain to
Mr. Yeltsin," Nemtsov said. "When he goes to the regions, he just
hands out cash." Thus, in 1995, at the local level, Russia presented a
strange picture: some local governments pushing their own plans forward helter-skelter, others dragging their feet as much as possible,
and the central government, committed to reform in its own sphere of
activity but failing to change the local government system. Reform of
that system remained, in 1995, one of the biggest outstanding tasks of
the Russian reform program.

Evaluation

If the government can improve the federal system, it will take a substantial step toward consolidating its own authority. While, as this chapter has argued, the local governments have played a big role in the development of Russia's post-communist reforms, the central government was still more important. In the early 1990s Russia's central government was performing a task in some ways similar to the job that America's federal government did in the 1930s. That is, it was the body coming to grips with the great problems of the day, which the local governments had proved unable to address. The New Deal began the great shift in power that took place in America between the 1930s and the 1960s, marking the erosion of the dominant position of the states and the gradual rise in the influence of the federal government.

In the long run, this will help the integrity and unity of Russia and will overcome the first effects of the Russian reform: that regions will become more and more varied. While their differences are unlikely to outweigh the unifying forces of language, ethnicity, and culture, in the short term it will nevertheless make sense to think of Russia not just as a single, unitary state but as a series of regions. Some may well be economic failures, such as the Far North and parts of the Northeast, where economic activity, conducted in extremes of cold and geological difficulty, was based on Stalin's slave labor camps. The entrenched power of conservatives is also likely to hold back regions like the Kuban, Russia's corn belt, or some cities along the Volga, like Ulyanovsk.

Alongside these failures will come successes: Tyumen, the main oil-producing region, is likely to look like a boom oil town such as Houston, but as reform began it looked like a dusty, small town based on light engineering. St. Petersburg, with its port, its huge science expertise, and tourism, should thrive. Karelia, bordering on Finland, is likely to receive Finnish investment. Nizhny Novgorod's reformist administration may show how to counteract the effects of deindustrialization.

Reform, then, is likely to be patchy at best. Russia's sheer size makes that inevitable. But it also makes it tolerable. It will be easier to let successful regions thrive while accepting, if not correcting, the failures, than it would be to attempt to impose a uniform pace of change on the whole of the vast Russian Federation.

Chapter 12

Will Russia rebuild the empire?

Was the Soviet collapse different from the collapse of the Russian empire? ·
Were the new states viable? · The economic pressure to restore the empire ·
Russia's psychological problems · Will there be conflicts over the
Russians abroad? · Russia as Big Brother · Not so tough with the near abroad ·
The end of the ruble zone · Was Russian peacekeeping justified? ·
Will any state rejoin Russia? · Evaluation

"Russia will never be an empire," Boris Yeltsin proclaimed in his state-of-the-nation address of 1993. At that time Russia found itself reduced almost to its late-seventeenth-century borders. With the loss of Ukraine and Belarus in the west, it had been pushed back from Central Europe (at its greatest extent, Russia had reached into what is now Germany). With the loss of Moldova, it had been pushed back from Europe to the southwest and the Balkans (Russia had once had a border with Hungary and Romania). With the loss of the Baltic states, much of its Scandinavian territory had gone. And with the loss of Central Asia, it had been stripped of its nineteenth- and early-twentieth-century eastern conquests.

The retreat from empire was a change of immense historical significance. It ended the Cold War balance of power that had prevailed for nearly half a century after 1945. For Europe, it altered a power balance that had lasted even longer. Since the Congress of Vienna in 1815, Europe had been living with the huge Russian empire on its eastern flank. If Russia's retreat from empire is permanent, then not only do Americans no longer have a superpower rival to fear, but Eu-

247

ropeans may have to reconsider whether their continent ends with Germany, or with Poland, or includes Russia itself.

But is the retreat from empire permanent? In the four years after the Soviet collapse, Russia intervened militarily in four former Soviet republics, reestablished military bases throughout much of the old empire, and agreed to establish a monetary and customs union with Belarus, its western neighbor. To many in the West Russia seemed well on the way to reestablishing hegemonic influence in the "near abroad," as it insouciantly calls the former Soviet Union. This chapter looks at whether Russia's actions really showed that it was trying to rebuild the lost empire or whether the actions were evidence of something else: the extreme difficulty of negotiating a postimperial settlement. It does so by looking at five questions: Why did the Soviet Union collapse? Were the new states really viable? Will there be conflicts over the Russians abroad? Was Russian peacekeeping justified? Will any state rejoin Russia?

Was the Soviet collapse different from the collapse of the Russian empire?

The Soviet Union was the last of the great nineteenth-century empires. It was different from most in that it was a contiguous area, not an overseas empire, like that of Britain and France. It was different from all of them in that, in its Soviet guise, it was held together by a political party and an ideology. It was also the only one that collapsed and was then reestablished.

Two months after the Revolution of 1917 the nine provinces that make up modern Ukraine declared the independence of the Ukrainian People's Republic. The Cossacks set up the semblance of two independent states in southwest Russia. Georgia established the world's only Menshevik state on May 26, 1918. Azerbaijan declared independence two days later; Armenia followed suit on May 30. In Central Asia, the All-Turkestani Muslim Congress declared the autonomy of Southern Central Asia at the end of November 1917 at the city of Kokand and demanded recognition from Moscow. In the west, Poland, Finland (then parts of the Russian empire), and the three Baltic states all won independence, while Bessarabia (now Moldova) was annexed by Romania.

The independence of all but the final group of countries was fleeting. The Bolsheviks responded to the Muslim Congress's demand for recognition by destroying Kokand. The Red Army overran the city in February 1918 and massacred 60 percent of its inhabitants in three days. Soviet power was soon extended throughout Central Asia, including, for good measure, two Khanates, Khiva and Bukhara, which had had a degree of independence under the Russian empire. The treatment meted out to the other independent states was equally swift. The Red Army recaptured Kiev on June 11, 1920, two months after conquering Azerbaijan. Armenia fell in December of that year, and Georgia in February 1921. By September 1924 when Bukhara's independence came to an end, the young Soviet state had almost entirely reversed the collapse of the Russian empire. It had taken six years.

On the face of it, there are some parallels between the collapse of the Russian empire and the collapse of the Soviet Union. First, the breakup occurred in both partly because the central government had been weakened by something other than revolt in the provinces. In 1917 it had been undermined by the costs of World War I, and in 1991, by communism's economic failures. The establishment of independent states was partly an opportunistic response by countries at the empire's edge. Second, the countries that emerged into independence were weak and unstable, and contained powerful groups opposing the new governments: Bolshevik supporters in the provinces in 1917 and some Russian-speakers in the new states in 1991. Third, there were groups in Russia itself not reconciled to the loss of the empire and bent on reconquest.

Yet, though parallels exist, the differences are more important. The most obvious is that the Russians opposed to the loss of empire were not in government in 1991. The Bolsheviks were ideologically opposed to the very idea of nationalism. Lenin thought that classes, not nations, were the basic social units. Ideally, they were hoping to start a worldwide revolution; failing that, they would create a communist Soviet Union. In contrast, the ideology of Yeltsin and the Russian government in 1991 predisposed them to accept the breakup of the empire. The empire had been established and run by autocrats. Russia's new rulers wanted to behave democratically, which required them to accept the referendums supporting independence in Ukraine and elsewhere. Their commitment to economic reform pointed the same way. Most of the other states proved less committed to reform than Russia itself, at least in the first instance. At the same time, because the Soviet economic system had been highly integrated, it was possible for the other states to undermine Russia's reforms (by, for instance issuing credits in rubles). That meant economic reform was possible only in an independent, separate Russia. So the new Russian government recognized the other independent states and accepted their boundaries as inviolable. This gave the states a few crucial years in which to start building stronger governments.

That points to the second big difference: Russia's neighbors were not so catastrophically weak in 1991 as they had been in 1917, which was especially noticeable in the largest and most important of them, Ukraine. The first unhappy period of Ukrainian independence saw three governments forcibly overthrown and German, Polish, French, and Bolshevik troops, as well as Ukrainian forces, fighting over the new state. The early years of its post-Soviet independence were difficult, but not as hard as that. Everywhere, the new governments were able to call on the resources and advice of such international institutions as the International Monetary Fund and the World Bank; economically at least, they were not isolated. It remains true that the new states were unstable, and their weaknesses posed problems for Russia. But the largest of them, at least, were not in conditions of virtual anarchy, nor did they turn into battlefields for competing powers.

The third difference between 1917 and 1991 was that nationalism played a much greater role in the collapse of the Soviet Union than it did in the collapse of the Russian empire. In 1988 the largest popular demonstrations seen in the Soviet Union for decades took place in Armenia, where nationalists demanded the return of Nagorno-Karabakh, an Armenian-populated enclave inside Azerbaijan. In Ukraine in 1991, 3 million people joined hands in a human chain between Kiev and Lvov in support of Ukrainian independence, copying a similar event, the Baltic Chain, that linked the Lithuanian, Latvian, and Estonian capitals the previous year.

It is true that the reactions to nationalism both of the populations and of some republic governments were mixed. In a referendum in March 1991 over 70 percent of the Soviet electorate voted for the continuation of the Union, albeit as a loose confederation. Most of the leaders of the now independent states were prepared to sign the Union Treaty, which codified such a decentralized system (the exceptions were the Baltic states and Ukraine). Yeltsin was a consistent supporter of a decentralized Soviet Union. He began advocating purely Russian policies—a separate currency, a Russian army—only after he came to power. In practice, though, the requirements of economic reform plus the power of nationalism in other republics would have made a looser confederation highly unstable. So, on balance, it remains true that nationalism was more important in breaking up the Soviet Union than it had been in breaking up the tsarist empire.

Lastly, there was something driving the Soviet dissolution that was not present in 1917: the distorting costs of central planning. Under the old economic system, trade within the Soviet Union was conducted at fixed prices. They were very different from prices that prevailed on world markets, both absolutely and relatively. Some goods were artificially cheap, especially oil, raw materials, and food. Others, such as consumer durables, were relatively expensive. Russia, as the biggest producer of oil and such raw materials as steel and coal, suffered more than any other republic, because the goods it produced were artificially depressed in price and the goods it bought from elsewhere were artificially expensive. In 1988 Russia ran a 31-billion-ruble trade deficit with the rest of the Soviet Union. Had the same trade been conducted at world prices instead of Soviet ones, Soviet statisticians calculated, Russia would have run a 33-billion-ruble surplus. Obviously, had trade actually been conducted at those prices, the pattern of trade would have changed drastically. Nevertheless, Russia was, in effect, subsidizing the rest of the country. In 1990 Yeltsin claimed that those subsidies amounted to 70 billion rubles a year. Russia had little economic interest in maintaining an empire that cost it so much.

The comparison between the collapse of the Russian and Soviet empires suggests that the forces at work in 1991 were profound. The last of the great empires had fallen apart. Suddenly Russia was faced with the problems of a postimperial settlement. Such problems are hard enough for an imperial power to cope with even when it loses an empire overseas. France came to terms with losing its overseas possessions only after it had fought a war in Indochina and one in Algeria, which brought down the Fourth Republic and created France's biggest postwar crisis. The Dutch fought and lost a war of independence in Indonesia. Though most of the British empire became independent without wars—Kenya and Aden (and America) are exceptions—Britain's loss of empire was barely less traumatic. Britain, in Dean Acheson's words, "lost an empire but has not yet found a role." Postimperial traumas are even greater when contiguous land empires break up. Every constituent part of the Ottoman empire fought a civil war after its collapse.

And the Soviet Union was not merely a land-based empire; it was, formally, a unitary state. That meant post-Soviet imperial disengagement was likely to be immensely problematic. On the face of it, therefore, many of Russia's problems in the near abroad might well have been caused by the sheer difficulty of managing a postimperial settlement, rather than by neo-imperialism. The problems were threefold. First, there were objective ones, to do with the instability of the new states. Second came the psychological problems connected with losing an empire and not finding a role. Third, Russia faced the problem of kith and kin in the near abroad.

Were the new states viable?

In parts of the Soviet Union, as in former Yugoslavia, the collapse of communism provided opportunities to revive long-suppressed ethnic rivalry. Two countries, Tajikistan and Georgia, collapsed into civil war. In Tajikistan the war was fought between rival clans, whose conflicts were exacerbated by differences between those waving the red banner of communism and those with the green one of Islam. In Georgia a small ethnic group in the west of the country called the Abkhaz rose up in arms against the national government, as they had done the last time Georgia had declared independence. Well armed and with support from Russia, the rebels took control of Abkhazia and established a separatist government. The Georgian president and former Soviet foreign minister, Eduard Shevardnadze, narrowly escaped death, fleeing Abkhazia's besieged capital, Sukhumi, only hours before it fell to the rebels. Georgia also experienced a military coup against its first president, Zviad Gamsakhurdia, and a war between his followers and Shevardnadze's. Azerbaijan experienced one military coup and two changes of government while continuing a war with its neighbor, Armenia, over Nagorno-Karabakh. In Moldova, as in Georgia, a separatist group, this time of Russian-speakers, set up a rebel government on the right bank of the Dniestr River. In all, the former Soviet republics experienced fourteen changes of government in 1991–95, five of them violent.

So, in the first years after the Soviet collapse, Russia found itself surrounded by some of the most unstable countries on earth. There were flashpoints everywhere, not just in the volatile Caucasus but also in Ukraine and Belarus, Russia's Slavic neighbors to the west. Russia and Ukraine wrangled over the nuclear weapons based in Ukraine but due to be sent to Russia for dismantling under the nuclear nonproliferation treaty. They argued about the division of the Black Sea Fleet based in Sebastopol, in Ukraine, but claimed by Russia. The Russian parliament even issued a claim to Sebastopol. Both were faced with the problem of Crimea, a peninsula mostly populated by Russians and once part of the Russian republic, but given to Ukraine by Nikita Khrushchev in 1954 "as a new clear illustration of the limitless trust and sincere love of the Russian people for the Ukrainian people" (as a resolution of the Ukrainian parliament put it). In 1994 the Crimeans elected as president Yury Meshkov, whose party called for independence from Ukraine as a step toward reunification with Russia. On the same day, in Belarus, the electorate chose as president Aleksandr Lukashenka, who also ran on a platform of reunification. That was the opposite of anti-Russian confrontation, but it was just as far away from the ideal of a Russia surrounded by stable, self-confident, cooperative neighbors.

The economic pressure to restore the empire

The other objective problem bedeviling the postimperial settlement concerned the economic costs of the Soviet breakup. For Russia, as we have seen, the maintenance of the Soviet Union involved large costs. Ironically, so did its collapse—at least in the short term.

The Soviet Union had been a market as well as a country. Factories in one republic were the suppliers of factories in another. To make cigarettes, for example, the filters came from Armenia, the paper from Latvia, and the tobacco from Georgia. Interrepublic trade links were badly disrupted when the Soviet Union broke down. Trade between the republics collapsed between 1990 and 1994. That hurt Russia directly, because the other republics no longer had money to buy Russian oil (Russia was their largest, often their only, fuel supplier). The president of the Russian Union of Industrialists, Arkady Volsky, claimed that 40 percent of the fall of Russian output in 1992 could be attributed to the breakdown of Soviet trade, while the president of Kazakhstan claimed in 1992 that the trade slump accounted for two-thirds of the total fall in output of all the republics.[1] To prevent the neighbors' slump from becoming even worse, Russia subsidized the other states. It exported much of its oil to them cheaply and provided subsidized credits. In 1992 Russia exported 11.7 percent of its GDP to the other ex-Soviet states, an enormous amount, especially for a country whose own output was falling fast.

The slump had an impact on the second group of problems that bedeviled Russia's search for a postimperial settlement: the attitude of the Russians themselves.

Russia's psychological problems

Two powerful groups were directly hurt by the post-Soviet economic collapse: the chairmen of the huge factories with branches spread over the former Soviet Union, and the generals of the Red Army. Together they formed a large part of the so-called nomenklatura.

"The nomenklatura of the former USSR," writes Dmitri Furman, a member of the Institute of Europe, a think tank in Moscow, "is a vast network of personal relationships and clans. Two former secretaries of regional Communist party committees or two factory managers will continue to maintain normal relations even if they find themselves in different states."[2] They will continue to behave in the old ways, that is, doing deals, buying and selling where they can, and using their contacts to advance their own careers. As captains of the old integrated Soviet economy, they found the post-Soviet disintegration hard to accept.

The nomenklatura included the generals of the old Red Army. As with the old industrial elite, much of the military top brass resented the Soviet collapse, and especially the carving up of the Red Army. The instability of the near abroad affected Russia's generals both because they were charged with trying to defend the country's new borders and because they were soon asked to send peacekeeping forces to their turbulent neighbors.

The discontent of those two groups further complicated Russia's postimperial problems. Even without them those problems would have been complex enough because of the psychology involved.

Like the citizens of most imperial nations, the Russians found the loss of empire hard to understand. Their difficulty was worse than most, because for centuries they had lived in one state with their neighbors and because the Soviet Union broke up so quickly that there was no time for the Russian public to get used to the idea.

Before the Soviet breakup a prominent philosopher, Aleksandr Tsipko, argued that "many Russians have forgotten not only that they are Russians but that they are Slavs and are bound by one common fate to the Ukrainians and Belorussians."[3] Afterward, as Boris Fedorov, a leading reformer, put it, "A lot of my friends find it very difficult to think of Kazakhs or Ukrainians as members of a truly independent country. To them, this independence is make-believe." The Ukrainians are in no doubt of Russia's attitude. "I have many friends in top positions in Moscow," Ukraine's deputy foreign minister, Andrei Makarenko, said in early 1994. "After the third glass of vodka they always ask me the same question: 'What do you need this independence for?'" So there was a psychological barrier to the post-Soviet settlement, as well as problems of political instability and slump.

Will there be conflicts over the Russians abroad?

The third of Russia's problem was that of its kith and kin in the near abroad. There were roughly 11 million Russians in Ukraine, most of them in the industrialized east of the country. In Latvia they formed one-third of the population and over half of the capital city, Riga. There were relatively few Russians in the turbulent Caucasus, but in Central Asia they formed a high-profile minority: Most of the managers and skilled industrial workers were Russians who had been sent to the poorest parts of the Soviet Union to build an industrial base there. "We left at least 25 million of our compatriots behind," Sergei Stankevich, a former deputy mayor of Moscow, says. "They all have relatives in Russia. These family ties mean there is an immediate and emotional reaction as soon as there is conflict around them."

In 1992 Estonia, attempting to reestablish indigenous Estonian law quickly, applied the citizenship law that had been in force before the invasion of the country by the Soviet army, that is, a law of 1938. Only those who had been Estonian citizens at that time, or their direct descendants, could claim citizenship as of right. Others had to apply, which took at least a year and required a language test. Estonia held an election in September 1992. Only citizens could vote. None of the ethnic Russians who had settled in Estonia when it was part of the Soviet Union had acquired citizenship by then, so none could vote. In all, 42 percent of the Estonian population, mostly Russians, were disfranchised in the first post-communist election.

Estonia was not the most troublesome problem for the ethnic Russians abroad, nor was eastern Ukraine, where the largest number of Russians lived. In both countries the local Russians, after initial disputes, began to accommodate themselves to the new regimes. In Moldova, however, the Russian-speakers rebelled against the government and, with the help of Russian troops from the former Soviet garrison, set up a secessionist state. More worrisome still, at least potentially, was Kazakhstan, the giant of Central Asia. That country is almost divided in half: 40 percent of the population is Kazakh and 38 percent is Russian (a hundred other ethnic groups account for the remainder). The Russians are overwhelmingly concentrated in the north of the country, on the border with Russia itself. The province of North Kazakhstan is 90 percent Russian; every province in the northern half of the country, which includes the second largest town, Karaganda, is over two-thirds Russian. That problem could become hard to manage. In the first five years after independence, there were increasing demands for a vigorous "Kazakhstan for the Kazakhs" policy. Even Nursultan Nazarbaev, the Kazakh president, who mostly managed to keep ethnic tensions low, gave a warning to Russia, couched in deliberately offensive terms: "Any talk about the protection of Russians living in Kazakhstan," he said, "reminds one of the times of Hitler, who also started off with the question of protecting the Sudeten Germans."4 If he were ever to pursue a strongly pro-Kazakh, anti-Russian policy, he risks provoking a Russian backlash in the part of the country that Aleksandr Solzhenitsyn calls "southern Siberia."

In short, then, the collapse of the Soviet Union left Russia facing three problems: instability and economic travails among its neighbors; its own citizens' psychological reluctance to accept the loss of empire; and the special problem of kith and kin left in the near abroad. The difficulties were always going to be immense. The question was how Russia would respond to them. Would it keep calm, ignore the problems, and seek a negotiated postimperial settlement? Or would it use the problems as excuses to reestablish the empire?

Russia as Big Brother

In 1993 and 1994 the worst fears appeared to be borne out. This was what might be called the saber-rattling phase of Russian policy, a period of aggression and expansionism. It was dictated largely by the army and was characterized by military destabilization of the neighbors, fierce defense of kith and kin abroad, and, in domestic political debate, by demands to rebuild a Great Russia.

The outbreak of Russian toughness began quite suddenly in the summer of 1993. In the spring of that year relations between the former Soviet states seemed to be in virtual deadlock over the future of the Commonwealth of Independent States. This was the organization hurriedly set up in December 1991 to oversee the dismantling of the Soviet Union. Russia's foreign minister, Andrei Kozyrev, had claimed that "the main priority of Russian diplomacy is the formation of the Commonwealth of Independence States." Several Central Asian states, notably Kazakhstan, wanted a strong CIS. But Ukraine wanted a weak one, fearing that it would be an instrument for Russian control. With Russia hesitating to take a strong lead lest it drive Ukraine out, countless CIS meetings came and went, producing either nothing at all or agreements that were ignored in practice.

By early autumn the picture had been transformed. Six of the non-Russian states had signed defense treaties with Russia. Five sought to set up a new currency area with Russia and promised to coordinate their monetary, fiscal, banking, and foreign-exchange relations with it. Two nonmembers, Georgia and Azerbaijan, were asking to join the CIS. Of the fifteen former Soviet republics, it seemed that only the Baltic three—Lithuania, Latvia, and Estonia—had managed to make a clean break. And even they received the unsubtle reminder from Russia's Foreign Minister "not to forget certain geopolitical realities"—i.e., that Russia is huge and well armed. It was a little like watching a nest of Matryoshka dolls, which had broken apart upon the collapse of the Soviet Union, reassemble itself, with all but the three smallest dolls jumping back inside Mother Russia.

The process began in Central Asia. There, the former communist government of Tajikistan, which was engaged in a civil war with Muslim rebels supported from Afghanistan, called in Russian forces. All the Central Asian governments welcomed Russia's involvement. For them, Russia stood as a defender of the region's old communist regimes against Muslim rebels. Russia's Deputy Defense Minister Andrei Kokoshin likened Russia's attitude toward Central Asia to that of France toward its former colonies in Africa: close both commercially and militarily.[5] Russia's defense ministry saw the local acquiescence in its intervention in Tajikistan as confirmation of the army's view that Russia's most defensible southern border was the Oxus (Amu-Darya) River between Tajikistan and Afghanistan, not the steppe between Kazakhstan and Russia itself.

On May 15th the Central Asian states, plus Russia and Armenia, signed a mutual defense treaty. Given the huge disparity of size and military might between Russia and the rest, such a treaty could only mean, of course, that Russia would come to the smaller states' defense on its own terms. On August 24 those same states agreed to set up a collective security council of their foreign and defense ministers, with attendant bureaucracy.

Even nonmembers of the CIS began edging closer to Russia. Georgia had been among the most militantly anti-Russian of all former Soviet states. In 1991 it had elected as its first president Zviad Gamsakhurdia, a former political prisoner and a passionate believer that his country faced twin evils: communism and Russia. His policies led first to civil war and then to Russian intervention in Abkhazia. His successor, Eduard Shevardnadze (Gorbachev's foreign minister), made far-reaching concessions to Russia in the hope of bringing peace. In August 1993 he accepted Russian peacekeepers' control over Abkhazia. And in February 1994 he and Yeltsin (by then nicknamed the Tsar of Transcaucasus) signed a treaty giving Russia military bases in Georgia, allowing it to station troops on Georgia's frontier with Turkey, and committing it to train and arm the Georgian army. The treaty in effect confirmed the former Soviet republic's reentry into the Russian orbit.

Azerbaijan had also stayed out of the CIS, as its parliament had refused to ratify its president's decision to join. It, too, faced turmoil. Military reverses in its war with Armenia over Nagorno-Karabakh soon led to the electoral defeat of the first post-Soviet government. A nationalist regime took over and led the country even farther from the CIS, forging close ties with Turkey. Then, further military losses precipitated a coup against the government and brought back the man ousted as Azerbaijani leader as long ago as 1985: Heidar Aliev, who had been Communist party boss under Leonid Brezhnev. Many Azerbaijanis claimed that both the coup and Aliev's return had been engineered by the Russian army. If so, it was the third time Russia had intervened against an elected nationalist to ensure his replacement by a former communist prepared to bring his country back into Moscow's orbit. First there was Tajikistan, then Georgia, now Azerbaijan. Aliev promptly announced that his country would attend the next CIS summit in Moscow.

In December all the states of the former Soviet Union except the Baltic three and Moldova signed a collective security treaty, which in effect subordinated the signatories' defense and military policies to Russia. Moldova, meanwhile, was dragooned into the CIS. After its parliament had failed to ratify CIS membership in August, it was told that unless it reconfirmed its membership by November 1993 it would face punitive tariffs.

By early 1994, then, all the former Soviet republics except the Baltic three had been browbeaten or cajoled into tolerating a degree of Russian involvement in their affairs that none would have considered acceptable in 1992. Before Russia's intervention, for example, neither Moldova nor Georgia wished to join the CIS or accept Russian military bases. After Russia's intervention, both had agreed to both. The scene, it appeared, was being set for the re-creation of a new Greater Russia.

Not so tough with the near abroad

During 1994, however, there were signs of change. The saber-rattling period of involvement began to end, giving way to what might be called an arm-twisting federalism. The new policy continued to project Russian power. The difference was a matter of emphasis and means. Now Russia began to stress economic pressure rather than military intervention, trade rather than destabilization, the manipulation of local rivalries rather than the direct imposition of might and will. Attempts at economic integration to create a Russian ruble zone failed. A doctrine of lebensraum (carving out "room to live") gave way to a kind of Monroesky doctrine (stay out of our backyard).

In August almost all Russian troops left the Baltic states, more or less on schedule.[6] In Moldova, Russia disbanded its local army, which had been propping up the rebels of Transdnestria. In February 1994 senior Russian officials refused to see Yury Meshkov, the president of Crimea, who visited Moscow in February 1994, a month after his election, to drum up support for his policy of reunifying the peninsula with Russia. Yeltsin and Chernomyrdin both refused to see him, and Chernomyrdin reiterated that Russia had no claims on Crimea. When the city council of Sebastopol (Crimea's largest port) declared that it was legally part of Russia, the Russian government and parliament brushed the declaration aside, saying they had no desire to warm their hands on the misfortunes of others.

Where once the army had been the most influential maker of policy, in 1994 business and economic interests came to the fore. In Azerbaijan, a Russian oil company, LUKoil, dismissing objections from Russia's foreign ministry, joined Azerbaijan's government and a Western-led consortium in the "deal of the century," a $5-billion agreement to drill for oil in the Caspian Sea. And when, in October 1994, the new president of Ukraine, Leonid Kuchma, began serious radical economic reform, Russia (Ukraine's largest creditor) offered large trade credits to help back the reform and help ensure that it would not be derailed by the country's need to buy imports.

The end of the ruble zone

Most important, Russian reformers managed to thwart attempts to integrate the finances of the former Soviet Union in a ruble zone that would have extended administrative control by Russia throughout the region. The ruble zone fell apart in four stages between April 1993 and July 1994.

In early 1993 ten of the former Soviet republics, including Russia, were still using old Soviet rubles. With the cooperation of the Russian Central Bank, the other nine countries were able to print money to finance their imports from Russia and then pass much of the inflationary consequences back to Russia itself. In April 1993, after a battle with the bank and its allies in parliament, Boris Fedorov, then finance minister, managed to end those inflationary credits from Russia. Thereafter the other republics could not print money at will, though they continued to use the ruble.

Then, on Saturday morning, July 24, the Russian Central Bank suddenly announced that all banknotes issued before 1993 would become worthless on July 26 and that Russians alone would be permitted to exchange old banknotes for new. Because there were restrictions placed on the exchange of notes, the decision was immensely unpopular in Russia, but its biggest impact was on the other nine republics. The decree forced them either to submit their monetary policy to Russian control or to set up their own currencies. Four of them—Azerbaijan, Georgia, Moldova, and Turkmenistan—took the latter course. Completely unprepared for the switch, they experienced instant hyperinflation. The other countries continued to use the ruble, but now, because Russia decided to supply them only with pre-1993 rubles, they faced severe cash shortages. By early August, then, only six countries were still using the ruble, and Russia alone was using the new rubles.

On September 7 the six —Russia, Armenia, Belarus, Kazakhstan,

Tajikistan, and Uzbekistan—attempted to re-create what they called "a ruble zone of a new type." They signed an agreement which aimed to set up a reunified currency area and promised to coordinate their monetary, fiscal, banking, and customs policies.

On the face of it, this was a little like the European Union's attempt to create a single currency. The EU's project, however, is to take place between countries that are far more stable than any in the former Soviet Union, is subject to more stringent conditions, and is spread out over many years. It is also supposed to create a rock-solid new common currency. The post-Soviet deal was quite different. It said that the Russians would control the supply of rubles but that others "will carry out credit emission within limits agreed to with the Russian side." Had that condition been put into effect, Fedorov argued, the others could have printed money at Russia's expense, debauching the ruble further. In practice, the agreement foundered because it depended on overly ambitious and vague promises about economic coordination, which were supposed to be fulfilled within a matter of months, even weeks. The reformers were able to insist that the other countries meet strict criteria before using the ruble. None was able to meet them. In the autumn of 1993 three more countries (Kazakhstan, Uzbekistan, and Armenia) abandoned the ruble zone and introduced their own currencies.

That left two: Tajikistan and Belarus. Tajikistan was a special case. Russia supplied it with new rubles for humanitarian and security reasons. It was Belarus that saw the last gasp of the ruble zone. On January 5, 1994, Russia's prime minister, Viktor Chernomyrdin, signed a declaration with his opposite number in Belarus, Vyacheslav Kebich, saying the two countries would use a common currency issued by Russia but with Belarus (again) able to issue credits. Russian reformers again opposed the currency union on the grounds that it would cost Russia millions. This time there were other considerations as well: The declaration breached the Russian constitution, which said that only the Russian Central Bank could issue rubles. It also envisaged implementation of the currency union without parliamentary ratification. The Russian parliament objected to both ideas. In Belarus, the central bank said it regretted the loss of sovereignty. Attempts to renegotiate the arrangement finally produced a tame and ill-defined agreement on "economic union" in April 1996, which promised much but committed its signatories to little.

Was Russian peacekeeping justified?

Did all this mean a real change of heart by the Russians? Economically, it surely did. By 1995 the ruble zone had failed, undermining attempts to introduce discretion and administrative controls into the economies of the former Soviet Union.

But when it came to Russia's political and military involvement in the near abroad, many in the West argued that there had been no real change. All that had happened, they said, was that the Russians had got what they wanted—for the moment. Russian peacekeeping troops remained in Moldova, Georgia, and Tajikistan. The issue of Crimea had not been settled. Russia was continuing to strong-arm Azerbaijan. Kozyrev had said Russia wanted thirty military bases in the republics of the former Soviet Union, and in 1991–95 it made considerable progress toward that goal.

The fact that Russian interests were served by peacekeeping, however, did not in itself prove that the peacekeeping operations were merely pretexts to restore Russian control. In 1994 America intervened in Haiti, and France in Rwanda. The interests of both countries were served by those operations, but that did not mean the operations (to restore the elected president to Haiti and to stop genocide in Rwanda) were unjustified. Could Russia make similar claims? To answer that question, it is worth applying three tests.

First, were the disputes so bad that negotiation was impossible? Most were. The three chief military operations took place in Tajikistan, Moldova, and Georgia. In Tajikistan, a full-blown civil war was raging. In Moldova the Russian-speakers on the eastern side of the Dniestr River had grabbed control of their region by violence and had set up their own government. Even in Georgia, the dispute looked intractable: The two sides had been fighting intermittently since 1989; the Abkhaz had never accepted Georgian sovereignty.

Second, did the intervention increase the chances of a settlement?

In Moldova and Tajikistan, the answer was yes. The bitterness of the fighting in both countries before Russia intervened precluded quick settlement, but the Russian-imposed truce at least made peace possible. In Tajikistan the underlying causes of the ethnic and clan conflict remained unresolved. But in Moldova, where the arrival of Aleksandr Lebed as commander of the Russian troops had stopped the fighting in three days, matters improved significantly. The main fear of the Russian-speaking rebels had been that Moldovan politicians would seek to reunify the country with Romania, of which Moldova had once been part. But the political party that supported this idea, the National Front, did badly in parliamentary elections in 1994. That made compromise possible. In 1995 the rebel region made a significant economic concession in adopting the Moldovan currency as its own. The two sides also signed an agreement promising not to use force to settle their dispute. In Abkhazia, however, the Russian intervention made a settlement harder to reach than it might otherwise have been. Though fighting between the two sides might well have been unavoidable, Russia supported the Abkhaz with fighter aircraft and information, helping them to military victory and making them less inclined to look for peace. Here, Russian intervention was far from evenhanded.

Third, did the intervention serve the interests of locals as well as Russians? That is perhaps the most important test by the standard of international diplomacy. It was a big worry in the saber-rattling stage, because the fear then was that Russia would destabilize its neighbors and then use peacekeeping forces to put puppet governments in power. That seemed to be happening in Azerbaijan in 1993, when the elected president, a dissident former professor of Turkish named Abdulfaz Elchibey, was overthrown by local rebels with the help, according to some, of Russia. But his replacement, Heidar Aliev, was later confirmed by election. It was not clear that Azerbaijanis' wishes had been flouted. In the three places where its soldiers intervened, Russia had the support of some local figures but not others. In Moldova, Russian troops had support among local Russian-speakers but were condemned by the government of Moldova itself. In Georgia, though Russia backed the Abkhazian rebels against him, Eduard Shevardnadze also benefited, because Russian troops helped him put down another rebellion, this one by the supporters of the predecessor whom he had ousted as president in 1993, Zviad Gamsakhurdia. "I trust Russia," Shevardnadze repeated frequently on Georgian television. In Tajikistan the Russians persuaded the government to hold a contested presidential election in 1994 after it had first attempted to arrange one in which the local opposition was not permitted to put up candidates.

In Tajikistan, then, Russia passed the tests of intervention reasonably clearly, even though it did not settle the clan war. In Moldova the Russian involvement helped advance a peace settlement, even though the Moldovan government initially opposed Russia's actions. In Georgia the Russians did have the president's support, even though they made the prospects of settling the dispute with Abkhazia more distant. The pattern, in other words, was mixed. Given that some confusion and mismanagement was inevitable, the mix suggests that Russia was not trying to reconquer the empire. It put at least as much emphasis on trying to achieve a postimperial settlement as on imperial ambition. And the difficulties it encountered can be traced to the sheer scale of the post-Soviet problems.

Will any state rejoin Russia?

The first few years of post-Soviet independence wrought two important changes that made the re-creation of the empire less likely.

The first was that Russia's neighbors began to pull themselves together, both economically and politically. In 1994 most of their economies hit rock bottom after the ruble zone collapsed. They then began to improve. Inflation began to fall, production to rise. That was important, because much depends on the stability of the former Soviet republic themselves: The more stable they are, the more unlikely it is that Russia will attempt to intervene in their affairs and the higher the cost of doing so. The weaker and more unstable they are, the more Russia will be tempted to meddle.

New countries become real states simply by being so. Over the years, they develop more stable institutions, which can appeal for support to the population. And, with the development of real politics with local support, the states are seen as legitimate by outsiders, too.

The most important change of that kind took place in Ukraine. "It cannot be stressed too much," the American foreign-policy expert and scholar Zbigniew Brzezinski argues, "that ... Ukraine is the single most important test of Russia's willingness to accept the end of empire; without Ukraine Russia ceases to be an empire."[7] Unless it contains Little Russia (as Ukraine was sometimes called), there will be no Great one. Russia would be like a latter-day Byzantine empire, shorn of its most valuable provinces in the west and doomed to succumb to more dynamic forces from the east.

In 1994 the election of a new Ukrainian president and his espousal of economic reform made possible Ukraine's rescue from the hyperinflationary collapse it had faced in 1993. Such a collapse would have been the surest recipe for Russian intervention in Ukraine. Instead, nationalists in western Ukraine rallied behind the free-market reforms of Kuchma, even though he came from the Russified east of the country. This began to heal the rift that runs through Ukraine, dividing the rural, nationalist west from the industrial, Russified east. Ukraine signed the nuclear nonproliferation treaty in December 1994, after two years of prevarication, settling another cause of friction between it and Russia. By becoming nonnuclear, Ukraine removed the main barrier to better relations with the West and opened the way to aid and advice. By 1995 that left only Crimea to divide the countries. Solving the peninsula problem will depend on tolerance on both sides. In 1995 that tolerance survived its first test, when Russia refused to panic after Ukraine suspended the Crimean government in the wake of inter-Crimean infighting. Russia's own logic in Chechnya suggests Crimea should not leave Ukraine. The two sides' continued calm behavior, however, cannot be relied upon.

By 1995 some of the other new states had not reached Ukraine's stage of nation-building. Kazakhstan had yet to face its potentially explosive test over ethnic tensions between Russians and Kazakhs. In Belarus politics seemed almost schizophrenic: On the one hand, the country had voted for a president who campaigned for reunification with Russia; on the other, every attempt to implement that policy (such as the currency union) met with dogged opposition. Belarus is the country nearest to Russia in language; it is also the country with the weakest sense of nationalism. During the 1990s, domestic politics there were highly unstable, riven by conflicts between an authoritarian president and a communist-dominated parliament. The close ties between the two countries and the domestic conflicts within Belarus itself made that country the one most likely to rejoin Russia. But even there, everything depended on Belarus itself. And, as Boris Fedorov remarked, "The easiest way to create Belarussian nationalism would be for us to take over the place again."

By 1995 Russia was beginning to treat the various republics of the former Soviet Union not as a single lump called "the near abroad" but separately. Its relations with Ukraine were dominated by its bilateral problem over Crimea and, to a lesser extent, nuclear weapons. Relations with the Baltic states were dominated by the Balts' desire to join NATO and the European Union and were strongly influenced by the close ties between the Baltic trio and Scandinavia. In the Caucasus, the basic issue was that of oil pipelines, especially whether the pipelines for pumping oil from the Caspian Sea would run through Russia.

A second change lay within Russia itself. A potentially momentous change seemed to be taking place in the attitude of Russians toward their former colonies. The change was indicated by the public outcry over Russia's invasion of Chechnya. More than 85 percent of the population opposed it, even though Chechnya was actually part of the Russian Federation. An opinion poll by the All-Russia Center for Public Opinion Research in August 1995 suggested that opposition to force on behalf of Russians in the near abroad was just as overwhelming. Asked whether they would support sending troops if there were a dispute and negotiation had failed to resolve it, 83 percent said no. Nationalism, it seemed, was an elite concern, not a popular one.

Emil Pain, a sociologist and Boris Yeltsin's adviser on interethnic affairs, spent 1993 and 1994 studying Russian attitudes toward their ill-defined national identity. In 1993, he found, over 80 percent of Russians, asked what they thought of as their real homeland, replied, "the Soviet Union." At the end of 1994 the answer, for over 80 percent, had shrunk to the Slav areas: Russia itself, Ukraine, Belarus, and northern Kazakhstan. More than 80 percent of those polled said they did not want to live in the same state as the Central Asians; over three-quarters excluded the Transcaucasian states.

Evaluation

It was still not Russia, of course, but it was a step toward Russia. The step was reflected in the changing political lobbies in favor of getting the empire back. In 1992 and 1993 the 25 million Russians abroad were a stick with which the opposition beat the government. In 1995 only one serious politician was openly advocating the restoration of the Soviet Union: Gennady Zyuganov, the leader of the Communist party. The parliamentary opposition concentrated instead on domestic issues: crime, corruption, and privatization.

It is true that parliament still contained imperialists. In March 1996 the communists pushed through a vote reasserting the "legitimacy" of the former Soviet Union and denouncing the CIS. But the vote was itself denounced by all the ex-Soviet republics concerned (except Belarus) and by parliament's upper house. Taken aback, the communists declared the vote "nonbinding." At the same time, Russia also had an articulate body of opinion arguing for "isolationism," that is, promoting the interests of Russians in Russia. That was the policy of Yegor Gaidar and others who opposed the ruble zone on the ground that the cost to Russia of bolting on the unreformed economies of Belarus and Ukraine would be ruinous.

The deeper researchers dug into popular sentiment, the more evidence they found that people were beginning to think of Russia, and only Russia, as their home. Asked whether they would be willing to see Russian lives lost or money spent for unification with the Slav republics, Russians overwhelmingly said no. The residual feeling of pan-Slavism is contracting. What began as a political tactic to embarrass Gorbachev in 1990—Russia's declaration of sovereignty—was becoming something real in 1995. "I am sure" concluded Pain, "that in the end Russians will consider Russia to be their homeland."

Chapter 13

Russia and the West:
Friends or foes?

How much did Russian policy change? · Did Kozyrev do a U-turn? ·
What happened to the window of opportunity? · Why the West distrusts
Russia · Why Russia distrusts the West · Russia's non-Western concerns ·
What Russia and the West have in common · Evaluation

The end of the Cold War promised to remake the world by creating a "new world order." No longer were countries corralled into opposing armed camps. Russia was governed by people who shared the West's basic values of democracy, free markets, and respect for human rights. The new Russian government was committed to regional stability in the near abroad and cooperation with the West; it had shed its imperial pretensions. Countries, freed from the ideological conflicts of superpowers, would now order their affairs according to the things they had in common rather than the things that divided them. Or so it seemed.

The high hopes were dashed. Between 1992 and 1995 Russia and the West became embroiled in a series of disputes in Eastern Europe and the former Soviet Union. They argued about the expansion of NATO, policy in the former Yugoslavia, and Russia's behavior in the near abroad. Why were the hopes dashed? Was a great opportunity wasted? Are Russia and the West now doomed to confrontation?

269

How much did Russian policy change?

The most common explanation for the disappointment was that Russia changed. On the face of it, that looks plausible: Russian foreign policy did indeed look very different in 1995 from what it had been in 1991.

To begin with, Russian policy had been extremely friendly toward the West. Before the collapse of the Soviet Union, the Russian leadership had espoused the most liberal of causes—Baltic independence, drastic arms cuts, and withdrawal of Soviet troops from Cuba. Immediately afterward, Russia's president and his foreign minister had articulated a strongly pro-Western foreign policy and called for a "strategic partnership" between Russia and America.

Boris Yeltsin had argued that Russia had joined (he said rejoined) the Western community of nations and that the historic conflicts between Russia and the West were over. Continuing Mikhail Gorbachev's nuclear policy, he had signed two new disarmament treaties and then negotiated the Washington charter, which promised to set up a "Euro-Atlantic peacekeeping capability." The Warsaw Pact, which had subordinated the armies of Eastern and Central Europe to Soviet command, had been scrapped. Russia had joined the main international economic institutions, the International Monetary Fund and World Bank, and had applied to join the World Trade Organization. It had even promised to join the Partnership for Peace program, the waiting room for NATO, the West's defensive shield.

Within the former Soviet Union, Andrei Kozyrev, the foreign minister, had vowed to respect the rights and boundaries of Russia's newly freed fellow Soviet republics, arguing that the best way to protect the rights of Russian-speakers abroad was to show respect for human rights in Russia itself, using the power of example. Even as late as 1993 he was still arguing that "Russia and its East European neighbors are grappling with the same strategic task, that of securing a worthy place in the club of highly developed, democratic states. The day of the . . . Brezhnev doctrine [that communist revolutions are irreversible] has passed." By then, however, something very strange was starting to happen.

Did Kozyrev do a U-turn?

On December 14, 1992, at a grand meeting of the Conference on Security and Cooperation in Europe, Kozyrev strode to the podium to address dozens of his fellow foreign ministers. This is what he said:

"First. While keeping to the course of joining Europe, we are distinctly conscious that our traditions are in large part, if not fundamentally, oriented toward Asia, and this determines the limits of our rapprochement with Western Europe. We see that although there has been some evolution in the aims of NATO and the Western European community, their basic policies remain unchanged, such as their plans for strengthening their military presence in the Baltic states and other parts of the former USSR and interference in Bosnia and in the internal affairs of Yugoslavia. It is apparent that the sanctions against the united republics of Yugoslavia were dictated by these policies. We demand that they be abolished, and, if this does not happen, we reserve the right to take necessary unilateral measures in protecting our interests, especially as the sanctions are inflicting economic damage upon us. Serbia can count on the support of great Russia in its struggle with the current government.

"Second. The territory of the former Soviet Union cannot be considered a zone in which CSCE norms are wholly applicable. It is in essence a postimperial area in which Russia must protect its own interests through the use of all available means, including those military and economic. We will firmly insist that the former republics of the USSR immediately join a new federation or confederation, and we will take a tough stance on this point.

"Third. Those who do not take these interests seriously and think that Russia is in for the same fate as the Soviet Union should remember that the state in question is capable of standing up for itself and its friends. It should be understood that we are ready to participate constructively in the work of the CSCE, although we will be very wary regarding ideas leading to interference in internal affairs."

He then walked off, leaving a distinguished audience with mouths agape. "Fundamentally oriented toward Asia . . . we reserve the right to take necessary unilateral measures in protecting our interests. . . .

The territory of the former Soviet Union . . . is in essence a postimperial area in which Russia must protect its own interests through the use of all available means. . . . We will firmly insist that the former republics of the USSR immediately join a new federation or confederation." Nothing like that had been heard from Moscow's foreign minister since the days of Andrei Gromyko, the Mr. Nyet of Soviet foreign policy in the Cold War. And this was the supposedly liberal Kozyrev, who at that very moment was fighting for his political survival back in Moscow against nationalists baying for his blood.

A few hours later, Kozyrev returned to the podium. That speech, he explained, did not reflect either official Russian policy or his own personal views. It was a dramatization of what might happen if hard-liners were to come to power in Moscow. The reaction of the assembled ministers now ranged from puzzlement and relief to annoyance. Germany's foreign minister, Klaus Kinkel, upbraided Kozyrev. Such behavior, he said, was not a serious way of conducting foreign policy.

The occasion for Kozyrev's outburst had been a dispute over how to handle the unfolding war in former Yugoslavia. The Russians felt they were being excluded by America and Europe from peacemaking efforts in the conflict. Kozyrev was, in effect, making a plea for consultation over Bosnia. In mistaking the manner for the matter, the Western ministers seemed to confirm Russia's feeling that the West was not taking it seriously and did not understand its concerns about either NATO or the post-Soviet settlement. But the West's attitude was understandable. To Westerners, Kozyrev's speech could hardly be discounted as a joke. Many thought that the confrontational policy he was describing was not just a possibility: It seemed already to be taking place. The whole episode encapsulated the confusion, misunderstanding, and uncertainty that surrounded Russia and the West after the Cold War ended.

A year later, in February 1994, Kozyrev returned to Scandinavia. This time, in Copenhagen, he made a straightforward policy statement. "We are not allergic to NATO," he told the Danish Foreign Policy Society, "but we don't understand the discussions to the effect that NATO must give security guarantees to the countries of Central Europe and in the long term accept them as members of the alliance. How are these states threatened, and by whom?"

Suddenly Russia was becoming much more assertive in its dealings with the West. Faced now with another crisis in former Yugoslavia, Russia adopted unilateral action. NATO had threatened to bomb the Bosnian Serbs besieging Sarajevo, Bosnia's capital. Just before the ultimatum expired, Russia negotiated a cease-fire. Bosnian Serb gunners agreed to pull back their artillery, and Russian troops went to the city as peacekeepers. It was an intriguing and defining moment in Russian diplomacy. The West had threatened the Serbs, historic allies of Russia. Russia had forestalled the threat. The West had attempted to act on its own in former Yugoslavia. Russia had shown the West that it could not ignore Russian power. Yet at the same time the West's aim—the withdrawal of Serb heavy weapons and their placement under UN supervision—had been achieved. Russia had implemented a Western policy and had served its own purpose (projecting Russian power abroad) in doing so. As Kozyrev's deputy for Bosnia, Vitaly Churkin, remarked, "The West should learn a lesson from the current Bosnian crisis. The lesson is that Russia should be treated as an equal partner, not the way some of them did."

By then Russia's attitude toward the states of the former Soviet Union had also become more assertive. On September 28, 1993, Kozyrev told the General Assembly of the United Nations that "no international organization can replace our peacekeeping efforts in this specific post-Soviet space." That was the summer Russia spent twisting the arms of its neighbors to acquire military bases on their soil. A little later, in a newspaper interview, Kozyrev called withdrawing troops from the surrounding former Soviet republics "an unwarranted loss of influence."[1] A year further on, the West insisted on putting forward proposals for expanding NATO that the Russians had not had time to study. Offended, Kozyrev said Russia would not implement its partnerships-for-peace program with NATO. "In the future, our foreign policy will continue to defend Russia's vital interests," he said, "even in those cases where it is contrary to the interests of the West." Just in case anyone was not clear about this, he reiterated: "Russia will not listen to the West's lessons and lectures."

All this undoubtedly marked a change. In the course of about a year, Russian foreign policy had gone from being pro-Western and dominated by negotiations over aid to self-confidently assertive. It had also changed from being controversial domestically, assailed on all sides by Yeltsin's opponents, to commanding near-consensus. In the spring of 1993 two of Kozyrev's most prominent critics, the chairman of parliament's foreign affairs committee and Russia's former ambassador to the United Nations, both said that the change of policy should be welcomed, not made an excuse for demanding further changes.[2]

Certainly, the turnaround was striking. But did it mean that Russia was turning into an adversary of the West? Some Westerners argued that it did. They said Russia's reforms were failing economically and politically, and as a result Great Russian nationalists were becoming more influential, driving Russia into a confrontation with the West. That argument was heard frequently after the electoral victory of Vladimir Zhirinovsky in December 1993. Yet the conclusion was greatly exaggerated.

In 1994 Russia supported American and international attempts to make the renegade government of North Korea open up its nuclear facilities to international inspection. On the matter of Iraq, a country that had been one of the Soviet Union's allies in the Middle East, Russia supported the Western alliance during the Gulf War and after.

Russia and the West certainly came into conflict over expanding NATO. Russia vehemently opposed the expansion of NATO eastward to include Poland, arguing that this represented an attempt by Westerners to encircle Russia militarily. On the other hand, the country made no attempt to rush into the great power vacuum left in Eastern and Central Europe after the collapse of Soviet power and the dissolution of the Warsaw Pact. On a visit to Budapest in November 1992, Boris Yeltsin was unequivocal in denouncing the Soviet Union's occupation of Hungary, especially its suppression of the 1956 uprising. "The 1956 uprising was not in vain," he said. "It showed that not only individuals but an entire people understood they have no future without ridding themselves of Communist dictators."[3] Russia brought its last troops out of eastern Germany on schedule in 1994.

In former Yugoslavia, Russia did not attempt to disrupt the peace-making efforts of the International Contact Group, which it formed with America, Britain, France, and Germany in 1994. Yegor Gaidar once described Serbia, a Slavic, Orthodox country, as "one of the core issues that the West has to understand Russia cannot budge on." In fact, in the UN Security Council, Russia did not veto various resolutions aimed at restraining the Serbs in Bosnia. When, in the late summer of 1995, NATO started aerial bombardments of the Bosnian Serbs, Russia huffed and puffed, but did nothing. And in November 1995, Russia said it would provide at least 1,500 troops to the international force sent to implement the Bosnian peace agreement initialed that month in Dayton, Ohio; those troops served (what symbolism) under an American general.

In short, though Russian policy did change, that can account for only a small part of the disappointment over the "strategic partnership" between Russia and the West.

What happened to the window of opportunity?

The real cause of the disappointment was that the partnership was based on unrealistic expectations from the start.

There are two broadly differing ways of managing international security. One is the standard balance-of-power approach, whereby stability is achieved by a balance of equal and opposing forces and countries, especially large ones, engage in power politics without much regard for international law or for legal commitments. The balance of terror in the Cold War was an extreme example of this approach. The other is the "institutional approach," whereby groups of countries bind themselves together with legal obligations to ensure their security, and economic and even domestic policies conform with one another. The European Union is the classic example of that approach. Russia began by seeking to adopt the institutional approach in world affairs but ended up being drawn back toward the traditional system of power balances.

The "strategic partnership" envisaged in 1991 was that of a Russia closely bound into an international alliance, rather as Germany had been bound into the Western alliance after 1945. The comparison between the two countries was seductive. Both were weakened, defeated states with long histories of aggressive militarism, in need of help and professing a commitment to liberalism and democracy.

There were, clearly, great differences between the two. The scale of

Germany's defeat in World War II was far greater than Russia's after the Cold War. The Western allies had been left in virtually complete command of Germany in 1945, which they were not, obviously, in Russia in 1991. And post-Soviet Russia remained a world power, which post-Nazi Germany was not.

There were also marked differences between the approach to building institutions for the post–World War II era and what happened after 1991. The years after 1945 were a period of intense institution-building. The United Nations, NATO, and the IMF were all created at that time. The seeds of what became the European Union were planted a little later. There was no comparable effort to build an institutional architecture for the post–Cold War world. The only new body set up after 1991 was the European Bank for Reconstruction and Development, designed to lend money to the former communist east. Russia proposed that NATO and the Warsaw Pact be put under the umbrella of the CSCE, which would become a sort of super-NATO, responsible for maintaining security in America, Europe, and Eurasia. That idea was rejected out of hand, because it would have extended Russia's influence into the West. So, while Germany got full membership in NATO and, later, the fledgling European Union after 1994, Russia was offered only "cooperation agreements" with those bodies after 1991; membership itself was ruled out.

The fate of the Partnership and Cooperation Agreement with the European Union was instructive. The agreement committed the Russians and Europeans to eventual free trade and, in the interim, codified Russia's commercial relations with the EU, its biggest trading partner. The agreement also linked the economic provisions to politics and human rights. It committed both sides to support of democratic and human rights and said that if one breached the commitment, the other could resort to "appropriate measures" (i.e., suspend the agreement). Some Russian hard-liners grumbled about the political provisions, but the Europeans insisted on them: The linkage was characteristic of the European Union's "institutional approach."

The ink was hardly dry on the treaty when war broke out in Chechnya. The European Commission promptly suspended the treaty on human rights grounds. European foreign ministers said it could be reactivated only if there were a cease-fire, humanitarian assistance, progress toward political settlement, and a role as intermediary for the Organization for Security and Cooperation in Europe (the successor to the CSCE). Despite more opposition from Russian hard-liners, the OSCE did set up an office in Grozny. Six months later, in June, the EU signaled that progress had been made on its four conditions, and Kozyrev signed the trade parts of the treaty in July. In the event, then, the episode was a test of Russia's relations with Western Europe; after a rocky start, Russia passed the test. The Europeans had insisted that, if Russia wanted to integrate itself into the West, it had certain standards of behavior to maintain. And the Russians had managed to maintain them—barely. On the other hand, the treaty still fell short of implementing an "institutional approach" to Russo-European relations: It did not clear the way for eventual EU membership for Russia, as analogous treaties with Eastern European countries had, and it still kept up significant trade barriers to Russian products. That was the closest Russia came in 1991–95 to the "institutional approach" to international relations.

The trouble with this approach was that it was predicated on Russia's behaving just like the countries of the West and neglected differences between the two sides that were bound to surface sooner or later.

Why the West distrusts Russia

Most Westerners feared a strong Russia because they saw it as a rival. They hoped that the relatively weak, cooperative Russia of the early 1990s would be a permanent feature of the diplomatic landscape. That hope was always in vain. Even stripped of its former empire, Russia remained a formidable power, with the world's second largest arsenal of nuclear weapons. The collapse of the Soviet Union had reduced Russia's historic power, but not destroyed it.

Russia has been a great power in Europe since about 1700, when Peter the Great defeated Sweden, then one of the strongest military powers in Europe. In 1813, after driving Napoleon from Moscow, Russian armies were camped outside the gates of Paris, and Tsar Alexander I was being hailed as the liberator of Europe. For the first half of the nineteenth century, Russia was the dominant force on the continent, and Nicholas I earned the nickname "the gendarme of Europe." In 1835 Tocqueville made his famous remark: "There are, at the present time, two great nations in the world, which seem to tend towards the same end, although they started from different points: I allude to the Russians and the Americans . . . they have suddenly assumed a most prominent place amongst the nations."[4] As the Hungarian historian Tibor Szamuely pointed out, the striking part of that prediction was the one concerning America; by 1835 Russia was already a great power.[5] It had defeated the Napoleonic empire and would save the Austro-Hungarian one by crushing the Hungarian uprising of 1848. It dismissed the Ottoman empire as the "sick man of Europe." Poland and Finland had actually been part of Russia. "When the Tsar is fishing," Alexander III is supposed to have retorted to a flunky anxious for a reply to the latest Euro-crisis, "Europe can wait." Lenin's withdrawal from World War I began a period of isolation from Western European affairs, but between 1941 and 1945 Russia had resumed its central role: the overwhelming part of the Wehrmacht's forces were occupied on the eastern front in World War II.

Many of those most suspicious of Russia remembered that throughout its history this state without natural borders has flowed back and forth—mostly forth—across the wide plains of Eastern Europe. In 1829 Fyodor Tyuchev described in *Russian Geography* an empire that would reach

From the Nile to the Neva, from the Elbe to China
From the Volga to the Euphrates, from the Ganges to the Danube.[6]

The traditional fear of how Russia would achieve this empire was wryly summed up nearly a quarter of a century after that poem as follows: "It would appear that the natural frontier of Russia runs from Danzig or perhaps Stettin to Trieste. And as sure as conquest follows conquest and annexation follows annexation, so surely would the conquest of Turkey by Russia be only the prelude to the annexation of Hungary, Prussia, Galicia, and the ultimate realization of the Slavonic empire. . . . Having come thus far on the way to universal empire is it probable that this gigantic, swollen state will pause in its career?" Thus declared the *New York Tribune* in 1853, carrying a dispatch from its Europe correspondent, none other than Karl Marx.[7]

Russia in the early 1990s had inherited many of the attributes of a great power from the former Soviet Union and the tsarist empires. Even without Ukraine it is still by far the largest territorial unit in the world, with a population of 150 million. Russia in 1995 had 726 intercontinental nuclear missiles, 95 nuclear bombers, and 45 nuclear submarines, giving it the world's second largest nuclear arsenal after America. It also had the largest army in Europe, with 1.5 million men under arms, and an extensive arms business, with exports all around the world. A quarter of the budget and 5 percent of the nation's income goes for defense.[8] Like all great powers, Russia has its traditional allies, such as Serbia, Greece, and Armenia, and its historical enemies, such as Poland, Turkey, and Germany. And, like all great powers, it is deeply suspected by all its neighbors.

Russia not only preserved great-power attributes. It also maintained great-power ambitions. In his state of the union speech of 1993, Yeltsin proclaimed that "Russia has not yet taken its proper place in the world. . . . Only a strong Russia can guarantee stability in the former Soviet Union. The world also needs a strong Russia." That is a second clear difference between Russia and Germany. Germany was, in political terms, merely a regional European power, a great Switzerland. Russia wanted to be a great power on the world stage. Optimists thought this meant it could be a powerful partner for the West. Pessimists thought it would prove a formidable foe. Both recognized it as a rival.

That is quite a different matter from a partnership in which Russia obediently backs up Western policy in exchange for aid. No one really wants a rival. A strong Russia implies one capable of vying for influence among the West's allies in the Middle East, Africa, and Eastern Europe, just as it was in the Cold War. So it seemed far from certain that Western interests really were served by a powerful Russia, especially if it was in the grip of an expansionist, perhaps military, government.

So much for Western suspicions of Russia. Seen from Russia's side of the partnership, the prospects for close ties were also poor.

Why Russia distrusts the West

From Russia's point of view, the most obvious attraction of the West in 1991–95 was the aid it could offer. The West's aid program was badly botched. Help would have done most good at the very start of the reforms, in November and December 1991, when it might have given the reformers something concrete to show for their efforts. Instead, the IMF wrongly advised the Russians not to set up a separate currency of their own, fearing the impact that would have on the Soviet market.[9] The IMF also insisted, again wrongly, that Russia did not need balance of payments support in 1992, though its imports had fallen by nearly half in 1991. Advisers from the group of seven largest industrial countries ignored Yeltsin's decision to adopt radical economic reform and insisted that the main problem was the financing of the Soviet Union's foreign debt. They sent in debt collectors, demanding Russia hand over its last kopek's worth of foreign exchange. No one in those early days seriously discussed how to help the new Russian reform policies. "Aid" meant food parcels. When aid programs did appear, in 1992 and 1993, they fell far short of what had been promised. President Bush announced Russia would get $24 billion in 1992; $15 billion actually arrived, of which $12.5 billion consisted of government-backed export credits: help to exporters to Russia rather than to Russia itself. Of the real aid ($4.5 billion from the IMF and World Bank) only $1 billion arrived, and that went into building up foreign exchange reserves. Matters improved in 1995, but the failure to deliver aid in the first three years of the reform program undermined the reformers politically and discredited the West in the eyes of many Russians.

Russia's non-Western concerns

It was hardly surprising, then, that Russians decided they could not trust the West to produce the sort of aid they needed. That being so, it followed that it was not worth aligning their country closely with the West.

The argument—frequently asserted in the Russian press—was that Russia had been tricked into subordinating its interests and forced to play second fiddle and got nothing in return. Russia's former ambassador to America, Vladimir Lukin, put it this way: "In recent times there seems to have been two images of my country ingrained in the American political mind. One is of the global Cold War rival. The other is a democratic, Westernized country playing the role of America's junior partner." By sometime in 1993, he said, Russia was getting the worst of both worlds. "At first, Russia was feared but not respected. Then it was respected but not feared. Now Russia is neither respected nor feared."

There were deeper reasons for distrusting the West than feelings of inferiority or disappointment over aid. Even if Russia were able to trust the West, some Russians argued, it should not. Such was the line taken by a group that became influential in foreign policy-making in 1993–95, the so-called Eurasians.[10]

The Eurasians emphasized Russia's unique geographical position and argued that shifts in the balance of power in the world should dictate a foreign policy less closely aligned with the West. Over the four decades of the Cold War, they said, the world was divided between capitalist West and communist East. As that division disappears, it will be replaced by a division between rich North and poor South. Russia straddles the divide. Geographically northern, Russia, the Eurasians said, is more like part of the South economically. Even if reform goes well, they claimed, thirty years will go by before Russia can join the club of rich countries. Even then, Russia's interests will still differ from those of other northern states. Russia is up against the challenge of the poor South in a way that no other northern country is. In particular, it has long borders with the poor South—the Transcaucasus, the states of Central Asia, and China. And it has to be especially careful about its relations with Islamic nations, because seven of its neighbors are Muslim and because Russia itself contains 18 million Muslims. As it was, by 1995 Russia was embroiled in three wars involving Muslim nations—in Tajikistan, Chechnya, and Bosnia. In contrast, other "northern states" are conveniently separated from the South by immutable geography (America's border with Mexico excepted). That means that, in case of a North–South confrontation, or a confrontation between the West and Islam over, for instance, Israel or Algeria, a Russia that was part of the northern club would be on the front line, a dangerous place to be.

Thus Russia has no interest in closely identifying itself with the North if it means open confrontation with the South. To take one example of how it could be threatened, two of its richest agricultural regions are the Kuban and the area around Stavropol (Gorbachev's birthplace). Both are in the South, on the borders of the turbulent Transcaucasus. For its own security, therefore, Russia cannot afford to ignore its neighbors to the south and southeast. It cannot be too pro-Western, if that means outraging Islamic sensibilities. In particular, the Eurasians said, Russia needs to pursue a more active policy toward its neighbors in the near abroad.

Three other strategic changes reinforce these arguments. First, the growth of Japan and the dragons of Southeast Asia and China is tipping the balance of world economic power eastward. Unlike any other European country, Russia has a Pacific coastline, an immeasurable advantage. Russia should therefore be seeking to develop its closest ties there. That is especially true because the Asian dragons are the countries nearest to Russia's own far east, and their economies are a good match for Russia's own: They need its energy and raw materials; it needs their technology. Yeltsin claimed in January 1993 that his "recent series of visits to South Korea, China, and now India is indicative of the fact that we are moving away from a Western emphasis."[11]

Second, Russia's "westward ho" policy is, to be more exact, an Atlantic policy. It is dominated by relations with America and the countries of Western Europe. But just as the increasing power of the Pacific rim provides a reason why Russia should not hitch its wagon too closely to America, so the likely recovery and growth of Eastern Europe provides reasons for caution in its approach to the European Union. On this argument, united Germany and its economic hinterland (the Czech republic, Hungary, Poland), rather than the European Union itself, will in practice be the linchpin of Russia's future relations with Europe. The last time there was real free trade throughout Europe from the Atlantic to the Urals, as long ago as 1913, 45 percent of Russia's trade was with Germany. Germany in 1991–94 was Russia's largest trading partner. If Russia's economy recovers, Russo-German trade will boom and encourage, the Russians say, closer ties between Europe's two largest countries. In practice, of course, neither Germany nor the Eastern European states want to weaken their commitment to the European Union for Russia's sake. Nevertheless, for Russia, what matters in Europe will be its relations with Germany and Eastern Europe, rather than the European Union and the Atlantic. The argument over the former Yugoslavia was important because it dramatized the dilemma: Would Russia go along with America and the West in their hostility to the Serbs? Or would Russia's traditional great-power interests in the Balkans—and its traditional alliance with Serbia—prevail? The outcome showed Russia trying to straddle the fence.

The third reason that the Eurasians said Russia could not pursue a "strategic partnership" with the West had to do with the breakup of the Soviet Union. The emergence of Ukraine as an independent state on Russia's western border meant that Russia now felt geographically farther from the center of Europe than at any time since the eighteenth century. Moreover, the long-term foreign policy aim of Ukraine is to join the European Union. Though its sheer size and military muscle will always command the respect of European governments, Russia can never hope to become an EU member. It is simply too big and too complex for the organization to swallow. Insofar as it is in competition with Ukraine for the EU's attention, it will fail. Ergo, it should not let Europe dominate its foreign policy.

For all those reasons, the relationship between the West and Russia was never likely to be easy. Those tensions would explain why Russian rhetoric and policy changed between 1992 and 1994. Given the historic pattern of mutual suspicion and the West's reluctance to create a new institutional framework to defuse it (as was done with Germany after 1945), "strategic partnership" does seem to have been too optimistic an initial goal. It may follow that Russia and the West are doomed to be rivals. It does not follow that they are doomed to be enemies.

What Russia and the West have in common

In practice, both sides managed to avoid open conflict. Russia supported Western policy in the Persian Gulf and North Korea. It did not oppose it in Bosnia. For its part, the West accepted Russia as the successor state to the Soviet Union and all the international obligations the Soviet Union had entered into, not only arms control treaties but the Middle East peace conference. The West did not seriously attempt to reverse the reassertion of Russian influence in the near abroad and gave little more than formulaic cluckings of diplomatic disapproval even when Russian soldiers supported the secession of Abkhazia or when Russia engaged in covert destabilization in Azerbaijan. Less than a month after the destruction of Grozny, the IMF signed a $6.4 billion loan to Russia (in contrast to the European Union's suspension of its cooperation agreement). It is hard to think of a single foreign policy issue in which the West forced Russia to do something that it wasn't planning to do anyway. Nor did Russia actually subordinate any of its national interests during the period of cooperation with the West.

The West has an interest in the success of Russian reform both altruistically (democracy and free markets are good for the Russians) and directly (not only will those things create markets for Western products, they should guard against a return to confrontational autocracy). The interest in the success of reform was a reason why the West was unclear about whether a strong Russia was in its interest. All things being equal, having a strong rival is not normally desirable. But all things were not equal. The failure of Russian reform would raise the prospect of instability in a nuclear country, with all that implies for Russia's neighbors, near neighbors, and the world. The desirability of avoiding nuclear-powered instability in Russia was one of the few certainties in international diplomacy. Thus both countries have an interest in the successful outcome of Russian economic reform, the Russians for direct reasons, the West for indirect ones: a reformed Russia is likely to be a stable one. A strong and stable Russia was preferable to a weak one, for it would be predictable.

On Russia's side, its non-Western concerns did not mean turning against the West. It proved a reason for supplementing an Atlantic policy. On Russian television on August 2, 1992, Kozyrev claimed that if Russian policy turned against America and other Western countries, it would lead the country into isolation. This, he argued in an article for the American journal *Foreign Affairs* in the spring of 1992, would have disastrous consequences for Russian reform. Unlike all other periods of reform, he argued, the "second Russian revolution unfolded in a favorable foreign policy setting."[12] All other periods of Russian reform had taken place against a background of conflict: Peter the Great's reforms (war with Sweden); the liberation of the serfs (the Crimean War); Stolypin's land reforms (war with Japan and then hostility with Germany); Lenin's new economic policy (hostility with the

West). The external conflicts contributed to the reforms' failures. For the first time in history, this was not happening. If the West could not ensure the reforms' success, it could at least avoid the mistakes that contributed to the previous failures.

Both sides have an interest in avoiding another arms race, Russia especially. In 1993, 20 percent of its budget spending went for defense, and even this seemed more than it could afford. Russia simply cannot finance another arms buildup. Despite the change in foreign policy, this aspect of Russian policy has not been affected: The most important arms control agreements were signed before the change in policy in 1993, by presidents Yeltsin and Bush. But there has been no backsliding since. The West's first interest in Russia lies in having a stable nuclear superpower.

Both Russia and America have the same interest in preventing nuclear proliferation. Russia's interest is perhaps even keener than America's, because three new possessors of nuclear weapons are neighbors: Belarus, Kazakhstan, and Ukraine. Russia wanted their weapons destroyed; the various post-Soviet arms agreements arranged for this.

Both sides, moreover, have an interest in insuring the stability of Eastern and Central Europe—Russia just as much as, if not more than, Western Europe—though they differ about whether NATO membership for Poland and other countries will help achieve such stability. That difference, however, is partly a reflection of the wider difference between the West and Russia. The colder relations between Russia and the West are, the more Poland and others who want close ties with the West will demand membership in the Western alliance. The closer the ties between Russia and the West, the less membership will be the all-important guarantor of security for the Poles. It is also an open question how much of its relationship with Russia America is willing to sacrifice for Polish membership of NATO: If America is forced to choose between Poland and Russia, it is not at all self-evident, given the wider interests linking the two big nuclear powers, that America will choose Poland.

Lastly, Russia and the West have an interest in Russia's policing the unstable countries around its rim. That is partly because instability there threatens not only Russia but also Western interests and partly because the West is unwilling to commit more than a handful of peacekeeping troops to the region. For example, in 1992 civil war broke out in Tajikistan. It soon spilled over into Afghanistan and could have drawn in Pakistan, a traditional American ally. More generally, Central Asia is a strategic black hole between the old Russian, Chinese, Indian, Persian, and Ottoman empires. Most Western governments would much rather see Russian troops involved there than, say, Iranian or Chinese ones. Eventually the West and Russia may need each other's help in managing what could be, potentially, a yet more difficult relationship: a rich, powerful, and assertive China.

Evaluation

All these are strong reasons for thinking that Russia and the West should be able to manage a relationship that lies somewhere between the traditional balance-of-power approach, based on equal and opposite forces, and the "institutional approach," based on common values and legal commitments. Over some issues—nuclear proliferation, for example, or, later, China—the institutional approach will prevail. Over others—perhaps the near abroad or Eastern Europe—Russia will remain outside the Western alliance, though necessarily confronting it, as it did during the Cold War.

In the long run, however, the balance between the two different approaches to international relations could shift toward the institutional one. If Russian democracy takes root, if its free market flourishes, and if its basic interest in the near abroad and Eastern Europe is regional stability (as this book has argued), then a real strategic partnership will become feasible.

Chapter 14

Executive summary and future scenarios

*Is Russia different? · Why did communism fail? · Too much shock therapy? ·
Has the West done enough? · How do people live? · Will Russia prosper? ·
Can Russia beat the mafia? · The economic balance sheet · Will political
deadlock recur? · Can democracy survive? · Will Russia break up? ·
Will Russia rebuild the empire? · Russia and the West: Friends or foes? ·
The political balance sheet · The future · Economic prospects ·
Political prospects · Scenarios*

So what have we learned? First, we are going to summarize the answers to our original twelve questions. Then from page 323 onward we shall gaze more intently into the future. We shall review the positive and negative forces at work, both in the economy and on the political scene. Using this review, we shall describe four main possible scenarios for the next ten years—and the likelihood of each.

Is Russia different?

We begin with the biggest question of all: Is Russia different in some way that will keep it from becoming a "normal" country? Is it naturally collectivist, so that the market economy will not operate properly? Is it naturally autocratic, so that democracy will fail? And is it inherently anti-Western? Many people, including many Russians, would answer yes to these questions. They point to the historical record.

Collectivist? The collective element is indeed strong in Russian history. Since 1861 most agricultural land has been collectively owned, though it was worked privately until Stalin formed the collective farms in the late 1920s. But life in the towns was always more individualistic. Though the Industrial Revolution came late to Russia, by the first decade of this century Russia's was the fastest growing industry in the world.[1]

Even under communism, much happened to erode the collectivist spirit. The population shifted from the countryside to the towns, and 73 percent of Russians now live in towns, a higher proportion than in Italy. The population became educated. Literacy is more universal than in Britain or the United States. Russia's educational progress was in fact faster under communism than it would have been under capitalism, and the same is true of the development of the physical sciences. That one success of communism was also the most potent of the forces that destroyed it. For educated people are thinking people, and in the end they rejected those who told them lies.

Surveys show that Russians are not more hostile to profit and self-advancement than Americans are. Those surveys were done before the economic reform began. But even then millions of Russians were involved in market-type transactions on behalf of themselves or their enterprises, and since the reform Russians have shown increasing commercial versatility. That is true of individuals and enterprises alike. The best evidence is the constant protests of the minority who oppose the "speculators." In fact, the combination of a weak state and a strong commercial spirit provides the ideal basis for a market economy (provided rights of property and contract can be enforced).

Autocratic? On the political front Russia has never been a democracy before. In the nineteenth century it had the most autocratic rulers of all major European countries. The same was true in the twentieth century.

Of course, absolutist rule was never fully accepted, and in the nineteenth century there were regular surges of revolutionary sentiment in the intelligentsia. But those were often focused on ideas of violent change rather than on the painstaking detail of reform. Eventually revolution happened in 1917, but it was violent revolution, again leading to absolutist rule.

Does that mean violence is still the natural Russian method of achieving change? On the contrary. In 1919–21 Russia was racked by civil war, and in 1941–45 Russia lost at least 20 million people. What ordinary Russians now fear more than anything is war—world war and civil war. That helps to explain why, once communism was established, Russians did so little to overthrow it by force.

Today's reformers never initiated violence. Once peaceful opposition was allowed, they behaved just like democrats elsewhere. The conservatives who initiated violence in August 1991 and in October 1993 gathered little support.

Russia today is not an autocracy. The government is so weak that it cannot enforce its own decrees. Today's Russians are not obedient sheep looking for a leader. There are, of course, some sheep, and every Russian would like to see a tougher fight against crime. But the old idea that Russians are either passive serfs or violent revolutionaries should be abandoned. It was swept away by the bad experience of violence and the good experience of freedom and democracy.

Anti-Western? Finally, there is the fear that Russia is innately anti-Western and not really European. Certainly most Russians have elements of ambivalence about Westerners and the West. But are those feelings much different from what the French feel about the Americans? In most cases, probably not. However, in some Russians there is a feeling about the uniqueness of Russia that perhaps exceeds what Frenchmen feel about France. These people are the heirs of the nineteenth-century Slavophiles, of whom Fyodor Dostoevsky was one of the leaders. Today they include figures like Aleksandr Solzhenitsyn, whose return to Russia reopened the debate about what it means to be Russian.

According to the Slavophiles, the Russian soul is fundamentally different from the European. It places a higher value on things of the spirit and less on material success. Russians of this sort find the prospect of increasing assimilation into Europe distasteful. They would prefer to retain more control over their own affairs rather than subscribe to the common rules that are increasingly used among the countries of Europe.

How important will this powerful element in the Russian tradition prove in the future? The answer is that it is much more powerful among the old than the young, and therefore (for good or ill) it is probably on the wane. True, people once said the same about Islamic fundamentalism, and they were wrong. But Islamic fundamentalism thrives only in a fundamentally non-European context and contains a strong element of anti-feminism. Slavophilia is quite different.

Of course the Slavophiles lament the universal presence of Western pop songs. But who can stop that? In fact the Western pop song has been one of the more revolutionary forces in Russia. While older people in Russia very rarely know English, even if they are highly educated, thousands of youngsters have learned English in order to understand those songs. If Brezhnev decided he could not keep out the Western pop song, it is unlikely that the Slavophiles will make much headway in doing so.

Indeed, among young Russians one of the most powerful desires is to be a part of the West. Most do not want to emigrate. They want to move Russia into Europe—which is where Russia belongs. If a Westerner lists the makers of European culture he will surely list many Russians: Tolstoy, Dostoevsky, Chekhov, Tchaikovsky, Rachmaninov, Stravinsky, Prokofiev, Shostakovich, Diaghilev, Stanislavsky, Eisenstein. How many people would he list from Poland, Hungary, Czechoslovakia, Romania, Bulgaria, and Yugoslavia put together? If those countries belong in Europe, then surely so does Russia.

In what follows we examine more deeply the preceding three issues—the development of markets, the establishment of democracy, and the conduct of relations with the West. We take the economics first, because it is the failure of communist economics that has been the prime mover of all the other changes.

Why did communism fail?

Communism failed because it was inherently inefficient. Planning did not work because it provided weak incentives and required more information than anyone could ever collate. Moreover the communist economies became largely isolated from the great stream of world trade through which most technological progress becomes diffused. On top of that, Russia came to be saddled with a crippling burden of defense costs, which led to a low, and eventually stagnant, standard of living for the ordinary Russian.

Increasingly Russians became aware that life was much better in the West. They demanded an improvement. Mikhail Gorbachev, appointed Communist party secretary in 1985, offered them perestroika (economic reconstruction) and glasnost (political openness). Economic reform was minimal, but glasnost transformed Russia. It led by 1990 to free elections for the parliaments of each of the Soviet Union's fifteen republics and to declarations of "sovereignty" by most of those republics.

At the same time the economic crisis deepened. Perestroika made it more difficult for the state to collect revenue from enterprises, and glasnost made it more difficult for the Union government to collect revenue from the republics. To bridge the gap the government simply printed money. Once in people's pockets, this increased their demand for goods, leading to longer and longer queues in the shops.

Faced with the republics' demands for more autonomy, Gorbachev proposed a new Union Treaty giving them much of what they wanted. For the conservatives that was the last straw, and on August 19, 1991, Gorbachev was put under house arrest. But Yeltsin survived in the White House, and within three days it was the leaders of the coup who were under arrest.

The August coup finished off the Soviet Union, and Russia came to be ruled by its own government and its own parliament, not by the government of the Soviet Union. Economic reform was now possible.

Yeltsin interviewed a number of candidates for the post of economic overlord and selected Russia's leading young radical economist, Yegor Gaidar. For some years Gaidar and his friends had been debating, first in secret and then more openly, how to reform the Russian economy. Now they became ministers in all the top economic departments. Their time had come.

Too much shock therapy?

The overarching question was how to transform Russia into a free market economy, based on private enterprise. But there was also the immediate issue of the shortages in the shops, where people often queued all day and ugly incidents became a regular occurrence. The strategy Gaidar chose was later criticized by President Clinton's adviser, Strobe Talbott, as "too much shock and too little therapy." Was he right?

On the overarching question there had been years of debate in Russia and elsewhere. Some had argued that before markets were freed, monopolies should be dismantled and firms privatized; otherwise the free market would never be efficient. Others had argued that freeing markets was the top priority in order to provide incentives and liberate energies. Most of the debate was quite sterile, and in any case it proved completely irrelevant. The crisis in the shops dictated the strategy.

There were only two ways of eliminating the queues. One was to reduce the amount of money people had. That was not on, because Stalin had done it and so had Valentin Pavlov, the last communist prime minister; both were hated men. The other way was through higher prices. Pavlov had tried that too, but he had simply reset the prices, which still failed to bring demand into balance with supply. Much better to free the prices, so that demand would automatically be brought back in line with supply. Free prices also had the large political advantage that they are set by the market and not the government.

Freeing prices. So the decision was taken to free most prices on January 2, 1992. That was surely one of the bravest decisions ever taken by any government. Some ministers had argued for a two-stage operation, where only some prices are freed at first. But, once people know that other prices are going to rise later, they will stop selling those other goods. So the decision was made to abolish federal price controls on nearly all items, except bread, milk, sugar, telephones, transport, housing, and energy.

When the shops closed on December 31, 1991, it was bitterly cold and the shops were bare. When they reopened on January 2, people were stunned. Prices had risen on average 3.5 times. Wages had less than doubled. Those were hard times for most Russians. But the foundations of the market economy had been laid. Over time the queues disappeared, and the shops looked more Western, with decent stocks on the shelves, goods the customers wanted, and a better quality of service. From a market where sellers could sell anything, however shoddy, Russia has moved to a market where the wishes of the customer matter.

This does not mean customers now bought more than they did before the reform. The stage of higher supplies was still to come. But the price reform achieved its first objective: to bring demand into line with supply and eliminate the humiliating tedium of the queues. People no longer spent hours, days, and weeks looking for goods. They knew that the goods were available at a price, just as in the West.

So the freeing of prices did what it was meant to. In the short run it got rid of the queues, but, more important, it created a market economy in which goods were freely bought and sold through voluntary agreements between buyer and seller. The system of "state orders" directing who supplied what to whom had been shattered at a blow.

But freeing the prices *was* shock therapy. We have described the good effects. But the price reform also led to a fall in real purchasing power, as people's savings were wiped out. More important, it initiated a free-for-all in which old patterns of supply (based on the command economy) were broken and years were needed to build new ones (based on market relations). In consequence output and living standards fell sharply. As Figure 14–1 shows, the fall was sharper than in much of Eastern Europe.[2]

Figure 14-1. The fall in output (1989 = 100)

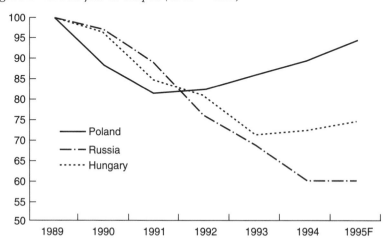

Source: Goskomstat and EBRD, *Transition Report, 1995.*

Why output fell. Why did output fall so much, and could that have been avoided? Almost nobody forecast that economic transition would be as painful as it has proved to be in all the post-communist countries.[3] Some people even imagined there would be an abrupt, immediate increase in output, since the market system is so much more efficient than the command economy.

Since that did not happen, was it wrong to move so rapidly to the market? By avoiding "inappropriate" use of free market economics, could Russia and Eastern Europe have made a transition like China, in which there has been continuous growth of output?

Unfortunately, the answer is no. One reason is precisely that these countries are post-communist and free, whereas China is communist and authoritarian. In China wages are tightly controlled, while in Russia, like the West, wages are completely free, and workers can go on strike. In any free society it is impossible to control inflationary pressure without some slack in the economy. Spain discovered that after the death of Franco, and Eastern Europe found it out after the opening of the Berlin Wall.

But, perhaps more important, China is a rural society, with 73 percent of its workers in agriculture. Its economic miracle comes about as people move from low-productivity agriculture into higher-productivity "township and village enterprises." By contrast Russia and Eastern Europe had only about 20 percent of their working people in agriculture; most of the rest were employed in traditional "state enterprises." In such a situation progress requires a radical restructuring of those traditional enterprises, a much more difficult task. As any businessman knows, when a business is restructured, its output falls before it bounces back. The fall has been no less in Hungary, which has followed Chinese-style gradualism, than in Poland, which had a big price shock.

The cause of the restructuring is the shift from a command system, where all output could be sold, to a market system, where output can be sold only if a customer is willing to pay the price. This is a painful transition.

In the opinion of some it is best done gradually. As an academic proposition that is highly doubtful (see the Hungarian experience), but as a proposition about Russia it is largely irrelevant. The com-

mand system, after all, broke down only partly because of policy decisions. It had already partly broken down because of the collapse of
Soviet power.

There were three main aspects of that collapse. The first was within
Russia. Farms were refusing to supply products at what they considered unfair prices; factories were refusing to accept inadequate inputs;
and so on. Second, there was the breakup in early 1991 of the COME-
CON system of managed trade among the Warsaw Pact countries. That
led to a shortage of critical imports in Russia and a shortage of customers for Russian products. Third, there was the breakup of the Soviet Union one year later. That had catastrophic effects, with suppliers
in other states often refusing to supply Russian customers, and former
customers of Russia often unable to pay for Russian products.

It is difficult to evaluate the relative importance of the three
sources of change, but it is striking how much Finland has suffered
from the changes in the Soviet Union. Finland, normally one of the
most successful Western countries, suffered a 13 percent fall in output
(1990–93) in part as a result of the dislocation of trade on its south-
eastern borders.

But, on top of all this, Russia had one extra problem. Disarmament
had a quite different significance for Russia from that for any other
country, because so high a proportion of its economy was diverted to
the defense effort. In 1992 the reform government cut the purchase of
military hardware by 85 percent. It had to do so in order to control
the yawning budget deficit. But the short-run effect on output can easily be imagined.

Compared with Eastern Europe, Russia was a much more deeply
communist country, with a bigger defense sector. Changing all that
was bound to be painful. There is no evidence that a slower shift
would have involved less pain in total. The worst place to be is in between one system and another, so it is best to hurry through the intermediate phase. That is what Poland did, and Poland is now one of the
fastest-growing countries in Europe.

Inflation. The Polish prototype had an enormous impact on policy-
making in Russia. But Russia did *not* follow one key element in the
Polish shock therapy: a rapid move to low inflation using a fixed ex-

change rate. In consequence, inflation in Russia was still, in the summer of 1995, higher than it was in Poland six months into the reform. This financial instability has been a major disincentive to investment in Russia for both Russians and foreigners.

Why did Russia fail to control inflation where Poland succeeded? First, Russia began with much more excess money and much longer queues than Poland ever had. Thus when prices were freed in Russia they rose by 250 percent (or 3.5 times), as against 80 percent in Poland in January 1990. To move rapidly to low inflation after such a price jump would have been extremely difficult.

It could probably have been done with a heavy input of foreign finance, but that was never on offer. The West treated Russia quite differently from Poland. For heroic Poland, newly free of the Soviets, the West had been willing to devise jointly a stabilization strategy involving an IMF loan and a Stabilization Fund that became available within four months of the change of government. But Russia was the former enemy, and the West's attitude was essentially: "Wait and see—we'll help you when you've shown you can do it on your own."

Even so, Russia did reduce its monthly inflation to around 10 percent by the end of the summer in 1992. But that was not to last. The demands for cheap credit for the military-industrial and agrarian lobbies were irresistible. Of course, the reformers in the government could have resigned, but they rightly figured that, in order to get Russia privatized, they ought to stay on. The success of the privatization program (discussed later) fully justifies their decision.

So in the period 1992–94 Russia lurched between 10 and 25 percent monthly inflation. It is not an impressive story. However, in late 1994 a new phase began. A much firmer budget was adopted with the explicit commitment of the president, leading to a budget deficit for 1995 of around 3 percent of GDP. The deficit was in part financed by an IMF loan of $6.8 billion. In July 1995 Russia moved to a pegged exchange rate. By February 1996 inflation was down to 3 percent per month. The shift, however, has been gradual. Even in 1995 there was no sudden financial standstill.

So has there been shock therapy? Yes and no. The price shock was one of the biggest ever administered to an economy, but there has been no monetary shock therapy. The dismantling of state controls has been slower than in Poland and the Czech Republic, but privatization has been much faster.

"Too much shock and too little therapy"? No. President Yeltsin was right: "The mistake has been to go too slow and not too fast."

Has the West done enough?

From the point of view of the West, the transformation of Russia is the opportunity of the decade. If things go well, we shall no longer have an enemy, which will save us billions on defense. And we shall have a new partner for trade and investment, which will increase our own prosperity.

But how has the West responded to this challenge? The answer is mixed. The moment of truth came in November 1991, when Gaidar became deputy prime minister with a mandate from Yeltsin to carry out the reform. The Supreme Soviet and the president were still on good terms, and there was clearly a window of opportunity to launch a successful reform in which prices were freed and then stabilized through a proper financial package. That was the strategy that had been followed in Poland in January 1990. It could have been tried also in Russia. But the window of opportunity was small. Unless the package was launched by April 1992 at the latest, the chances of success were small, because by then the opposition would clearly be on the warpath.

Requests for a financial package went from Yeltsin to the G7 group of leading Western countries in December 1991. Almost nothing happened. The main Westerner to come to Moscow in the key weeks before Christmas was David Mulford, the U.S. Treasury's undersecretary for international affairs, leading a G7 delegation of debt collectors worried about who would pay the debts of the Soviet government. No higher-ranking U.S. official came, nor did the managing director of the International Monetary Fund (IMF).

In fact, there was never any question of Western involvement in a Polish-style package to go with the reform. The G7 offered no money at that stage, and the IMF could not do so, because Russia was not a member of the IMF till the spring of 1992. It is difficult to explain the G7's inertia at that time. Quite possibly President Bush simply failed to understand how much had changed in Russia. Or, despite all the talk about a "new world order," he could not help thinking of Russia as the enemy. Everybody's excuse, of course, was that they had budget deficits. But 2 percent of NATO's defense expenditure would have been a massive financial package for Russia.

Of course, the success of a package could not have been guaranteed, but the G7 should have made the attempt, providing the money only step by step as the conditions were satisfied. A success would have advanced by three years the time when Russia became financially normal. Instead, the G7 asked the IMF to advise them what to do. In lending its own money, the IMF was bound to apply its standard criteria regardless of the strong political arguments for special treatment of a nuclear superpower. It could perhaps have publicly thrown the issue back to the G7, but it did not. Thus after three months of fact-finding, the IMF in February 1992 thrashed out with the Russian government a Memorandum of Economic Policy in which the Russians committed themselves to all sorts of things and the IMF to nothing. Not surprisingly, the Russians did not subsequently deliver on many of their undertakings.

Thus began the uneasy relationship between the IMF and the Russian government. Until 1994 it was essentially arm's-length, and only after that did it move to the level of constructive partnership, leading to a $6.8 billion "standby" loan in 1995.

Yet if we ask, "Who in the West did most for Russia?" we would have to say the IMF. Through its regular exchanges with the Russians it did more than any other Westerners to impress on disbelieving Russians that only monetary control would reduce inflation. Eventually it won the confidence of the Russian Central Bank. If one looks back to the original Memorandum of February 1992 one can see how clearly it set out what needed to be done—and by 1995 nearly all of it had been carried out.

And what of the record of the G7? There has been a lot more sound than substance. Twice, when President Yeltsin seemed under threat, huge packages of Western aid were announced: $24 billion in April 1992 and $28 billion in July 1993. What actually arrived was $15 billion and $8 billion[4] respectively, most of it consisting of export credits, which benefited Western exporters as much as Russia, if not more. Actual grants from Western governments in 1992 and 1993 amounted to only $2 billion in all. In retrospect, as many thought at the time, it was a mistake to mention huge sums that would not materialize. The impact on Russian public opinion was very bad, when the people first saw their president going to the West with a begging bowl and then found that the West did not fill it up.

Yet there has been substantial Western technical assistance of great value, especially in the process of privatization. Some of it has come from the World Bank, the European Commission, and the European Bank (EBRD), and some from national aid programs like USAID and the British Know-How Fund. In general the technical assistance has been poorly administered. There has inevitably been much muddle at the Russian end, but things have been scarcely better at the Western end. The West should have realized that to be effective in Russia its technical assistance programs needed to be run from Moscow. Instead the Western agencies operated the traditional "mission" system, where teams make short visits often followed by other teams, which repeat the same questions. Thus much time and money have been wasted. But some results of extreme worth have been achieved. To give an example, the Hungarian-American philanthropist George Soros used his money most imaginatively to help preserve Russian science and to reform the school curriculum.

But, of course, as time passes technical assistance by official agencies is exceeded by technical assistance through regular business contacts. The private sector replaces the public sector as the main method of transferring Western technology and Western business practice into Russia.

How do people live?

Amid all these changes, how do people manage to survive? For most Russians the last five years have been a traumatic experience. Almost everybody has had to change their life in some drastic way.

Death. The clearest evidence of hardship comes from the evidence on mortality. The death rate in Russia has been rising steadily, while the number of births has been falling (see Figure 14–2). The upward trend in the death rate set in before the reform, but it accelerated sharply

Figure 14-2. Birth and death rates (per thousand people)

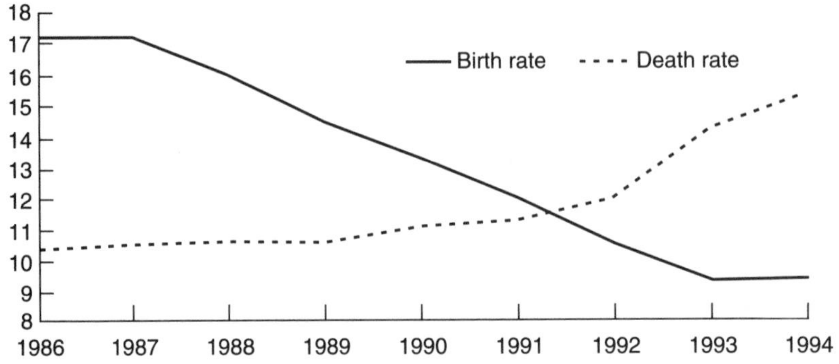

Source: Goskomstat, *Current Statistical Report*, 1995, no. 3, p. 7.

between 1992 and 1993 and is only now beginning to decelerate. Most of the extra deaths are due to heart disease, stroke, violent death, or alcoholism—all symptoms of stress. Reduced efficiency of the health service must also be partly to blame. The change has particularly affected men, whose life expectancy fell in one year (1993) from 62 to 59, the same now as in Egypt and India.

It is easy to understand why men have suffered more during the transition than women. Almost everybody has had to change his or her pattern of work to try to preserve the family income. But women have also experienced real gains from the reform. Women and pensioners do almost all the shopping in Russia. In the past women queued for an average of perhaps twenty hours a week, often outdoors in the snow. Now the queues are similar to those in the West.

Living standards. But there is less real money to spend. Just how far have household living standards fallen (ignoring the gain from reduced queues and easier availability of wanted goods)? In 1995 households bought (or produced for themselves) about 65 percent of the amount they did in 1991. In the first year of the reform the figure had been rather worse (around 60 percent), rising thereafter. However, these figures grossly underrepresent the importance of housing and heating. These have been (and remain) virtually free, so that real living standards have in fact fallen less than the figures we have quoted.

The most absurd of all Western misrepresentations is the idea of starving Russians. There were, it is true, in the winter of 1991–92 serious anxieties about food supplies to Moscow and St. Petersburg. But in fact total food consumption in Russia never fell sharply. And for most items it was by early 1994 back to the 1991 level, except for milk. But people were poorer in other ways. They saved on clothes, on durables, and on holidays. And they ate 25 percent more potatoes, a clear sign of lower living standards. Even so, life continues with dignity in most cases, and the average young woman is more attractively dressed than in Britain or America (and more beautiful!).

Inequality. If the average Russian is somehow getting by, what about the least fortunate? There has certainly been a big increase in inequality. Beggars can now been seen on the streets, though in fewer numbers than in London. And old people can be seen looking in trash bins.

At the other end of the income scale, the incomes of the very rich have rocketed. The new rich are better-heeled than the nomenklatura ever were. They buy houses in London, Cyprus, and the Côte d'Azur. But even so, inequality still falls short of that in the United States; it is close to the level in Britain.

The main increase in inequality came about because wages have become much more unequal. In prosperous industries (such as energy) linked to the world market, workers have done much better than in hard-hit industries like textiles. In fact, workers in textiles, clothing, and footwear now get under 30 percent of wages in the energy sector, as against 60 percent before the reform. And many workers get no wages for a month or more by reason of unpaid leave or straightforward nonpayment.

The Russian government has a poverty standard that can be used to identify who is most likely to be poor. It shows that children are more likely to be in poverty than pensioners. That is because there are many poor working families, but they get the same children's benefits as richer families that need the benefits less.

Social safety net. So did the social safety net fail? It depends on what standard you apply. The starting point is that average living standards fell—the inevitable result of shifting from a command economy toward a market system of relations between enterprises. At the same time tax receipts fell even faster. So it is not surprising that pensions fell more than average incomes.

The most avoidable failures were the scale of child poverty and the problems of health care. The health care system was already in terrible trouble before the reform began, but now many hospitals suffer from a grievous lack of funds, so that they often cannot afford even aspirin to relieve the patients' pain. Operations have constantly to be postponed for lack of supplies. A two-class system has emerged, where those who can pay get a different standard of treatment from those who cannot. This systemic failure is certainly one reason for Russia's extraordinarily low life expectancy.

Unemployment. Many people expected that unemployment would be a terrible problem, but so far it has been quite moderate. Unemployment (by international definitions) was up from 4.5 percent when the reform began to 8.5 percent by 1996. But only 3 percent of the workforce is registered at Russia's two thousand employment offices as looking for work.

What explains such a slow increase, when compared, for example, with the Polish experience, where unemployment rose in three years to 15 percent of the workforce? Basically it reflects the intense aversion in Russia to the whole idea of unemployment. Workers dread it because they get much more than wages from their enterprises. They often get housing, subsidized kindergarten facilities, and cheap holidays that they would not otherwise have. If instead they are unemployed, they get benefits between 45 and 100 percent of their former wage, which sounds good, except that inflation soon drives its value down toward zero. Thus most of the unemployed in fact get the guaranteed minimum benefit, which is only 10 percent of the average wage.

In order to keep their jobs Russian workers are willing to accept cuts in living standards that would be rejected by workers in any other country. Strikes have been extraordinarily few and far between (about 1 percent of the OECD level), and, unlike in Poland, workers generally accept whatever the managers offer.

The result is in many ways a Thatcherite's dream. When an enterprise finds it cannot sell as much as it used to, it pays lower real wages. That makes immediate layoffs unnecessary. But the workers start looking around for better work. Eventually some of them leave, and it is this process of voluntary quitting which brings about the redeployment of labor. Instead of having workers pushed into unemployment until a new job comes along, they stay in their old jobs until a more attractive one pulls them away.

The managers too have their own reasons for wishing to limit layoffs. Up to now layoffs have been regarded as a mark of managerial failure. Managers anywhere like to be liked. So enterprises in trouble devise forms of work-sharing to avoid layoffs. In late 1995, 3 percent of all Russian workers were on short-time working, and 1 percent had been sent home for a period of leave, typically around a month, on negligible pay, a form of hidden unemployment.

Has Russia overdone its job protection, as judged by the need for Russia to restructure but without unnecessary pain? There has in fact been a lot of restructuring. Employment in services is growing, while employment in industry falls. Labor mobility is high, with 20 percent of workers moving into different jobs. So job protection has not produced stagnation, and it has reduced the pain.

Western observers often wonder why the pains of economic transition have led to so little organized protest. The answer is partly that most Russians have some way of coping. Most have a plot of land where they grow potatoes, vegetables, and often fruit. Over 20 percent have a second job. And in cases of real hardship the extended family is a much more important form of social security than in the West.

Even so, there has been real hardship. The absence of protest is mainly because almost no one believes that any politician can improve things. Even the vote for Zhirinovsky in the December 1993 elections turns out to have come from people of above-average income and below-average age. It was more a protest against crime and indiscipline than against economic reform.

The most encouraging news from Russia is that average living standards are higher than in 1992. The trend will continue, and by 1997 total output is likely to be rising also. But will Russia become really prosperous?

Will Russia prosper?

The general answer is yes. Russia has greater natural resources than any other country in the world. Compared with the United States, it produces (per capita) more natural gas, oil, steel, aluminum, nickel, platinum, diamonds, gold, uranium, and copper. Though a country can become rich without natural resources (like Japan and Italy), most countries that have great resources do prosper if market forces are allowed to work.

The only exceptions are where the educational level of the population is really low. But that is not the case in Russia. Its level of literacy is higher than the West's, and it has a good general level of mathematical and scientific education. What it desperately lacks is professional competence in the arts of commerce. But the appetite is there to learn. When modern textbooks become more readily available, millions of Russians will reeducate themselves for the jobs where money is to be made.

But if Russia will prosper, the question is when? It depends, of course, on the speed of institutional change—the spread of private ownership and the development of a proper market system. Russia's record on privatization is quite remarkable; in fact, it is the biggest single reason for expecting rapid economic growth. On market reform the record so far is more patchy, with still too much regulation, inadequate law enforcement of contracts and property rights, and pervasive interference of the mafia in economic life.

Going private. Like most post-communist countries, Russia has now sold off well over half its shops and small businesses, but the difference comes in its approach to big business. In the first three years Russia had only one privatization minister, Anatoly Chubais, an outstanding economist with extraordinary determination and political skills. Backed by President Yeltsin, he drove through his program almost singlehanded. By mid-1994, 80 percent of Russia's industrial companies had been privatized (as against 28 percent in Poland, 42 percent in Hungary, and a majority in the Czech Republic).[5]

So who were the new owners? Most of the capital was given away.

Just enough was given to the managers and workers to disarm their opposition, and just enough to the population at large to satisfy the claims of those who did not happen to work in industry. Thus in the typical firm the workers and managers got 51 percent of the shares at a knockdown price (though in the largest firms the figure was 35 percent). Most of the rest of the shares were auctioned to the public, not for money but for "vouchers," which had been given free to every citizen in the land. Despite dire warnings that the system would fail, it worked, and by mid-1994, when voucher auctions ended, nearly all the vouchers had been exchanged for shares in Russian industry.

Who ended up controlling the firms? In more than half of them a substantial block of shares (over 5 percent) was in the hands of a single owner, often one of the funds. But, of course, an outsider could exercise control only with support from some of the insiders, who now own on average 59 percent of shares: managers with 17 and workers 43 percent.[6] The battle of reorganization is still being played out in shareholders' meetings and boardrooms up and down the country. The balance of power is changing as workers who are short of cash sell out, generally to outsiders. The outsider element will also grow as new shares are issued in order to raise more capital. Some of them will go to foreigners.

Foreign investment and trade. The foreign connection will be critical for Russia's economic growth. The reason is that you can learn capitalism only from capitalists. The greatest weaknesses in Russian business are in marketing, financial management, and technology—in that order. Russian businesses need to produce only what can be sold, and then sell it. That means learning general skills in marketing and specific facts about the world market for their products. Only firms already in that market can really help. The help may come from a trade partner or a foreign investor. Money is not the main issue, and quite small sums of foreign investment can make an enormous difference (and earn a high return) if they come with some key item of know-how.

Already there have been many small pockets of foreign investment. It can be found in almost every industry, but especially in those oriented toward Russia's huge domestic market. Western companies can now be found operating in about every sector of the economy. Total foreign investment is believed to have been around $4 billion by 1994, half of it "direct" investment and half of it simply the purchase of shares on the open market. The numbers are still small, just over 1 percent of Russia's national income. Because of uncertainty, shares of Russian companies are currently very cheap. In mid-1995 they equaled roughly two years' profits. But as soon as the climate is right, Russia will see a prolonged investment boom.

If foreign investment is important, so too is trade. In the West the expansion of trade has been a key component in the postwar economic miracle. This has been significantly spurred by the progressive dismantling of trade barriers. Russia needs to reduce its own trade barriers (especially import taxes) but also to have open access to Western markets. In some products (uranium, aluminum, space launchers) Russia is such a major world producer that temporary obstacles have been erected, perhaps inevitably. But a large step forward has been taken in the Partnership and Cooperation Agreement with the European Union. It sets the ultimate goal of free trade. That is not the same as membership in the European Union, of course, which has been offered as a goal to the Eastern European nations. But it offers an important new vision not unlike the vision offered to Spain after the death of Franco. It says that, if Russia continues to develop as a democratic market economy, it will become a full-fledged member of the European economy. In Spain the vision had a strong impact on business decisions and political outcomes. When the colonels took over the Spanish parliament, the Spanish people rejected them because they had something to lose—their future membership in Europe and the prosperity that would bring. The same incentive will play an important role in Russia.

Regulations, taxes, and legal rights. It is not mainly a shortage of money that is holding back investment, either by foreigners or by Russians. The money is there. Russians own more than $40 billion in foreign assets: $9 billion in Russian bank accounts, $16 billion in currency, and $18 billion abroad.[7] Much of that money is waiting to be used in Russia when good opportunities exist.

So what is holding up the investment boom? Financial instability is still a deterrent, but inflation rates of 50 percent a year are far less bothersome than 1,000 percent. Political instability is another deterrent, and the outcome of the 1996 presidential election will affect the speed of recovery. But the biggest problem is simply the difficulties of doing business.[8]

Business is hard in Russia. There is still a great deal of regulation, especially about the use of premises and land, but also still about the right to produce and to export. Regulations get changed by many different authorities, often in contradictory directions, and it is a nightmare to find who is the key bureaucrat to persuade or bribe. There are also very high tax rates, made necessary by excessive tax evasion. The tax structure is itself highly unpredictable.

Worse than all this, however, is the inadequate legal framework. If a contract is broken, it is extremely difficult to obtain legal redress, which is one reason why illegal redress and threats of violence are so common. Property rights are often unclear. Firms that think they own something often find that someone else thinks the same.

The greatest obscurity remains the ownership of land. In the countryside the privatization of land ownership is going very slowly and will be the last privatization to be completed. In towns businesses in principle can buy their own land.[9] But local authorities own all unsold land and are often unwilling to make it available for new development. All land use is subject to zoning restrictions.

Bit by bit, however, all this is improving. A registry of land ownership is being compiled in some areas. Stage by stage, laws and degrees that were originally extremely vague become more precise and codified. By 1995 the first part of the new Civil Code had been adopted.

In Russia there will always be attempts to halt economic change and even to reverse it. But regardless of the ripples on the political surface, there is a strong tide beneath, which is carrying Russia toward the market economy. Observers should be less excited about the inconsistent utterances of ministers, who (as anywhere in the world) have to maximize their political support. One should focus rather on the powerful tides of economic change, which are almost surely irreversible. Most young people support the market system, and bit by bit the young are taking over.

Can Russia beat the mafia?

The mafia, however, are a real problem. There is the big mafia, which has made huge fortunes through control of trade in oil, metals, cars and (more recently) drugs. And there are the local mafias, which control retail trade, construction and repair shops, making sure that new entrants either pay up or keep out. Every day you hear of new businesses nipped in the bud by the restrictive force of the mafia.

So are the mafia in Russia to stay, as they have stayed in Sicily? Or are they just a feature of the transition?

Though there was plenty of corruption under communism (often backed by force), things have become steadily worse since 1985, and it is easy to see why. The main reason is not the decline of police power (which is more a symptom than a cause). It is the ending of the state monopoly of jobs and of property.

Under communism there was only one employer, so you had better behave properly or otherwise you would find it very difficult to get a satisfactory job. The state monopoly of jobs meant that if you wanted a successful career, you should not offend against the party code; if you got caught, there was nowhere outside the system where you could go. That was a very strong sanction supporting good behavior.

At the same time the state monopoly of property meant that there was no private property and no private contracts. So there was no problem of how to protect your property or how to enforce a contract on someone who owed you money.

As communism fell, both situations changed, with the same results as in Sicily in the mid-nineteenth century, when the feudal system gave way to individual landholding. As private property proliferated, there was a demand for people to protect property and to help collect debts. In addition there was in Russia, as in Sicily, an ample supply of people with good military or paramilitary training, willing to earn money by providing protection.

The answer to the mafia is, of course, for the state to supply the protection. A law-based society is one where the state has the monopoly of force and where there is a working system of law courts. Now that the state monopoly of jobs is gone, the legal system has to be the main sanction enforcing good behavior.

Can the state rise to the occasion? There is some evidence that shopkeepers increasingly use the police rather than the mafia to protect them, because they charge a lower fee, their protection is more dependable, and there is less chance that they will arbitrarily increase the fee. That is exactly what is needed. The police are gradually reestablishing their superior force by buying better equipment and paying their officers better.

Sicily never threw off the Mafia, but in Russia there are two grounds for hope. First, many of the problems that nourished the growth of the mafia were manifestly transitional and short-lived. One was the problem of the black market in the perestroika period. It developed from the attempt to fix prices at below market-clearing levels. The incentives for illegal selling at higher prices were thus enormous, and the mafia determined who made those gains. More recently the existence of an overregulated economy with export quotas and other licenses created the possibility of huge "rents," and again the mafia came into play as the organization that determined who got the proceeds. For example, there was a huge incentive to smuggle out metals and oil bought in Russia at one-tenth of world prices. Estonia became the world's leading net exporter of nonferrous metals, even though it produced none itself. The protection of those illegal export routes was an important field for mafia activity. Today, however, licensing is in retreat, and the black market stems mainly from tax evasion, as in any normal country. That is the first ground for hope.

The second ground for hope is that Russia is becoming a more settled society. In settled societies people take far more care to build solid reputations than they do in unsettled times. In unsettled times the natural thing is to make your fortune by a quick act of robbery. In more settled times you need a sound reputation if you want a steady income. As Russia becomes more settled, this will become a dominant influence. Those who made their fortunes by robbery already want to develop reputations for more respectable practice, and they want a strong legal system to protect the property they previously stole.[10]

The economic balance sheet

It is time for a stock-taking on the economic reform. How has it gone? As we have said, the initial conditions in Russia were exceptionally

Table 14–1. An economic balance sheet

Freeing prices and markets	Quite good, including foreign exchange. Still excessive licensing (of production and distribution)
Privatizing state property	Industry: excellent, but some theft Agriculture: virtually no change Urban land: limited success Housing: gradual
Controlling inflation	Poor: but inflation down to 3 percent per month by early 1996
Supporting the weak	Real wages: fell Inequality: increased greatly Unemployment: contained within firms Pensions: fell against average incomes Child benefits: fell Health care: serious deterioration Mortality: up by 36 percent (1991–94)
Promoting legality	Very weak Corruption of officials: rampant Protection rackets: pervasive Property rights: often unclear Law courts: weak law enforcers
Economic prospects	Good GDP stopped falling during 1994 Massive natural resources Highly educated population No shortage of investment finance

difficult. But, if a Westerner is interested in doing business in Russia he is entitled to ask how things stand, regardless of the reasons. He wants to know the reality, as Oliver Cromwell said, "warts and all."

We attempt to provide such a balance sheet in Table 14–1. Inevitably the record is mixed. There are two big successes: Markets have replaced the command economy, and most of industry and trade has been privatized. In four years that is quite an achievement. But high inflation persisted for most of that period, and the financial environment remained unpredictable. During the transition real incomes inevitably fell in line with output, and, since wage inequality increased, some people suffered greatly. The worst poverty was among large families. Health care deteriorated, and mortality increased hugely.

But perhaps the greatest problem in the economy now is the lack of a clear legal framework, upheld by the courts. Apart from that, Russia is now poised for a sizable economic upsurge. It has natural resources unparalleled in the world, a well-educated workforce, and plenty of liquid finance waiting to be invested.

Will political deadlock recur?

But may not political failure put all this in peril? What are the prospects for political stability and democracy in Russia? The historical record between 1991 and 1993 is not encouraging, but most people in the West misunderstand quite badly what in fact happened. They see it as a typical example of Russian muddle and violence, rather than a trauma caused by an unworkable constitution, which somehow had to be replaced.

At the beginning of the reform Russia had a constitution based on the sovereignty of parliament. Of course, under communism everything was decided by the Communist party, and the parliament was told just how to vote. So there was a coherent government and a clear locus of decision-making.

But once the Communist party had collapsed, there was a power vacuum. The parliament wanted to exercise its rights. At the same time the president expected to govern. If the policy prescriptions of parliament and the president had been the same, that just might have worked for a time. But they were not. The president, who had been elected by direct popular vote in June 1991, believed in private ownership and the market economy. The parliament, by contrast, had been elected one year earlier, only six weeks after the Communist party agreed that anybody could run in the election regardless of their standing with the party. Many of those elected were directors of enterprises or farms and stood to lose from the process of reform. Conflict between parliament and the president was inevitable.

From April 1992 on Russia lurched from crisis to crisis. In April 1993 Yeltsin won a referendum calling for new parliamentary elections. But, as was its constitutional right, the parliament refused to agree to elections. In September the parliament proposed to double the budget deficit and attempted to make the managers the main beneficiaries of privatization. At the same time it turned the parliament building into an armed camp.

After eighteen months of compromise Yeltsin appealed once more to the people. On September 21 he suspended the parliament and called for new elections. The parliament refused to be disbanded and appointed Vice President Rutskoi as president. Yeltsin sent troops to encircle the parliament building (otherwise known as the White House).

At this stage, opinion polls showed that below 10 percent of Russians supported the parliament, but the parliamentary leaders believed otherwise. On the afternoon of October 3, Rutskoi appeared on the balcony of the White House calling on Russians to rise up and urging the army to mutiny. Parliamentary troops broke out of their cordon. They seized the office of the Moscow mayor and tried all night to fight their way up the main television tower.

At dawn Yeltsin struck back. Tanks pounded the White House. There was never any doubt of the outcome. In the crowds you could ask people what they thought. Many said, "It is the end of communism." They were right. For the second time in twenty-six months the communists had misjudged the people and had used force in pursuit of their ends, as communism had taught them to do. They have not tried again.

Many people thought that fighting in Moscow could settle nothing. In fact it settled a lot. The elections were in held in mid-December. The reformers fought a weak and divided campaign, and did quite poorly. Yet the new parliament never confronted the president, as the old one had. It elected well-qualified people (and not Zhirinovsky) to chair its committees, and by April 1995 it had passed a budget of quite unprecedented austerity.

So what had changed? The answer was simple: the constitution. At the same time as the mid-December elections there had been a referendum on a new constitution, and it had been adopted. Though it still has some ambiguities (most constitutions do), it is a workable arrangement.

It is a hard thing when a president is driven to break a constitution. But if that is what the people want, it must be the democratic thing to do. De Gaulle did it. And what of the future? Since the conflicts of the recent years stemmed from an unworkable constitution, such violent conflicts are unlikely to recur. But smaller conflicts and even the collapse of democracy cannot be ruled out.

Can democracy survive?

How robust is Russian democracy? Indeed, is Russia really democratic yet, and will it remain so?

Although the president is very powerful, Russia is a democracy by any reasonable definition.[11] First, there are free elections. The president is elected, and so is the parliament. The president has slightly more power than a French president but serves a term of five years rather than seven. In general, elections have been conducted fairly, with no restrictions on who could stand. The only political parties not permitted are those advocating violent overthrow of the state.

Second, there is free speech. There are a multitude of antigovernment newspapers, though they receive less financial support than those supporting the government. The first television channel is controlled by the president, but the others are not, and in Moscow there are five of them. Private money, rather than government connections, determines access to those channels. Public meetings can be freely held, with minimal restraints on venues. And, though the renamed KGB is still busy keeping records, its impact on political activity is probably limited.

But how secure is all this? Does Russia have the strength of political and other civic institutions to resist a would-be dictator? Unfortunately, the political parties in Russia are not strong. None have real grassroots organization, except the communists. Instead the members of the Duma are spread over many blocs. Within most parties there is little voting discipline, and alliances between parties tend to be ephemeral.

That has been a serious weakness of the reform cause: Its leaders have not been able to sink their personal differences and work within a common framework to secure the support of the Russian people.[12] This reflects partly lack of adequate finance but also a lack of the instinctive respect for voters that is acquired over time by politicians in settled democracies.

Some people blame Yeltsin for not himself founding a political party. That is unjustified. In any divided society, heads of state try to ride above factions. When France was nearly riven apart in the late 1950s, De Gaulle did just that, and Yeltsin probably did well to stay above the fray, ruling through a broadly based coalition government.

Just as Russia lacks powerful political parties, it also has still to develop many of the other institutions of a fully civic society that are in the last resort bastions against dictatorship. The courts command little respect, and institutions like universities, learned societies, trade unions, employers' associations, sports clubs, and so on are still developing their sense of themselves as institutions independent of the state. For many purposes, any Russian organization wanting to do anything still goes straight to the local mayor.

With this level of vulnerability, what are the chances for Russian democracy? On many criteria the outlook is good. Democracies on average are more educated than autocracies: Russia is well educated. Democracies tend to be complex, urban, societies with a modicum of wealth; so is Russia. And most democracies (though not all) are ethnically homogeneous, as is Russia, where 82 percent of the citizens are ethnic Russians.

Today Russia's most obvious problems are crime and corruption, and most Russians would like a strong president who would tackle those problems. They indicate their preference with a clench of the fist. Can such a president rule within a democratic context? It is certtainly possible.

But what about the army? The army has been unwilling to get involved in politics. In August 1991 it would not attack the White House and only agreed to do so in October 1993 under protest. A pure military coup is therefore most unlikely, and if it were successful its leaders would almost certainly end up controlling only a limited domain around Moscow and perhaps a few other cities. More possible is the election of a legitimate president who tries to use the Communist party apparatus or the army to increase his power.

But even then, one should never underestimate the regions of Russia. They will strongly resist any effort to increase the power of Moscow. Thus a key advantage of Russia's size is that the regions are an important source of countervailing power. Because no one wants to be a dictator whose will is flouted, the regions are perhaps the main bulwark against dictatorship in Russia.

The backstop is the international community. Russians want to trade with the West and to be accepted by the West. They know that under an autocracy such contacts, though they might continue, would be diminished. That too is a new force supporting democracy.

There is no certainty in these matters, but despite the communist resurgence we would still bet on the survival of Russian democracy.[13] But will Russia itself hold together?

Will Russia break up?

The handling of the regions has been one of Yeltsin's success stories, except for Chechnya. When the Soviet Union broke up into fifteen separate states, many people forecast that Russia would follow suit. They pointed to the size of Russia, which makes it difficult to control; to the economic differences between regions, which make for internal conflicts; and to the ethnic diversity.

Russia is indeed huge, with territory spanning ten time zones. But in reality most of the territory is empty, and most Russians live either in the European heartland of Russia or not far from the Trans-Siberian Railway. About 90 million Russians live in the European heartland, an area three times the size of France running from the Caucasus Mountains in the south to St. Petersburg in the north, and bordered on the east by the Volga hinterland.[14] Most other Russians live within 200 miles of the Trans-Siberian Railway, with further pockets around ports, mines, or gasfields in the Far North.

But distance as such is not the main problem in maintaining the union, especially as communications improve. A more serious obstacle is the growing difference in income levels across Russia (see Figure 14–3). Broadly, Moscow is the richest city, with St. Petersburg some distance behind. The other richest parts of Russia are the oil areas (mostly in Siberia) and those rich in minerals (also mostly in Siberia). Income inequalities will cause difficulty only if the central government redistributes from rich to poor regions.

The biggest problem, however, is the ethnic factor, which mainly arises from the fact that 12 percent of the population of Russia is Mus-

Figure 14-3. Income levels in 1994 by regions (in brackets: 1994 population in millions)

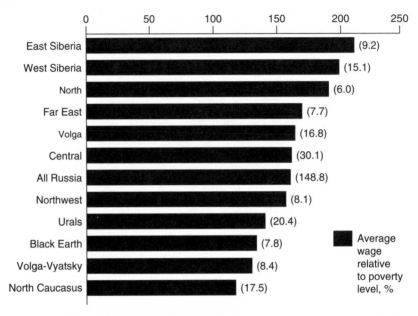

Sources: Population—Goskomstat, 1994, pp. 441-43. Average wage—Goskomstat, 1995, pp. 219–21; takes into account local price level.

lim. The majority of Muslims live in one of the twenty-one so-called republics of the federation, which have rather more autonomy than the sixty-six oblasts that constitute the other main regional govern-ments.[15] The Muslim republics fall into two main groups: those along the Volga, and those along the southern frontier beneath the slopes of the Caucasus Mountains. The Volga republics, like Tatarstan (capital: Kazan) and Bashkortostan (capital: Ufa), have oil and straddle the east–west railways. Their oil provides them with incentives to avoid taxes, while their position gives them political leverage. But on the other hand, ethnic Russians make up 40–60 percent of the local popu-lation, and the landlocked position of these republics makes a genuine bid for independence implausible. Even so, for two years Tatarstan in-sisted that it was a sovereign state.

The republics of the North Caucasus are better placed to break free. They were always difficult for Russia to control, the typical frontier area populated by independent clansmen. But none of those republics is homogenous, even though Russians are in a small minority there. Only in a few of the republics does the majority of the population come from the ethnic group after which the republic is named. One such area is Chechnya. In August 1991 it declared its independence, and for five years it has defied the authority of Moscow.

But despite a challenge from Chechnya, the issue of regional independence has ceased to be a major issue elsewhere in the Federation—at least up until 1996 with Yeltsin at the helm.

How did Yeltsin hold Russia together, where Gorbachev failed to hold together the Soviet Union? It was surely an easier task. Russia was an old entity, ethnically homogeneous, whereas the Soviet Union included diverse states, some recently conquered, like the Baltics, and others conquered earlier, like Georgia, Armenia, and the Muslim republics of Asia.

But Yeltsin also learned from Gorbachev's mistakes. He always gave the issue high priority and was always willing to share power from the beginning. In March 1992 he persuaded all the regions (except for Tatarstan and Chechnya) to sign a Federation Treaty. That gave the central government responsibility for defense, national security, monetary policy, long-distance communications and transport, pensions, basic science, and the like, while the regions were responsible for most health, education, law and order, and privatization. By 1994 half of all public expenditure was in the hands of regional and local authorities. Central subsidies to regional governments amounted to only 3 percent of the GDP.

On the tax side, most taxes are split between the center and the regions in fixed proportions. That is a good approach, because it gives local tax officials an incentive to collect as many taxes as possible, including the central government's share. As oil and gas prices rise, profits taxes in the energy sector will surely cause problems, because they will lead to a major redistribution of regional income. Nevertheless, though in the past some regions have refused to implement national tax laws, they now carry out the law.[16] And even Tatarstan agreed in February 1994 that it was "united" with Russia and accepted the obligations of the Federation Treaty.

So it seemed by 1994 that the regional issue had been more or less settled, except for the Muslim republic of Chechnya, which still claimed independence and paid no taxes. The elected ruler of Chechnya, Jokar Dudaev, had assumed dictatorial power in the fall of 1991. He then declared independence but was never willing to put that proposition to the electorate. He was a controversial figure even within Chechnya. But the old guard around Yeltsin felt he should be taught a lesson, which would be remembered in the future by any would-be secessionist. In December 1994 the Russian Army went in, expecting a quick victory and the support of the Russian people. They got neither. The war was hard and bloody, and over 80 percent of Russians said they opposed it. Westerners were horrified at what they saw on their TV screens, but most drew the wrong conclusion. The war reinforced their view that Russians were a violent and aggressive people, but they failed to notice that the war was also condemned by most Russians.

The war had three important effects. First, it reinforced Western suspicions of Russia, making a "new world order" much less likely. Second, it discredited the old guard in Russia and led to the economic policy victory of the reformist ministers in early 1995, which in turn led to the IMF standby agreement. And, third, it committed Russia to the logic of the sanctity of international frontiers. Thus, for the time being at least, Russia abandoned any thought that Crimea should leave Ukraine. Thus one bloody war made less likely an even bloodier one between Russia and Ukraine.

Will Russia rebuild the empire?

When the Soviet Union split up, many people feared a repetition of Yugoslavia, especially a war between Russia and Ukraine. There were certainly reasons to worry. There are 25 million Russians living in other republics, especially in Ukraine and Kazakhstan, kith and kin beyond the borders, analogous to the Serbs in Bosnia and Croatia. Ukraine has 11 million Russians, mostly in Crimea and the Donets River Basin, and in both areas Russians form a majority. Most Russians had never even considered Ukraine a separate entity. In 1954, when Khrushchev gave Crimea to Ukraine, it was to demonstrate the friendship of Russia and Ukraine. In almost every republic of the former Soviet Union there are areas where Russians are in the majority.

That would have caused no problem if Russians had been able to continue to live as before, but in many areas (especially the Baltics) their civil rights were limited by voting restrictions or linguistic requirements in education and employment.

So the first question is, How did the Soviet Union break up without any major conflict between Russia and the other former republics? For the future, there is a second question: Will Russia restore the Empire?

The key to both questions lies in the manner in which the Soviet Union fell apart. It was not mainly destroyed by nationalism. It was destroyed by hatred of centralized communist rule in Moscow. Russia itself left the Soviet Union in order to escape from its communist government. The other countries, more communist in their thinking, left in order to escape from Moscow. The Russians were as happy to see the others go as were those who went. The Empire was destroyed on December 8, 1991, by an agreement between the presidents of Russia, Ukraine, and Belarus in a hunting lodge near Minsk.

Thus at the start the Russians and the other new states had a common interest in leaving the Soviet Union. But will Russia now wish to reestablish its authority? For Russia there are of course pros and cons. The economic arguments are against a new imperialism, but there are political factors pushing the other way.

Russia is far richer than the other states. Though most Russians and many Westerners assumed that Russia had been exploiting the rest of the Empire and, indeed, the whole COMECON area, it turned out that the opposite was true. The Empire and COMECON had been draining Russia. The reformers understood that and therefore wanted to reduce Russia's responsibilities for the other countries to the barest minimum.

That has always been a strong argument against a new economic union. Yet proposals for economic union have kept recurring, due to Russia's desire to exert influence in its own backyard. Russia's first overwhelming interest was to neutralize the nuclear weapons in Ukraine, Belarus, and Kazakhstan. That was done temporarily in return for various handouts. But the ongoing interest is to make sure that Russians abroad get a reasonable deal and that there is no serious disorder in the countries close to Russia.

This has led to the use of strong-arm tactics on a number of occasions. In Moldova the Russian Army openly supported the Russians on the eastern side of the Dniestr, who demanded more autonomy than the Moldovian government was willing to provide. In Tajikistan the Russian Army carried out a CIS-agreed mission to impose peace on warring clans and to insist on a proper election. In Azerbaijan Russia (probably) supported an armed coup against the elected president, though the new president was later confirmed by election. And in Georgia Russian troops openly supported the successful revolt of the Abkhaz people against the national government. It is not easy to judge most of those episodes, but the Abkhaz incident clearly went far beyond the bounds of peacekeeping.

However, when all is said, the overall record is good: no fighting between Russia and the other successor states, and (except over the Black Sea fleet) barely a crisis. After strong international pressure Russian troops left the Baltics on time in 1994. Under Russian pressure all the other republics joined the Commonwealth of Independent States, and most gave Russia bases on their territory. But any great power tries to exert influence in its hinterland, and the Russian record is not bad by international standards, except for Chechnya, which is nominally a Russian domestic question.

Only two major Russian parties are pledged to reunite the Empire, the communists and Zhirinovsky's Liberal Democrats. Such an attempt would almost certainly involve bloodshed and would probably therefore be unpopular (as the Chechen war was). But events can always take unexplained turns, and sentiments can change. One cannot rule out the possibility of conflict with either Ukraine or Kazakhstan, though both are unlikely.

Russia and the West: Friends or foes?

More uncertain, and more vital for the whole world, is the relation between Russia and the West. In the Cold War the richer part of the world was divided into two camps, and peace was preserved by the balance of terror. Though nuclear weapons added to the dangers, the arrangement was not altogether different from the traditional European system of alliances, where each country had friends and enemies, and peace was preserved by the balance of power—with wars preceded by a buildup of arms.

Suddenly, between 1985 and 1992 this mold was cracked. Under Gorbachev Russia recognized that it had lost the capacity to compete in the arms race. Once the old warriors in Russia were ousted in late 1991, there was suddenly a world in which the West had no enemy. People talked of a "new world order" in which the great nations would concentrate on the objectives they shared rather than on those where they differed. The hope was that Russia would become a "normal" country, like Germany, say, rather than behave like a superpower; only the United States would retain that status.

During 1992 the Russian government was extremely friendly to the West. Boris Yeltsin was saying that Russia had rejoined the Western community of nations and that the historic tension between Russia and the West was over. He surely meant it, though it was also a prudent posture for a country seeking foreign aid. Many Russians disliked the posture, and through 1992 their voices grew louder. Andrei Kozyrev, Russia's internationally minded foreign minister, tried hard to impress on the West that Russia needed to be treated as an equal partner if the honeymoon was to continue.

In fact it was almost inevitable that elements of tension would return, especially after Zhirinovsky's successes in the elections of December 1993, which forced the Russian government to adopt a more strident tone in foreign affairs. Much of the trouble came from Western actions perceived by Russia as uncollegial. The first problem was Serbia, a Slavic, Orthodox country traditionally allied to Russia. To deal with Bosnian Serb aggression in Bosnia, NATO decided in February 1994 to send air strikes against Serb positions around Sarajevo. Russia was not consulted and was furious. But Russia showed impressive statesmanship when in 1995 it agreed that Russian peace-keeping troops in Bosnia could serve under an American general.

By far the biggest problem so far has been the proposed enlargement of NATO. Poland has always feared Russia—quite understandably, since Russia has carved it up many times. It wants the security guarantee that NATO membership would confer. So do the other countries of Eastern Europe.

But one also has to look at the matter from the Russian angle. Russia has been invaded from Poland twice this century, losing more than 35 million people as a result. NATO membership would put NATO tanks, artillery, and infantry on the eastern border of Poland. What is the purpose? The main reason must be that Russia is a potential enemy.

But alliances have their own logic and can exacerbate the very enmity they are meant to guard against. Russia in early 1996 is ruled by a government that would never menace Poland. The best way to install a more hostile government in Moscow would be to expand NATO.

After the end of the last war NATO was created to oppose Russia. But it was also designed in a way that included and contained the former enemy, Germany. That act itself changed the nature of Germany. With this in mind, Russia has itself proposed a European security system of which *it* would be a member and has suggested building up for this purpose the Organization for Security and Cooperation in Europe (OSCE). OSCE by this proposal would replace NATO.

But NATO is not willing to die, even though at present it has no enemy. "Realist" Americans like Kissinger and Brzezinski insist that Russia's past record must preclude it from the key security organizations, even though the same argument would surely have led also to the exclusion of Germany. Apparently some countries can be expected to change and others not.

Faced with this impasse, the West has proposed a Partnership for Peace in which NATO is free to make bilateral treaties with any other member outside NATO. Such an arrangement can certainly lead to confidence-building exchanges of information and personnel, and (after some difficulties) Russia has joined the Partnership.

But the issue of NATO expansion will rumble on. It has a formidable momentum. American Polish voters and old Cold Warriors provide the emotional force—not to mention the armaments industry. The encouraging thing is that so much of the European diplomatic community senses the dangers. With luck Western voters will in the end question whether they want to spend money and risk lives on a far-off frontier.[17] But on the outcome of this debate will depend how far Russia develops into a "normal" member of the community of nations and whether Europe is governed by a new principle of "partnership" or by the old and costly principle of the "balance of power."

But how "normal" could Russia ever be? Russia will always be different. It is huge in population and in land, and has often in the past been viewed as a superpower in Europe, even before the Revolution. It has a long and difficult frontier with the world of Islam and China, which makes it careful of too strong an alliance with the West and makes the West careful of too strong an alliance with Russia. Besides, Russia is still unstable.

So what principle should be followed at this delicate moment in history? It must surely be, "Never close off options." Why say that Russia could *never* join NATO or the European Union? Of course, if Russia joined, the organizations would change their character. But the right course is surely to see what happens if both sides are as friendly to each other as possible.

The political balance sheet

So let us take a political stock-taking since 1991. How far has Russia progressed in the direction of democracy and world citizenship? Considering that Russia was never a democracy, even before the Revolution, the progress is remarkable (see Table 14–2). Russia has a freely elected government based on contested elections. It has free speech, with no more government interference in the media than occurs at times in France and Italy. The Soviet Union was split up without bloodshed. And in world affairs Russia has tried to behave as a proper partner of the West within the framework of the United Nations.

But there are still also glaring weaknesses. The workings of government are confused and dominated somewhat erratically by the presidency. Political parties are weak, and it is not clear who would organize any resistance to a more autocratic president. Chechnya, though ruled by a dictator, was brutally invaded. Russia has on occasion exerted more influence on its neighbors than is reasonable, especially in supporting the Abkhaz rebels in Georgia. And there remains the whole question of Russian nationalism.

The future

It is time to peer more systematically into the future. Will economic reform continue, with Russia ever more open to trade and investment

Table 14–2. The political balance sheet

Democratic elections	Contested and fair elections for presidency and parliament
Free speech	Freedom of assembly; free press, with state subsidies; independent, as well as state, TV
Rule by due process	Confused issuing of decrees and laws Dominance of presidency over government Constitutional court reactivated in 1995 only
Sources of countervailing power	Political parties weak; absence of strong bulwarks against autocratic rule
Local democracy	Elected councils Brutal suppression of Chechnya's secession under dictator Dudayev
Treatment of former Soviet states	Successful breakup of Soviet Union without bloodshed Some subsequent bullying, and support of Abkhaz rebels in Georgia
World citizenship	A good start, but bedeviled by Western and Russian ambivalence about full partnership; NATO expansion would undermine it

from the West, or will there be more controls and a return to "fortress Russia"? Will democracy become more firmly entrenched, with Russia friendly to the West, or will autocracy increase, fueled by Russian nationalism?

A simplistic answer is to say there are two possibilities: economic and political freedom, or economic and political dictatorship. But the history of other countries shows that many combinations are possible: A political dictator like Pinochet can sponsor economic freedom. So we have to think about Russia's future in terms of at least two different dimensions: economic and political.

We shall begin with the economic prospects and then examine the political prospects. Finally we shall review the main specific scenarios that could come about, assigning a likelihood to each.

Economic prospects

On the economic front much is clear.

• *The market has taken over from the state.* There is virtually no chance that Russia will revert to a state-controlled economy or even move back at all far in that direction. The voters will not vote for state control, though they might vote for some increase in regulation and for more state subsidies and social spending. But most attempts at reregulation would fail, because market forces are too powerful and the state apparatus too weak. The banks, the traders, and all the new business interests would find a way around. And the very size of Russia works strongly against effective regulation from the center, so any reregulation will be mainly local in character.

Private ownership is strongly entrenched by now. More of the urban economy is in private hands than in Italy. The new owners would resist to the maximum any effort to remove their property. Having said that, there are some significant qualifications. Property rights are still not well defined, and it is extremely difficult to secure legal redress for breach of contract. Bit by bit, shareholders' rights will improve, the Civil Code will be completed, lawyers and judges will be trained, and business will become more "normal." Those who obtain property by dubious methods now have a strong interest in the development of normality, since it will make it easier for them to hold on to what they have gained.

It will be some time before there is widespread private ownership of land. In the cities local authorities will continue to drag their feet over the sale of land, though it will accelerate. In the countryside it may take decades before all collective farms are broken up. The weakness of the real estate market will thus be one of the main impediments to new business development. The other main impediment is the mafia. Popular resentment is likely in the end to weaken the local mafia, though the big mafia in drugs, finance, and international trade may be harder to crack. But all in all, we can be sure that the domestic economy will look increasingly like economies in the West. But what of Russia's attitude to Western business?

• *Most Russians want to belong to the world economy.* They know that the West is rich, and they feel that the way to become rich is to join the club. There is, of course, massive ambivalence on this point. People do not like having to join someone else's club. When the question is put, however, most Russians would prefer a leadership that was liked by the West than one that was ostracized. That applies equally to the privileged, who have most of their property abroad, and to the underprivileged.

Thus Yeltsin almost always responded to Western pressure. When the West lamented the loss of Gaidar in December 1992, Yeltsin brought in Fedorov. When the West lamented the loss of Fedorov and Gaidar in January 1994, Yeltsin courted the IMF, and Chernomyrdin took the IMF chief for a weekend's shooting. And when the West was outraged at the attack on Chechnya, Yeltsin made major concessions to the IMF and the World Bank in order to get their blessing for his economic program. There has always been a powerful reform minister in the government, and this is quite likely to continue. But even if Russia reverted to a government of bureaucrats only, the desire to belong to the world community would remain a strong force affecting economic policy. Even bureaucrats want foreign investment of the "right" kind, and "fortress Russia" is an unlikely scenario. One should not rule out periods in which Russian economic policy moves backward for a time and is heavily criticized by the West, as happened to Ukraine in 1992–94. But such periods are not likely to last long; the political process will react appropriately to the economic failure that results.

Simple expropriation of Western property is unlikely. Tax treatment will remain uncertain, but tax laws are unlikely to change as often in the future as in the past. But greater protectionism is quite likely, so that Western business would be well advised to base itself inside Russia where possible. But how worthwhile is it to invest?

• *Russia has high growth potential, compared with most countries.* Any country that starts off behind can expect to grow faster than others, by the simple process of technological 'catch-up'—provided other things are equal. But in the case of Russia most things point to faster growth than could be expected for the average country (such as Brazil) that is at the same income level as Russia.

First, communism distorted the economy much more than inappropriate policies did in other emerging economies (like Brazil) that are already capitalist. Second, like other communist countries, Russia has a highly educated workforce. Third, Russia has exceptional natural resources. Fourth, compared with other countries, Russia used a much higher fraction of its resources on defense; those resources (especially the intellectual skills available for redeployment) are now helping to build capitalism. And fifth, Russia used to be remote from the centers of world prosperity, but not anymore. When Russia was last a capitalist country, it took three days to reach Moscow from London by train; now it takes three hours by plane. Thus Moscow is now in effect no farther from the West than Warsaw, Budapest, or Helsinki.

Against this, Russia has obvious disadvantages. Seventy-five years of communism generated a deeper cynicism and a sloppier attitude to work than did forty years of communism in Eastern Europe. Even so, the last three factors above make it highly likely that in the next fifteen years Russia will grow faster than most of Eastern Europe.

How fast will depend on the economic policies followed, which in turn will depend on the politics. Will Russia continue down the path of economic reform, or will it ride a perpetual see-saw caused by political instability?

Political prospects

There is much more uncertainty over the future of politics than over the future of the economy. The future of the economy is largely determined by the individual pursuit of wealth, which has predictable effects. Moreover, different political regimes will have more similar policies on the economy than on political freedom or defense. No politician would try to establish totalitarian control over the economy, however autocratic he might be. The logic of the market solution will always reassert itself.

Thus in economic life there is an inbuilt equilibrating force, but in politics that is less true. Here we are in the realm where forceful individuals and random events can have a powerful influence, whatever the underlying forces. Indeed, some people see Russian politics as a train moving along a railroad track with "points" at intervals along it; a small difference in the disposition of the points can lead the train to vastly different destinations.

This picture is probably exaggerated. Even in politics there are some strong equilibrating forces.

• *Russians are deeply cynical about politicians' ability to improve their lot.* This is a strong buffer against extremism.

• *Russians also care significantly about Western opinion.* This is partly because they want Western trade and finance, but they also like to see their president on good terms with the West and accepted as an equal at summit meetings. If Russia's leaders were tempted toward autocracy, the reaction of international institutions and business would exert an important counterinfluence. With modern communications such reactions feed through fast. Another important source of countervailing power is Russia's regions.

• *The regions have the last word.* In the end anyone who wants to rule all of Russia must pay enormous attention to the views and interests of the regions. Unlike the Soviet Union, which was an ethnic patchwork, Russia is homogeneous and will not break up. But the strength of the regions means that any autocrat in Moscow who attempts a general repression will be almost certain to fail. (Repression of a minority like the Chechens might, of course, succeed.) Local autonomy makes a substantial national political relapse unlikely. But, equally, some quite bad things could happen in some regions without being controlled by Moscow.

Those, then, are the forces for stability. But there are many potential sources of instability.

• *The weakness of Russian democracy.* Though Russia now has a constitution similar to the French, it has been in place only since late 1993. If the constitution were broken, there are few groups well organized to oppose this. The political parties are fragmented, and the legal profession disorganized.

Russian democracy is more likely to be undermined by a gradual process than by a sudden coup. At some point, a strong ruler such as Lebed could be elected president, and then gradually assume increased power to deal with manifest problems. The most obvious problems are the mafia and corruption. To deal with the mafia, President Yeltsin has already broken the constitution by allowing detention without trial for up to thirty days, even though the constitution allows only forty-eight hours. That produced almost no protest.

More far-reaching infringements of freedom might well be accepted in the name of strong government. Indeed, one can even imagine cases where the Duma would itself confer extreme powers on the president. The most obvious occasion would be a problem in the "near abroad."

• *Trouble in the "near abroad."* There are 25 million Russians living in other states of the near abroad. They are the Sudeten Deutsche of Russia, with the same destabilizing potential. The greatest problem lies in Ukraine. Most Russians feel that Crimea is part of Russia, not Ukraine. And there are millions more Russians in the Donets Basin nearby, who face severe economic difficulties that could easily be exploited to produce unrest. Though relations between Russia and Crimea have been quite well handled so far, problems could always recur, as they did in Northern Ireland after years of quiescence. It is easy to see how the problem of Russians in Ukraine could be exploited by Russian nationalists.

There is also the chance of unrest in North Kazakhstan, which is overwhelmingly Russian, and in the Baltics, where, for example, the second largest town in Estonia, Narva, is 95 percent Russian. Andrei Kozyrev, Russia's foreign minister, said that Russia reserves the right to use force to protect Russians in the near abroad. He was clearly playing to the domestic gallery, but his remarks sent tremors through the West.

From the standpoint of the West a foreign minister like Kozyrev is the best that can be hoped for. His actions from 1991 onward showed a willingness to cooperate with the West and to help build a new world order of nations that cooperate to preserve peace rather than rely on the balance of terror. But whether such an attitude continues to prevail in Russia's Foreign Ministry will depend very much on how skillfully the West handles the new Russia.

• *Russian nationalism.* The West must expect Russia to behave like a great power. Russia always was a great power from the eighteenth century on. The aberration was 1992, when Russia was so weak that it appeared totally compliant. By 1993 it was beginning to behave again like any great power. That meant attempting to exert influence in neighboring countries, as the United States does in the Americas (Panama, Nicaragua, Grenada, Haiti). Sometimes, as in Georgia, Russia has overstepped reasonable levels of intervention, but rarely has a great power relinquished an empire with so little bloodshed or malpractice.

The incident that most alarmed the West was, of course, the brutal invasion of the Russian province of Chechnya in late 1994. Such violence was surely unjustified and revived Cold War memories in the West. Unfortunately, most Westerners failed to notice the accompanying good news: that the majority of Russians strongly opposed the war.

In any case, from the West's point of view the key issue is how Russia has been in its dealings with the West. The answer is that it has sought a partnership in which great powers work together, as France and Germany work together, rather than a relationship based on the traditional balance of power. The response of the West has been uncertain and gives grounds for unease over the future.

• *Western reactions.* To make an old enemy into a partner requires a major act of faith of the kind practiced by France and Germany after 1945. It does not come naturally, and on two issues the West has offended Russian pride in ways that could be dangerous.

The first is the enlargement of NATO, and the second is the conflict in the Balkans. Unless the West and Russia can find agreed approaches to these problems, the kickback in Russia is unpredictable.

• *Weariness with reform?* The other obvious area of uncertainty is whether the Russians will tire of reform and how much that will matter.

In most of Eastern Europe, except the Czech Republic, reformist governments by now have been succeeded by left wing parties descended from the former Communist party. Reform has not been reversed anywhere, but it has been slowed. Will the same thing, or worse, happen in Russia?

There has indeed already been a strong swing against reform—and even more against corruption in government. In the elections to the Duma in December 1995, the largest number of seats went to the Communist party, who with their allies control 40 percent of the seats. At the same time there was a substantial fall in the support for the nationalist party, led by Vladimir Zhirinovsky, which now controls 11 percent of the seats. Altogether the combined proportion of the (party list) votes going to the Communists, Agrarians, and nationalists did not increase between the two elections of 1993 and 1995. But the 1995 election was a major setback for Yeltsin—especially because it brought to the forefront a much more organized opposition party (the Communists) and a much more plausible rival for president (the Communist leader, Gennady Zyuganov).

Yeltsin's reaction was to dump two of his key reformist ministers, Anatoly Chubais and Andrei Kozyrev, and to replace them with more traditionalist members of the old Soviet establishment. He also made populist noises about the need for more social spending and closer links with former Soviet republics, especially Belarus. But most of these changes were made for purposes of the presidential election campaign; there was little change in the substance of policy.

On the economic front Russia continued to stick to the financial targets agreed with the IMF in early 1995, and in March 1996 the government committed itself to a further 3-year program of disinflation and radical structural reform. In return the IMF promised a further $10.2 billion loan—a resounding vote of confidence. One reason for the IMF's confidence was the strength of the Central Bank, to which a new reformist governor, Sergei Dubinin, had been appointed in October 1995 for a four-year term of office.

By March 1996 it appeared that the most likely frontrunners for the June presidential election were Yeltsin himself and the Communist Zyuganov, though the prospects for Yeltsin could always falter if his health deteriorated or if there was a major reversal in Chechnya. If Yeltsin were to win, one could expect a continuation of current policies. If the Communists win, it is much less clear what to expect. Zyuganov has been talking with many voices, including a reassuring voice to Westerners. But there is clearly a battle between the moderates within the party, like Zyuganov, and the hard-liners. The party policy includes substantial renationalization (especially of oil and gas), more social spending, the use of price controls, and the voluntary restoration of the Soviet Union. It is clear that some of these policies would have to be attempted, putting in peril the program of disinflation and generating inevitable tensions between Moscow and the regions. Eventually, in all probability, the policies would be reversed, but in the meantime there could be a substantial setback to the economic recovery.

Scenarios

So much for the immediate prospects in early 1996. But for many purposes it is important to take a longer view, over say the next ten years. What are the main possibilities, and what are the chances attaching to each?

More of the same. During the next ten years the most likely prevailing scenario is "more of the same." The government would be led from the center but would remain a broad-based coalition, including some reform ministers as well as representatives of conservative groups. Progress would continue, but in the accustomed manner of two steps forward, one step back. The location of decision-making would remain unclear, but the legal system would improve steadily, with more codification of the law and better-functioning courts. However, much regulation would continue, especially at the local level, and corruption and the mafia would remain pervasive. Privatization would go on, but by lurches, with much of the agricultural land still unprivatized in ten years' time.

Under this scenario inflation would be in the range of 30 to 150 percent a year. Investment would recover, especially in natural resource industries, and the forces of the market would be strong. Thus economic growth would be good, averaging at least 5 percent a year. Relations with the West would be reasonably friendly.

That is what would happen if the existing governing group led by Yeltsin and Chernomyrdin continued in power. It is illustrated by the dark area in Figure 14-4. But other outcomes are also possible.

Neocommunism. The next most likely outcome is some form of left-wing nationalism of the kind now represented by the Communist party. Inflation would almost inevitably increase, since higher spending on social programs and subsidies to the military-industrial com-

Figure 14-4. Scenarios

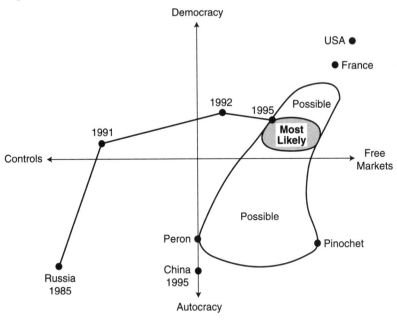

plex could not easily be matched by higher taxes. Price controls might then be introduced but would certainly fail. In other words, we would see the kind of populist statism pursued by Peron in Argentina.

There would be no further privatization, and some private wealth might be taken back into state hands. The power of the ministries would increase, and there would be increasing conflict between Moscow and the regional governments—leading at worst to an attempt by some parts of the country to split off.

To impose its will, the Center might use local Communist party secretaries as a kind of parallel government. Freedom of TV and radio would be severely limited. The mafia might have a harder time.

At the same time there would be more explicit pressure on the former Soviet republics to become client states. This could include more support for Crimean independence from Ukraine, and more use of oil and gas supplies as instruments of diplomatic pressure. But any attempt to woo the former republics toward voluntary reunion would be costly (in terms of financial transfers) and thus eventually rejected by the Russian people, who though they want Russia to be great do not want to pay billions of dollars to others, especially if they are Muslims. Meanwhile relations with the West would worsen.

A development of this kind would have strong support from older Russians but much less from the young. It would be ultimately doomed because of economic failure and because the young will eventually take over. It would be unlikely to last more than five years.

The return to financial orthodoxy would probably come sooner than that. Economic recovery would be muted, but would be likely to average at least 4 percent a year.

Noncommunist nationalism. A third possible outcome within the next ten years is authoritarian rule, coming not from the political left but from the center, or even from the right. This could happen through an outburst of simple nationalism or of revulsion against corruption and lawlessness. The chief threat of this kind comes at present from Vladimir Zhirinovsky, but new threats could arise over the next decade. The most dangerous moment is not necessarily at the depth of recession. As expectations begin to rise, the danger of political unrest often increases. A series of bad experiences in the "near abroad" could create a very nasty climate in Russia—with refugees fleeing to Russia while at the same time the West condemns Russian aggression. Nationalism and anti-Semitism are never far below the surface, and one cannot rule out a period of rule by a fascist populist. The president might seize extra powers or even have them conferred on him by the Duma or by referendum. Though a simple military coup is unlikely, media freedom would be curtailed.

But what would happen to economic policy? It could be centrist or it could even be strongly pro-business like that of Pinochet in Chile. After all, Zhirinovsky has declared himself to be the businessman's friend. In such a world business might eventually do better than under a more muddled government, but it would surely take a few years before Western business recovered its confidence in Russia after the failure of democracy.

Reform, pure and simple. The least likely outcome is a government united behind economic reform. Russia has never yet had such a government, and the pressure of vested interests makes it unlikely. But if

Yeltsin won the presidential election his position would be remarkably strong, since the Russian president has even more power relative to parliament than France or the United States has. (A similar opportunity with a different president and a different Duma might occur in 2001.) Under such a scenario there would surely be a surge of foreign investment, which could rise to over $10 billion a year, with economic growth at over 6 percent a year.

Envoi. So the most likely outcome is a continuation of "muddling through" in politics, and market deepening in economics.[18] Though there is a real chance that the politics will turn bad, in all probability Russia will become increasingly integrated into the international system, eventually joining the World Trade Organization and becoming a full member of the G7.

It will remain a great power with a large nuclear arsenal, but if the West can make it a partner, this will help toward a more stable world. At home, political and legal processes will gradually become more normal, though it will take years before corruption and the mafia are substantially cut back.

Meanwhile, whatever happens to the politics, there will be strong economic growth, based on private enterprise. Russia's economy, which is now the size of California's,[19] will grow faster over the next twenty years than that of most OECD countries and probably faster than most emerging markets (outside the Far East). It will remain a hard place to do business, but foreigners will reap good returns from investing in the large domestic market and in Russia's amazing natural resources. Those who move fast will gain a special advantage from being first—and from the current undervaluation of Russian assets.[20]

When Westerners visit Russia they regularly say, "Is this the country I have been reading about?" Compared with its image in the Western media, Russia is a much more normal place. When Westerners realize this, they will make good money. But, more important, we shall have a safer world and a more prosperous Russia.

Calendar of Events

1917	*Nov.*	October Revolution
1921	*Feb.*	Creation of Gosplan
1922	*Dec.*	Formation of the Union of Soviet Socialist Republics
1928	*Oct.*	Beginning of First Five Year Plan
1941	*Jun.*	German invasion of USSR
1953	*Mar.*	Death of Stalin
	Sept.	Khrushchev confirmed as first secretary of Communist party
1964	*Oct.*	Brezhnev replaces Khrushchev
1979	*Dec.*	Soviet military intervention in Afghanistan
1982	*Nov.*	Death of Brezhnev. Andropov becomes general secretary
1984	*Feb.*	Death of Andropov. Chernenko becomes general secretary
1985	*Mar.*	Death of Chernenko. Gorbachev becomes general secretary
1986	*Apr.*	Chernobyl disaster
1989	*May/Jun.*	Meeting of Congress of People's Deputies (elected in March)
	Jul.	Coal miners' strike
	Nov.	Fall of Berlin Wall
1990	*Feb.*	Communist party renounces its leading role
	Mar.	Election of Russian Congress of People's Deputies (dissolved September 1993)

May	Russian Congress elects Yeltsin as chairman
Jun.	Russian Congress declares sovereignty of Russia
1991	*Jan.*	Soviet forces attack public buildings in Vilnius and Riga
	Jun. 12	Yeltsin elected president of Russia by direct election
	Aug. 19–21	Abortive coup
	Oct. 28	Yeltsin announces the policy of radical economic reform in his address to Congress of People's Deputies of Russia
	Nov. 1	The parliament grants Yeltsin extraordinary powers to be exercised in the course of radical economic reform. Drafts of the presidential decrees on economic policy become effective, if not rejected by the parliament within seven days
	Nov. 6–8	Reform government appointed. Deputy prime ministers are Burbulis (first deputy), Gaidar, and Shokhin
	Nov. 15	Liberalization of wages and salaries; freedom to export and import established
	Dec. 5	VAT, excise, and profit taxes introduced
	Dec. 8	Leaders of Russia, Ukraine, and Belarus meet near Minsk and sign agreement to abolish the USSR and found the Commonwealth of Independent States
	Dec. 25	USSR president Mikhail Gorbachev announces his resignation and the end of the USSR
1992	*Jan. 2*	Price liberalization
	Jan. 29	Decree on liberalization of trade
	Feb. 27	Agreement with the IMF on economic policy for 1992
	Mar. 31	All the former autonomous republics within Russia (except Chechnya and Tatarstan) sign the Federation Treaty
	Apr. 1	Western governments announce a $24 billion aid package for Russia, including a $6 billion stabilization fund
	Apr. 3	Burbulis dropped as first deputy prime minister
	Apr. 6	Congress of People's Deputies attacks government
	Apr. 29	Gaidar participates in meeting of G7 finance ministers in United States
	Jun. 15	Yeltsin names Gaidar as acting prime minister
	Jul. 10	Russia and IMF sign a standby agreement
	Jul. 17	Gerashchenko appointed chairman of Central Bank
	Aug. 15	Yeltsin announces voucher privatization
	Dec. 12	Yeltsin agrees with the parliament on holding a referendum
	Dec. 14	Chernomyrdin replaces Gaidar as prime minister

	Dec. 23	Fedorov appointed deputy prime minister for economy and finance
1993	*Mar. 11*	Congress of People's Deputies passes draft resolution limiting powers of the president and the government to implement reforms
	Mar. 20	Yeltsin introduces "special presidential rule"
	Mar. 23	Parliamentary Speaker Khasbulatov calls for impeachment of Yeltsin
	Mar. 28	Congress fails to impeach Yeltsin
	Apr. 3–4	U.S.–Russia summit in Vancouver, Canada
	Apr. 13–14	Meeting of G7 ministers of foreign affairs in Japan with participation of Russian finance minister Fedorov and foreign minister Kozyrev. The G7 propose a $28 billion package. United States also proposes $4 billion Privatization Fund
	Apr. 25	Referendum expresses confidence in the president, supports the socio-economic policy of government and the president, does not favor earlier presidential elections, but favors earlier elections for the Congress
	Jul. 2	The IMF approves first part ($1.5 billion) of $3 billion "systemic transformation facility" (STF) loan
	Jul. 24	Demonetization of old Soviet banknotes
	Sept. 18	Gaidar rejoins government as first deputy prime minister
	Sept. 21	Yeltsin dissolves parliament and calls elections for a new legislative body for December 11–12
	Sept. 22	In response to president's action, Russian parliament appoints Rutskoi as president
	Oct. 3	Parliamentary forces attack the television tower and the Moscow mayor's office
	Oct. 4	Government forces storm parliament buildings
	Dec. 12	Parliamentary elections and a referendum on the constitution
1994	*Jan. 16*	Gaidar resigns as first deputy prime minister
	Jan. 20	Fedorov resigns. Shokhin becomes first deputy prime minister responsible for economy
	Mar. 22	IMF managing director Michel Camdessus announces that second tranche of the STF loan, worth $1.5 billion, will be released
	Jun. 24	Partnership and Cooperation Agreement with the European Union initialed
	Oct. 12	Following the ruble crash of October 11, Yeltsin dismisses acting finance minister Dubinin

	Oct. 18	Paramonova appointed by President Yeltsin to replace Gerashchenko
	Nov. 4	Panskov becomes finance minister. Shokhin resigns
	Dec. 12	Russia moves troops into Chechnya
1995	*Jan. 27*	Parliament passes the Law on the Central Bank of Russia by which the Central Bank is banned from lending to the government without parliamentary sanction
	Jan. 28	Russia, Belarus, and Kazakhstan sign an agreement to establish a customs union
	Apr. 11	The IMF approves a $6.8 billion standby loan
	Apr. 25	Chernomyrdin announces the creation of his own electoral bloc
	Jul. 5	Exchange rate corridor of R4,300 to R4,900 to the dollar introduced by the Central Bank
	Aug. 24	Exchange rate corridor extended to end year
	Oct. 26	President Yeltsin suffers second, more serious, heart attack
	Nov. 22	Dubinin approved by the Duma as chairman of Central Bank
	Nov. 28	Russia agrees that its peacekeeping troops in Bosnia can serve under an American general
	Nov. 30	Exchange rate corridor of $4,550–5,150 announced for first half of 1996
	Dec. 6	1996 Budget approved by Duma
	Dec. 17	Duma elections. Big Communist gains.
1996	*Jan. 5*	Kozyrev resigns as foreign minister (shortly afterwards replaced by Primakov)
	Jan. 16	Chubais resigns as deputy prime minister (shortly afterwards replaced by Kadannikov)
	Feb. 15	Yeltsin and Zyuganov announce their candidacy for the presidential election.
	Feb. 22	Agreement between Russia and IMF initialed for 3-year Extended Fund Facility of $10.1 billion (subsequently ratified by the Russian government and IMF Board).
	Mar. 15	Duma votes to reassert the legitimacy of the Soviet Union and to denounce treaty setting up CIS. Vote has no constitutional force.

Notes

Chapter 2. Is Russia different?

1. Published in George Gibian, ed., *The Portable Nineteenth-century Russian Reader* (London, 1993), p. 237.
2. Anna Akhmatova, "I am not with those who abandon their land," from *Anno Domini MCMXXI* (St. Petersburg, 1922).
3. Aleksandr Herzen, *The Other Shore* (London, 1956), p. 179.
4. Pyotr Chaadayev, *Filosoficheskiye Pisma* (Philosophical Letters) (Moscow, 1908), p. 100. Quoted in Tibor Szamuely, *The Russian Tradition* (London: Secker & Warburg, 1974), p. 269.
5. Ruslan Khasbulatov, *The Struggle for Russia* (London: Routledge, 1993), p. 57.
6. Szamuley points out that other countries grant their most influential figures ages and eras (the Elizabethan or Victorian ages in Britain, France's Napoleonic era, or Wilhelmine Germany). Russia organizes its whole history around Peter, dividing it into pre- and post-Petrine periods. Szamuely, *Russian Tradition*, p. 122.
7. Aleksandr Herzen, *Polnoye sobraniye sochinenii i pisem*, ed. M. K. Lemke (St. Petersburg, 1919), vol. IX, p. 1.
8. Reinhard Wittram, *Russia and Europe* (London, 1973), p. 61.
9. Ilya Krichevsky, "Exhausted by Depression," trans. Albert C. Todd. In Albert C. Todd and Max Hayward, eds., *Twentieth-century Russian Poetry*, selected by Yevgeny Yevtushenko (London, 1993).
10. Quoted in Jeffrey Sachs and David Lipton, *Prospects for Russia's Economic Reforms* (Washington, DC: Brookings Institution, 1993).
11. Nikolai Berdyaev, *The Russian Idea*, trans. R. M. French (London: Londisfarne Press, 1992).

12. See Richard Pipes, *Russia Under the Old Regime*, 2d ed. (Harmondsworth: Penguin, 1995).

13. Marquis de Custine, *Empire of the Czar* (Garden City, NY: Doubleday, 1989), p. 16.

14. Andre Gide, *A Retour de URSS* (Paris: Livres de Poche, 1938), p. 15.

15. Gide, *A Retour de URSS*, p. 66.

16. Custine, *Empire of the Czar*, p. 129, and Gide, *A Retour de URSS*, p. 46.

17. Custine, *Empire of the Czar*, p. 588, and Gide, *A Retour de URSS*, p. 48.

18. Custine, *Empire of the Czar*, p. 619, and Gide, *A Retour de URSS*, p. 79.

19. Quoted by David Remnick, "Autumn of the Patriarch," *New Yorker*, May 9, 1994, p. 100.

20. Boris Yeltsin, *The View from the Kremlin*, trans. Catherine A. Fitzpatrick. London: HarperCollins, 1994, p. 288.

21. Thomas Garrigue Masaryk, *The Spirit of Russia*, 3 vols., trans. Eden Paul and Cedar Paul (London: George Allen & Unwin, 1919).

22. Masaryk, *Spirit of Russia*, vol. 1, p. 5.

23. *Ibid.*, vol. 2, p. 528, and Szamuely, *Russian Tradition*, p. 240.

24. Masaryk, *Spirit of Russia*, vol. 2, p. 113, and Szamuely, *Russian Tradition*, pp. 241–42, 217.

25. Szamuely, *Russian Tradition*, p. 465, and Masaryk, *Spirit of Russia*, vol 2, p. 543.

26. Szamuely, *Russian Tradition*, p. 305.

27. Masaryk, *Spirit of Russia*, vol. 2, pp. 92–93, and Szamuely, *Russian Tradition*, pp. 388–89.

28. Szamuely, *Russian Tradition*, p. 7.

29. Masaryk, *Spirit of Russia*, vol. 2, p. 527.

30. Quoted in Isaiah Berlin, *Russian Thinkers* (London: Hogarth, 1978), p. 165.

31. Masaryk, *Spirit of Russia*, vol. 2, p. 545.

32. Masaryk, *Spirit of Russia*, p. 133, and Szamuely, *Russian Tradition*, p. 243.

33. Szamuely, *Russian Tradition*, pp. 380–82.

34. *Ibid.*, p. 243.

35. Berdyaev, *Russian Idea*, p. 104.

36. Sergei Filatov and Lyudmila Vorontsova, "In Search of an Identity," in *Remaking Russia*, ed. Heyward Isham. (Armonk, NY: IEWS M.E. Sharpe, 1995).

37. Robert Schiller, Maxim Boycko, and Vladimir Korobov, "Popular Attitudes Toward Free Markets: the Soviet Union and the United States Compared," *The American Economic Review*, June 1991.

38. Anders Aslund, *How Russia Became a Market Economy* (Washington, DC: Brookings Institution, 1995), p. 312.

39. Vyacheslav Ivanov, "In My End Is My Beginning," in Isham, ed., *Remaking Russia*.

40. See Szamuely, *Russian Tradition*, pp. 13–16.

41. Aleksandr Blok, "The Scythians," trans. Babette Deutsch, in Todd and Hayward, eds., *Twentieth-century Russian Poetry*.

42. Prince Nikolai Trubetskoi, George Florovsky, and Pyotr Savitsky, *Iskhod kvostoku* (Exodus to the East) (Sofia, 1921).
43. Masaryk, *Spirit of Russia*, vol. 1, pp. 242–43. See also Vera Tolz, "The Intellectual Debate over Russia's Future," RFE/RL Research Report, vol. 1, no. 49 (Munich: Radio Free Europe/Radio Liberty Research Institute, December 11, 1992).
44. Dmitry Likhachev, "I Object," in Isham, ed., *Remaking Russia*, pp. 51–63.
45. "A Silent Revolution: A Survey of Russia's Emerging Market, *The Economist*, April 8, 1995, p. 4.
46. Aleksei Khomyakov, *To Russia*, quoted in Masaryk, *Spirit of Russia*, vol. 1, p. 322.
47. Fyodor Dostoevsky, "On the Mission of Russia," in Gibian, ed., *Nineteenth-century Russian Reader*, p. 433.
48. Fyodor Dostoevsky, "Writer's Diary, August 1880," reprinted in Gibian, ed., *Nineteenth-century Russian Reader*, p. 434.
49. Pyotr Chaadeyev, *Filosoficheskiye pisma*, p. 104, quoted in Szamuely, *Russian Tradition*, p. 269.
50. N. K. Mikhailovsky, *Sochineniya*, vol. IV, p. 952, quoted in Szamuely, *Russian Tradition*, p. 202.
51. William Richardson, *Anecdotes of the Russian Empire* (New York: Da Capo, 1968), letters XXXIV and LIV. Emphasis in original.
52. Fyodor Dostoevsky. *Notes from Underground*, trans. Jesse Coulson (London, 1972), pp. 33–34.
53. *Ibid.*, p. 9.
54. Maria Avakkumova, "Russia can't be grasped by the mind . . ." trans. Albert C. Todd, in Todd and Hayward, eds., *Twentieth-century Russian Poetry*.
55. Filatov and Vorontsova, "In Search of Identity," pp. 279–87.
56. *Ibid.*

Chapter 3. Why did Communism fail?

1. Many excellent books have covered the breakdown of the communist system between 1985 and 1991. On the economic side there are Anders Aslund, *Gorbachev's Struggle for Economic Reform* (London: Pinter, 1991); *idem, How Russia Became a Market Economy* (Washington, DC: Brookings Institution, 1995), ch. 2; and R. Skidelsky, T*he World After Communism: A Polemic for Our Times* (London: Macmillan, 1995). On the political side, see G. Hosking, *A History of the Soviet Union 1917–1991* (London: Fontana, 1992); J. B. Dunlop, *The Rise of Russia and the Fall of the Soviet Empire* (Princeton, NJ: Princeton University Press, 1993); and D. Remnick, *Lenin's Tomb* (New York: Random House, 1993).
2. See Anders Aslund, "How Small Is the Soviet National Income?" in Henry S. Rowen and Charles Wolf, Jr., *The Impoverished Superpower* (San Francisco: ISC Press, 1990). There was of course some defense spending by other Warsaw Pact countries.

3. For a time in the 1970s Voice of America was not jammed.
4. For a description of his life up till 1990, see Boris Yeltsin, *Against the Grain* (London: Pan Books, 1990), and for 1990 to 1994, see *idem, The View from the Kremlin* (New York: Random House, 1994).

Chapter 4. Too much shock therapy?

1. At the suggestion of Ljubo Szirc, in 1983 the director of the Institute of Economic Affairs, Lord Harris of High Cross, founded the Centre for Research into Communist Economies. That organization then helped to found in Moscow in 1989 the International Center for Research into Economic Transformation, directed by Konstantin Kagalovsky.
2. All the leaders subsequently held office. The leading members of the Gaidar group were Yegor Gaidar (later acting prime minister), Vladimir Mashchits (minister for CIS Affairs), Andrei Nechayev (minister of economy), Pyotr Aven (minister of foreign economic relations), Konstantin Kagalovsky (Russian director of the IMF), Andrei Vavilov (first deputy minister of finance), and Sergei Glasiev (deputy minister and then minister of foreign economic relations). Another key figure was Yevgeny Yasin, teacher of many of the reformers and later minister of economy. The leading members of the St. Petersburg group included Anatoly Chubais (deputy prime minister in charge of privatization and then first deputy prime minister in charge of economic affairs), Dmitri Vasiliev (deputy minister of privatization, and then deputy chairman of the Federal Securities Commission), Sergei Ignatiev (a deputy chairman of the Central Bank and then deputy minister of economy), Sergei Vasiliev (director of the Government's Working Center for Economic Reform and then deputy minister of economy), and Andrei Illarionov (chief economic adviser to the prime minister).
3. Also important behind the scenes was Aleksei Golovkov, economic adviser to Yeltsin and a member of Gaidar's Institute of Economic Policy.
4. The speech was to the Fifth Congress of People's Deputies.
5. The main members of the team were Kagalovsky, Vavilov, and Golovkov, with visits from Shokhin, Nechayev and others.
6. The president was prime minister, and there were three deputy prime ministers: Burbulis (first deputy), Gaidar (responsible for economic affairs), and Shokhin (responsible for social affairs).
7. The Supreme Soviet was a smaller body than the Congress of People's Deputies, and in continuous session except during vacations.
8. Western critics of the Gaidar policy include Marshall I. Goldman, *Lost Opportunity: Why Economic Reforms in Russia Have Not Worked* (New York: Norton, 1994); J. Gray, *Post-Communist Societies in Transition: A Social Market Perspective* (London: Social Market Foundation, 1994); M. Ellman, "Shock Therapy in Russia: Failure or Partial Success?" *Radio Free Europe/Radio Liberty Research Report*, April 3, 1992; and J. Steele, *Eternal Russia: Yeltsin, Gorbachev, and the Mirage of Democracy* (London: Faber & Faber, 1994). For good defenses, see J. Sachs, *Understanding Shock Ther-*

apy (London: Social Market Foundation, 1994); Anders Aslund, *How Russia Became a Market Economy* (Washington, DC: Brookings Institution, 1995); and R. Skidelsky, *The World After Communism: A Polemic for Our Times* (London: Macmillan, 1995). See also D. Gros and A. Steinherr, *Winds of Change: Economic Reform in Central and Eastern Europe* (London: Longman, 1995).

9. The extent of monopoly is discussed in Chapter 7.

10. This was mainly due to Boris Fedorov, as was the abolition of the Price Committee.

11. While the foreign exchange market had a freely determined and unified exchange rate from the beginning, there were also an export levy of about 40 percent for raw material exporters and (originally) massive import subsidies.

  On the export side, the export levy for the first six months consisted of a 20 percent tax plus a 40 percent surrender requirement at roughly half price; that was then replaced by a 40 percent tax. The government used these dollars to service the foreign debt and to buy centralized imports (which were also bought on trade credit). The centralized imports were then sold in Russia at far below the ruble equivalent of world prices, implying massive import subsidies. The subsidies were phased out during 1993.

  Exporters also had to sell a fraction of their export earnings in Russia, at the market rate, as follows:

  Jan.–July 1992 10% to the Central Bank (at roughly the market rate)
  July 1992–94   20% to the Central Bank, 30% to the foreign exchange market
  July 1994 on   50% to the foreign exchange market

Foreigners have been able to operate freely in rubles only since mid-1993, when they were permitted to have capital and current ruble accounts and to operate on MICEX. A capital account (or "I" account) is needed in order to conduct investments in Russia, and to open such an account Central Bank permission is required.

12. The black market rate in the street was 30 rubles to the dollar in April 1991, rising to 60 by the end of October.

13. N. Petrakov, "The Crisis of Economic Reform in Russia," *Voprosy ekonomiki*, 2 (1993): 64–65.

14. Yegor Gaidar, "Russian Reform," in Y. Gaidar and O. Pöhl, *Russian Reform/International Money* (Cambridge, MA: MIT Press, 1995).

15. R. Layard, S. Nickell, and R. Jackman, *Unemployment: Macroeconomic Performance and the Labour Market* (Oxford: Oxford University Press, 1991).

16. Burbulis had been dropped just before the Congress.

17. Former chairman of the USSR Gosbank (Central Bank) 1989–91.

18. G. Alfandari and M. Schaffer, "On 'Arrears' in Russia," paper, World Bank/Ministry of Economy of Russian Federation conference, "Russia: Economic Policy and Enterprise Restructuring," St. Petersburg, June 12–13, 1995, Table 4.

19. R. Layard and A. Richter, "Who Gains and Who Loses from Russian Credit Expansion?" *Communist Economies and Economic Transition*, 6, no. 4 (1994): 459–72, and P. Teplukhin, *Economic Policy Instruments for Russia* (Moscow: Progress-Academia, 1994), p. 23.
20. In January 1993, M2 equaled 17 percent of annualized national income. By March 1995 it had fallen to 9 percent.
21. USSR minister of the Gas Industry, 1985–89; chairman of the state concern "Gazprom," 1989–92.
22. Institute for World Economy and International Relations.
23. In 1992 the IMF had favored this as a goal, but it became more skeptical after the Mexican crisis and the apparent success of floating exchange rates in some other FSU states.
24. See paper by Layard presented in October 1993: R. Layard, "Can Russia Control Inflation?" in J.A.H. Beaufort Wijnholds, S.C.W. Eijffinger, and L. H. Hoogduin, eds., *A Framework for Monetary Stability* (Dordrecht: Kluwer Academic, 1994).
25. On the ruble zone, see B. Granville, "Farewell, Ruble Zone," in A. Aslund, ed., *Russian Economic Reform at Risk* (London: Pinter, 1995).
26. Russia had always sold more to the other republics than it bought from them (because of the abundance of its oil and gas). But this export surplus was a planned transfer of resources within one country. Now it became an unplanned transfer, which depended on the rate of money creation in the other republics. For example, the Ukrainian Central Bank would issue credit to a Ukrainian enterprise. This enterprise could then use those rubles to buy Russian oil—paying them to the Russian enterprise. The result was a transfer of resources to the Ukraine and an inflationary growth of money in Russia. Thus Russia's unplanned export surplus to the CIS countries became an automatic source of monetary growth in Russia, equal in the first half of 1992 to nearly 10 percent of the GDP.
27. This fundamental reform was instigated by Sergei Ignatyev, an insightful monetary economist from St. Petersburg serving as a deputy chairman of the Central Bank.
28. On the notion of equilibrium unemployment (or slack) see Layard, Nickell, and Jackman, *Unemployment*.
29. Because of Russia's size, Russian imports in 1990 were only 16 percent of its GDP (9 percent from the rest of the USSR; and 7 percent from elsewhere).
30. *The Economist*, July 22, 1995. Most of the rest said spontaneously, "There's been no reform."
31. For some critics, see note 8 for this chapter.

Chapter 5. Has the West done enough?

1. As early as September the World Bank had aborted a mission to advise on the Soviet economy because the Union government was no longer functioning.

2. Under the formula, the new states were "jointly and severally responsible." This meant that the debt was split up, but if one state defaulted on its share all the others would take over the responsibility.

3. It should also be noted that a given budget deficit will always be less inflationary if based on borrowed foreign exchange (rather than the printing of money), even if the foreign exchange goes entirely in capital flight.

4. The GDP is measured at the market rate because we are interested in how many rubles of expenditure the government could have financed with the money. Of course a loan of that scale would have somewhat reduced the ruble price of dollars.

5. For a fuller discussion see J. Sachs, "Russia's Struggle with Stabilization: Conceptual Issues and Evidence," in *Proceedings of the World Bank Conference on Development Economics* (Washington, DC: World Bank, 1994). See also E. Hernandez-Cata, "Russia and the IMF: The Political Economy of Macro Stabilization," IMF paper on Policy Analysis and Assessment, Washington, DC, 1994, for the view of the chief IMF negotiator (1993–94).

6. This changed in mid-1992, when the resident professional staff rose to three; in 1993 it rose to four. The World Bank had three resident professionals in 1992, rising to five from 1993 on. Though the IMF missions in 1992 were led by a senior figure, John Odling-Smee, the managing director of the IMF did not visit Moscow at all during the "heroic" period between October 1991 and June 1992.

7. If the IMF is to blame, it may be for not pointing out publicly enough the need for G7 government action.

8. Slightly different statements were issued by President Bush and Chancellor Kohl. Later the Japanese complained that they had not been consulted.

9. About $40 billion was owed to governmental creditors (the Paris Club), $26 billion to foreign banks (the London Club), and the rest to nonorganized creditors, like providers of trade credit.

10. His influence can be seen by looking at two of the many remarkable papers he wrote charting the steps necessary for a properly-functioning financial system; see J. D. Sachs and D. Lipton, "Remaining Steps to a Market-based Monetary System," in A. Aslund and R. Layard, *Changing the Economic System in Russia* (London: Pinter, 1993), and J. D. Sachs, "Prospects for Monetary Stabilization in Russia," in A. Aslund, ed., *Economic Transformation in Russia*. (London: Pinter, 1994). At a later stage, Charles Wyplosz of INSEAD became the main Western economist working on monetary policy.

11. The Macroeconomic and Finance Unit was supported by the Ford Foundation and the Swedish government; the LSE's Centre for Economic Performance group was supported by the TACIS Program of the European Commission and located since 1995 in RECEP.

12. In addition it provided $1.2 billion of general budget support.

13. In September 1992 the World Bank financed the London School of Economics to organize for deputy prime minister Saltykov a Commission of

twenty-four Western and Russian experts to work out what texts and curricula were needed, but no funds could be found to implement the findings.

14. Another obvious high-return policy would have been to send many students abroad, as China did. But Russia did not request such a program.

15. The choice of the consultant also often reflects greater concern for which country the consultant comes from than for the wishes of the Russians. That gives the impression that a main aim of the program is to provide jobs in the West. This problem clearly arises strongly in bilateral aid programs but it also arises in multilateral programs, especially those financed by the European Commission.

16. There was also delay over the "negative pledge," by which the World Bank requires its loans to have priority position over the claims of other creditors. The Bank dropped this requirement in December 1993 for all transition economies.

17. See R. Layard, "Eldorados in Russia," in A. Raphael, ed., *Debrett's Euro-Industry 1993* (London: Debrett's Peerage, 1992).

18. EBRD, *Transition Report*, 1994, Table 8.6.

19. C. Michalopoulos and D. G. Tarr, eds., *Trade in the New Independent States* (Washington, DC: World Bank, 1994), p. 14.

20. Russia was not yet treated as an equal in the economic discussions.

Chapter 6. How do people live?

1. The material in this section is based on the World Bank's *World Development Report, 1994*, World Development Indicators; The Economist, *Pocket World in Figures* (London: Hamish Hamilton, 1994), and the *Economist Diary*. Using purchasing power parity (PPP) exchange rates Russia was richer than Greece, but this almost certainly gives insufficient weight to differences in the quality of products. (Russia had only one-third of Greece's telephones per capita and cars per capita, though almost 70 percent more TV and radio sets.) At PPP exchange rates the Russian GDP per capita was one-third of the U.S. figure; see Economist, *Pocket World in Figures*, p. 25.

2. *Economist Diary*, 1993, p. 111.

3. *Ogonyok*, May 1995, p. 48.

4. On newspaper readership and TV sets, see *Economist Diary*, 1993, p. 111.

5. The Economist, *The Economist Book of Vital World Statistics* (London: Hutchinson Business Books, 1990), p. 216.

6. Goskomstat, *Russian Statistical Yearbook* (Moscow: State Committee on Statistics, 1994), p. 55.

7. World Bank, *Russian Federation—Restructuring the Coal Industry: Putting People First* (Washington, DC: World Bank, 1994), p. 163.

8. On alcohol, see Goskomstat, *Russian Statistical Yearbook*, p. 200, and on smoking and accidents, see Economist, *Pocket World in Figures*, pp. 77

and 57. The following table compares male deaths by violence in Russia and the United States.

Male deaths by violence or accident (per 100,000 males)

	Russia 1991	United States 1990
Motor traffic accidents	42.6	26.1
Accidental poisoning	32.5	3.5
Accidental drowning	16.9	2.6
Suicide	44.5	20.4
Homicide	24.9	15.9
Other	74.3	20.6
	235.7	89.1

Source: World Health Organization, *Statistics Annual*, 1993.

9. M. Ellman, "The Increase of Death and Disease Under 'Katastroika,'" *Cambridge Journal of Economics*, 18 (1994): 329–55.
10. Economist, *Pocket World in Figures*, p. 71, and Goskomstat, *Russian Statistical Yearbook*, p. 45.
11. Much of this section and the next is based on Illarionov, Layard, and Orszag, "The Conditions of Life," in Anders Aslund, ed., *Economic Transition in Russia* (London: Pinter, 1994). This has been updated using subsequent issues of *Russian Economic Trends*.
12. They probably exaggerate the fall, even here. The prices used to deflate expenditure before the reform were listed prices only (i.e., lower than actual prices).
13. *Russian Economic Trends*, 3, no. 4 (1994): 128.
14. Number of plots from Anders Aslund; *How Russia Became a Market Economy* (Washington, DC: Brookings Institution, 1995), p. 262; the total area in January 1994 was 5.4 million hectares. Goskomstat, *Russian Statistical Yearbook*, p. 349.
15. Goskomstat, *Russian Statistical Yearbook*, pp. 357, 364. Data are for 1993. Update. Other high percentages are for vegetables (65), fruit (69), milk (35), and eggs (27).
16. The measured real wage was 25 percent lower in mid-1994 than in 1985—exactly the same fall as for the real pension. But, because of novel sources of income, wage growth understates the growth of nontransfer household income.
17. Like everybody, pensioners gained from the ending of the queues. For those old people who were weak or ill, queues were a real nightmare. But since the pension age is sixty for men and fifty-five for women, there are also many able-bodied pensioners. For them queues were less irksome than for working people, since they had fewer other demands on their time. Thus on average the ending of the queues probably benefited old and young in roughly equal measure.

18. See B. Popkin, M. Mozhina, and A. Baturin "The Development of a Subsistence Income Level in the Russian Federation," mimeograph, 1992. The income assumed to be needed in each age group was the following proportion of the average: children ages 0–6, 0.78; children 7–17, 1.16; adult males, 1.26; adult females, 1.05; and pensioner adults, 0.71.
19. Applies to end of 1994. The pension consists of your individual minimum pension plus an earnings-related element. If you have worked all your life, your individual minimum is 1.2 times the official "minimum pension."
20. Applies to 1994. See *Russian Economic Trends*, vol. 3, no. 2, chapter 4, Table 3.
21. It would also be bad for the budget deficit.
22. The data shown relate to individuals distributed according to monthly household income per capita. Using these data one can also calculate the more comprehensive Gini coefficient of inequality, which varies between 0 (complete equality) and 1 (all income to one person). The figures for Russia:

1991	0.26
1992	0.29
1993	0.33
1994	0.39
1995 (Q1)	0.39

See *Russian Economic Trends*, vol. 3, no. 4 (1994), Table 42.
23. These numbers are based on standard labor force surveys akin to the European Labor Survey, and the unemployment definition is the ILO/OECD definition: did no paid work in last week, available for work, and sought work in last four weeks.
24. What follows is heavily based on R. Layard and A. Richter, "How Much Unemployment Is Needed for Restructuring: The Russian Experience," *Economics of Transition*, 3, no. 1 (1995): 39–58.
25. This is the average for those enterprises that were in arrears; see *Russian Economic Trends*.
26. In Russia strike days per 1,000 workers were 1.2 during 1994; *Russian Economic Trends*, vol. 4, no. 1 (1995). In the OECD countries the corresponding annual average was 310 days in 1989–93. UK Employment Department, *Employment Gazette*, 1994, p. 434.
27. After that he goes onto the minimum wage, which is only 10 percent of the average.
28. There was a period of three years (1987–90) when the workers appointed the managers, but that was soon revised.
29. The Excess Wage Tax has varied in form. In 1995 firms paid an Excess Wage Tax equal to the rate of profit tax times all wages paid in excess of six times the minimum wage (i.e., in excess of roughly 60 percent of the national average wage). It could therefore pay a firm to keep a worker on, if it cut his wage to the bone; see W. Roxborough and J. C. Shapiro, "Excess Wages Tax," *Socio-economic Survey*, no. 17 (Moscow, 1994), and Layard and Richter, "How Much Unemployment," Appendix. But that rarely

happened. A more important result of the Excess Wage Tax was simply general downward pressure on wages. R. Layard, S. Nickell, and R. Jackman, *Unemployment: Macroeconomic Policy and Economic Performance* (Oxford: Oxford University Press, 1991), pp. 485–90. In addition, since the tax was on weekly wages per worker (rather than hourly), it encouraged work-sharing, because a firm could cut its tax liability by reducing hours per worker, with a similar cut in pay.

30. A. N. Brown, B. Ickes, and R. Ryterman, "The Myth of Monopoly: A New View of Industrial Structure in Russia," World Bank Policy Research Working Paper no. 1131, 1994, Table 24.
31. The main reason for the lower life expectancy of men as compared with women is the frequency of death by external causes (i.e. violence or poisoning) between the ages of 15 and 59. Most such deaths are alcohol-related (Ellman, "Increase in Death and Disease," p. 335). See also note 8 for this chapter.
32. UNICEF, "Crisis in Mortality, Health and Nutrition: Central and Eastern Europe in Transition—Public Policy and Social Conditions," *Economic and Transition Studies: Regional Monitoring*, no. 2, August 1994, p. 24.
33. *Ibid.*, p. 92.
34. For a good discussion see J. C. Shapiro, "The Russian Mortality Crisis and Its Causes," in Anders Aslund, ed., *Russian Economic Reform at Risk* (London: Pinter, 1995), and UNICEF, "Crisis in Mortality."
35. Between 1989 and 1993 deaths of men rose by 69 percent (at ages 20–39) and 54 percent (at ages 40–59), and of women by 55 percent (at ages 20–39) and 37 percent (at ages 40–59), see UNICEF, "Crisis in Mortality," p. 38.
36. *Ibid.*
37. The health service suffered from a serious shortage of drugs in 1992, but by 1994 the situation was back to normal.
38. Both figures relate to men of working age. UNICEF, "Crisis in Mortality," p. 53.
39. *Ibid.*; Ellman, "Increase in Death and Disease," p. 333, and U.K., *Social Trends*, 1994. The figures for homicide and suicide per 100,000 men and women were

	1990	1991	1992	1993
Homicide	14.3	15.2	22.8	30.6
Suicide	26.4	26.5	31.0	38.1

Source: Goskomstat, 1994, p. 50.

40. Goskomstat, *Russian Statistical Yearbook*, 1994, p. 51.
41. The number of true doctors (with medical degrees) per 1,000 people is 3.6 in Russia, 1.6 in the U.K. and 2.0 in the United States. Chernichovsky *et al.*, "Reform of the Russian Health Sector," World Bank report, mimeographed, 1994, p. 32, and Economist, *Vital World Statistics*, p. 216.
42. In 1991, 67 percent of public recurrent expenditure was on hospitals, compared with around a half in the West; 3 percent was on public health. Chernichovsky *et al.*, "Reform of Russian Health Sector," p. 58.

43. Though 8.5 percent of beds are in enterprise-owned hospitals, the recurrent expenditure is mainly met from local government budgets. *Ibid.*, p. 51.

44. Some areas, but not many, shifted over to regional Health Maintenance Organizations in which polyclinics performed a leading role, as budget holders. *Ibid.*, p. 66.

45. Goskomstat, *Russian Statistical Yearbook*, 1994, p. 101.

46. *Ibid.*, p. 105. During 1993, some 9 percent of families waiting were provided with a flat; 18 percent of families were on the waiting list. In Moscow the criteria for joining the waiting list was that there was less than 9 square meters of living space per person (excluding kitchen, toilets and corridors).

47. J. D. Braithwaite, "The Old and New Poor in Russia: Trends in Poverty" 1994, Table 3.A.

48. World Bank, *Russian Economic Reform: Crossing the Threshold of Cultural Change* (Washington, DC: World Bank, 1992); 5 percent were owned by co-ops and 17 percent privately.

49. Source: World Bank.

50. Goskomstat, *Russian Statistical Yearbook*, 1994, p. 762.

51. In 1993, a World Bank study of five cities recorded "residential mobility" of only 3.1% a year.

52. *Ibid.*, p. 108.

53. At present the procedures for foreclosure have still to be clarified, and housing is still an imperfect collateral.

54. Goskomstat, *Russian Statistical Yearbook*, 1994, p. 103.

55. There was no formal system of child benefits, but enterprise directors commonly allowed for children in their distribution of noncash benefits.

56. For a fuller discussion, see Braithwaite, "Old and New Poor."

Chapter 7. Will Russia prosper?

1. On the determinants of economic growth, see R. J. Barro and X. Sala-i-Martin, *Economic Growth* (New York: McGraw-Hill, 1995), summarized in R. J. Barro, "Democracy and Growth, in R. J. Barro and R. Marmion, eds., *Growth and Political Institutions* (Bucharest: Centre de Recerca en Economica Internacional, Universitat Pompeu Fabra, 1995); and J. D. Sachs and A. M. Warner, "Economic Convergence and Economic Policy," Harvard Institute for International Development paper, mimeographed, 1995.

2. As Sachs and Warner, "Economic Convergence," point out, natural resources that are already being exploited can be a hindrance since they lead to a lower share of manufacturing in total output (manufacturing being the sector where growth is faster), and the income they generate can be squandered through bad policy. Russia's natural resources, however, are underexploited; as regards policy, the outcome remains to be seen.

3. The other standard factor is population growth. In some (but not all) studies this is harmful to the growth of per capita income. Russia's population is roughly stable, with the excess of deaths over births offset by immigra-

tion from the "near abroad." See Goskomstat, *Current Statistical Survey*, 1995.

4. World Bank, *World Development Report*, 1995, Table 1.
5. For an excellent account of privatization in Russia, see Maxim Boycko, A. Shleifer, and R. Vishny, *Privatizing Russia* (Cambridge, MA: MIT Press, 1995).
6. J. Kornai, *The Road to a Free Economy* (New York and London: W. W. Norton, 1991).
7. In Poland this was achieved without privatization by allowing state enterprises to sell their assets by open competition.
8. Employees got preferential treatment in auctions and were also allowed to undertake employee buyouts after leasing. Of all retail outlets privatized by May 1993, 70 percent were bought by employees. Anders Aslund, *How Russia Became a Market Economy* (Washington, DC: Brookings Institution, 1995).
9. *Ibid.*, p. 255.
10. Wolf and Freeland in *Financial Times*, March 7, 1995.
11. J. Blasi and A. Shleifer, "Corporate Governance in Russia: An Initial Look," paper for World Bank/Central European University conference "Governance in Central Europe and Russia," Washington, DC, December 15–16, 1994.
12. Blasi and Shleifer, "Corporate Governance." Data relate to December 1994 and are based on a sample of 61 firms. In those firms the state still owned 10 percent of shares, and outsiders 29 percent. The general findings are very similar to Earle and colleagues (see note 13 below), whose data relate to 215 firms in the summer of 1994.
13. J. S. Earle, S. Estrin, and L. Loshchenko, "Ownership Structure, Patterns of Control, and Enterprise Behavior in Russia," paper for World Bank/Russian Federation Ministry of Economy conference "Russia: Economic Policy and Enterprise Restructuring," St. Petersburg, June 12–13, 1995.
14. Blasi and Schleifer, "Corporate Governance."
15. *Russian Economic Barometer*, 3, no. 1 (1994): 52.
16. *Russian Economic Barometer*, 3, no. 2 (1994): 12–19.
17. G. Alfandari and M. Schaffer, "On 'Arrears' in Russia," paper for June 1995 St. Petersburg conference (note 13 above), Table 4. For France, Britain, Germany, and Italy the average is 1.2 months. Russia's was 0.8 months. Updated using *Russian Economic Trends*.
18. Coal-related subsidies amounted to 1.7 percent of the GDP in 1993 and 1.3 percent of the GDP in 1994. World Bank, *Russian Federation—Restructuring the Coal Industry: Putting People First* (Washington, DC: World Bank, 1994), pp. 9, 20.
19. Goskomstat, *Russian Statistical Yearbook* (Moscow: State Committee on Statistics, 1994), pp. 341, 349.
20. Since July 1994 firms can buy the land from their local authority and then sell it. But it is often not easy for them to obtain legal validation of title, and there had been few purchases by early 1996.

21. According to the official statistics, family farms produce only 2 percent of agricultural output, while private plots produce 35 percent. Goskomstat, *Russian Statistical Yearbook*, pp. 341, 349 (1993 data). This is because the land allocated to private farms is often marginal.

22. S. Commander and U. J. Lee, "Social Benefits and the Russian Industrial Firm, paper for the June 1995 St. Petersburg conference (see note 13), Table 10.

23. In Moscow 40 percent; Commander and Lee, "Social Benefits." Also, wages are subject to heavy additional taxation.

24. A. N. Brown, B. W. Ickes, and R. Ryterman, "The Myth of Monopoly: A New View of Industrial Structure in Russia," World Bank Policy Research Working Paper no. 1331, 1994. U.S. data include only employees working in the United States. The data on Russia relate to 1989 and firms are defined according to the Law of Enterprises of 1987. An earlier study by Pryor relates to an earlier concept of the firm, when the economy was more centralized: F. L. Pryor, *Property and Industrial Organization in Communist and Capitalist Nations* (Bloomington: Indiana University Press, 1973).

25. Brown, Ickes, and Ryterman, "Myth of Monopoly," show that, if products are divided into 350 "four-digit" industries, the fraction of workers employed in the four largest firms in their industry is no higher in Russia than the United States. Scare stories in Russia are based on the statistic that of 7,664 products, 77 percent were produced by one firm. But many of these products are highly specialized, and similar results might well be found in the West.

26. Goskomstat, *Russian Statistical Yearbook*, p. 394, and *Economist Diary*, 1995. We include only transport by road, rail, or water, not by pipeline.

27. M. Schaffer, Q. Fan, and U. J. Lee, "Bank–Enterprise Relations and Credit Allocation in Russia," paper for June 1995 St. Petersburg conference (see note 13 above). Also on Russian banks, see World Bank, *Russia: The Banking System During Transition*, WB Country Study (Washington, DC: World Bank, 1993).

28. As already noted, there is high international capital mobility, so that real interest rates in Russia (averaged over one or two years) are little affected by Russian monetary or fiscal policy.

29. See Chapter 4.

30. The government deficit can be financed by printing money or by borrowing. If it is financed by printing money, this causes inflation, which in turn causes households to use their savings to accumulate money with which to maintain their "real" money balances. That is what happened in 1992–94, when the budget deficit (including cheap credits) was much higher than now. It is possible that if inflation is lower, saving will be lower, but up to mid-1995 there was no sign of this.

31. *Russian Economic Trends*, Monthly Update, April 14, 1995.

32. This is confirmed by the strong effect of the real interest rate on the real exchange rate. See *Russian Economic Trends*, 3, no. 3 (1994): 31–32.

33. *Economist*, April 8, 1995.

34. CSFB, "Russia Is Bright Star for CS First Boston," *CS First Boston Newsletter*, March 1995, pp. 3–5.

35. Joint ventures are now frequently getting into trouble because the Russian partner feels more confident and tries to rewrite the terms. If this becomes a significant problem, 100 percent Western ventures may become more common.
36. Estimates based on EBRD, *Transition Report*, p. 123, and Goskomstat *Current Statistical Survey*, 1995, no. 3, p. 37.
37. In banking, foreign banks need to be licensed to undertake retail operations; only six such licenses were initially given.
38. Moscow, where all land is leasehold, is an exception (1995 position).
39. For further detail see P. Teplukhin and L. Halligan, "Investment Disincentives in Russia," *Russian Economic Trends*, vol. 4, no. 1 (1995). The survey was done between February and May 1995.
40. See *Russian Economic Trends*, vol. 4, no. 2 (1995), Special Report.
41. See *ibid.*, p. 1.
42. On firms see Nickell (1995).
43. Western protectionism is discussed in Chapter 5.
44. 1994 data.
45. Russian firms tend to overprice their exports rather than get what they can for them.
46. In 1994 the GDP per capita at PPP exchange rate is estimated as follows (US=100): Russia 18, Poland 21, Hungary 25, Brazil 22, Mexico 28 (adapted from World Bank *World Development Report*, 1995, p. 221, using Figure 1). This probably exaggerates comparative consumption standards in Russia since investment is a fairly high share of national income in Russia and the quality of goods and services is comparatively poor. But Russia is much farther below its potential than are Brazil and Mexico, and probably also Poland and Hungary.

Chapter 8. Can Russia beat the mafia?

1. This figure would imply that something like twenty times as many women were murdered by their partners in Russia as in America. That is possible, but an alternative explanation is that some of the victims were murdered by people other than the partners suspected of the murders. At any rate, it seems that few of these unfortunates were victims of mafia-style contract killings.
2. As opposed to robbery, which is more like a one-shot theft of capital.
3. DIA annual report, 1995. Reported in *The Economist*, July 29, 1995, p. 31. These figures show membership of three different organized-crime groups: the Mafia (Sicily, 181 families, 5,487 members); the Camorra (Campania; 145 families, 7,000 members) and the 'Ndrangheta (Calabria; 80 families, 5,000 members).
4. S. Handelman, *Comrade Criminal* (London: Michael Joseph, 1994), p. 11.
5. *Izvestia*, December 30, 1993, summarized by *RFE/RL Research Report*, vol. 3, no. 2 (January 14, 1994).
6. Viktor Ilyukhin, the chairman of the security committee of the lower house of parliament and a leading communist deputy, claimed that criminals control 81 percent of the shares in all privatized firms. Ilyukhin's tes-

timony, however, was suspect, since he wanted to stop privatization and may have been using this assertion to discredit the process.

7. Andrei Shleifer and Robert Vishny, "Corruption," *Quarterly Journal of Economics*, Autumn 1993.

8. Arkady Vaksberg, "Crime and Punishment," in Heyward Isham, ed., *Remaking Russia* (Armonk, NY: M. E. Sharpe, 1995). For a fuller account, see Arkady Vaksberg, *The Soviet Mafia* (London: Weidenfeld & Nicolson, 1991).

9. Lev Timofeyev, *The Secret Rulers of Russia* (New York: Knopf, 1992), pp. 98–99. Quoted in Handelman, *Comrade Criminal*.

10. Handelman, *Comrade Criminal*, p. 22.

11. *Ibid.*

12. Valery Chalidze, *Criminal Russia: Essays in Crime in the Soviet Union* (New York: Random House, 1977), p. 342. Quoted in Handelman, *Comrade Criminal*, p. 24.

13. Handelman, *Comrade Criminal*, pp. 23–24.

14. For an account of this meeting, see *ibid.*, pp. 18–20.

15. Boris Yeltsin, *The View from the Kremlin* (London: HarperCollins, 1994), pp. 229–30.

16. "Crime in Russia: The High Price of Freeing Markets," *The Economist*, February 19, 1994.

17. Diego Gambetta, *The Sicilian Mafia* (Cambridge, MA: Harvard University Press, 1994).

18. *Ibid.*, p. 15.

19. *Ibid.*, p. 21.

20. This is a distinction used by Mancur Olsen in "Dictatorship, Democracy, and Development," *American Political Science Review*, vol. 87, no. 3 (September 1993).

21. Gambetta, *Sicilian Mafia*, p. 252.

22. Federico Varese, "Is Sicily the Future of Russia? Private Protection and the Rise of the Russian Mafia," mimeo.

23. *Moscow News*, quoted in David Remnick, "The Tycoon and the Kremlin," *New Yorker*, February 20, 1995, pp. 128–30.

24. Handelman, *Comrade Criminal*, p. 257.

25. "Russia's Mafia: More Crime than Punishment," *The Economist*, July 9, 1994.

26. Remnick, "Tycoon and Kremlin," p. 136.

27. *Ibid.*, p. 132.

Chapter 9. Will political deadlock recur?

1. Kennan was the author of the famous "Long Telegram" warning the Truman administration of the coming Stalinist threat.

2. Hélène Carrère d'Encausse, *The End of the Soviet Empire* (New York: Basic Books, 1993), p. 177.

3. Ruslan Khasbulatov, *The Struggle for Russia* (London: Routledge, 1993), p. 46.

4. Yegor Gaidar, *Russian Reform*. (Cambridge, MA: MIT Press, 1995), p. 22.
5. In only one case did Yeltsin attempt to introduce emergency rule. That was in Chechnya, immediately after the republic's declaration of independence. His attempt failed after being overruled by parliament, a failure that would have big consequences later.
6. Alexis de Tocqueville, *Democracy in America*, vol. 1 (New York: Knopf, 1945), pp. 251–52.
7. The reason was that aggrieved shareholders in an investment company that had just been closed down were threatening to use this law to force a politically embarrassing referendum.
8. The full list was the president; the vice president; the prime minister; all first deputy prime ministers; the chairman of the Supreme Soviet; the chairmen of both its houses, the Councils of the Republic and the Council of Nationalities; and the deputy chairman of the Council of Nationalities.
9. *Marshall Plan for the Mind*, Radio Russia.
10. *Literaturnaya gazeta*, July 28, 1993.
11. *The Economist*, November 19, 1994.
12. *Rossiiskiye vesti*. August 7, 1993. See also Dominic Gualtieri, "Russia's New War of Laws," *RFE/RL Research Report*, vol. 2, no 35.
13. Reuters, November 11, 1994.
14. Robert Dahl, *Who Governs?* (New Haven, CT: Yale University Press, 1961).
15. "Talking to Gaidar," *The Economist*, April 25, 1992.
16. Valentin Pavlov, the last Soviet prime minister, had sought the same privilege just before supporting the attempted coup of August 1991.
17. By seventy-two votes.
18. *Megapolis-Express*, September 1, 1993.
19. *Moscow News*, no. 32, August 8, 1993.
20. For a fuller account of the evidence, see Alexander Rahr, "The October Revolt: Mass Unrest or Putsch?" *RFE/RL Research Report*, vol. 2, no. 44 (1993).
21. Russian television (*Vesti*), July 21, 1993.
22. ITAR-TASS, September 7, 1993, and *Radio Rossiya*, September 9, 1993. Quoted in Rahr, "October Revolt."
23. *Nezavisimaya gazeta*. September 23, 1993. Quoted in *RFE/RL Research Report*, 2, no. 40 (1993): 6.
24. Public opinion polls by the Public Opinion Foundation, published in *V pole zreniya*, nos. 42, 43, and 44, and summarized in Mary Cline, Amy Corning, and Mark Rhodes, "The Showdown in Moscow: Tracking Public Opinion," *RFE/RL Research Report*, vol. 2, no. 43 (1993).
25. *Ibid.*
26. The final results were: Liberal Democratic party, 22.79 percent; Russia's Choice, 15.38 percent; Communist party, 12.35 percent; Women of Russia, 8.10 percent; Agrarians, 7.90 percent; Yabloko, 7.83 percent; Party of Russian Unity and Accord, 6.76 percent; Democratic Party of Russia, 5.50 percent; Democratic Russia Movement plus Russian Movement for Democratic Reforms (ran together) and others, 13.39 percent.
27. *Der Spiegel*, no. 4, 1994.

Chapter 10. Can democracy survive?

1. They "settled on cat fur, the finest cat they could find in the shops and which could easily be mistaken for marten from a distance." Nikolai Gogol, *Diary of a Madman and Other Stories*, trans. Ronald Wilks (London: Penguin, 1972).
2. Robert D. Putnam, *Making Democracy Work: Civic Traditions in Modern Italy*. (Princeton: Princeton University Press, 1993), pp. 184–185.
3. Samuel P. Huntington, *The Third Wave: Democratization in the Late Twentieth Century* (Norman: University of Oklahoma Press, 1991), pp. 266–267.
4. Robert A. Dahl, *Polyarchy: Participation and Opposition* (New Haven: Yale University Press, 1971).
5. A general election to the Soviet parliament in April 1989; an election to the Russian parliament in 1990; a presidential election in June 1991; two nationwide referendums on relations between Russia and the Soviet Union in April 1991; a referendum on Boris Yeltsin's performance and his policies in April 1993; a general election to the new parliament in December of that year, plus a referendum on a new Russian constitution; and last, a round of local elections in 1994.
6. The vote was described as a plebiscite, not a referendum, which meant that a simple majority was enough for it to pass, assuming a majority of eligible voters took part (a referendum would have required the agreement of 50 percent plus one of all eligible voters). The official results were not announced for a week after the vote, which led some Western monitors of the election to suspect vote rigging (*The Times* [London], December 18, 1993). When the preliminary results were announced, the number of registered voters was 2 million fewer than the figure given for the electoral roll in the referendum of 1993. That was relevant because of the rule requiring a majority of eligible voters to take part to make the vote valid. When the final results were announced, the number of registered voters was not given at all; the actual number of votes in favor was 32.9 million, which was wrongly said to be 58.4 percent of votes cast (in fact, it is 56.6 percent); the number of votes against was 23.4 million, or 40.3 percent (official figures gave this as 41.6 percent). The turnout was claimed to be a 55 percent of those voters estimated in the preliminary results. So, of potential voters, less than a third (31 percent) actually voted for the new constitution. The charge of electoral irregularity was never proved, but five months later a team set up by Yeltsin to investigate the poll found that the turnout had actually been only 46 percent, which, a presidential spokesman admitted, meant that the constitutional poll had failed (*Izvestia*, May 4, 1994).
7. The president may not dissolve parliament in its first year of office, in the last six months of its normal term, and if it is deliberating his impeachment.
8. In a reshuffle in late in 1994, Yeltsin chose the ministers without consulting Prime Minister Chernomyrdin (Reuters, November 10, 1994).
9. Alexander Rahr, "Russia's Future: With or Without Yeltsin," *RFE/RL Research Reports*, vol. 3, no. 17 (1994).

10. Richard Sawka, *Russian Politics and Society* (London: Routledge, 1993), p. 166.
11. *Argumenty i fakty*, August 16, 1994.
12. *The Economist*, September 3, 1994, p. 40.
13. Alexis de Tocqueville, *Democracy in America*, vol. 2 (New York: Knopf, 1995), Second Book, ch. 3.
14. James W. Prothro and Charles M. Grigg, "Fundamental Principles of Democracy: Bases of Agreement and Disagreement," in *Empirical Democratic Theory*, ed. Charles F. Cnudde and Dean E. Neubauer.
15. According to Radio Liberty, Russia's Central Electoral Commission gave the figure as 58.4 percent.
16. Conversation with the author, September 23, 1994.
17. *American Political Science Review*, vol. 58, no. 2 (June 1964).
18. David Remnick, *Lenin's Tomb* (New York: Random House, 1993), pp. 415–19.
19. Boris Yeltsin, *The View from the Kremlin* (London: HarperCollins, 1994), pp. 276–77.
20. Sergei Filatov and Lyudmila Vorontsova, "In Search of an Identity," in Heyward Isham, ed., *Remaking Russia* (Armonk, NY: IEWS, M. E. Sharpe, 1995).
21. Alexis de Tocqueville, *The Ancien Régime* (London: J. M. Dent, 1988), p. 141.
22. Seymour Martin Lipset, "Some Social Requisites of Democracy: Economic Development and Political Legitimacy," *American Political Science Review*, vol. 53, no. 1 (March 1959).
23. Phillips Cutright, "National Political Development: Measurement and Analysis," *American Sociological Review*, 28, pp. 253–264.
24. Gabriel A. Almond and Sidney Verba, *The Civic Culture* (Boston: Little, Brown, 1963).
25. *Rossiya: partii, assotsiatsii, soyuzy, kluby* (Moscow: Russian-American University, publication ongoing). See also Geoffrey Hosking, *The Awakening of the Soviet Union* (London: Heinemann, 1990).

Chapter 11. Will Russia break up?

1. "A Silent Revolution: A Survey of Russia's Emerging Market, *The Economist*, April 8, 1995, p. 2.
2. Emil Payin, "Separatism and Federalism," in Heyward Isham, ed., *Remaking Russia* (Armonk, NY: IEWS, M. E. Sharpe, 1995), p. 194.
3. "Now What? A Survey of the Soviet Union," *The Economist*, October 20, 1990, p. 10.
4. *Ibid.*
5. Philip Hanson, "The Center Versus the Periphery in Russian Economic Policy," *RFE/RL Research Report*, vol. 3, no. 7 (April 29, 1994). See also M. J. Bradshaw and Philip Hanson, "Regions, Local Power, and Reform in

Russia," in R. W. Campbell, ed., *Issues in The Transformation of Centrally Planned Economies: Essays in Honor of Gregory Grossman* (Boulder, CO: Westview Press, 1994).

Chapter 12. Will Russia rebuild the empire?

1. *Literaturnaya gazeta*, August 19, 1992.
2. Quoted in *RFE/RL Research Report*, vol. 3, no. 1 (January 7, 1994).
3. *The Economist*, December 7, 1991, p. 28.
4. Interfax, November 24, 1993.
5. *Le Figaro*, November 27, 1993.
6. A few were left to guard a missile plant in Latvia and an intelligence-gathering station in Estonia.
7. Zbigniew Brzezinski, "The Premature Partnership," *Foreign Affairs*, March–April 1994, p. 80.

Chapter 13. Russia and the West: Friends or foes?

1. *Nezavisimaya gazeta*, November 24, 1993.
2. Interview with Yevgeny Ambartsumov on Russian television, April 3, 1993; remarks by Vladimir Lukin in Interfax, March 29, 1993.
3. Richard Sawka, *Russian Politics and Society* (London: Routledge, 1993), p. 305.
4. Alexis de Tocqueville, *Democracy in America*, vol. 1 (New York: Knopf, 1945), ch. 18.
5. Tibor Szamuely, *The Russian Tradition* (London: Secker & Warburg, 1974), pp. 179–80.
6. Quoted in Richard Hare, *Pioneers of Russian Social Thought* (Oxford: Oxford University Press, 1951), p. 132.
7. *New York Tribune*, April 12, 1853.
8. The IMF estimated defense at 5 percent of the GDP in 1995. The International Institute for Strategic Studies gives a figure of 8.8 percent. See *The Military Balance 1995–96.* (London: IISS, 1995), p. 122.113.
9. As late as the spring of 1992, the IMF warned Estonia against setting up its own currency because it thought the Soviet ruble and the Soviet trading system had a better future. In the event, the creation of the Estonian kroon was an economic as well as a political triumph (inflation came down to zero within months, and the economy began to recover within a year, faster than in any other Soviet republic). The IMF was forced to concede the effect.
10. The term "Eurasian" did not refer only to the geographical emphasis of this school. The term referred back to the original "Eurasians," who were Russians driven into exile by the Bolsheviks in the 1920s and who were both anti-Bolshevik and anti-Western.
11. ITAR-TASS, January 30, 1993.
12. Andrei Kozyrev, "Russia: A Chance of Survival," *Foreign Affairs*, Spring 1992, p. 4.

Chapter 14. Executive summary and future scenarios

1. Richard Pipes, *The Russian Revolution* (London: Collins Harvill, 1990), and *Russia Under the Old Regime*, 2d. ed. (Harmondsworth: Penguin, 1995).
2. For an IMF assessment of the true output fall, see V. Koen and E. Gavrilenkov, "How Large Was the Output Collapse in Russia? Alternative Estimates and Welfare Implications," IMF report, mimeographed, 1994. Clearly the prereform figures were also exaggerated.
3. For a fairly early assessment see O. Blanchard *et al., Reform in Eastern Europe* (Cambridge, MA: MIT Press, 1991), updated in O. Blanchard *et al., Post-Communist Reform: Pain and Progress* (Cambridge, MA: MIT Press, 1993). A good account of Russia's first year is in D. Lipton and J. D. Sachs, "Prospects for Russia's Economic Reform," *Brookings Papers on Economic Activity*, 2 (1992): 213–65.
4. J. D. Sachs, "Russia's Struggle with Stabilization: Conceptual Issues and Evidence," *Proceedings of World Bank Conference on Developmental Economics* (Washington, DC: World Bank, 1994), Table 5. There was also of course significant debt-rescheduling.
5. EBRD, *Transition Report Update*, April 1995, Appendix II.
6. J. Blasi and A. Shleifer, "Corporate Governance in Russia: An Initial Look," paper for World Bank/Central European University conference, Washington, DC, December 15–16, 1994. Data relate to December 1994 and are based on a sample of sixty-one firms. In these firms the state still owned 10 percent of shares and outsiders 29 percent. The general findings are very similar to Earle and colleagues, whose data relate to 215 firms in the summer of 1994. J. S. Earle, S. Esfrin, and L. Leshchenko, "Ownership Structures, Patterns of Control and Enterprise Behavior in Russia," paper for World Bank/Russian Ministry of Economy conference, St. Petersburg, June 12–13, 1995.
7. End of 1994. See *Russian Economic Trends*, monthly update, April 14, 1995. There was a further $10 billion capital flight in 1995.
8. See *Russian Economic Trends*, vol. 4, no. 1 (1995), Special Report on Investment Disincentives.
9. A decree in early 1996 reinforced this right.
10. On these issues, see C. M. Asilis and V. H. Juan-Ramon, "On Corruption and Capital Accumulation," IMF Working Paper no. 94/86, 1994.
11. For a useful definition, see, for example, R. A. Dahl, *Democracy and Its Critics* (New Haven, CT: Yale University Press, 1991).
12. Of the five most celebrated reformers (Gaidar, Fedorov, Shokhin, Chubais and Yavlinsky), each except Chubais founded a different party.
13. For a contrary view, see R. D. Blackwell, "Russian Foreign Policy: Trilateral Interests and Policies," in R. D. Blackwell, R. Braithwaite, and A. Tanaka, eds., *Engaging Russia* (New York, Paris, and Tokyo: Trilateral Commission, 1995).
14. These statistics relate to the six regions known as Northwest, Central, Black Earth, Volga-Vyatka, Povolzhky, and North Caucasus. Altogether 110 million Russians live on the continent of Europe.

15. The "sixty-six oblasts" include some krais and okrugs. In addition to Moscow and St. Petersburg, regional cities are also jurisdictions, making eighty-nine in all.

16. A few have reached private agreements with Moscow for some special arrangement.

17. Another obvious way in which European taxpayers could save money is by buying the Russian Sukhoy fighter plane rather than spend over 30 billion ECUs developing a Euro-fighter that will probably be no better than the Sukhoy. The supply of spare parts could be secured if Russia provided a factory to make them in the West, as it has with spare parts for the MiGs bought by Malaysia.

18. The phrase "muddling down" is effectively used by D. Yergin and T. Gustafson, *Russia 2120 and What It Means for the World* (New York: Random House, 1993), in their insightful analysis of Russia's prospects, written as early as 1993.

19. Evaluated at purchasing power parity exchange rate; see World Bank, *World Development Report*, 1995, p. 220. California has 20 percent of Russia's population, and Russia has 20 percent of California's per capita income. On the same basis, the size of the Russian economy is one-third the Chinese.

20. See page 143.

References

Alfandari, G., and M. Schaffer. 1995. "On 'Arrears' in Russia," World Bank/Ministry of Economy of Russian Federation conference, "Russia: Economic Policy and Enterprise Restructuring," St. Petersburg, June 12–13.

Asilis, C. M., and V. H. Juan-Ramon. 1994. "On Corruption and Capital Accumulation," International Monetary Fund Working Paper no. 94/86.

Aslund, A. 1990. "How Small Is the Soviet National Income?" in Henry S. Rowen and Charles Wolf, Jr., eds., *The Impoverished Superpower*. San Francisco: ICS Press.

———. 1991. *Gorbachev's Struggle for Economic Reform*. London: Pinter Publishers.

———. 1995. *How Russia Became a Market Economy*. Washington, DC: Brookings Institution.

Aslund, A., ed. 1994. *Economic Transformation in Russia*. London: Pinter Publishers.

———, ed. 1995. *Russian Economic Reform at Risk*. London and New York: Pinter.

Aslund, A., and R. Layard, eds. 1993. *Changing the Economic System in Russia*. London: Pinter Publishers.

Atkinson, A. B. Forthcoming. "Income Distribution in Europe and the United States." Nuffield College, Oxford, mimeographed.

Barro, R. J. 1995. "Democracy and Growth," in R. J. Barro and R. Marimon, eds., *Growth and Political Institutions*. Bucharest: Centre de Recerca en Economia Internacional, Universitat Pompeu Fabra.

Barro, R. J., and X. Sala-i-Martin. 1995. *Economic Growth*, New York: McGraw-Hill.

Berlin, I. 1978. *Russian Thinkers*. London: Hogarth Press.

Blackwell, R. D. 1995. "Russian Foreign Policy: Trilateral Interests and Poli-

363

cies," in R. D. Blackwell, R. Braithwaite, and A. Tanaka, eds., *Engaging Russia*. New York, Paris, and Toyko: Trilateral Commission.

Blanchard, O., *et al.* 1991. *Reform in Eastern Europe*. Cambridge, MA: MIT Press.

———. 1993. *Post-Communist Reform: Pain and Progress*. Cambridge, MA: MIT Press.

Blasi, J., and A. Shleifer. 1994. "Corporate Governance in Russia: An Initial Look," World Bank/Central European University Privatization Project conference "Corporate Governance in Central Europe and Russia," Washington, DC, December 15–16.

Boycko, M.; A. Shleifer; and R. Vishny. 1995. *Privatizing Russia*. Cambridge, MA: MIT Press.

Braithwaite, J. D. 1994. "The Old and New Poor in Russia: Trends in Poverty," World Bank, mimeographed.

Braithwaite, Sir R. 1995. "Russia's Future and Western Policy: A European View," in R. D. Blackwell, R. Braithwaite, and A. Tanaka, eds., *Engaging Russia*. New York, Paris, and Toyko: Trilateral Commission.

Brown, A. N.; B. W. Ickes; and R. Ryterman. 1994. "The Myth of Monopoly: A New View of Industrial Structure in Russia," World Bank, Policy Research Working Paper no. 1331.

Chernichovsky, D., *et al.* 1994. "Reform of the Russian Health Sector," World Bank, mimeographed.

Commander, S., and U. Lee. 1995. "Social Benefits and the Russian Industrial Firm," World Bank/Ministry of Economics of the Russian Federation Conference, "Russia: Economic Policy and Enterprise Restructuring," St. Petersburg, June 12–13.

CSFB. 1995. "Russia Is Bright Star for CS First Boston," *CS First Boston Newsletter*, March, pp. 3–5.

Custine, Astolphe, Marquis de. 1843. *The Empire of the Czar*, translation of *La Russie en 1839*. Reprint, Garden City, NY: Doubleday, 1990.

Dahl, R. A. 1971. *Polyarchy: Participation and Opposition*. New Haven: Yale University Press.

———. 1989. *Democracy and Its Critics*. New Haven: Yale University Press.

Dunlop, J. B. 1993. *The Rise of Russia and the Fall of the Soviet Empire*. Princeton, NJ: Princeton University Press.

Earle, J. S.; S. Estrin; and L. Leshchenko. 1995. "Ownership Structures, Patterns of Control, and Enterprise Behavior in Russia," World Bank/Ministry of Economy of the Russian Federation Conference, "Russia: Economic Policy and Enterprise Restructuring," St. Petersburg, June 12–13.

Economist. 1990. *The Economist Book of Vital World Statistics*, 1990. London: Hutchinson Business Books.

———. 1994. *Pocket World in Figures*. London: Hamish Hamilton.

Ellam, M., and R. Layard. 1993. "Prices, Incomes, and Hardship," in A. Aslund and R. Layard, eds., *Changing the Economic System in Russia*. London: Pinter Publishers.

Ellman, M. 1992. "Shock Therapy in Russia: Failure or Partial Success?" *Radio Free Europe/Radio Liberty Research Report*, April 3.

————. 1994. "The Increase in Death and Disease Under 'Katastroika,' " *Cambridge Journal of Economics*, 18: 329–55.

European Bank for Reconstruction and Development. 1994. *Transition Report*. London, October.

————. 1995. *Transition Report Update*. London, April.

Gaidar, Y. 1995. "Russian Reform," in Y. Gaidar and O. Pöhl, *Russian Reform/International Money*. Cambridge, MA: MIT Press.

Gambetta, D. 1994. *The Sicilian Mafia*. Cambridge, MA: Harvard University Press.

Gide, A. 1938. *À la Retour de URSS*. Paris: Livres de Poche.

Gogol, N. V. 1842. *The Overcoat*.

Goldman, Marshall I. 1994. *Lost Opportunity: Why Economic Reforms in Russia Have Not Worked*. New York and London: W. W. Norton.

Goskomstat. 1994. *Russian Statistical Yearbook*. Moscow: State Statistical Committee.

————. 1995. *Social and Economic Situation in Russia in 1994*, Moscow: State Statistical Committee.

————. *Current Statistical Survey*, monthly, various issues.

Granville, B. 1995. "Farewell, Ruble Zone," in A. Aslund, ed., *Russian Economic Reform at Risk*. London and New York: Pinter.

Gray, J. 1994. *Post-Communist Societies in Transition: A Social Market Perspective*. London: Social Market Foundation.

Gros, D., and A. Steinherr. 1995. *Wind of Change. Economic Transition in Central and Eastern Europe*. London and New York: Longman.

Handelman, S. 1994. *Comrade Criminal*. London: Michael Joseph.

Hernández-Catá, E. 1994, "Russia and the IMF: The Political Economy of Macro-Stabilization," IMF Paper on Policy Analysis and Assessment. Washington DC: International Monetary Fund.

Hosking, G. 1990. *The Awakening of the Soviet Union*. London: Heinemann.

————. 1992. *A History of the Soviet Union: 1917–1991*. London: Fontana Press.

Illarionov, A.; R. Layard; and P. Orszag. 1994. "The Conditions of Life," in A. Aslund, ed., *Economic Transformation in Russia*. London: Pinter Publishers. Also in *Russian Economic Trends*, vol. 2, no. 2 (1993).

International Monetary Fund. 1995. "Macroeconomic Stabilization in Russia and the Federal Budget for 1995 and Thereafter," presentation at EBRD, January 17.

Islam, S., and M. Mandelbaum. 1993. *Making Markets: Economic Transformation in Eastern Europe and the Post-Soviet States*. New York: Council on Foreign Relations Press.

Kaminski, B. 1994. "Trade Performance and Access to OECD Markets," in C. Michalopoulos and D. G. Tarr, eds., *Trade in the New Independent States*. Washington, DC: World Bank.

Khasbulatov, R. I. 1993. *The Struggle for Russia*. London: Routledge.

Koen, V., and Gavrilenkov, E. 1994. "How Large Was the Output Collapse in Russia? Alternative Estimates and Welfare Implications," International Monetary Fund, mimeographed.

Kornai, J. 1990. *The Road to a Free Economy*. New York and London: W. W. Norton.

Layard, R. 1992. "Eldorados in Russia," in A. Raphael, ed., *Debrett's Euro-Industry 1993*. London: Debrett's Peerage Limited.

———. 1994. "Can Russia Control Inflation?" in J. A. H. Beaufort Wijnholds, S. C. W. Eijffinger, and L. H. Hoogduin, eds., *A Framework for Monetary Stability*. Dordrecht: Kluwer Academic Publishers.

Layard, R., and A. Richter. 1994. "Who Gains and Who Loses from Russian Credit Expansion?" *Communist Economies and Economic Transition*, 6, no. 4: 459–72. Also in *Russian Economic Trends*, vol. 2, no. 4 (1993).

———. 1995. "How Much Unemployment Is Needed for Restructuring? The Russian Experience," *Economics of Transition*, 3, no. 1: 39–58, and related articles in *Russian Economic Trends*, vol. 3, no. 2 (1994), and in A. Aslund, ed., *Russian Economic Reform at Risk*. London and New York: Pinter.

Layard, R.; S. Nickell; and R. Jackman. 1991. *Unemployment: Macroeconomic Performance and the Labour Market*. Oxford: Oxford University Press.

———. 1994. *The Unemployment Crisis*. Oxford: Oxford University Press.

Layard, R., *et al.* 1992. *East–West Migration: The Alternatives*. Cambridge, MA: MIT Press.

Lipset, S. M. 1959. "Some Social Requisites of Democracy: Economic Development and Political Legitimacy," *American Political Science Review*, vol. 53, no. 1.

Lipton, D., and J. D. Sachs. 1992. "Prospects for Russia's Economic Reforms," *Brookings Papers on Economic Activity*, 2: 213–65.

Masaryk, T. G. 1919. *The Spirit of Russia*. 3 vols. London: George Allen & Unwin.

Nickell, S. J., *The Performance of Companies* (Oxford: Basil Blackwell, 1995).

Payin, E. 1995. "Separatism and Federalism in Contemporary Russia," in H. Isham, ed., *Remaking Russia*. Armonk, NY: M. E. Sharpe.

Petrakov, N. 1993. "The Crisis of Economic Reform in Russia," *Voprosy ekonomiki*, 2: 64–65.

Pipes, R. 1990. *The Russian Revolution*. London: Collins Harvill.

———. 1995. *Russia Under the Old Regime*. 2d ed., London: Penguin.

Popkin, B.; M. Mozhina; and A. Baturin. 1992. "The Development of a Subsistence Income Level in the Russian Federation," mimeographed.

Pryor, F. L. 1973. *Property and Industrial Organisation in Communist and Capitalist Nations*. Bloomington: Indiana University Press.

Remnick, D. 1993. *Lenin's Tomb*. New York: Random House.

Richardson, W. 1968. *Anecdotes of the Russian Empire*. New York: Da Capo Press.

Roxburgh, W., and J. C. Shapiro. 1994. "Excess wages tax," *Socio-economic Survey* (Moscow), no. 17.

Russian Economic Barometer, various issues, 15-b Orenburgskaya st., Moscow, 111621, Russia, fax: 007 (095) 310-7027. US fax: 913-843-1274.

Russian Economic Trends, Whurr Publishers Ltd., 19B Compton Terrace, London N1 2UN, UK, fax: (0171) 226-5290. US fax: 913-843-1274.

Sachs, J. D. 1993. "Western Financial Assistance and Russia's Reforms," in

S. Islam and M. Mandelbaum, eds., *Making Markets: Economic Transformation in Eastern Europe and the Post-Soviet States*. New York: Council on Foreign Relations Press.

———. 1994. "Prospects for Monetary Stabilization in Russia," in A. Aslund, ed., *Economic Transformation in Russia*. London: Pinter Publishers.

———. 1994. *Understanding Shock Therapy*. London: Social Market Foundation.

———. 1994. "Russia's Struggle with Stabilization: Conceptual Issues and Evidence," in *Proceedings of the World Bank Annual Conference on Development Economics*, supplement to *The World Bank Economic Review* and *The World Bank Research Observer*. Washington, DC: World Bank.

Sachs, J. D., and D. Lipton. 1993. "Remaining Steps to a Market-based Monetary System," in A. Aslund and R. Layard, eds., *Changing the Economic System in Russia*. London: Pinter Publishers.

Sachs, J. D., and A. M. Warner, 1995. "Economic Convergence and Economic Policies," Harvard Institute for International Development, mimeographed.

———. 1994. "Natural Resources and Economic Growth," Harvard University, mimeographed.

Sawka, R. 1993. *Russian Politics and Society*. London: Routledge.

Schaffer, M.; Q. Fan; and U. J. Lee. 1995. "Bank–Enterprise Relations and Credit Allocation in Russia," World Bank/Ministry of Economy of the Russian Federation Conference, "Russia: Economic Policy and Enterprise Restructuring," St. Petersburg, June 12–13.

Shapiro, J. 1995. "The Russian Mortality Crisis and Its Causes," in A. Aslund, ed., *Russian Economic Reform at Risk*. London and New York: Pinter.

Shleifer, A., and R. W. Vishny. 1993. "Corruption," *Quarterly Journal of Economics*, no. 435, August: 599–617.

Skidelsky, R. 1995. *The World After Communism: A Polemic for Our Times*. London: Macmillan.

Steele, J. 1994. *Eternal Russia: Yeltsin, Gorbachev and the Mirage of Democracy*. London: Faber & Faber.

Szamuely, T. 1974. *The Russian Tradition*. London: Secker & Warburg.

Teplukhin, P. 1994. *Economic Policy Instruments for Russia* (in Russian). Moscow: Progress-Academia.

Teplukhin, P., and L. Halligan. 1995. "Investment Disincentives in Russia," *Russian Economic Trends*, vol. 4, no. 1.

Tocqueville, Alexis de. 1840. *Democracy in America*. New York: Knopf, 1945.

UNICEF. 1994. "Crisis in Mortality, Health and Nutrition: Central and Eastern Europe in Transition—Public Policy and Social Conditions," *Economic and Transition Studies: Regional Monitoring*, Report no. 2, August.

Wallich, C. I., ed. *Russia and the Challenge of Fiscal Federalism*. Washington, DC: World Bank.

World Bank. 1992. *Russian Economic Reform: Crossing the Threshold of Structural Change*, Washington, DC: World Bank.

———. 1993. *Russia: The Banking System During Transition*, World Bank Country Study. Washington, DC: World Bank.

———. 1994. *Russian Federation—Restructuring the Coal Industry: Putting People First.* Washington, DC: World Bank.

Yeltsin, B. N. 1991. *Against the Grain.* London: Pan Books.

———. 1994. *The View from the Kremlin.* London: HarperCollins.

Yergin, D., and T. Gustafson. 1993. *Russia 2010 and What It Means for the World.* New York: Random House.

Index